THE
POETRY OF
PABLO NERUDA

TRANSLATED BY

MIGUEL ALGARÍN   TERESA ANDERSON   APRIL BERNARD

ROBERT BLY   RAFAEL CAMPO   MARK EISNER

MARTÍN ESPADA   JOHN FELSTINER   BETTY FERBER

ANGEL FLORES   EDWARD HIRSCH   JANE HIRSHFIELD

MARÍA JACKETTI   GALWAY KINNELL   KEN KRABBENHOFT

PHILIP LEVINE   DENNIS MALONEY   W. S. MERWIN

STEPHEN MITCHELL   PAUL MULDOON   ELSA NEUBERGER

JAMES NOLAN   WILLIAM O'DALY   ALASTAIR REID

MARGARET SAYERS PEDEN   RICHARD SCHAAF

JACK SCHMITT   GREG SIMON   GARY SOTO   ILAN STAVANS

MARK STRAND   NATHANIEL TARN   STEPHEN TAPSCOTT

DONALD D. WALSH   STEVEN F. WHITE   JAMES WRIGHT

CLARK M. ZLOTCHEW

THE

POETRY OF

PABLO NERUDA

edited and with an

introduction by

ILAN STAVANS

FARRAR, STRAUS AND GIROUX

NEW YORK

FARRAR, STRAUS AND GIROUX
19 Union Square West, New York 10003

This work contains poems from the following original volumes by Pablo Neruda: *Crepusculario* (1923), *Veinte poemas de amor y una canción desesperada* (1924), *Residencia en la tierra* (1933), *Tercera residencia* (1947), *Canto general* (1950), *Los versos del capitán* (1952), *Odas elementales* (1954), *Nuevas odas elementales* (1956), *Tercer libro de odas* (1957), *Estravagario* (1958), *Navegaciones y regresos* (1959), *Cien sonetos de amor* (1959), *Canción de gesta* (1960), *Las piedras de Chile* (1961), *Cantos ceremoniales* (1961), *Plenos poderes* (1962), *Memorial de Isla Negra* (1964), *Arte de pájaros* (1966), *Una casa en la arena* (1966), *La barcarola* (1967), *Las manos del día* (1968), *Fin del mundo* (1969), *Maremoto* (1970), *Aún* (1970), *La espada encendida* (1970), *Las piedras del cielo* (1970), *Geografía infructuosa* (1972), *La rosa separada* (1972), *Incitación al Nixonicidio y alabanza de la revolución chilena* (1973), *El mar y las campanas* (1973), *2000* (1974), *Elegía* (1974), *El corazón amarillo* (1974), *Jardín de invierno* (1974), *Libro de las preguntas* (1974), *Defectos escogidos* (1974).

Owing to limitations of space, all acknowledgments for permission to reprint previously
published material can be found on pages 980–86.

Library of Congress Cataloging-in-Publication Data
Neruda, Pablo, 1904–1973.
[Poems. Selections]
The poetry of Pablo Neruda / edited and with an introduction by Ilan Stavans.
p. cm.
Includes bibliographical references and index.
ISBN 0-374-29995-1 (hc. : alk. paper)
1. Neruda, Pablo, 1904–1973—Translations into English. I. Stavans, Ilan. II. Title.

PQ8097.N4 A2 2003
861'.62—dc21

2002032548

Designed by Gretchen Achilles

www.fsgbooks.com

3   5   7   9   10   8   6   4

Y digo que os dispongáis para oír a un auténtico poeta de los que tienen sus sentidos amaestrados en un mundo que no es el nuestro y que poca gente percibe. Un poeta más cerca de la muerte que de la filosofía, más cerca del dolor que de la inteligencia; más cerca de la sangre que de la tinta.

And I tell you that you should open yourselves to hearing an authentic poet, of the kind whose bodily senses were shaped in a world that is not our own and that few people are able to perceive. A poet closer to death than to philosophy, closer to pain than to intelligence, closer to blood than to ink.

—FEDERICO GARCÍA LORCA, 1934
(Translated by Steven F. White)

CONTENTS

from **RESIDENCE ON EARTH/**
RESIDENCÍA EN LA TIERRA (1925–1945)

I.

II.

III.

IV.

RESIDENCE II

RESIDENCE III

from **CANTO GENERAL/**
CANTO GENERAL (1938–1949)

THIRD BOOK OF ODES

from EXTRAVAGARIA/
ESTRAVAGARIO (1957–1958)

from **SONG OF PROTEST/**
CANCIÓN DE GESTA (1958–1968)

from **THE STONES OF CHILE/**
LAS PIEDRAS DE CHILE (1959–1961)

from **THE BOOK OF QUESTIONS/**
LIBRO DE LAS PREGUNTAS (1971–1973)

from **SELECTED FAILINGS/**
DEFECTOS ESCOGIDOS (1971–1973)

HOMAGE:
FOURTEEN OTHER WAYS OF LOOKING AT PABLO NERUDA

"I have always wanted the hands of people to be seen in poetry," Pablo Neruda wrote in 1966. Then he added, "I have always preferred a poetry where the fingerprints show. A poetry of loam, where water can sing. A poetry of bread, where everyone may eat." This intuitive connection to the masses was a feature of his oeuvre from early on in his career, with his groundbreaking *Residence on Earth.* Not only did it persist throughout his life but the connection actually became more intense, turning him into a biblical prophet of sorts, the voice of the voiceless. It also made him a favorite target of attacks. Gabriel García Márquez once depicted him as "the greatest poet of the twentieth century—in any language." Conversely, Juan Ramón Jiménez said that Neruda was "a great bad poet." It is clear that the Chilean knew how to make waves. So much so that when the Swedish Academy granted him the Nobel Prize for Literature in 1971, the official announcement itself was bellicose in tone: This year's award, it stated, has been given "to a contentious author who is not only debated but for many is also debatable. This debate has been going on for the past forty years, which demonstrates that his contribution is unquestionable."

The strident debate has at times threatened to simplify Neruda's contribution. His public persona is legendary. He is, arguably, the ultimate *poet engagé,* whose words were tools for radical transformation. But there was a private person behind, one watchful of the disturbances of life. He stated in 1935 in a manifesto called "Towards an Impure Poetry": "It is useful at certain hours of the day and night to look closely at the world of objects at rest: wheels that have crossed long, dusty spaces with their huge vegetal and mineral burdens, bags of coal from the coal bins, barrels, baskets, handles, and hafts in a carpenter's tool chest. From them flow the contacts of man with the earth, like an object lesson for all troubled lyricists. The used surfaces of things, the wear that hands have given to things, the air, tragic at times, pathetic at others, of such things—all lend a curious attractiveness to reality that we should not underestimate." The two Nerudas, the outspoken and the private, do not always go together.

His odyssey is extraordinary. From the provincial boy named Neftalí Ricardo Reyes Basoalto, born on July 12, 1904, in the small village of Parral, Chile, to his Nobel Prize speech in Stockholm as the internationally renowned Pablo Neruda, two years prior to his death at the age of sixty-nine, and onward to the coup d'état in Santiago by General Augusto Pinochet that drove the democratically elected president Salvador Allende to his death and contributed to the poet's own demise of cancer at 10:30 p.m. on September 23, 1973, is a consummate voyage of awakening: to the possibilities of art, to the elasticity of language, to the consciousness of self, and to the responsibility of the intellectual to society and to history. Decades go by and his poetry, a perennial favorite of young and old, always feels as if it were just off the press. Translations of Neruda, in official and pirated editions, abound in dozens of languages, including Uzbek, Latin, and Yiddish. In fact, years ago a Spanish newspaper concluded after a survey that he is "the most frequently translated poet on the globe."

Almost every significant event of the twentieth century palpitates in Neruda's poems: the Soviet Revolution; the Spanish Civil War; Nazism and Stalinism; the massacres of World War II perpetuated in the name of volatile utopias, imperialism, and colonialism; the Cold War; the political and economic insolvency of Latin America; Vietnam and the Age of Aquarius; Fidel Castro's revolution in Cuba; the student upheavals of 1968; and the arrival of Socialism in his native land. His work is at once a chronicle of tumultuous times and the intimate diary of a nomad.

Neruda showed up at the height of the *Modernista* literary movement in Latin America inspired by Symbolism, in which Rubén Darío and José Martí, among others, sought to purify the Spanish language of the stylistic excesses of the nineteenth century. Neruda's was a rebellious stand against abstract, evasive poetry in general, with swans and princesses as its leitmotivs. He toyed with Surrealism, too. In the end, he embraced the ode, a classic form with roots in Homer, Pindar, and Horace, as the finest way to sing of common things, but he used innovative strategies to create the down-to-earth effect he sought, as in his odes to the artichoke and to a pair of socks. He declared himself allergic to the "elevated" style practiced in ancient times. It was in the mundane that he found his subject matter, and he wanted to keep his poetry at that level. His strategy is easily summarized in three words: simplicity, honesty, and conviction.

I'm of a generation that came of age with a Neruda who was more about propaganda than about the inner search for truth. In the Mexico of the seventies, he was about not reason but impulse. I first became an avid reader when my fifth-grade teacher introduced her students to the twenty-year-old author of *Twenty Love Poems and a Song of Despair.* The class memorized several verses entire. At the time, none of us seized upon the eroticism in the volume, particularly its first poem: "Body of Woman." The epic and the metaphysical poet of later books was not part of the curriculum; he came in successive years, as my own quest evolved. I always read him fragmentarily, nonsequentially, as did my generation: in bits and pieces. There appeared to be a Neruda for all seasons, but what about a Neruda that was the sum of his parts?

This fracture was in part the result of the times. In the eighties and nineties, after Neruda was gone, others—Borges, for instance—held the spotlight. The Argentine, in an interview, disparaged the Chilean, whom he probably met briefly in 1927 in Buenos Aires, for "selective" activism, choosing to endorse a good cause only when his own reputation could not be compromised. Borges portrayed Neruda as a fine poet, then qualified the comment in cumbersome fashion: "I don't admire him as a man." Borges, of course, was allergic to the types of enthusiasms his target was famous for. As Volodia Teitelboim, Neruda's friend and most visible biographer, argued, Neruda in turn believed his colleague to be too "preoccupied with cultural problems, which didn't attract [him] because, in his opinion, they were not human (or at least, let *us* say it, not as human) . . . The exegetes, the explainers, the entomologists of literature, and the enigmas of knowledge," in the Chilean's view, "were "all vast and complex speculations, not without emptiness." Octavio Paz, the other canonical poet of the region, once described Neruda as "a servant of fascism."

It isn't at all surprising, therefore, that while these contemporaries reigned—Borges was Neruda's elder by five years and Paz his junior by a decade—other muses were invoked. These were conservative years, marked by a clear distaste for the marriage of activism and literature. Nothing is static in our universe, though: the stage is always the same, but the actors and set designs change. The new becomes old, and the old is in time reconsidered—reinvented, even. Today the fanciful guerrilla fighters of the sixties have been replaced by the logos of Microsoft and Nike. Portfolio-carrying executives believe that the revolution is possible within the transnational corporation, not from without. Images of "Che" Guevara, Subcomandante Marcos—and, yes, Pablo Neruda—are ubiquitous on T-shirts and coffee mugs.

The Chilean, it strikes me, is ready for a reappraisal. Or better, the time is ripe finally to appreciate him in full. The quality that has made him a classic is the sheer abundance of his talent. He works from the bottom up.

He resists and insists, always striving for the epiphany that will satisfy his curiosity. "Poetry is song and fertility," he once wrote. It "emerged from its secret womb and flows, fertilizing and singing. It kindles with its swelling waters, it works at milling flour, tanning hides, cutting wood, giving light to cities. It is useful, and awakens to find banners along its banks: festivals are celebrated beside the singing water." No wonder Neruda's ghost is, always and inevitably, at one's side. It takes his several dozen collections—let alone the only novel he wrote, along with his plays, autobiography, and volumes of prose—to realize that he used words to map out his people, from the local to the continental, from the one to the many, from the past to the future. *Residence on Earth* and *Canto General* alone are superb explorations that delve admirably into the condition of Latin America. In them, the critic Fernando Alegría once said, Neruda expressed, as nobody before, the anguish, terror, and superstition, the sense of guilt imposed on the region by foreign religions and the broken tradition of the Indian ancestors, the loneliness in the midst of a strange, misunderstood civilization, the consternation before Nature that crushes with its untamed jungles, oceans, and mountains, the decadence that comes from exploitation, malnutrition, alcoholism, poverty, and disease.

A sum of Nerudas, a Neruda in full view: the initial attempt at a comprehensive evaluation, in the form of the *Complete Works*, was published in Spanish when the poet was fifty-three, by Losada in Buenos Aires, under the authoritative editorship of Hernán Loyola. An updated second attempt appeared in Barcelona in 1999, under the aegis of Galaxia Gutenberg/Círculo de Lectores. Other cultures have fallen prey to the fragmentation I've talked about—among them, the United States. For a variety of reasons, Neruda's relationship to *los Estados Unidos* was marked by ambivalence: He was attracted to its citizenry but furious with its government. Thus goes a famous set of lines in the poem "I Wish the Woodcutter Would Wake Up": "What we love is your peace, not your mask. / Your warrior's face is not handsome."

This relationship was shaped, obviously, by geographical proximity, and also by the sense that the land of Neruda's idol, Walt Whitman, is and is not part of the Americas. Indeed, the United States isn't part of the panoramic landscape in *Canto General*. It appears as an invader in the book, in poems such as "Standard Oil Co." And later on in his poetry, it is the aggressor in Vietnam and the oppressor in the drama *Splendor and Death of Joaquín Murieta*, based on the mythical border outlaw often seen as

Chicano but whom Neruda portrayed as Chilean. And yet, it is not an exaggeration to say that nowhere outside his home has the poet been more influential than north of the Rio Grande.

My objective in *The Poetry of Pablo Neruda* is to offer the reader an image of Neruda's entire poetic arc. In his mature years he was slow-moving. This was a mirage, though, for his life is nothing but a peripatetic journey: from Parral he moved to Santiago, and from there to places in the Far East, such as Singapore and Batavia; he visited almost every nation in the Americas, as well as in Europe and the Soviet bloc. This hyperkinesis left a fecund legacy: the updated edition of 1973 of his *Complete Works* totals 3,522 pages; in the five-volume one of 1999, the first three tomes, in which his poetry is contained in toto, have 1,279, 1,453, and 1,067 pages respectively. Obviously, it would take several books the size of this one to present his whole oeuvre.

In search of the Neruda that is a sum of his parts, I have taken a more modest route: I have selected approximately 600 poems, ordering them chronologically by the original date of completion of the collections where they sit in Spanish. The dates are listed in the table of contents. For those interested in the specific years and bibliographic details of individual collections, information is provided in the notes. Only the youthful collections *El hondero entusiasta* (*The Ardent Slingsman*, 1923–1924) and *Tentativa del hombre infinito* (*Venture of the Infinite Man*, 1926), as well as the unconvincing middle-age volume *Las uvas y el viento* (*The Grapes and the Wind*, 1950–1953)—are not represented; I have also left out all the uncollected poems. Of the nearly three dozen collections that make up the contents, I have offered a larger harvest from the most significant ones, such as *Residence on Earth* and *Canto General* earlier on, and *Fully Empowered* and *Isla Negra*, written in the poet's late fifties.

These criteria guided my editorial choices: diversity, representation, and translatability. I have sought to offer the reader a sense of Neruda's abundance and inquisitiveness and the search for epiphanies in every period of his career. I have also gone in pursuit of sharp, elegant translations, trustworthy at least, if not perfect. Obviously, it is difficult, though not always impossible, to find the entirely satisfying version—the "perfect" example of transposition from one language to another. In Neruda's case, this difficulty is exacerbated by the fact that the poet's output is clearly uneven. The first book-length rendition of his poetry in English was by Angel Flores, privately printed in 1944 and expanded two years later. It included portions of *Residence on Earth* and *Spain in the Heart*. Since then I've counted over a hundred translators who have done two or more poems, released in periodicals, anthologies, and separate volumes.

The Chilean himself encouraged this multiplicity: he allowed various translators to work over the same poem, at times even concurrently. As is to be expected, the quality isn't uniform. Furthermore, the field of Neruda's translators is a particularly belligerent, acrimonious one. Since the late sixties, the debate on what constitutes a fine translation has been strident. Michael Wood said in 1974 that "only Robert Bly and Anthony Kerrigan make Neruda sound in English as if he might be a good poet in Spanish." The previous year Bly himself attacked Donald D. Walsh as "a poor translator" because "he doesn't feel emotional intensity." Walsh responded by describing Bly's attack as "slashing and slandering," then pointed out various errors made by Bly. The debate brings forth the question: Can a translation be truly error-free? Alastair Reid, arguably one of the best of Neruda's translators, said years ago that translation has a mysterious alchemy. "Some poems survive it to become poems in another language," he argued, "but others refuse to live in any language but their own, in which case the translator can manage no more than a reproduction, an effigy, of the original." To this I would add that the right measure of freedom is the result of sheer intuition: too much is disruptive, too little is confining. In between the two is the deceitful, ungraspable ideal of perfection.

For *The Poetry of Pablo Neruda* I threw as wide a net as possible in the hunt for available material. Many renditions in the volume I adore without reservations; others I have reservations about. No doubt I would have the same reaction if any one translator, or I myself, had, in a Quixotic reverie, embarked on the entire enormous project alone. For better or worse, my own taste and judgment served me as a compass. I commissioned new work. Where possible, I also revisited some established renditions with the translators. Thirty-six writers, young and old, lent their ability. Their names appear at the end of each poem they reinvented into Shakespeare's tongue.

A fully bilingual edition was unfortunately beyond reach. To compensate partially for this limitation, I have seeded the book with examples of Neruda's original poems throughout. And since here and elsewhere I have emphasized the magic of translation, on half a dozen occasions more than one version is offered. The purpose is purely comparative: in the case of "Ode to Federico García Lorca," for instance, the reader has available a couple of English-language interpretations next to the Spanish source.

The last section is called "Homage: Fourteen Other Ways of Looking at Pablo Neruda." To shape it, I invited a number of leading poets in the English-speaking world to return to the master. The invitation was delineated in clear and open fashion: find one or more favorite poems, then bring them afresh into English. I have also included here a few previously published translations by other poets, such as those by Miguel Algarín in *Song of Protest*, and Robert Bly and James Wright in *Neruda and Vallejo: Selected Poems.*

Finally, an explanation about my role as editor. This is not, nor does it intend to be, a critical edition of Neruda's complete poetry. In the back of the book I offer a list of available translations, biographies, musical and cinematic adaptations, significant critical sources, translations done by the poet himself, and a succinct description of each of the poet's books represented, often accompanied by a quotation that provides context. I have also included explanations for some recurring references. I have deliberately sought to keep my intervention to a minimum. My goal isn't to force a particular doctrine on the reader, nor has it been to censor one Neruda in favor of another. It is no secret that his work is unbalanced. How could it be otherwise given his astonishing output? The lyrical poet at times clashes with the pamphleteer. Fortunately, the incisive, humane Neruda eclipses his counterpart.

Not too long ago, a friend of mine, finding that I had been faithfully making my way through the Chilean's legacy, asked me: "Ay . . . He condemned Hitler but embraced Stalin, didn't he? And didn't he embrace Fidel Castro, only to be betrayed by the Cuban leader and his people later on, as a result of a speech Neruda delivered at the P.E.N. Club in New York?" These are important questions. Everybody is responsible for choices made in life. Subsequent generations shall judge us under a different light, one none of us is able to predict. How would Neruda have reacted to the fall of the Berlin Wall and the ruins of Marxism? My instinct is that, at the core, his nonreligious messianism—his belief in basic fairness—would have remained intact.

Pablo Neruda *en persona*: vulnerable, sentimental, antagonistic, mellifluous, right *and* wrong . . . "If the poetry I've written has any virtue," he told an interviewer shortly before his death, "it is only as an organism." *Organic* is the key term. There is an intrinsic self-reflective dialogue at the heart of the poet's legacy: as the world around him rotates, he rotates too; his verses react to external changes by explaining how those changes affect him and his poetry. He puts it inspiringly in "Ars Poetica":

. . . the truth is that suddenly the wind that lashes my chest,
the nights of infinite substance fallen in my bedroom,
the noise of a day that burns with sacrifice,
ask me mournfully what prophecy there is in me,
and there is a swarm of objects that call without being answered,
and a ceaseless movement, and a bewildered man.

—ILAN STAVANS

THE
POETRY OF
PABLO NERUDA

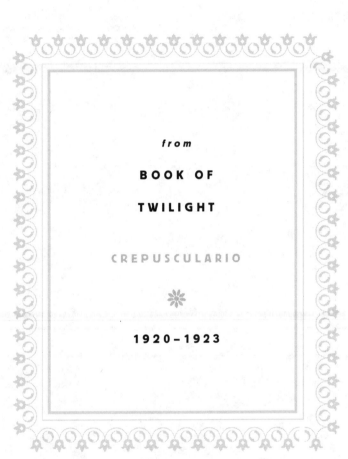

from

BOOK OF

TWILIGHT

CREPUSCULARIO

✳

1920–1923

LOVE

Woman, I would have been your child, to drink
the milk of your breasts as from a well,
to see and feel you at my side and have you
in your gold laughter and your crystal voice.

To feel you in my veins like God in the rivers
and adore you in the sorrowful bones of dust and lime,
to watch you passing painlessly by
to emerge in the stanza—cleansed of all evil.

How I would love you, woman, how I would
love you, love you as no one ever did!
Die and still
love you more.
And still
love you more
                    and more.

ILAN STAVANS

IF GOD IS IN MY VERSE

Dog of mine,
if God is in my verse,
I am God.

If God is in your distressed eyes,
you are God.

No one exists in this immense world of ours
that might kneel before us two!

ILAN STAVANS

MY SOUL

My soul is an empty carousel at sunset.

ILAN STAVANS

from

TWENTY LOVE
POEMS AND A SONG
OF DESPAIR

VEINTE POEMAS DE AMOR
Y UNA CANCIÓN
DESESPERADA

1923–1924

✳

I

Body of woman, white hills, white thighs,
you look like the world in your posture of surrender.
My savage peasant body digs through you
and makes the son leap from the depth of the earth.

I went alone as a tunnel. Birds fled from me,
and night invaded me with her powerful force.
To survive myself I forged you like a weapon,
like an arrow in my bow, like a stone in my sling.

But the hour of vengeance falls, and I love you.
Body of skin, of moss, of avid, steady milk.
Ah the goblets of the breasts! Ah the eyes of absence!
Ah the roses of the pubis! Ah your voice slow and sad!

Body of my woman, I will persist in your grace.
My thirst, my boundless yearning, my indecisive path!
Dark riverbeds where eternal thirst follows,
and fatigue follows, and infinite sorrow.

MARK EISNER

II

The light wraps you in its mortal flame.
Abstracted pale mourner, standing that way
against the old propellers of the twilight
that revolves around you.

Speechless, my friend,
alone in the loneliness of this hour of the dead

and filled with the lives of fire,
pure heir of the ruined day.

A bough of fruit falls from the sun on your dark garment.
The great roots of night
grow suddenly from your soul,
and the things that hide in you come out again
so that a blue and pallid people,
your newly born, takes nourishment.

Oh magnificent and fecund and magnetic slave
of the circle that moves in turn through black and gold:
rise, lead, and possess a creation
so rich in life that its flowers perish
and it is full of sadness.

W. S. MERWIN

IX

Drunk with pines and long kisses,
like summer I steer the fast sail of the roses,
bent towards the death of the thin day,
stuck into my solid marine madness.

Pale and lashed to my ravenous water,
I cruise in the sour smell of the naked climate,
still dressed in gray and bitter sounds
and a sad crest of abandoned spray.

Hardened by passions, I go mounted on my one wave,
lunar, solar, burning and cold, all at once,
becalmed in the throat of the fortunate isles
that are white and sweet as cool hips.

In the moist night my garment of kisses trembles
charged to insanity with electric currents,
heroically divided into dreams
and intoxicating roses practicing on me.

Upstream, in the midst of the outer waves,
your parallel body yields to my arms
like a fish infinitely fastened to my soul,
quick and slow, in the energy under the sky.

W. S. MERWIN

X

Hemos perdido aun este crepúsculo.
Nadie nos vio esta tarde con las manos unidas
mientras la noche azul caía sobre el mundo.

He visto desde mi ventana
la fiesta del poniente en los cerros lejanos.

A veces como una moneda
se encendía un pedazo de sol entre mis manos.

Yo te recordaba con el alma apretada
de esa tristeza que tú me conoces.

Entonces, dónde estabas?
Entre qué gentes?
Diciendo qué palabras?
Por qué se me vendrá todo el amor de golpe
cuando me siento triste, y te siento lejana?

Cayó el libro que siempre se toma en el crepúsculo,
y como un perro herido rodó a mis pies mi capa.

Siempre, siempre te alejas en las tardes
hacia donde el crepúsculo corre borrando estatuas.

X

We have lost even this twilight.
No one saw us this evening hand in hand
while the blue night dropped on the world.

I have seen from my window
the fiesta of sunset in the distant mountaintops.

Sometimes a piece of sun
burned like a coin between my hands.

I remembered you with my soul clenched
in that sadness of mine that you know.

Where were you then?
Who else was there?
Saying what?
Why will the whole of love come on me suddenly
when I am sad and feel you are far away?

The book fell that is always turned to at twilight
and my cape rolled like a hurt dog at my feet.

Always, always you recede through the evenings
towards where the twilight goes erasing statues.

W. S. MERWIN

XII

Your breast is enough for my heart,
and my wings for your freedom.
What was sleeping above your soul will rise
out of my mouth to heaven.

In you is the illusion of each day.
You arrive like the dew to the cupped flowers.

You undermine the horizon with your absence.
Eternally in flight like the wave.

I have said that you sang in the wind
like the pines and like the masts.
Like them you are tall and taciturn,
and you are sad, all at once, like a voyage.

You gather things to you like an old road.
You are peopled with echoes and nostalgic voices.
I awoke and at times birds fled and migrated
that had been sleeping in your soul.

W. S. MERWIN

XIII

I have gone marking the atlas of your body
with crosses of fire.
My mouth went across: a spider, trying to hide.
In you, behind you, timid, driven by thirst.

Stories to tell you on the shore of evening,
sad and gentle doll, so that you should not be sad.
A swan, a tree, something far away and happy.
The season of grapes, the ripe and fruitful season.

I who lived in a harbor from which I loved you.
The solitude crossed with dream and with silence.
Penned up between the sea and sadness.
Soundless, delirious, between two motionless gondoliers.

Between the lips and the voice something goes dying.
Something with the wings of a bird, something of anguish and oblivion.
The way nets cannot hold water.
My toy doll, only a few drops are left trembling.
Even so, something sings in these fugitive words.
Something sings, something climbs to my ravenous mouth.
Oh to be able to celebrate you with all the words of joy.

Sing, burn, flee, like a belfry at the hands of a madman.
My sad tenderness, what comes over you all at once?
When I have reached the most awesome and the coldest summit
my heart closes like a nocturnal flower.

W. S. MERWIN

XIV

Every day you play with the light of the universe.
Subtle visitor, you arrive in the flower and the water.
You are more than this white head that I hold tightly
as a cluster of fruit, every day, between my hands.

You are like nobody since I love you.
Let me spread you out among yellow garlands.
Who writes your name in letters of smoke among the stars of the south?
Oh let me remember you as you were before you existed.

Suddenly the wind howls and bangs at my shut window.
The sky is a net crammed with shadowy fish.
Here all the winds let go sooner or later, all of them.
The rain takes off her clothes.

The birds go by, fleeing.
The wind. The wind.
I can contend only against the power of men.
The storm whirls dark leaves
and turns loose all the boats that were moored last night to the sky.

You are here. Oh, you do not run away.
You will answer me to the last cry.
Cling to me as though you were frightened.
Even so, at one time a strange shadow ran through your eyes.

Now, now too, little one, you bring me honeysuckle,
and even your breasts smell of it.
While the sad wind goes slaughtering butterflies
I love you, and my happiness bites the plum of your mouth.

How you must have suffered getting accustomed to me,
my savage, solitary soul, my name that sends them all running.
So many times we have seen the morning star burn, kissing our eyes,
and over our heads the gray light unwinds in turning fans.

My words rained over you, stroking you.
A long time I have loved the sunned mother-of-pearl of your body.
I go so far as to think that you own the universe.
I will bring you happy flowers from the mountains, bluebells,
dark hazels, and rustic baskets of kisses.
I want
to do with you what spring does with the cherry trees.

W. S. MERWIN

XV

Me gustas cuando callas porque estás como ausente,
y me oyes desde lejos, y mi voz no te toca.
Parece que los ojos se te hubieran volado
y parece que un beso te cerrara la boca.

Como todas las cosas están llenas de mi alma
emerges de las cosas, llena del alma mía.
Mariposa de sueño, te pareces a mi alma,
y te pareces a la palabra melancolía.

Me gustas cuando callas y estás como distante.
Y estás como quejándote, mariposa en arrullo.
Y me oyes desde lejos, y mi voz no te alcanza:
déjame que me calle con el silencio tuyo.

Déjame que te hable también con tu silencio
claro como una lámpara, simple como un anillo.
Eres como la noche, callada y constelada.
Tu silencio es de estrella, tan lejano y sencillo.

Me gustas cuando callas porque estás como ausente.
Distante y dolorosa como si hubieras muerto.

Una palabra entonces, una sonrisa bastan.
Y estoy alegre, alegre de que no sea cierto.

XV

I like for you to be still: it is as though you were absent,
and you hear me from far away and my voice does not touch you.
It seems as though your eyes had flown away
and it seems that a kiss had sealed your mouth.

As all things are filled with my soul
you emerge from the things, filled with my soul.
You are like my soul, a butterfly of dream,
and you are like the word Melancholy.

I like for you to be still, and you seem far away.
It sounds as though you were lamenting, a butterfly cooing like a dove.
And you hear me from far away, and my voice does not reach you:
Let me come to be still in your silence.

And let me talk to you with your silence
that is bright as a lamp, simple as a ring.
You are like the night, with its stillness and constellations.
Your silence is that of a star, as remote and candid.

I like for you to be still: it is as though you were absent,
distant and full of sorrow as though you had died.
One word then, one smile, is enough.
And I am happy, happy that it's not true.

W. S. MERWIN

XVII

Thinking, tangling shadows in the deep solitude.
You are far away too, oh farther than anyone.
Thinking, freeing birds, dissolving images,
burying lamps.

16

Belfry of fogs, how far away, up there!
Stifling laments, milling shadowy hopes,
taciturn miller,
night falls on you face downward, far from the city.

Your presence is foreign, as strange to me as a thing.
I think, I explore great tracts of my life before you.
My life before anyone, my harsh life.
The shout facing the sea, among the rocks,
running free, mad, in the sea-spray.
The sad rage, the shout, the solitude of the sea.
Headlong, violent, stretched towards the sky.

You, woman, what were you there, what ray, what vane
of that immense fan? You were as far as you are now.
Fire in the forest! Burn in blue crosses.
Burn, burn, flame up, sparkle in trees of light.

It collapses, crackling. Fire. Fire.
And my soul dances, seared with curls of fire.
Who calls? What silence peopled with echoes?

Hour of nostalgia, hour of happiness, hour of solitude,
hour that is mine from among them all!
Hunting horn through which the wind passes singing.
Such a passion of weeping tied to my body.

Shaking of all the roots,
attack of all the waves!
My soul wandered, happy, sad, unending.

Thinking, burying lamps in the deep solitude.

Who are you, who are you?

W. S. MERWIN

Here I love you.
In the dark pines the wind disentangles itself.
The moon glows like phosphorus on the vagrant waters.
Days, all one kind, go chasing each other.

The snow unfurls in dancing figures.
A silver gull slips down from the west.
Sometimes a sail. High, high stars.

Oh the black cross of a ship.
Alone.
Sometimes I get up early and even my soul is wet.
Far away the sea sounds and resounds.
This is a port.
Here I love you.

Here I love you and the horizon hides you in vain.
I love you still among these cold things.
Sometimes my kisses go on those heavy vessels
that cross the sea towards no arrival.
I see myself forgotten like those old anchors.
The piers sadden when the afternoon moors there.
My life grows tired, hungry to no purpose.
I love what I do not have. You are so far.
My loathing wrestles with the slow twilights.
But night comes and starts to sing to me.

The moon turns its clockwork dream.
The biggest stars look at me with your eyes.
And as I love you, the pines in the wind
want to sing your name with their leaves of wire.

W. S. MERWIN

XX

Tonight I can write the saddest lines.

Write, for example, "The night is starry
and the stars are blue and shiver in the distance."

The night wind revolves in the sky and sings.

Tonight I can write the saddest lines.
I loved her, and sometimes she loved me too.

Through nights like this one I held her in my arms.
I kissed her again and again under the endless sky.

She loved me, sometimes I loved her too.
How could one not have loved her great still eyes.

Tonight I can write the saddest lines.
To think that I do not have her. To feel that I have lost her.

To hear the immense night, still more immense without her.
And the verse falls to the soul like dew to the pasture.

What does it matter that my love could not keep her.
The night is starry and she is not with me.

This is all. In the distance someone is singing. In the distance.
My soul is not satisfied that it has lost her.

My sight tries to find her as though to bring her closer.
My heart looks for her, and she is not with me.

The same night whitening the same trees.
We, of that time, are no longer the same.

I no longer love her, that's certain, but how I loved her.
My voice tried to find the wind to touch her hearing.

Another's. She will be another's. As she was before my kisses.
Her voice, her bright body. Her infinite eyes.

I no longer love her, that's certain, but maybe I love her.
Love is so short, forgetting is so long.

Because through nights like this one I held her in my arms
my soul is not satisfied that it has lost her.

Though this be the last pain that she makes me suffer
and these the last verses that I write for her.

W. S. MERWIN

✳

Emerge tu recuerdo de la noche en que estoy.
El río anuda al mar su lamento obstinado.

Abandonado como los muelles en el alba.
Es la hora de partir, oh abandonado!

Sobre mi corazón llueven frías corolas.
Oh sentina de escombros, feroz cueva de náufragos!

En ti se acumularon las guerras y los vuelos.
De ti alzaron las alas los pájaros del canto.

Todo te lo tragaste, como la lejanía.
Como el mar, como el tiempo. Todo en ti fue naufragio!

Era la alegre hora del asalto y el beso.
La hora del estupor que ardía como un faro.

Ansiedad de piloto, furia de buzo ciego,
turbia embriaguez de amor, todo en ti fue naufragio!

En la infancia de niebla mi alma alada y herida.
Descubridor perdido, todo en ti fue naufragio!

Te ceñiste al dolor, te agarraste al deseo.
Te tumbó la tristeza, todo en ti fue naufragio!

Hice retroceder la muralla de sombra,
anduve más allá del deseo y del acto.

Oh carne, carne mía, mujer que amé y perdí,
a ti en esta hora húmeda, evoco y hago canto.

Como un vaso albergaste la infinita ternura,
y el infinito olvido te trizó como a un vaso.

Era la negra, negra soledad de las islas,
y allí, mujer de amor, me acogieron tus brazos.

Era la sed y el hambre, y tú fuiste la fruta.
Era el duelo y las ruinas, y tú fuiste el milagro.

Ah mujer, no sé cómo pudiste contenerme
en la tierra de tu alma, y en la cruz de tus brazos!

Mi deseo de ti fue el más terrible y corto,
el más revuelto y ebrio, el más tirante y ávido.

Cementerio de besos, aún hay fuego en tus tumbas,
aún los racimos arden picoteados de pájaros.

Oh la boca mordida, oh los besados miembros,
oh los hambrientos dientes, oh los cuerpos trenzados.

Oh la cópula loca de esperanza y esfuerzo
en que nos anudamos y nos desesperamos.

Y la ternura, leve como el agua y la harina.
Y la palabra apenas comenzada en los labios.

Ése fue mi destino y en él viajó mi anhelo,
y en él cayó mi anhelo, todo en ti fue naufragio!

Oh sentina de escombros, en ti todo caía,
qué dolor no exprimiste, qué olas no te ahogaron.

De tumbo en tumbo aún llameaste y cantaste
de pie como un marino en la proa de un barco.

Aún floreciste en cantos, aún rompiste en corrientes.
Oh sentina de escombros, pozo abierto y amargo.

Pálido buzo ciego, desventurado hondero,
descubridor perdido, todo en ti fue naufragio!

Es la hora de partir, la dura y fría hora
que la noche sujeta a todo horario.

El cinturón ruidoso del mar ciñe la costa.
Surgen frías estrellas, emigran negros pájaros.

Abandonado como los muelles en el alba.
Sólo la sombra trémula se retuerce en mis manos.

Ah más allá de todo. Ah más allá de todo.

Es la hora de partir. Oh abandonado!

The memory of you emerges from the night around me.
The river mingles its stubborn lament with the sea.

Deserted like the wharves at dawn.
It is the hour of departure, oh deserted one!

Cold flower heads are raining over my heart.
Oh pit of debris, fierce cave of the shipwrecked.

In you the wars and the flights accumulated.
From you the wings of the songbirds rose.

You swallowed everything, like distance.
Like the sea, like time. In you everything sank!

It was the happy hour of assault and the kiss.
The hour of the spell that blazed like a lighthouse.

Pilot's dread, fury of a blind diver,
turbulent drunkenness of love, in you everything sank!

In the childhood of mist my soul, winged and wounded.
Lost discoverer, in you everything sank!

You girdled sorrow, you clung to desire,
sadness stunned you, in you everything sank!

I made the wall of shadow draw back,
beyond desire and act, I walked on.

Oh flesh, my own flesh, woman whom I loved and lost,
I summon you in the moist hour, I raise my song to you.

Like a jar you housed the infinite tenderness,
and the infinite oblivion shattered you like a jar.

There was the black solitude of the islands,
and there, woman of love, your arms took me in.

There were thirst and hunger, and you were the fruit.
There were grief and the ruins, and you were the miracle.

Ah woman, I do not know how you could contain me
in the earth of your soul, in the cross of your arms!

How terrible and brief was my desire of you!
How difficult and drunken, how tensed and avid.

Cemetery of kisses, there is still fire in your tombs,
still the fruited boughs burn, pecked at by birds.

Oh the bitten mouth, oh the kissed limbs,
oh the hungering teeth, oh the entwined bodies.

Oh the mad coupling of hope and force
in which we merged and despaired.

And the tenderness, light as water and as flour.
And the word scarcely begun on the lips.

This was my destiny and in it was the voyage of my longing,
and in it my longing fell, in you everything sank!

Oh pit of debris, everything fell into you,
what sorrow did you not express, in what sorrow are you not drowned!

From billow to billow you still called and sang.
Standing like a sailor in the prow of a vessel.

You still flowered in songs, you still broke in currents.
Oh pit of debris, open and bitter well.

Pale blind diver, luckless slinger,
lost discoverer, in you everything sank!

It is the hour of departure, the hard cold hour
which the night fastens to all the timetables.

The rustling belt of the sea girdles the shore.
Cold stars heave up, black birds migrate.

Deserted like the wharves at dawn.
Only the tremulous shadow twists in my hands.

Oh farther than everything. Oh farther than everything.

It is the hour of departure. Oh abandoned one.

W. S. MERWIN

from

RESIDENCE ON
EARTH

RESIDENCÍA EN
LA TIERRA

1925–1945

I

DEAD GALLOP

Like ashes, like oceans swarming,
in the sunken slowness, formlessness,
or like high on the road hearing
bellstrokes cross by crosswise,
holding that sound just free of the metal,
blurred, bearing down, reducing to dust
in the selfsame mill of forms far out of reach,
whether remembered or never seen,
and the aroma of plums rolling to earth
that rot in time, endlessly green.

All of it so quick, so livening,
immobile though, like a pulley idling on itself,
those wheels that motors have, in short.
Existing like dry stitches in the seams of trees,
silenced, encircling, in such a way,
all the planets splicing their tails.
Then from where, which way, on what shore?
The ceaseless whirl, uncertain, so still,
like lilacs around a convent,
or death when it gets to the tongue of an ox
who stumbles down unguarded, horns wanting to sound.

That's why, in what's immobile, pausing, to perceive
then, like great wingbeats, overhead,
like dead bees or numbers,
oh all that my spent heart can't embrace,
in crowds, in half-shed tears
and human toiling, turbulence,
black actions suddenly disclosed

like ice, immense disorder,
oceanwide, for me who goes in singing
with a sword among defenseless men.

Well then what is it made of—that spurt of doves
between night and time, like a damp ravine?
That sound so drawn out now
that drops down lining the roads with stones,
or better, when just one hour
buds up suddenly, extending endlessly.

Within the ring of summer,
once, the enormous calabashes listen,
stretching their poignant stems—
of that, of that which urging forth,
of what's full, dark with heavy drops.

JOHN FELSTINER

ALLIANCE (SONATA)

Of dusty glances fallen to the ground
or of soundless leaves burying themselves.
Of metals without light, with the emptiness,
with the absence of the suddenly dead day.
At the tip of the hands the dazzlement of butterflies,
the upflight of butterflies whose light has no end.

You kept the trail of light, of broken beings
that the abandoned sun, sinking, casts at the churches.
Stained with glances, dealing with bees,
your substance fleeing from unexpected flame
precedes and follows the day and its family of gold.

The spying days cross in secret
but they fall within your voice of light.
Oh mistress of love, in your rest
I established my dream, my silent attitude.

With your body of timid number, suddenly extended
to the quantities that define the earth,
behind the struggle of the days white with space
and cold with slow deaths and withered stimuli,
I feel your lap burn and your kisses travel
shaping fresh swallows in my sleep.

At times the destiny of your tears ascends
like age to my forehead, there
the waves are crashing, smashing themselves to death:
their movement is moist, drifting, ultimate.

DONALD D. WALSH

THE DAWN'S DEBILITY

The day of the luckless, the pale day peers out
with a chill and piercing smell, with its forces gray,
without rattles, the dawn oozing everywhere;
it is a shipwreck in a void, with a surrounding of tears.

Because the moist, silent shadow departed from so many places,
from so many vain cavilings, so many earthly places
where it must have occupied even the design of the roots,
from so many sharp and self-defending shapes.

I weep amid invasion, among confusion,
among the swelling taste, lending an ear
to the pure circulation, to the increase,
making pathless way for what arrives,
what comes forth dressed in chains and carnations,
I dream, enduring my mortal remains.

There is nothing precipitous, or gay, or proud in form,
everything appears, taking shape with obvious poverty,
the light of the earth comes from its eyelids
not like the stroke of a bell but rather like tears:
the texture of the day, its feeble canvas,

serves as a bandage for the patients, serves to make signs
in a farewell, behind the absence:
it is the color that wants only to replace,
to cover, swallow, conquer, make distances.

I am alone among rickety substances,
the rain falls upon me and it seems like me,
like me with its madness, alone in the dead world,
rejected as it falls, and without persistent shape.

DONALD D. WALSH

UNITY

There is something dense, united, seated in the depths,
repeating its number, its identical sign.
How clear it is that the stones have touched time,
in their fine substance there is a smell of age
and the water that the sea brings from salt and sleep.

I am surrounded by just one thing, a single movement:
the weight of the mineral, the light of the honey,
they stick to the sound of the word *night*:
the shade of wheat, of ivory, of tears,
things of leather, of wood, of wool,
aged, faded, uniform things
gather around me like walls.

I work silently, wheeling over myself,
like the crow over death, the crow in mourning.
I think, isolated in the expanse of the seasons,
central, surrounded by silent geography:
a partial temperature falls from the sky,
an ultimate empire of confused unities
gathers surrounding me.

DONALD D. WALSH

JOACHIM'S ABSENCE

From now, like a departure noticed from afar,
in funeral stations of smoke or solitary seawalls,
from now I see him plunging to his death,
and behind him I feel the days of time close in.

From now, brusquely, I feel him leave,
plunging into the waters, into certain waters, into a certain ocean,
and then, as he strikes, drops rise, and I hear
a sound, a persistent, deep sound come forth,
a huge wave, whipped by his weight,
and from somewhere, from somewhere, I feel these waters leaping and
    splashing,
these waters splash upon me, and they have acid lives.

His habit of dreams and measureless nights,
his disobedient soul, his prepared pallor
sleep with him at last, and he sleeps,
because his passion collapses into the sea of the dead,
violently sinking, coldly coalescing.

DONALD D. WALSH

FANTASMA

Cómo surges de antaño, llegando,
ecandilada, pálida estudiante,
a cuya voz aún piden consuelo
los meses dilatados y fijos.

Sus ojos luchaban como remeros
en el infinito muerto
con esperanza de sueño y materia
de seres saliendo del mar.

Del la lejanía en donde
el olor de la tierra es otro

y lo vespertino llega llorando
en forma de oscuras amapolas.

En la altura de los días inmóviles
el insensible joven diurno
en tu rayo de luz se dormía
afirmado como en una espada.

Mientras tanto crece a la sombra
del largo transcuro en olvido
la flor de la soledad, húmeda, extensa,
como la tierra en un largo invierno.

PHANTOM

How you rise up from yesteryear, arriving,
dazzled, pale student,
at whose voice the dilated and fixed months
still beg for consolation.

Their eyes struggled like rowers
in the dead infinity
with hope of sleep and substance
of beings emerging from the sea.

From the distance where
the smell of the earth is different
and the twilight comes weeping
in the shape of dark poppies.

At the height of motionless days
the insensible diurnal youth
was falling asleep in your ray of light
as if fixed upon a sword.

Meanwhile there grows in the shadow
of the long passage through oblivion

the flower of solitude, moist, extensive,
like the earth in a long winter.

DONALD D. WALSH

SLOW LAMENT

Into the night of the heart
your name drops slowly
and moves in silence and falls
and breaks and spreads its water.

Something wishes for its slight harm
and its infinite and short esteem,
like the step of a lost one
suddenly heard.

Suddenly, suddenly listened to
and spread in the heart
with sad insistence and increase
like a cold autumnal dream.

The thick wheel of the earth,
its tire moist with oblivion,
spins, cutting time
into inaccessible halves.

Its hard goblets cover your heart
spilt upon the cold earth
with its poor blue sparks
flying in the voice of the rain.

DONALD D. WALSH

How pure you are by sunlight or by fallen night,
how triumphal and boundless your orbit of white,
and your bosom of bread, high in climate,
your crown of black trees, beloved,
and your lone-animal nose, nose of a wild sheep
that smells of shadow and of precipitous, tyrannical flight.

Now, what splendid weapons my hands,
how worthy their blade of bone and their lily nails,
and the placing of my face and the rental of my soul
are situated in the center of earthly force.
How pure my gaze of nocturnal influence,
a fall of dark eyes and ferocious urge,
my symmetrical statue with twin legs
mounts toward moist stars each morning,
and my exiled mouth bites the flesh and the grape,
my manly arms, my tattooed chest
on which the hair takes root like a tin wing,
my white face made for the sun's depth,
my hair made of rituals, of black minerals,
my forehead, penetrating as a blow or a road,
my skin of a grownup son, destined for the plow,
my eyes of avid salt, of rapid marriage,
my tongue soft friend of dike and ship,
my teeth like a white clockface, of systematic equity,
the skin that makes in front of me an icy emptiness
and in back of me revolves, and flies in my eyelids,
and folds back upon my deepest stimulus,
and grows toward the roses in my fingers,
in my chin of bone and in my feet of richness.

And you, like a month of star, like a fixed kiss,
like a structure of wing, or the beginning of autumn,
girl, my advocate, my amorous one,
light makes its bed beneath your big eyelids,
golden as oxen, and the round dove
often makes her white nests in you.

Made of wave in ingots and white pincers,
your furious apple health stretches without limit,
the trembling cask in which your stomach listens,
your hands daughters of wheat and sky.

How like you are to the longest kiss,
its fixed shock seems to nourish you,
and its thrust of live coals, of fluttering flag,
goes throbbing in your domains and mounting trembling,
and then your head slenders into hairs,
and its warlike form, its dry circle,
collapses suddenly into lineal strings
like swords' edges or inheritance of smoke.

DONALD D. WALSH

TYRANNY

Oh heartless lady, daughter of the sky,
help me in this solitary hour
with your direct armed indifference
and your cold sense of oblivion.

A time complete as an ocean,
a wound confused as a new being
encompass the stubborn root of my soul
biting the center of my security.

What a heavy throbbing beats in my heart
like a wave made of all the waves,
and my despairing head is raised
in an effort of leaping and of death.

There is something hostile trembling in my certitude,
growing in the very origin of tears
like a harsh, clawing plant
made of linked and bitter leaves.

DONALD D. WALSH

SERENADE

On your brow rests the color of the poppies,
the mourning of widows finds echo, oh hapless one:
when you run behind the railroads, in the fields,
the slender worker turns his back on you,
from your footprints sweet toads sprout trembling.

The youth without memories greets you, asks you about his forgotten
    wish,
his hands move in your atmosphere like birds,
and there is great dampness surrounding him:
crossing his incomplete thoughts,
wishing to reach something, oh, seeking you,
his pale eyes blink in your net
like lost instruments that suddenly gleam.

Oh I remember the first day of thirst,
the shadow pressed against the jasmines,
the deep body in which you took refuge
like a drop that also trembles.

But you silence the great trees, and above the moon, far away above,
you spy upon the sea like a thief.
Oh, night, my startled soul asks you,
you, desperately, about the metal that it needs.

DONALD D. WALSH

ARS POETICA

Between shadow and space, between trimmings and damsels,
endowed with a singular heart and sorrowful dreams,
precipitously pallid, withered in the brow
and with a furious widower's mourning for each day of life,
ah, for each invisible water that I drink somnolently
and from every sound that I welcome trembling,
I have the same absent thirst and the same cold fever,

a nascent ear, an indirect anguish,
as if thieves or ghosts were coming,
and in a shell of fixed and profound expanse,
like a humiliated waiter, like a slightly raucous bell,
like an old mirror, like the smell of a solitary house
where the guests come in at night wildly drunk,
and there is a smell of clothes thrown on the floor, and an absence of
    flowers—
possibly in another even less melancholy way—
but the truth is that suddenly the wind that lashes my chest,
the nights of infinite substance fallen in my bedroom,
the noise of a day that burns with sacrifice,
ask me mournfully what prophecy there is in me,
and there is a swarm of objects that call without being answered,
and a ceaseless movement, and a bewildered man.

DONALD D. WALSH

ARS POETICA

Between shadow and space, between garrisons and maidens,
Endowed with singular heart and doleful dreams,
Precipitately pale, the forehead withered,
And with the mourning of an angry widower for each day of life,
Alas, for each invisible drop of water which I drink sleepily
And for each sound which I receive, trembling,
I have the same absent thirst and the same cold fever,
An ear that is born, an indirect anguish,
As if thieves or ghosts were approaching,
And in a shell of fixed and deep extent,
Like a humiliated waiter, like a bell slightly hoarse,
Like an old mirror, like the smell of a lonely house
Whose roomers enter by night dead drunk,
And there is a smell of clothing thrown about on the floor, and an
    absence of flowers,
Possibly in some other way even less melancholy,
But, in truth, suddenly, the wind that strikes my chest,
The nights of infinite substance dropped into my bedroom,

The noise of a day that burns with sacrifice,
Demand, sadly, whatever there is of prophetic in me,
And there is a knocking of objects which call without being answered,
And a ceaseless movement, and a confused name.

ANGEL FLORES

SONATA AND DESTRUCTIONS

After a good deal, after vague leagues,
confused about domains, uncertain about territories,
accompanied by faint hopes
and faithless companies and uneasy dreams,
I love the tenacity that still survives in my eyes,
I hear in my heart my horseman steps,
I bite the dormant fire and the ruined salt,
and at night, dark in atmosphere and fugitive mourning,
he who keeps vigil at the edge of camps,
the armed traveler of sterile resistances,
prisoner amid growing shadows and trembling wings,
I feel that I am he, and my arm of stone defends me.

There is among the sciences of weeping a confused altar,
and in my session of perfumeless twilights,
in my abandoned bedrooms where the moon dwells,
and inherited chandeliers, and destructions that are dear to me,
I adore my own lost being, my imperfect substance,
my silver set and my eternal loss.
The moist grape burned, and its funereal water
still wavers, still resides,
and the sterile patrimony, and the treacherous domicile.

Who made a ceremony of ashes?
Who loved the lost, who protected the last?
The bone of the father, the wood of the dead ship,
and its own ending, its very flight,
its sad force, its miserable god?

I spy, then, on the inanimate and the doleful,
and the strange testimony that I affirm,
with cruel efficiency and written in ashes,
is the form of oblivion that I prefer,
the name that I give to the earth, the value of my dreams,
the interminable quantity that I divide
with my winter eyes, during each day of this world.

DONALD D. WALSH

II

LA NOCHE DEL SOLDADO

Yo hago la noche del soldado, el tiempo del hombre sin melancolía ni exterminio, del tipo tirado lejos por el océano y una ola, y que no sabe que el agua amarga lo ha separado y que envejece, paulatinamente y sin miedo, dedicado a lo normal de la vida, sin cataclismos, sin ausencias, viviendo dentro de su piel y de su traje, sinceramente oscuro. Así, pues, me veo con camaradas estúpidos y alegres, que fuman y escupen y horrendamente beben, y que de repente caen enfermos de muerte. Porque, dónde están la tía, la novia, la suegra, la cuñada del soldado? Tal vez de ostracismo o de malaria mueren, se ponen fríos, amarillos, y emigran a un astro de hielo, a sus cadáveres, sus pobres cadáveres de fuego, irán custodiados por ángeles abastrinos a dormir lejos de la llama y la ceniza.

Por cada día que cae, con su obligación vesperal de sucumbir, paseo, haciendo una guardia innecesaria, y paso entre mercaderes mahometanos, entre gentes que adoran la vaca y la cobra, paso yo, inadorable y común de rostro. Los meses no son inalterables, y a veces llueve: cae del calor del cielo una impregnación callada como el sudor, y sobre los grandes vegetales, sobre el lomo de las bestias feroces, a lo largo de cierto silencio, estas plumas húmedas se entretejen y alargan. Aguas de la noche, lágrimas del viento monzón, saliva salada caída como la espuma del caballo, y lenta de aumento, pobre de salpicadura, atónita de vuelo.

Ahora, dónde está esa curiosidad profesional, esa ternura abatida que sólo con su reposo abría brecha, esa conciencia resplandeciente cuyo destello me vestía de ultraazul? Voy respirando como hijo hasta el corazón de un método obligatorio, de una tenaz paciencia física, resultado de alisus mentos y edad acumulados cada día, despojado de mi vestuario de venganza y de mi piel de oro. Horas de una sola estación ruedan a mis pies, y un día de formas diurnas y nocturnas está casi siempre detenido sobre mí.

Entonces, de cuando en cuando, visito muchachas de ojos y caderas jóvenes, seres en cuyo peinado brilla una flor amarilla como el relámpago. Ellas llevan anillos en cada dedo del pie, y brazaletes, y ajorcas en los tobillos, y además, collares de color, collares que retiro y examino, porque yo quiero sorprenderme ante un cuerpo ininterrumpido y compacto, y no mitigar mi beso. Yo peso con mis brazos cada nueva estatua, y bebo su remedio vivo con sed masculina y en silencio. Tendido, mirando desde abajo la fugitiva criatura, trepando por su ser desnudo hasta su sonrisa: gigantesca y triangular hacia arriba, levantada en el aire por dos senos globales, fijos ante mis ojos como dos lámparas con luz de aceite blanco y dulces energías. Yo me encomiendo a su estrella morena, a su calidez de piel, e inmóvil bajo mi pecho como un adversario desgraciado, de miembros demasiado espesos y débiles, de ondulación indefensa: o bien girando sobre sí misma como una rueda pálida, dividida de aspas y dedos, rápida, profunda, circular, como una estrella en desorden.

Ay, de cada noche que sucede, hay algo de brasa abandonada que se gasta sola, y cae envuelta en ruinas, en medio de cosas funerales. Yo asisto comúnmente a esos términos, cubierto de armas inútiles, lleno de objeciones destruidas. Guardo la ropa y los huesos levemente impregnados de esa materia seminocturna: es un polvo temporal que se me va uniendo, y el dios de la substitución vela a veces a mi lado, respirando tenazmente, levantando la espada.

THE NIGHT OF THE SOLDIER

I play the night of the soldier, the time of the man without melancholy or extermination, of the type cast far by the ocean and a wave, and who does not know that the bitter water has separated him and that he is growing old, gradually and without fear, dedicated to what is normal in life, without cataclysms, without absences, living inside his skin and his suit, sincerely obscure. So, then, I see myself with stupid and gay comrades, who smoke and spit and drink horribly, and who suddenly fall down deathly sick. Because, where are the aunt, the bride, the mother-in-law, the sister-in-law of the soldier? Perhaps they die of ostracism or malaria, they grow cold, yellow, and they emigrate to a star of ice, to a cool planet, to rest, at last, among girls and glacial fruits, and their corpses, their poor fiery corpses, will go guarded by alabaster angels to sleep far from the flame and the ash.

Through each day that falls, with its twilight obligation to succumb, I walk, performing an unnecessary watch, and I pass among Mohammedan merchants, among people who adore the cow and the cobra, I pass, unadorable and common faced. The months are not unalterable, and at times it rains; from the heat of the sky falls an infusion as silent as sweat, and over the great vegetables, over the backs of the fierce beasts, along a certain silence, these moist feathers interweave and lengthen. Waters of the night, tears of the monsoon wind, salt saliva fallen like the horse's spume, and slow to augment, poor in splash, astonished in flight.

Now, where is that professional curiosity, that abject tenderness that with its mere repose opened a breach, that resplendent conscience whose flash dressed me in ultrablue? I go breathing like a child to the heart of an obligatory way, of a tenacious physical patience, the result of food and age accumulated each day, stripped of my wardrobe of vengeance and of my golden skin. Hours of a single season roll at my feet, and a day of diurnal and nocturnal forms is almost always suspended over me.

Then, from time to time, I visit girls with young eyes and hips, beings in whose hair shines a flower yellow as the lightning. They wear rings on each toe, and bracelets, and bangles on their ankles, and besides, colored necklaces, necklaces that I remove and examine, because I want to discover myself before an uninterrupted and compact body, and not to mitigate my kiss. I weigh with my arms each new statue, and I drink its living remedy with masculine thirst and in silence. Stretched out, looking up at the fugitive creature, climbing up over her naked being to her smile; gigantic and triangular above, raised in the air by two global breasts, fixed before my eyes like two lamps with light of white oil and gentle energy. I commend myself to her dark star, to the warmth of her skin, and motionless beneath my chest like a fallen adversary, with members too thick and feeble, with defenseless undulation, or else revolving upon herself like a pale wheel, divided by crosspieces and fingers, rapid, profound, circular, like a disordered star.

Ah, of each night in succession there is something of abandoned coal that consumes itself and falls wrapped in ruins, in the midst of funereal things. I commonly attend those endings, covered with useless weapons, filled with destroyed objections. I watch over the clothes and the bones lightly impregnated with the seminocturnal material; it is a temporal dust that gradually collects on me, and the god of substitution keeps watch at times at my side, breathing tenaciously, raising his sword.

DONALD D. WALSH

CONTRADICTED COMMUNICATIONS

Those days led astray my prophetic sense, into my house entered the stamp collectors, and hidden, at all hours of the season, they assaulted my letters, tore from them fresh kisses, kisses subjected to a long maritime residence, and incantations that protected my luck with feminine science and defensive calligraphy.

I lived beside other houses, other persons, and trees tending to the grandiose, pavilions with passionate foliage, emerged roots, vegetal blades, straight coconut trees, and in the midst of these green foams, I would pass with my sharp-pointed hat and a heart completely fictional, with a splendor-heavy stride, because in proportion as my powers eroded and, destroyed in dust, sought symmetry like the cemetery dead, the known places, the extensions scorned up to that hour and the faces that like slow plants sprouted in my abandonment, varied around me with terror and silence, like quantities of leaves overturned by a sudden autumn.

Parrots, stars, and in addition the official sun and a brusque dampness brought out in me a meditative taste for the earth and whatever covered it, and the satisfaction of an old house in its bats, a naked woman's delicacy about her nails, arranged in me feeble and tenacious weapons of my shameful faculties, and melancholy put its stria in my web, and the love letter, pale-papered and fearful, removed its tremulous spider that scarcely weaves and ceaselessly unweaves and weaves. Naturally, from the lunar light, from its circumstantial prolongation, and still more, from its cold axis, which the birds (swallows, geese) cannot step on even in the deliriums of emigration, from its blue skin, smooth, thin, and without jewels, I fell toward mourning, as one who falls wounded by a sword. I am a fellow of special blood, and that substance at once nocturnal and maritime made me alter and suffer, and those subcelestial waters degraded my energy and the commercial part of my disposition.

In that historic way my bones acquired a great preponderance in my in-

tentions: the repose, the mansions at the seashore attracted me without se-
curity but with destiny, and once arrived at the enclosure, surrounded by
the mute and more motionless chorus, subjected to the final hour and its
perfumes, unjust to inexact geographies and a mortal partisan of the ce-
ment armchair, I await time militarily and with the foil of the adventure
stained with forgotten blood.

DONALD D. WALSH

THE YOUNG MONARCH

As a continuation of what has been read and preceding from the following
page, I must direct my star to amorous territory.

Fatherland limited by two long warm arms, of long parallel passion, and
a place of diamonds defended by system and mathematical warlike science.
Yes, I want to marry the most beautiful woman in Mandalay, I want to en-
trust my earthly wrapping to that noise of the woman cooking, to that
fluttering of skirt and bare foot that move and mix like wind and leaves.

A lovely girl with little feet and a big cigar, amber flowers in her pure
and cylindrical hair, and living dangerously like a heavy-headed lily of
thick consistency.

And my wife at my shore, at the side of my murmur so far-fetched, my
Burmese wife, daughter of the king.

Her coiled black hair I then kiss, and her sweet and perpetual foot; and
night already near, its mill unchained, I listen to my tiger and I weep for
my absent one.

DONALD D. WALSH

III
SINGLE GENTLEMAN

The homosexual young men and the amorous girls,
and the long widows who suffer from delirious insomnia,
and the young wives thirty hours pregnant,
and the raucous cats that cross my garden in the dark,

like a necklace of throbbing sexual oysters,
they surround my solitary residence,
like enemies established against my soul,
like conspirators in nightclothes
who had exchanged long thick kisses by command.

The radiant summer leads the loved ones
in uniform melancholy regiments,
made of fat and skinny and happy and sad couples:
beneath the elegant coconut trees, next to the ocean and the moon,
there is a continuous life of trousers and skirts,
a rustle of stroked silk stockings,
and feminine breasts that shine like eyes.

The little employee, after quite a while,
after the weekly tedium, and the novels read in bed at night,
has definitively seduced his neighbor,
and takes her to miserable movies
where the heroes are colts or passionate princes,
and he strokes her legs covered with soft down,
with his ardent moist hands that smell of cigarettes.

The twilights of the seducer and the nights of the spouses
unite like two sheets burying me,
and the hours after lunch when the young men students
and the young women students and the priests masturbate,
and the animals fornicate directly,
and the bees smell of blood, and the flies buzz angrily,
and boy cousins play strangely with their girl cousins,
and the doctors look furiously at the husband of the young patient,
and the morning hours when the teacher absentmindedly
fulfills his conjugal duty and has breakfast,
and still more, the adulterers, who love each other with true love
upon beds as lofty and lengthy as ships;
I am securely and eternally surrounded by
this great respiratory and entangled forest
with huge flowers like mouths and teeth
and black roots shaped like fingernails and shoes.

DONALD D. WALSH

Distance sheltered upon tubes of foam,
salt in ritual waves and defined orders,
and the smell and murmur of an old ship,
of rotten planks and broken tools,
and weary machines that howl and weep,
pushing the prow, kicking the sides,
chewing laments, swallowing, swallowing distances,
making a noise of bitter waters upon the bitter waters,
moving the ancient ship upon the ancient waters.

Inner vaults, twilight tunnels
visited by the intermittent day of the ports:
sacks, sacks accumulated by a somber god,
like gray animals, round and eyeless,
with sweet gray ears,
and estimable bellies filled with wheat or copra,
sensitive paunches of pregnant women
shabbily dressed in gray, patiently
waiting in the shadow of a dreary movie house.

The outer waters suddenly
are heard passing, running like an opaque horse,
with a noise of horsehoofs on the water,
swift, plunging again into the waters.
There is then nothing more than time in the cabins:
time in the ill-fated solitary dining room,
motionless and visible like a great misfortune.
The smell of leather and cloth worn to shreds,
and onions, and olive oil, and even more,
the smell of someone floating in the corners of the ship,
the smell of someone nameless
who comes down the ladders like a wave of air,
and crosses through corridors with his absent body,
and observes with his eyes preserved by death.

He observes with his colorless, sightless eyes,
slowly, and he passes trembling, without presence or shadow:

noises wrinkle him, things pierce him,
his transparency makes the dirty chairs gleam.
Who is that ghost without a ghostly body,
with his steps light as nocturnal flour
and his voice sponsored only by things?
The furniture moves along filled with his silent being
like little ships inside the old ship,
laden with his faint and uncertain being:
the closets, the green covers of the tables,
the color of the curtains and the floor,
everything has suffered the slow emptiness of his hands,
and his breathing has wasted things away.

He slides and slips, he descends transparent,
air with the cold air that runs across the ship,
with his hidden hands he leans against the railings
and looks at the angry sea that flees behind the ship.
Only the waters reject his influence,
his color and his smell of forgotten ghost,
and fresh and deep they develop their dance
like fiery lives, like blood or perfume,
new and strong they surge, joined and rejoined.

The waters, inexhaustible, without custom or time,
green in quantity, efficient and cold,
touch the black stomach of the ship and wash
its matter, its broken crusts, its iron wrinkles:
the living waters gnaw at the ship's shell,
trafficking its long banners of foam
and its salt teeth flying in drops.

The ghost looks at the sea with his eyeless face:
the circle of the day, the cough of the ship, a bird
in the round and solitary equation of space,
and he descends again to the life of the ship,
falling upon dead time and wood,
slipping in the black kitchens and cabins,
slow with air and atmosphere and desolate space.

DONALD D. WALSH

Oh evil one, you must by now have found the letter, you must have wept
    with fury,
and you must have insulted my mother's memory,
calling her rotten bitch and mother of dogs,
you must have drunk alone, all by yourself, your twilight tea,
looking at my old shoes forever empty,
and you won't be able any longer to recall my illnesses, my night dreams,
    my meals,
without cursing me aloud as if I were still there,
complaining about the tropics, about the *corringhis* coolies,
about the poisonous fevers that did me so much harm,
and about the frightful Englishmen that I still hate.

Evil one, really, what an enormous night, what a lonely earth!
I have come again to the solitary bedrooms,
to lunch on cold food in the restaurants, and again
I throw my trousers and shirts upon the floor,
there are no coat hangers in my room, no pictures of anyone on the
    walls.
How much of the darkness in my soul I would give to get you back,
and how threatening to me seem the names of the months,
and the word *winter*, what a mournful drum sound it has.

Buried next to the coconut tree you will later find
the knife that I hid there for fear that you would kill me,
and now suddenly I should like to smell its kitchen steel
accustomed to the weight of your hand and the shine of your foot:
under the moisture of the earth, among the deaf roots,
of all human languages the poor thing would know only your name,
and the thick earth does not understand your name
made of impenetrable and divine substances.

Just as it afflicts me to think of the clear day of your legs
curled up like still and harsh solar waters,
and the swallow that sleeping and flying lives in your eyes,
and the furious dog that you shelter in your heart,
so too I see the deaths that are between us from now on,

and I breathe in the air ashes and destruction,
the long, solitary space that surrounds me forever.

I would give this giant sea wind for your brusque breath
heard in long nights with no mixture of oblivion,
merging with the atmosphere like the whip with the horse's hide.
And to hear you making water in the darkness, at the back of the house,
as if spilling a thin, tremulous, silvery, persistent honey,
how many times would I give up this chorus of shadows that I possess,
and the noise of useless swords that is heard in my heart,
and the bloody dove that sits alone on my brow
calling for vanished things, vanished beings,
substances strangely inseparable and lost.

DONALD D. WALSH

IV

IT MEANS SHADOWS

What hope to consider, what pure presage,
what definitive kiss to bury in the heart,
to yield in the origins of rejection and intelligence,
soft and safe upon the eternally troubled waters?

What vital, rapid wings of a new angel of dreams
to install on my sleeping shoulders for perpetual security,
in such a way that the road among the stars of death
shall be a violent flight begun many days and months and centuries ago?

Perhaps the natural weakness of suspicious and anxious beings
suddenly seeks permanence in time and limits on earth,
perhaps the tediums and the ages implacably accumulated
extend like the lunar wave of an ocean newly created
upon shores and lands grievously deserted.

Ah, let what I am go on existing and ceasing to exist,
and let my obedience be ordered with such iron conditions

that the tremor of deaths and of births will not trouble
the deep place that I wish to keep for myself eternally.

Let him be, then, what I am, in some place and in every time,
an established and assured and ardent witness,
carefully destroying himself and preserving himself incessantly,
clearly insistent upon his original duty.

DONALD D. WALSH

I

ONE DAY STANDS OUT

From resonance come numbers,
dying numbers and dung-covered ciphers,
dampened thunderbolts and dirty lightningflashes.

From resonance, growing, when
night comes out alone, like a recent widow,
like a dove or a poppy or a kiss,
and her marvelous stars expand.

In resonance light takes place:
vowels are drowned, weeping falls in petals,
a wind of sounds crashes like a wave,
it shines and cold elastic fishes dwell in it.

Fishes in sound, slow, sharp, moist,
arched masses of gold with drops on their tails,
scaly sharks and trembling foam,
bluish salmon with congealed eyes.

Tools that fall, vegetable carts,
rustles of trampled flowers,
violins filled with water, fresh explosions,
submerged motors and dusty shadow,
factories, kisses,
throbbing bottles,
throats,
around me sounds the night,
the day, the month, the time,
sounding like sacks of wet bells,
or frightening mouths of fragile salts.

Sea waves, landslides,
fingernails, sea steps,
coiled currents of destroyed animals,
whistle blasts in the raucous fog
determine the sounds of the gentle dawn
waking in the abandoned sea.

To resonance the soul rolls
falling from dreams,
still surrounded by its black doves,
still lined with its rags of absence.

To resonance the soul rushes
and celebrates and hastens its swift wedding.

Husks of silence, of turbid blue,
like flasks from dark, shut drugstores,
silence wrapped in hair,
silence galloping on legless horses,
and machines asleep, and airless candles,
and trains of dejected jasmine and of wax,
and overladen ships filled with hats and shadows.

From silence the soul rises
with instant roses,
and in the morning of the day it collapses
and plummets into the sounding light.

Brusque shoes, beasts, utensils,
waves of harsh roosters overflowing,
clocks running like dry stomachs,
wheels unrolling on downcast rails,
and white water closets awaking
with wooden eyes, like one-eyed pigeons,
and their sunken throats
make sudden sounds like waterfalls.

See how the mold's eyelids lift
and the red lock is unchained

and the garland develops its affairs,
things that grow,
the bridges crushed by the big streetcars
creak like amatory beds,
night has opened its piano doors:
day runs like a horse in its courts.

From resonance comes the day
of increase and degree,
and also of cut violets and curtains,
of expanses, of shadow recently fleeing
and drops that from the heart of heaven
fall like celestial blood.

DONALD D. WALSH

SÓLO LA MUERTE

Hay cementerios solos,
tumbas llenas de huesos sin sonido,
el corazón pasando un túnel
oscuro, oscuro, oscuro,
como un naufragio hacia adentro nos morimos,
como ahogarnos en el corazón,
como irnos cayendo desde la piel al alma.

Hay cadáveres,
hay pies de pegajosa losa fría,
hay la muerte en los huesos,
como un sonido puro,
como un ladrido sin perro,
saliendo de ciertas campanas, de ciertas tumbas,
creciendo en la humedad como el llanto o la lluvia.

Yo veo, solo, a veces,
ataúdes a vela
zarpar con difuntos pálidos, con mujeres de trenzas muertas,
con panaderos blancos como ángeles,

con niñas pensativas casadas con notarios,
ataúdes subiendo el río vertical de los muertos,
el río morado,
hacia arriba, con las velas hinchadas por el sonido de la muerte,
hinchadas por el sonido silencioso de la muerte.

A lo sonoro llega la muerte
como un zapato sin pie, como un traje sin hombre,
llega a golpear con un anillo sin piedras y sin dedo,
llega a gritar sin boca, sin lengua, sin garganta.
Sin embargo sus pasos suenan
y su vestido suena, callado, como un árbol.

Yo no sé, yo conozco poco, yo apenas veo,
pero creo que su canto tiene color de violetas húmedas,
de violetas acostumbradas a la tierra,
porque la cara de la muerte es verde,
y la mirada de la muerte es verde,
con la aguda humedad de una hoja de violeta
y su grave color de invierno exasperado.

Pero la muerte va también por el mundo vestida de escoba,
lame el suelo buscando difuntos,
la muerte está en la escoba,
es la lengua de la muerte buscando muertos,
es la aguja de la muerte buscando hilo.

La muerte está en los catres:
en los colchones lentos, en las frazadas negras
vive tendida, y de repente sopla:
sopla un sonido oscuro que hincha sábanas,
y hay camas navegando a un puerto
en donde está esperando, vestida de almirante.

ONLY DEATH

There are lone cemeteries,
tombs filled with soundless bones,
the heart passing through a tunnel
dark, dark, dark;
like a shipwreck we die inward,
like smothering in our hearts,
like slowly falling from our skin down to our soul.

There are corpses,
there are feet of sticky, cold gravestone,
there is death in the bones,
like a pure sound,
like a bark without a dog,
coming from certain bells, from certain tombs,
growing in the dampness like teardrops or raindrops.

I see alone, at times,
coffins with sails
weighing anchor with pale corpses, with dead-tressed women,
with bakers white as angels,
with pensive girls married to notaries,
coffins going up the vertical river of the dead,
the dark purple river,
upstream, with the sails swollen by the sound of death,
swollen by the silent sound of death.

To resonance comes death
like a shoe without a foot, like a suit without a man,
she comes to knock with a stoneless and fingerless ring,
she comes to shout without mouth, without tongue, without throat.
Yet her steps sound
and her dress sounds, silent, like a tree.

I know little, I am not well acquainted, I can scarcely see,
but I think that her song has the color of moist violets,
of violets accustomed to the earth,
because the face of death is green,

and the gaze of death is green,
with the sharp dampness of a violet leaf
and its dark color of exasperated winter.

But death also goes through the world dressed as a broom,
she licks the ground looking for corpses,
death is in the broom,
it is death's tongue looking for dead bodies,
it is death's needle looking for thread.

Death is in the cots:
in the slow mattresses, in the black blankets
she lives stretched out, and she suddenly blows:
she blows a dark sound that puffs out sheets,
and there are beds sailing to a port
where she is waiting, dressed as an admiral.

DONALD D. WALSH

II

WALKING AROUND

Sucede que me canso de ser hombre.
Sucede que entro en las sastrerías y en los cines
marchito, impenetrable, como un cisne de fieltro
navegando en un agua de origen y ceniza.

El olor de las peluquerías me hace llorar a gritos.
Sólo quiero un descanso de piedras o de lana,
sólo quiero no ver establecimientos ni jardines,
ni mercaderías, ni anteojos, ni ascensores.

Sucede que me canso de mis pies y mis uñas
y mi pelo y mi sombra.
Sucede que me canso de ser hombre.

Sin embargo sería delicioso
asustar a un notario con un lirio cortado

o dar muerte a una monja con un golpe de oreja.
Sería bello
ir por las calles con un cuchillo verde
y dando gritos hasta morir de frío.

No quiero seguir siendo raíz en las tinieblas,
vacilante, extendido, tiritando de sueño,
hacia abajo, en las tripas mojadas de la tierra,
absorbiendo y pensando, comiendo cada día.

No quiero para mí tantas desgracias.
No quiero continuar de raíz y de tumba,
de subterráneo solo, de bodega con muertos
ateridos, muriéndome de pena.

Por eso el día lunes arde como el petróleo
cuando me ve llegar con mi cara de cárcel,
y aúlla en su transcurso como una rueda herida,
y da pasos de sangre caliente hacia la noche.

Y me empuja a ciertos rincones, a ciertas casas húmedas,
a hospitales donde los huesos salen por la ventana,
a ciertas zapaterías con olor a vinagre,
a calles espantosas como grietas.

Hay pájaros de color de azufre y horribles intestinos
colgando de las puertas de las casas que odio,
hay dentaduras olvidadas en una cafetera,
hay espejos
que debieran haber llorado de vergüenza y espanto,
hay paraguas en todas partes, y venenos, y ombligos.

Yo paseo con calma, con ojos, con zapatos,
con furia, con olvido,
paso, cruzo oficinas y tiendas de ortopedia,
y patios donde hay ropas colgadas de un alambre:
calzoncillos, toallas y camisas que lloran
lentas lágrimas sucias.

WALKING AROUND

I happen to be tired of being a man.
I happen to enter tailorshops and moviehouses
withered, impenetrable, like a felt swan
navigating in a water of sources and ashes.

The smell of barbershops makes me wail.
I want only a respite of stones or wool,
I want only not to see establishments or gardens,
or merchandise, or eyeglasses, or elevators.

I happen to be tired of my feet and my nails
and my hair and my shadow.
I happen to be tired of being a man.

Nevertheless it would be delightful
to startle a notary with a cut lily
or slay a nun with a blow to the ear.
It would be lovely
to go through the streets with a sexy knife
and shouting until froze to death.

I don't want to go on being a root in the dark,
vacillating, stretched out, shivering with sleep,
downward, in the soaked guts of the earth,
absorbing and thinking, eating each day.

I do not want for myself so many misfortunes.
I do not want to continue as root and tomb,
a solitary subterranean, a vault with corpses
stiff with cold, dying of distress.

That is why Monday day burns like petroleum
when it sees me coming with my prison face,
and it howls in its transit like a wounded wheel,
and it takes hot-blooded steps toward the night.

And it pushes me into certain corners, into certain moist houses,
into hospitals where the bones stick out the windows,
into certain shoestores with a smell of vinegar,
into streets as frightening as chasms.

There are brimstone-colored birds and horrible intestines
hanging from the doors of the houses that I hate,
there are dentures left forgotten in a coffeepot,
there are mirrors
that ought to have wept from shame and fright,
there are umbrellas everywhere, and poisons, and navels.

I walk around with calm, with eyes, with shoes,
with fury, with forgetfulness,
I pass, I cross by offices and orthopedic shoestores,
and courtyards where clothes are hanging from a wire:
underdrawers, towels, and shirts that weep
slow, dirty tears.

DONALD D. WALSH

WALKING AROUND

It so happens I am sick of being a man.
And it happens that I walk into tailorshops and movie houses
dried up, waterproof, like a swan made of felt
steering my way in a water of wombs and ashes.

The smell of barbershops makes me break into hoarse sobs.
The only thing I want is to lie still like stones or wool,
The only thing I want is to see no more stores, no gardens,
no more goods, no spectacles, no elevators.

It so happens I am sick of my feet and my nails
and my hair and my shadow.
It so happens I am sick of being a man.

Still it would be marvelous
to terrify a law clerk with a cut lily.

or kill a nun with a blow on the ear.
It would be great
to go through the streets with a green knife
letting out yells until I died of the cold.

I don't want to go on being a root in the dark,
insecure, stretched out, shivering with sleep,
going on down, into the moist guts of the earth,
taking in and thinking, eating every day.

I don't want so much misery.
I don't want to go on as a root and a tomb,
alone under the ground, a warehouse with corpses,
half frozen, dying of grief.

That's why Monday, when it sees me coming
with my convict face, blazes up like gasoline,
and it howls on its way like a wounded wheel,
and leaves tracks full of warm blood leading toward the night.

And it pushes me into certain corners, into some moist houses,
into hospitals where the bones fly out the window,
into shoeshops that smell like vinegar,
and certain streets hideous as cracks in the skin.

There are sulfur-colored birds, and hideous intestines
hanging over the doors of houses that I hate,
and there are false teeth forgotten in a coffeepot,
there are mirrors
that ought to have wept from shame and terror,
there are umbrellas everywhere, and venoms, and umbilical cords.

I stroll along serenely, with my eyes, my shoes,
my rage, forgetting everything,
I walk by, going through office buildings and orthopedic shops,
and courtyards with washing hanging from the line:
underwear, towels, and shirts from which slow
dirty tears are falling.

ROBERT BLY

DISACTION

The dove is filled with spilt papers,
its breast is stained with erasers and weeks,
with blotting paper whiter than a corpse
and inks frightened by their sinister color.

Come with me to the shadow of administrations,
to the weak, delicate, pallid color of the chiefs,
to the tunnels deep as calendars,
to the doleful thousand-paged wheel.

Let us examine now the titles and the conditions,
the special affidavits, the vigils,
the petitions with their teeth of nauseous autumn,
the fury of ashen destinies and sad decisions.

It is a tale of wounded bones,
bitter circumstances and interminable clothes,
and stockings suddenly serious.

It is the dead of night, the veinless head
from which day suddenly falls
as if from a bottle broken by a lightningbolt.

They are the feet and the clocks and the fingers
and a locomotive of dying soap,
and a bitter sky of soaked metal,
and a yellow river of smiles.

Everything reaches the tips of fingers like flowers,
and fingernails like lightningbolts, withered armchairs,
everything reaches the ink of death
and the violet mouths of the tax stamps.

Let us weep for the death of earth and fire,
swords, grapes,
the sexes with their tough realms of roots,
the alcohol ships sailing among ships

and the perfume that dances at night, on its knees,
dragging behind a planet of perforated roses.

With dog's suits and stains on our brows
let us fall into the depths of the papers,
into the anger of enchained words,
into demonstrations tenaciously defunct,
into systems wrapped in yellow leaves.

Come with me to the offices, to the uncertain
smell of ministries, and tombs, and postage stamps.
Come with me to the white day that is dying
screaming like a murdered bride.

DONALD D. WALSH

THE DESTROYED STREET

Through the insulted iron, through the plaster eyes
passes a tongue of years different
from time. It is a tail
of harsh hairs, hands of stone filled with anger,
and the color of the houses is hushed, and architectural
decisions burst forth,
a terrible foot dirties the balconies:
slowly, with accumulated shadow,
with masks bitten by winter and slowness,
the lofty-browed days walk about
among moonless houses.

Water and custom and the white mud
that the star emits, and especially
the air that the bells have struck furiously,
exhaust things, touch
the wheels, stop
in cigar stores,
and the red hair grows in the cornices
like a long lament, while down to the depths

fall keys, clocks,
flowers resembling oblivion.

Where is the newborn violet? Where
the necktie and the virginal red zephyr?
Over the towns
a tongue of rotted dust advances,
breaking rings, gnawing painting,
making the black chairs howl voiceless,
covering the cement rosettes, the bulwarks
of shattered metal,
the garden and the wool, the enlargements of ardent photographs
wounded by the rain, the thirst of the bedrooms, and the huge
movie posters on which struggle
the panther and the thunder,
the geranium's lances, the stores filled with spoiled honey,
the cough, the suits of shiny weave,
everything is covered with a mortal taste
of retreat and dampness and injury.

Perhaps the stifled conversations, the rustle of bodies,
the virtue of the weary ladies who nest in the smoke,
the tomatoes implacably assassinated,
the passage of the horses of a sad regiment,
the light, the pressure of many nameless fingers
use up the flat fiber of the lime,
surround the facades with neutral air
like knives: while
the air of danger gnaws at circumstances,
bricks, salt, spills like water
and the fat-axled wagons lurch.

Wave of broken roses and holes! future
of the fragrant vein! Pitiless objects!
Let nobody wander about! Let nobody open his arms
within the blind water!
Oh movement, oh ill-wounded name,
oh spoonful of confused wind

and flogged color! Oh wound into which fall
to their deaths the blue guitars!

MELANCHOLY IN THE FAMILIES

I keep a blue flask,
inside it an ear and a portrait:
when night forces
the owl's feathers,
when the raucous cherry tree
shatters its lips and threatens
with husks that the ocean wind often penetrates,
I know that there are great sunken expanses,
quartz in ingots,
slime,
blue waters for a battle,
much silence, many
veins of retreats and camphors,
fallen things, medals, acts of tenderness,
parachutes, kisses.

It is only the passage from one day toward another,
a single bottle moving across the seas,
and a dining room to which come roses,
a dining room abandoned
like a thorn: I refer
to a shattered goblet, to a curtain, to the depths
of a deserted room through which a river flows
dragging the stones. It is a house
set on the foundations of the rain,
a two-storied house with compulsory windows
and strictly faithful climbing vines.

I go in the evening, I arrive
covered with mud and death,

dragging the earth and its roots,
and its vague belly where corpses
sleep with wheat,
metals, overturned elephants.

But on top of everything there is a terrible,
a terrible abandoned dining room,
with broken jugs
and vinegar flowing under the chairs,
a rather dark lightningbolt
stopped from the moon, and I look for
a comparison within myself:
perhaps it is a tent surrounded by the sea
and torn cloths oozing brine.
It is only an abandoned dining room,
and around it there are expanses,
submerged factories, boards
that only I know,
because I am sad and old,
and I know the earth, and I am sad.

DONALD D. WALSH

MATERNITY

Why do you rush toward maternity and check
your dark acid with frequently fatal grams?
The future of the roses has arrived! The time
of the net and the lightning! The soft petitions
of the leaves wildly nourished!
An excessively broken river
runs through rooms and baskets
instilling passions and misfortunes
with its heavy liquid and its abundance of drops.

It is about a sudden season
that peoples certain bones, certain hands,
certain sailor suits.

And since its sparkle makes the roses vary,
giving them bread and stones and dew,
oh dark mother, come,
with a mask in your left hand
and with your arms filled with sobs.

Through corridors where no one has died
I want you to pass, through a sea without fish,
without scales, without shipwrecked men,
through a hotel without steps,
through a tunnel without smoke.

It is for you, this world in which no one is born,
in which exist
neither the dead wreath nor the uterine flower,
it is yours, this planet filled with skin and stones.

There is shadow there for all lives.
There are circles of milk and buildings of blood,
and towers of green air.
There is silence in the walls, and great pale cows
with hoofs of wine.

There are shadows there so that the tooth
may continue in the jaw and one lip opposite another,
and so that your mouth may speak without dying,
and so that your blood may not be spilled in vain.

Oh dark mother, wound me
with ten knives in the heart,
toward that side, toward that bright time,
toward that springtime without ashes.

Until you break its black timbers,
knock on my heart, until a map
of overflowing blood and hair
stains the holes and the shadow,
until its windowpanes weep, knock,
until its needles melt.

Blood has fingers and it opens tunnels
underneath the earth.

DONALD D. WALSH

III

ODE WITH A LAMENT

Oh girl among the roses, oh crush of doves,
oh fortress of fishes and rosebushes,
your soul is a bottle filled with thirsty salt
and your skin, a bell filled with grapes.

Unfortunately I have only fingernails to give you,
or eyelashes, or melted pianos,
or dreams that come spurting from my heart,
dusty dreams that run like black horsemen,
dreams filled with velocities and misfortunes.

I can love you only with kisses and poppies,
with garlands wet by the rain,
looking at ash-gray horses and yellow dogs.
I can love you only with waves at my back,
amid vague sulfur blows and brooding waters,
swimming against the cemeteries that run in certain rivers
with wet fodder growing over the sad plaster tombs,
swimming across submerged hearts
and pale lists of unburied children.

There is much death, many funereal events
in my forsaken passions and desolate kisses,
there is the water that falls upon my head,
while my hair grows,
a water like time, a black unchained water,
with a nocturnal voice, with a shout
of birds in the rain, with an interminable
wet-winged shadow that protects my bones:
while I dress, while
interminably I look at myself in mirrors and windowpanes,

I hear someone who follows me, sobbing to me
with a sad voice rotted by time.

You stand upon the earth, filled
with teeth and lightning.
You spread the kisses and kill the ants.
You weep with health, with onion, with bee,
with burning abacus.
You are like a blue and green sword
and you ripple, when I touch you, like a river.

Come to my heart dressed in white, with a bouquet
of bloody roses and goblets of ashes,
come with an apple and a horse,
because there is a dark room there and a broken candleholder,
some twisted chairs waiting for winter,
and a dead dove, with a number.

DONALD D. WALSH

MATERIAL NUPCIAL

De pie como un cerezo sin cáscara ni flores,
especial, encendido, con venas y saliva,
y dedos y testículos,
miro una niña de papel y luna,
horizontal, temblando y respirando y blanca
y sus pezones como dos cifras separadas,
y la rosal reunión de sus piernas en donde
su sexo de pestañas nocturnas parpadea.

Pálido, desbordante,
siento hundirse palabras en mi boca,
palabras como niños ahogados,
y rumbo y rumbo y dientes crecen naves,
y aguas y latitud como quemadas.

La pondré como una espada o un espejo,
y abriré hasta la muerte sus piernas temerosas,

y morderé sus orejas y sus venas,
y haré que retroceda con los ojos cerrados
en un espeso río de semen verde.

La inundaré de amapolas y relámpagos,
la envolveré en rodillas, en labios, en agujas,
la entraré con pulgadas de epidermis llorando
y presiones de crimen y pelos empapados.

La haré huir escapándose por uñas y suspiros
hacia nunca, hacia nada,
trepándose a la lenta médula y al oxígeno,
agarrándose a recuerdos y razones
como una sola mano, como un dedo partido
agitando una uña de sal desamparada.

Debe correr durmiendo por caminos de piel
en un país de goma cenicienta y ceniza,
luchando con cuchillos, y sábanas, y hormigas,
y con ojos que caen en ella como muertos,
y con gotas de negra materia resbalando
como pescados ciegos o balas de agua gruesa.

NUPTIAL SUBSTANCE

Standing like a cherry tree without bark or flowers,
special, burning, with veins and saliva,
and fingers and testicles,
I look at a girl of paper and moon,
horizontal, trembling and breathing and white
and her nipples like two separated ciphers,
and the rosy meeting of her legs where
her mound flutters with nocturnal eyelashes.

Pale, overflowing,
I feel words sink into my mouth,

words like drowned children,
and on we go and ships grow teeth,
and waters and breadth as if on fire.

I shall place her like a sword or a mirror,
and I shall open until death her fearful legs,
and I shall bite her ears and her veins,
and I shall make her retreat, her eyes closed
in a thick river of green semen.

I shall flood her with poppies and lightningbolts,
I shall wrap her in knees, in lips, in needles,
I shall enter her with inches of weeping epidermis
and pressures of crime and soaked hair.

I shall make her flee escaping through fingernails and sighs
toward never, toward nothing,
climbing up the slow marrow and the oxygen,
clutching memories and reasons
like a single hand, like a cleft finger
waving a fingernail of forsaken salt.

She must run sleeping along roads of skin
in a country of ashen gum and ashes,
struggling with knives, and sheets, and ants,
and with eyes that fall on her like dead men,
and with drops of black substance slipping
like blind fish or bullets of thick water.

DONALD D. WALSH

SEXUAL WATER

Rolling in big solitary raindrops,
in drops like teeth,
in big thick drops of marmalade and blood,
rolling in big raindrops,
the water falls,

like a sword in drops,
like a tearing river of glass,
it falls biting,
striking the axis of symmetry, sticking to the seams of the soul,
breaking abandoned things, drenching the dark.

It is only a breath, moister than weeping,
a liquid, a sweat, a nameless oil,
a sharp movement,
forming, thickening,
the water falls,
in big slow raindrops,
toward its sea, toward its dry ocean,
toward its waterless wave.

I see the vast summer, and a death rattle coming from a granary,
stores, locusts,
towns, stimuli,
rooms, girls
sleeping with their hands upon their hearts,
dreaming of bandits, of fires,
I see ships,
I see marrow trees
bristling like rabid cats,
I see blood, daggers, and women's stockings,
and men's hair,
I see beds, I see corridors where a virgin screams,
I see blankets and organs and hotels.

I see the silent dreams,
I accept the final days,
and also the origins, and also the memories,
like an eyelid atrociously and forcibly uplifted
I am looking.

And then there is this sound:
a red noise of bones,
a clashing of flesh,

and yellow legs like merging spikes of grain.
I listen among the smack of kisses,
I listen, shaken between gasps and sobs.
I am looking, hearing,
with half my soul upon the sea and half my soul upon the land,
and with the two halves of my soul I look at the world.

And though I close my eyes and cover my heart entirely,
I see a muffled waterfall,
in big muffled raindrops.
It is like a hurricane of gelatin,
like a waterfall of sperm and jellyfish.
I see a turbid rainbow form.
I see its waters pass across the bones.

DONALD D. WALSH

V

ODA A FEDERICO GARCÍA LORCA

Si pudiera llorar de miedo en una casa sola,
si pudiera sacarme los ojos y comérmelos,
lo haría por tu voz de naranjo enlutado
y por tu poesía que sale dando gritos.

Porque por ti pintan de azul los hospitales
y crecen las escuelas y los barrios marítimos,
y se pueblan de plumas los ángeles heridos,
y se cubren de escamas los pescados nupciales,
y van volando al cielo los erizos:
por ti las sastrerías con sus negras membranas
se llenan de cucharas y de sangre,
y tragan cintas rojas, y se matan a besos,
y se visten de blanco.

Cuando vuclas vestido de durazno,
cuando ríes con risa de arroz huracanado,

cuando para cantar sacudes las arterias y los dientes,
la garganta y los dedos,
me moriría por lo dulce que eres,
me moriría por los lagos rojos
en donde en medio del otoño vives
con un corcel caído y un dios ensangrentado,
me moriría por los cementerios
que como cenicientos ríos pasan
con agua y tumbas,
de noche, entre campanas ahogadas:
ríos espesos como dormitorios
de soldados enfermos, que de súbito crecen
hacia la muerte en ríos con números de mármol
y coronas podridas, y aceites funerales:
me moriría por verte de noche
mirar pasar las cruces anegadas,
de pie y llorando,
porque ante el río de la muerte lloras
abandonadamente, heridamente,
lloras llorando, con los ojos llenos
de lágrimas, de lágrimas, de lágrimas.

Si pudiera de noche, perdidamente solo,
acumular olvido y sombra y humo
sobre ferrocarriles y vapores,
con un embudo negro,
mordiendo las cenizas,
lo haría por el árbol en que creces,
por los nidos de aguas doradas que reúnes,
y por la enredadera que te cubre los huesos
comunicándote el secreto de la noche.

Ciudades con olor a cebolla mojada
esperan que tú pases cantando roncamente,
y silenciosos barcos de esperma te persiguen,
y golondrinas verdes hacen nido en tu pelo,
y además caracoles y semanas,
mástiles enrollados y cerezos
definitivamente circulan cuando asoman

tu pálida cabeza de quince ojos
y tu boca de sangre sumergida.

Si pudiera llenar de hollín las alcaldías
y, sollozando, derribar relojes,
sería para ver cuándo a tu casa
llega el verano con los labios rotos,
llegan muchas personas de traje agonizante,
llegan regiones de triste esplendor,
llegan arados muertos y amapolas,
llegan enterradores y jinetes,
llegan planetas y mapas con sangre,
llegan buzos cubiertos de ceniza,
llegan enmascarados arrastrando doncellas
atravesadas por grandes cuchillos,
llegan raíces, venas, hospitales,
manantiales, hormigas,
llega la noche con la cama en donde
muere entre las arañas un húsar solitario,
llega una rosa de odio y alfileres,
llega una embarcación amarillenta,
llega un día de viento con un niño,
llego yo con Oliverio, Norah,
Vicente Aleixandre, Delia,
Maruca, Malva Marma, María Luisa y Larco,
la Rubia, Rafael Ugarte,
Cotapos, Rafael Alberti,
Carlos, Bebé, Manolo Altolaguirre,
Molinari,
Rosales, Concha Méndez,
y otros que se me olvidan.

Ven a que te corone, joven de la salud
y de la mariposa, joven puro
como un negro relámpago perpetuamente libre,
y conversando entre nosotros,
ahora, cuando no queda nadie entre las rocas,
hablemos sencillamente como eres tú y soy yo:
para qué sirven los versos si no es para el rocío?

Para qué sirven los versos si no es para esa noche
en que un puñal amargo nos averigua, para ese día,
para ese crepúsculo, para ese rincón roto
donde el golpeado corazón del hombre se dispone a morir?

Sobre todo de noche,
de noche hay muchas estrellas,
todas dentro de un río
como una cinta junto a las ventanas
de las casas llenas de pobres gentes.

Alguien se les ha muerto, tal vez
han perdido sus colocaciones en las oficinas,
en los hospitales, en los ascensores,
en las minas,
sufren los seres tercamente heridos
y hay propósito y llanto en todas partes:
mientras las estrellas corren dentro de un río interminable
hay mucho llanto en las ventanas,
los umbrales están gastados por el llanto,
las alcobas están mojadas por el llanto
que llega en forma de ola a morder las alfombras.

Federico,
tú ves el mundo, las calles,
el vinagre,
las despedidas en las estaciones
cuando el humo levanta sus ruedas decisivas
hacia donde no hay nada sino algunas
separaciones, piedras, vías férreas.

Hay tantas gentes haciendo preguntas
por todas partes.
Hay el ciego sangriento, y el iracundo, y el
desanimado,
y el miserable, el árbol de las uñas,
el bandolero con la envidia a cuestas.

Así es la vida, Federico, aquí tienes
las cosas que te puede ofrecer mi amistad
de melancólico varón varonil.
Ya sabes por ti mismo muchas cosas,
y otras irás sabiendo lentamente.

ODE TO FEDERICO GARCÍA LORCA

If I could weep with fear in a solitary house,
if I could take out my eyes and eat them,
I would do it for your black-draped orange-tree voice
and for your poetry that comes forth shouting.

Because for you they paint hospitals bright blue,
and schools and sailors' quarters grow,
and wounded angels are covered with feathers,
and nuptial fish are covered with scales,
and hedgehogs go flying to the sky:
for you tailorshops with their black skins
fill up with spoons and blood,
and swallow red ribbons and kiss each other to death,
and dress in white.

When you fly dressed as a peach tree,
when you laugh with a laugh of hurricaned rice,
when to sing you shake arteries and teeth,
throat and fingers,
I could die for how sweet you are,
I could die for the red lakes
where in the midst of autumn you live
with a fallen steed and a bloodied god,
I could die for the cemeteries
that pass like ash-gray rivers
with water and tombs,
at night, among drowned bells:
rivers as thick as wards
of sick soldiers, that suddenly grow
toward death in rivers with marble numbers
and rotted crowns, and funeral oils:

I could die to see you at night
watching the sunken crosses go by,
standing and weeping,
because before death's river you weep
forlornly, woundedly,
you weep weeping, your eyes filled
with tears, with tears, with tears.

If at night, wildly alone, I could
gather oblivion and shadow and smoke
above railroads and steamships,
with a black funnel,
biting the ashes,
I would do it for the tree in which you grow,
for the nests of golden waters that you gather,
and for the vine that covers your bones,
revealing to you the secret of the night.

Cities with a smell of wet onions
wait for you to pass singing raucously,
and silent sperm boats pursue you,
and green swallows nest in your hair,
and also snails and weeks,
furled masts and cherry trees
definitively walk about when they glimpse
your pale fifteen-eyed head
and your mouth of submerged blood.

If I could fill town halls with soot
and, sobbing, tear down clocks,
it would be to see when to your house
comes summer with its broken lips,
come many people with dying clothes,
come regions of sad splendor,
come dead plows and poppies,
come gravediggers and horsemen,
come planets and maps with blood,
come buzzards covered with ashes,
come masked men dragging damsels

pierced by great knives,
come roots, veins, hospitals,
springs, ants,
comes night with the bed where
a solitary hussar is dying among the spiders,
comes a rose of hatred and pins,
comes a yellowish vessel,
comes a windy day with a child,
come I with Oliverio, Norah,
Vicente Aleixandre, Delia,
Maruca, Malva Marina, María Luisa, and Larco,
the Blond, Rafael Ugarte,
Cotapos, Rafael Alberti,
Carlos, Bebé, Manolo Altolaguirre,
Molinari,
Rosales, Concha Méndez,
and others that slip my mind.

Come, let me crown you, youth of health
and butterflies, youth pure
as a black lightningflash perpetually free,
and just between you and me,
now, when there is no one left among the rocks,
let us speak simply, man to man:
what are verses for if not for the dew?
What are verses for if not for that night
in which a bitter dagger finds us out, for that day,
for that dusk, for that broken corner
where the beaten heart of man makes ready to die?

Above all at night,
at night there are many stars,
all within a river
like a ribbon next to the windows
of houses filled with the poor.

Someone of theirs has died, perhaps
they have lost their jobs in the offices,
in the hospitals, in the elevators,

in the mines,
human beings suffer stubbornly wounded
and there are protests and weeping everywhere:
while the stars flow within an endless river
there is much weeping at the windows,
the thresholds are worn away by the weeping,
the bedrooms are soaked by the weeping
that comes wave-shaped to bite the carpets.

Federico,
you see the world, the streets,
the vinegar,
the farewells in the stations
when the smoke lifts its decisive wheels
toward where there is nothing but some
separations, stones, railroad tracks.

There are so many people asking questions
everywhere.
There is the bloody blindman, and the angry one, and the
disheartened one,
and the wretch, the thorn tree,
the bandit with envy on his back.

That's the way life is, Federico, here you have
the things that my friendship can offer you,
the friendship of a melancholy manly man.
By yourself you already know many things,
and others you will slowly get to know.

DONALD D. WALSH

ODE TO FEDERICO GARCÍA LORCA

If I could weep with fear in an empty house,
if I could feast on the eyes I plucked from my head,
I'd do it for the mourning orange tree of your voice
and your poetry, shouting its way into the world.

Because of you the hospitals are painted blue
and the schools and the shantytowns by the sea are swelling,
and the wounded angels are inhabited by feathers,
and the fish are covered with scales on their weddings,
and the sea urchins go flying into the sky;
for you the tailors' shops full of black membranes
are filled with spoons and blood,
and swallow red ribbons, and kiss each other to death,
and dress themselves in white.

When you fly dressed as a peach tree,
when you laugh like rice driven by the wind,
when, just to sing, you shake your arteries and teeth,
your throat and your fingers—
I could die for your sweetness,
I could die for the red lakes
where you lived at the height of autumn
with a fallen steed and a bloodstained god,
I could die for the cemeteries
that pass like rivers of ash
with water and tombs,
at night, among drowned bells;
rivers as thick as infirmaries
full of soldiers, who suddenly grow
toward death in rivers with marble numbers
and rotten crowns, and funereal oils;
it would be worth dying to see you at night
watching the crosses pass in the high water,
standing up and in tears,
because you cry before the river of death
hopelessly, wounded,
tearstained and weeping, eyes full
of tears, and tears, and tears.

If only in the night of being, so lost and alone,
I could gather oblivion, shadow, and smoke
from trains and ocean liners,
with a black funnel,
with ashes in my teeth,

I'd do it for the tree in which you grow,
for the nests of golden water you've gathered,
and for the vine that covers your bones,
revealing to you the secret of the night.

Cities that reek like wet onions
wait for you to go by singing in a hoarse voice,
and silent boats of sperm pursue you,
and green swallows have nested in your hair,
not to mention snails and weeks,
masts coiled like snakes, and the cherry trees'
vital movement as they glimpse
your pale head with fifteen eyes
and the submerged blood in your mouth.

If I could fill the town halls with soot,
and sobbing, demolish the clocks,
it would be to see your house when
summer comes with its cracked lips,
and people dressed in dying suits,
regions in splendid sadness,
dead plows and poppies,
gravediggers and horsemen,
planets and bloodstained maps,
divers coated with ash,
and masked men dragging girls
pierced by great knives,
and then roots, veins, hospitals,
headwaters, and ants come,
and night arriving with the bed
in which a lonely hussar dies among the spiders,
then come pins and a rose of hatred,
a sallow vessel,
a windy day with a child,
and I come with Oliverio, Norah,
Vicente Aleixandre, Delia,
Maruca, Malva, Marina, María Luisa and Larco,
La Rubia, Rafael Ugarte,
Cotapos, Rafael Alberti,

Carlos, Bebé, Manolo Altolaguirre,
Molinari,
Rosales, Concha Méndez,
and others I can't remember.

Come closer so I can crown you, embodiment of health
and the butterfly, youth as pure
as a black lightning bolt, always free,
and talking with each other
now that no one else is left on these rocks,
let's use simple words in keeping with your character and mine:
What good is poetry if it isn't for the dew?

What good is poetry if it isn't for that night
when we can't escape the knife, and that day,
that twilight, that broken corner
where someone's beaten heart prepares to die?

At night, oh yes,
at night there are many stars,
all of them in a river
like a ribbon at the windows
of those houses harboring the poor.

One of them has died, perhaps
others have lost their jobs in the offices,
in the hospitals, in the elevators,
in the mines—
human beings suffer stubborn wounds
and there is design and crying everywhere;
while the stars flow along in an endless river
everyone cries at the windows,
thresholds are worn out by the crying,
the bedrooms are soaked by the crying
that comes like a wave to gnaw the rugs away.

Federico,
you see the world, the streets,
the vinegar,

the farewells in the stations
when the smoke lifts its decisive wheels
toward nothing but a few
separations, stones, railroad tracks.

There are so many people asking questions
everywhere.
There are the blind and bloody, the enraged and the
discouraged,
and the miserable, the tree of fingernails,
the highway robber who carries his envy on his back.

That's life, Federico, and here you have
all that my friendship can offer,
all from a melancholy, manly man.
You've already learned a lot of things on your own
and others you will come to know, slowly.

GREG SIMON AND STEVEN F. WHITE

THE DISINTERRED ONE

Homage to the Count of Villamediana

When the earth full of wet eyelids
becomes ashes and harsh sifted air,
and the dry farms and the waters,
the wells, the metals,
at last give forth their worn-out dead,
I want an ear, an eye,
a heart wounded and tumbling,
the hollow of a dagger sunk some time ago
in a body some time ago exterminated and alone,
I want some hands, a science of fingernails,
a mouth of fright and poppies dying,
I want to see rise from the useless dust
a raucous tree of shaken veins,
I want from the bitterest earth,
among brimstone and turquoise and red waves

and whirlwinds of silent coal,
I want to see a flesh waken its bones
howling flames,
and a special smell run in search of something,
and a sight blinded by the earth
run after two dark eyes,
and an ear, suddenly, like a furious oyster,
rabid, boundless,
rise toward the thunder,
and a pure touch, lost among salts,
come out suddenly, touching chests and lilies.

Oh day of the dead! Oh distance toward which
the dead spike lies with its smell of lightning,
oh galleries yielding up a nest
and a fish and a cheek and a sword,
all ground up amid confusion,
all hopelessly decayed,
all in the dry abyss nourished
between the teeth of the hard earth.

And the feather to its soft bird,
and the moon to its film, and the perfume to its form,
and, among the roses, the disinterred one,
the man covered with mineral seaweed,
and to their two holes his eyes returning.

He is naked,
his clothes are not in the dust
and his broken skeleton has slipped to the bottom of hell,
and his beard has grown like the air in autumn,
and to the depths of his heart he wants to bite apples.

From his knees and his shoulders hang
scraps of oblivion, fibers of the ground,
areas of broken glass and aluminum,
shells of bitter corpses,
pockets of water converted into iron:
and meetings of terrible mouths

spilt and blue,
and boughs of sorrowful coral
make a garland on his green head,
and sad deceased vegetables
and nocturnal boards surround him,
and in him still sleep half-open doves
with eyes of subterranean cement.

Sweet Count, in the mist,
oh recently awakened from the mines,
oh recently dry from the riverless water,
oh recently spiderless!

Minutes creak in your nascent feet,
your murdered sex rises up,
and you raise your hand where still
lives the secret of the foam.

DONALD D. WALSH

VI

THE CLOCK FALLEN INTO THE SEA

There is so much dark light in space
and so many dimensions suddenly yellow
because the wind does not fall
and the leaves do not breathe.

It is a Sunday day arrested in the sea,
a day like a submerged boat,
a drop of time assaulted by scales
that are fiercely dressed in transparent dampness.

There are months seriously accumulated in a vestment
that we wish to smell weeping with closed eyes,
and there are years in a single blind sign of water
deposited and green,
there is the age that neither fingers nor light captured,

much more praiseworthy than a broken fan,
much more silent than a disinterred foot,
there is the nuptial age of the days dissolved
in a sad tomb traversed by fish.

The petals of time fall immensely
like vague umbrellas looking like the sky,
growing around, it is scarcely
a bell never seen,
a flooded rose, a jellyfish, a long
shattered throbbing:
but it is not that, it is something that scarcely touches and spends,
a confused trace without sound or birds,
a dissipation of perfumes and races.

The clock that in the field stretched out upon the moss
and struck a hip with its electric form
runs rickety and wounded beneath the fearful water
that ripples palpitating with central currents.

DONALD D. WALSH

AUTUMN RETURNS

A day in mourning falls from the bells
like a trembling vague-widow cloth,
it is a color, a dream
of cherries buried in the earth,
it is a tail of smoke that restlessly arrives
to change the color of the water and the kisses.

I do not know if I make myself clear: when from on high
night approaches, when the solitary poet
at the window hears autumn's steed running
and the leaves of trampled fear rustle in his arteries,
there is something over the sky, like the tongue of a thick
ox, something in the doubt of the sky and the atmosphere.

Things return to their places,
the indispensable lawyer, the hands, the olive oil,
the bottles,
all the traces of life: the beds, above all,
are filled with a bloody liquid,
people deposit their confidences in sordid ears,
assassins go down stairs,
it is not this, however, but the old gallop,
the horse of the old autumn that trembles and endures.

The horse of the old autumn has a red beard
and the foam of fear covers its cheeks
and the air that follows it is shaped like an ocean
and a perfume of vague buried putrefaction.

Every day down from the sky comes an ashen color
that doves must spread over the earth:
the cord that forgetfulness and weeping weave,
time that has slept long years within the bells,
everything,
the old tattered suits, the women who see snow coming,
the black poppies that no one can look at without dying,
everything falls into the hands that I lift
in the midst of the rain.

DONALD D. WALSH

THERE IS NO OBLIVION (SONATA)

If you ask me where I have been
I must say, "It so happens."
I must speak of the ground that the stones darken,
of the river that enduring is destroyed:
I know only the things that the birds lose,
the sea left behind, or my sister weeping.
Why so many regions, why does a day
join a day? Why does a black night
gather in the mouth? Why dead people?

If you ask me where I come from, I have to converse with broken things,
with utensils bitter to excess,
with great beasts frequently rotted,
and with my anguished heart.

Those that have crossed paths are not memories
nor is the yellowish dove that sleeps in oblivion,
they are faces with tears,
fingers at the throat,
and what falls down from the leaves:
the darkness of a day gone by,
of a day nourished with our sad blood.

Here are violets, swallows,
everything that pleases us and that appears
in the sweet calling cards
around which stroll time and sweetness.

But let us not penetrate beyond those teeth,
let us not bite the shells that silence gathers,
because I do not know what to answer:
there are so many dead,
so many seawalls that the red sun split,
and so many heads that beat against the ships,
and so many hands that have cradled kisses,
and so many things that I want to forget.

DONALD D. WALSH

I

THE DROWNED WOMAN OF THE SKY

Woven butterfly, garment
hung from the trees,
drowned in sky, derived
amid squalls and rains, alone, alone, compact,
with clothes and tresses torn to shreds
and centers corroded by the air.
                    Motionless, if you withstand
the raucous needle of winter,
the river of angry water that harasses you. Celestial
shadow, dove branch
broken by night among the dead flowers:
I stop and suffer
when like a slow and cold-filled sound
you spread your red glow beaten by the water.

DONALD D. WALSH

WALTZ

I touch hatred like a daily breast,
I ceaseless, from clothes to clothes, come
sleeping far away.

I am not, I am no good, I don't know anyone,
I have no weapons of sea or of wood,
I do not live in this house.

With night and water my mouth is filled.
The durable moon determines
what I do not have.

What I do have is in the midst of the waves.
A thunderbolt of water, a day for me:
an iron bottom.

There is no countersea, no shield, no suit,
there is no special unfathomable solution,
or vicious eyelid.

I live suddenly and at other times I follow.
I suddenly touch a face and it murders me.
I have no time.

Do not seek me, then, drawing back
the customary savage thread or the
sanguinary vine.

Do not call me: that is my occupation.
Do not ask my name or my estate.
Leave me in the midst of my own moon,
in my wounded terrain.

DONALD D. WALSH

BRUSSELS

Of all that I have done, of all that I have lost,
of all that I have won through fright,
in bitter iron, in leaves, I can offer a little.

A frightened taste, a river that the feathers
of burning eagles gradually cover, a sulfuric
retreat of petals.

      I am no longer forgiven by the entire salt
or the continuous bread, or the little church devoured
by the ocean rain, or the coal bitten
by the secret foam.

I have searched and found, heavily,
under the ground, among fearsome bodies,
a kind of tooth of pale wood
coming and going beneath the harsh acid,
next to the substances
of agony, between moon and knives,
dying of the night.

        Now, in the midst
of the disparaged speed, beside
the threadless walls,
in the depths cut by the ends,
here I am with that which loses stars,
vegetally, alone.

DONALD D. WALSH

NACIENDO EN LOS BOSQUES

Cuando el arroz retira de la tierra
los granos de su harina,
cuando el trigo endurece sus pequeñas caderas y levanta su rostro de mil
    manos,
a la enramada donde la mujer y el hombre se enlazan acudo,
para tocar el mar innumerable
de lo que continúa.

Yo no soy hermano del utensilio llevado en la marea
como en una cuna de nácar combatido:
no tiemblo en la comarca de los agonizantes despojos,
no despierto en el golpe de las tinieblas asustadas
por el ronco pecíolo de la campana repentina,
no puedo ser, no soy el pasajero
bajo cuyos zapatos los últimos reductos del viento palpitan
y rígidas retornan las olas del tiempo a morir.

Llevo en mi mano la paloma que duerme reclinada en la semilla
y en su fermento espeso de cal y sangre
vive Agosto,

vive el mes extraído de su copa profunda:
con mi mano rodeo la nueva sombra del ala que crece:
la raíz y la pluma que mañana formarán la espesura.

Nunca declina, ni junto al balcón de manos de hierro,
ni en el invierno marítimo de los abandonados, ni en mi paso tardío,
el crecimiento inmenso de la gota, ni el párpado que quiere ser abierto:
porque para nacer he nacido, para encerrar el paso
de cuanto se aproxima, de cuanto a mi pecho golpea como un nuevo
corazón tembloroso.

Vidas recostadas junto a mi traje como palomas paralelas,
o contenidas en mi propia existencia y en mi desordenado sonido
para volver a ser, para incautar el aire desnudo de la hoja
y el nacimiento húmedo de la tierra en la guirnalda: hasta cuándo
debo volver y ser, hasta cuándo el olor
de las más enterradas flores, de las olas más trituradas
sobre las altas piedras, guarda en mí du patria
para volver a ser furia y perfume?

Hasta cuándo la mano del bosque en la lluvia
me avecina con todas sus agujas
para tejer los altos besos del follaje?
Otra vez
escucho aproximarse como el fuego en el humo,
nacer de la ceniza terrestre,
la luz llena de pétalos,
                    y apartando la tierra
en un río de espigas llega el sol a mi boca
como una vieja lágrima enterrada que vuelve a ser semilla.

BORN IN THE WOODS

When rice withdraws from earth
the grains of its flour,
when wheat hardens its little flanks and lifts up its thousand-handed face,
I hasten to the arbor where man and woman are linked

to touch the innumerable sea
of what endures.

I am not brother of the tool carried on the tide
as if in a cradle of aggressive pearl:
I do not tremble in the region of dying despoliation,
I do not wake to the thump of the darkness frightened
by the raucous clapper of the sudden bell,
I cannot be, I am not the passenger
beneath whose shoes throb the last redoubts of the wind
and the rigid waves of time return to die.

I bear in my hand the dove that sleeps reclining on the seed
and in its thick ferment of lime and blood
lives August,
lives the month extracted from its deep goblet:
with my hand I surround the new shadow of the growing wing:
the root and the feather that tomorrow will form the thicket.

It never abates, neither next to the iron-handed balcony,
nor in the sea winter of the abandoned ones, nor in my slow step,
the immense swelling of the drop, or the eyelid that wants to be opened:
because I was born to be born, to cut off the passage
of everything that approaches, of everything that beats on my breast like
    a new
trembling heart.

Lives lying next to my costume like parallel doves,
or contained in my own existence and in my disordered sound
to be again, to seize the naked air of the leaf
and the moist birth of the earth in the garland: how long
must I return and be, how long does the fragrance
of the most buried flowers, of the waves most pounded
on the high rocks, keep in me its homeland
to be again fury and perfume?

How long does the hand of the woods in the rain
bring me close with all its needles
to weave the lofty kisses of the foliage?

Again
I hear approach like fire in smoke,
spring up from earthly ash,
light filled with petals,
                              and pushing earth away
in a river of flowerheads the sun reaches my mouth
like an old buried tear that becomes seed again.

DONALD D. WALSH

II: FURIES AND SORROWS

. . . In my heart there are furies and sorrows . . .

QUEVEDO

This poem was written in 1934. How many things have come to pass since then! Spain, where I wrote it, is a girdle of ruins. Ah, if with only a drop of poetry or love we could placate the anger of the world, but that can be done only by striving and by a resolute heart.

The world has changed and my poetry has changed. A drop of blood fallen on these lines will remain living upon them, indelible as love.

MARCH 1939

In the depths of our hearts we are together,
in the cane field of the heart we cross through
a summer of tigers,
watching over a meter of cold flesh,
watching over a bouquet of inaccessible skin,
with our mouths sniffing sweat and green veins
we find ourselves in the moist shadow that drops kisses.

You, my enemy of so much sleep broken just
like bristly plants of glass, like bells
destroyed menacingly, as much as shots
of black ivy in the midst of perfume,
my enemy with big hips that have touched my hair
with a harsh dew, with a tongue of water,
despite the mute coldness of the teeth and the hatred of the eyes,
and the battle of dying beasts that watch over oblivion,
in some summer place we are together

watching with lips invaded by thirst.
If there is someone that pierces
a wall with circles of phosphorus
and wounds the center of some sweet members
and bites each leaf of a forest giving shouts,
I too have your bloody firefly eyes
that can impregnate and cross through knees
and throats surrounded by general silk.

When in meetings
chance, ashes, drinks,
the interrupted air,
but there are your eyes smelling of the hunt,
of green rays that riddle chests,
your teeth that open apples from which blood drips:
your legs that stick moaning to the sun
and your pearly teats and your poppy feet,
like funnels filled with teeth seeking shade,
like roses made of whips and perfume, and even,
even more, even more,
even behind the eyelids, even behind the sky,
even behind the costumes and the travels, in the streets where people
    make water,
you sense the bodies,
in the sour half-destroyed churches, in the cabins that the sea bears in its
    hands,
you watch with your lips nonetheless florid,
you knife through wood and silver,
your great frightening veins swell:
there is no shell, there is no distance or iron,
your hands touch hands,
and you fall making the black flowers crackle.
You sense the bodies!
Like an insect wounded with warrants,
you sense the center of the blood and you watch over
the muscles that disregard the dawn, you attack shocks,
lightningflashes, heads,
and you touch lingering the legs that guide you.

Oh guided wound of special arrows!

Do you smell the damp in the middle of the night?

Or a brusque vase of burnt rosebushes?

Do you hear the drop of clothes, keys, coins
in the filthy houses where you come naked?
My hatred is a single hand that shows you
the silent road, the sheets where somebody has slept
in fear: you come
and roll on the floor handled and bitten,
and the old odor of semen like a clinging vine
of ashy flour slips from your mouth.

Ah light and mad goblets and eyelashes,
air that floods a half-open river
like a single dove of irate riverbed,
like an emblem of rebellious water,
ah substances, tastes, live-winged eyelids
with a trembling, with a blind fearful flower,
ah grave, serious breasts like faces,
ah huge thighs filled with green honey,
and heels and shadow of feet, and spent
breath and surfaces of pale stone,
and harsh waves that mount the skin toward death
filled with heavenly soaked flour.
Then, does this river
go between us, and do you along one shore
go biting mouths?

Then is it so that I am truly, truly distant
and a river of burning water flows by in the dark?
Ah how often you are the one that hatred does not name,
and how sunken in the darkness
and under what showers of mashed manure
your statue devours the clover in my heart.

Hatred is a hammer that strikes your gown
and your scarlet brow,
and the days of the heart fall on your ears
like vague owls with eliminated blood,
and the necklaces that were formed drop by drop with tears
encircle your throat burning your voice as if with ice.

It is so that you will
never, never speak, it is so that never, never
will a swallow come out of the tongue's nest
and so that its nettles will destroy your throat
and a bitter ship's wind will inhabit you.

Where do you undress?
In a railroad station, next to a red Peruvian
or with a harvester, in the fields, in the violent light of the wheat?
Or do you run around with certain fearful-looking lawyers,
you lengthily naked, at the edge of the water of night?
You look: you do not see the moon or the hyacinth
or the darkness dripping with dampness,
or the slimy train, or the split ivory:
you see waists as slender as oxygen,
breasts that wait getting heavier
and just like the sapphire of lunar avarice
you flutter from the sweet navel to the roses.

Why do you? Why not? The naked days
bring red sand ceaselessly shattered
to the pure propellers that inaugurate the day,
and a month goes by with tortoiseshell,
a sterile day goes by,
an ox, a corpse goes by,
a woman named Rosalie,
and in the mouth remains only a taste of hair
and of golden tongue nourished on thirst.
Nothing but that human pulp,
nothing but that goblet of roots.

I pursue as if in a broken tunnel, at another end,
flesh and kisses that I must forget unjustly,
and in the backwaters, when the mirrors now
liven the abyss, when fatigue, the sordid clocks
knock at the doors of suburban hotels, and the flower
of painted paper falls, and the velvet shit by the rats and the bed
a hundred times occupied by wretched couples, when
everything tells me that a day has ended, you and I
have been together knocking bodies down,
building a house that neither endures nor dies,
you and I together have gone down a single river
with linked mouths filled with salt and blood,
you and I have made tremble again the green lights
and we have asked once more for the great ashes.

I remember only a day
that perhaps was never intended for me,
it was an incessant day,
without origins, Thursday.
I was a man transported by chance
with a woman vaguely found,
we undressed
as if to die or swim or grow old
and we thrust ourselves one inside the other,
she surrounding me like a hole,
I cracking her like one who
strikes a bell,
for she was the sound that wounded me
and the hard dome determined to tremble.

It was a dull business of hair and caverns
and crushing tips of marrow and sweetness
I have reached the great genital wreaths
among stones and submitted subjects.

This is a tale of ports which
one reaches, by chance, and goes up to the hills,
so many things happen.

Enemy, enemy,
is it possible that love has fallen to the dust
and that there is only flesh and bones swiftly adored
while the fire is consumed
and the red-dressed horses gallop into hell?

I want for myself the oats and the lightning
flesh bottomed,
and the devouring petal unfolded in fury,
and the labial heart of the June cherry tree,
and the repose of slow paunches that burn without direction,
but I lack a floor of lime with tears
and a window at which to wait for foam.

That's the way life is,
you, run among the leaves, a black
autumn has come,
run dressed with a skirt of leaves and a belt of yellow metal,
while the mist of the station corrodes the stones.
Run with your shoes, with your stockings,
with the distributed gray, with the hollow of the foot, and with those
    hands that wild tobacco would adore,
strike staircases, knock down
the black paper that protects doors,
and enter amid the sun and the anger of a day of daggers
to throw yourself like a dove of mourning and snow upon a body.

It is a single hour long as a vein,
and between the acid and the patience of wrinkled time
we pass,
separating the syllables of fear and tenderness,
interminably exterminated.

DONALD D. WALSH

Who has lied? The foot of the lily
broken, inscrutable, darkened, all
filled with wound and dark splendor!
All, the norm from wave to wave to wave,
the imprecise tumulus of the amber
and the harsh drops of the flower!
I based my heart on this, I listened to all
the sorrowful salt: by night
I went to plant my roots.
I discovered the bitterness of the earth:
for me everything was night or lightningflash:
secret wax settled in my head
and scattered ashes in my tracks.

And for whom did I seek this cold pulse
if not for a death?
And what instrument did I lose in the forsaken
darkness, where no one hears me?
No,
     it was high time, flee,
shadows of blood,
starry ice, retreat at the pace of human steps
and remove from my feet the black shadow!

I have the same wounded hand that men have,
I hold up the same red cup
and an equally furious amazement:
                        one day
burning with human
dreams, a wild
oat reached
my devouring night
so that I could join my wolf steps
to the steps of man.
              And thus united,
sternly central, I seek no shelter
in the hollows of weeping: I show

the bee's root: radiant bread
for the son of man: in mystery blue prepares itself
to look at wheat distant from the blood.

Where is your place in the rose?
Where is your starry eyelid?
Did you forget those sweaty fingers mad
to reach the sand?
     Peace to you, dark sun,
peace to you, blind brow,
there is a burning place for you in the roads,
there are stones without mystery that look at you,
there are silences of a prison with a mad star,
naked, foulmouthed, contemplating hell.
Together, facing the sobbing!
      It is the high
hour of earth and perfume, look at this face
just come from the terrible salt,
look at this bitter mouth that smiles,
look at this new heart that greets you
with its overflowing flower, resolute and golden.

DONALD D. WALSH

IV: SPAIN IN OUR HEART
INVOCATION

To begin, pause over the pure
and cleft rose, pause over the source
of sky and air and earth, the will of a song
with explosions, the desire
of an immense song, of a metal that will gather
war and naked blood.
     Spain, water glass, not diadem,
but yes crushed stone, militant tenderness
of wheat, hide and burning animal.

RICHARD SCHAAF

BOMBARDMENT/CURSE

Tomorrow, today, in your steps
a silence, an astonishment of hopes
like a major air: a light, a moon,
a worn-out moon, a moon from hand to hand,
from bell to bell!
                        Natal mother, fist
of hardened oats,
                        dry
and bloody planet of heroes!
Who? by roads, who,
who, who? in shadows, in blood, who?
in a flash, who,
                        who? Ashes
fall, fall,
iron
and stone and death and weeping and flames,
who, who, mother, who, where?
Furrowed motherland, I swear that in your ashes
you will be born like a flower of eternal water,
I swear that from your mouth of thirst will come to the air
the petals of bread, the spilt
inaugurated flower. Cursed,
cursed, cursed be those who with ax and serpent
came to your earthly arena, cursed those
who waited for this day to open the door
of the dwelling to the Moor and the bandit:
what have you achieved? Bring, bring the lamp,
see the soaked earth, see the blackened little bone
eaten by the flames, the garment
of murdered Spain.

RICHARD SCHAAF

Cursed be those who one day
did not look, cursed cursed blind,
those who offered the solemn fatherland
not bread but tears, cursed
sullied uniforms and cassocks
of sour, stinking dogs of cave and grave.
Poverty was throughout Spain
like horses filled with smoke,
like stones fallen from the
spring of misfortune,
grainlands still
unopened, secret storehouses
of blue and tin, ovaries, doors, closed
arches, depths
that tried to give birth, all was guarded
by triangular guards with guns,
by sad-rat-colored priests,
by lackeys of the huge-rumped king.
Tough Spain, land of apple orchards and pines,
your idle lords ordered you:
Do not sow the land, do not give birth to mines,
do not breed cows, but contemplate
the tombs, visit each year
the monument of Columbus the sailor, neigh
speeches with monkeys come from America,
equal in "social position" and in putrefaction.
Do not build schools, do not break open earth's
crust with plows, do not fill the granaries
with abundance of wheat: pray, beasts, pray,
for a god with a rump as huge as the king's rump
awaits you: "There you will have soup, my brethren."

RICHARD SCHAAF

TRADITION

In the nights of Spain, through the old gardens,
tradition, covered with dead snot,
spouting pus, and pestilence, strolled
with its tail in the fog, ghostly and fantastic,
dressed in asthma and bloody hollow frock coats,
and its face with sunken staring eyes
was green slugs eating graves,
and its toothless mouth each night bit
the unborn flower, the secret mineral,
and it passed with its crown of green thistles
sowing vague deadmen's bones and daggers.

RICHARD SCHAAF

MADRID (1936)

Madrid, alone and solemn, July surprised you with your joy
of humble honeycomb: bright was your street,
bright was your dream.
                    A black vomit
of generals, a wave
of rabid cassocks
poured between your knees
their swampy waters, their rivers of spittle.

With eyes still wounded by sleep,
with guns and stones, Madrid, newly wounded,
you defended yourself. You ran
through the streets
leaving trails of your holy blood,
rallying and calling with an oceanic voice,
with a face changed forever
by the light of blood, like an avenging
mountain, like a whistling
star of knives.

When into the dark barracks, when into the sacristies
of treason your burning sword entered,
there was only silence of dawn, there was
only your passage of flags,
and an honorable drop of blood in your smile.

RICHARD SCHAAF

SONG FOR THE MOTHERS OF SLAIN MILITIAMEN

They have not died! They are in the midst
of the gunpowder,
standing, like burning wicks.
Their pure shadows have gathered
in the copper-colored meadowland
like a curtain of armored wind,
like a barricade the color of fury,
like the invisible heart of heaven itself.

Mothers! They are standing in the wheat,
tall as the depth of noon,
dominating the great plains!
They are a black-voiced bell stroke
that across the bodies murdered by steel
is ringing out victory.
                        Sisters like the fallen
dust, shattered
hearts,
have faith in your dead.
They are not only roots
beneath the bloodstained stones,
not only do their poor demolished bones
definitively till the soil,
but their mouths still bite dry powder
and attack like iron oceans, and still
their upraised fists deny death.
Because from so many bodies an invisible life
rises up. Mothers, banners, sons!
A single body as alive as life:

a face of broken eyes keeps vigil in the darkness
with a sword filled with earthly hopes!

Put aside
your mantles of mourning, join all
your tears until you make them metal:
for there we strike by day and by night,
there we kick by day and by night,
there we spit by day and by night
until the doors of hatred fall!
I do not forget your misfortunes, I know
your sons,
and if I am proud of their deaths,
I am also proud of their lives.

                    Their laughter
flashed in the silent workshops,
their steps in the subway
sounded at my side each day, and next
to the oranges from the Levant, to the nets from the South, next
to the ink from the printing presses, over the cement of the architecture
I have seen their hearts flame with fire and energy.

And just as in your hearts, mothers,
there is in my heart so much mourning and so much death
that it is like a forest
drenched by the blood that killed their smiles,
and into it enter the rabid mists of vigilance with the rending loneliness
    of the days.

But
more than curses for the thirsty hyenas, the bestial death rattle,
that howls from Africa its filthy privileges,
more than anger, more than scorn, more than weeping,
mothers pierced by anguish and death,
look at the heart of the noble day that is born,
and know that your dead ones smile from the earth
raising their fists above the wheat.

RICHARD SCHAAF

SONG TO THE MOTHERS OF DEAD LOYALISTS

They are not dead! They are in the midst
Of the gunpowder,
Erect, with match cords burning!
Their pure shadows have joined
In the copper-colored meadow
Like a curtain of armored air,
Like a barrier the color of fury,
Like the very invisible chest of the sky.

Mothers! They are standing in the wheatfields,
Tall as deep noon,
Dominating the vast plains!
They are the sound of bells of somber voice
Which across the bodies of murdered steel
Peal the victory.
    Sisters like the fallen
Dust, broken
Hearts,
Have faith in your dead!
They are not mere roots
Under the bloodstained stones,
Not only do their poor fallen bones
Definitively work the land,
But even their mouths bite the dry gunpowder
And attack like oceans of iron, and even
Their clenched fists on high contradict death.

For from so many bodies an invisible life
Arises. Mothers, flags, sons!
A single body alive as life:
One face of broken eyes watches the darkness
Like a sword filled with terrestrial hopes!

Throw aside
Your mourning mantles, gather together all
Your tears until they turn to metal:
So that we may strike day and night,

So that we may kick day and night,
So that we may spit day and night
Till the gates of hate be overthrown!

I have not forgotten your misfortunes, I know
Your sons,
And if I am proud of their deaths
I am also proud of their lives.
    Their laughter
Rang in the deafening factories,
In subway stations
Their feet sounded by mine every day, and among
The oranges of the East, by the fishing nets of the South, in
The ink of the print shops, upon the cement of buildings
I have seen the flame of their hearts of fire and strength.

And as in your hearts, mothers,
There is in my heart so much mourning and so much death
That it seems like a forest
Wet with the blood that quenched their smiles,
And over it comes the rabid mist of sleeplessness
With the lacerating loneliness of the days.

But
Over and beyond the curse on the thirsty hyenas, on the bestial death
    rattle
Which from Africa bays its filthy cries,
Over and beyond the anger, beyond the scorn, beyond the tears,
Oh mothers transfixed by anguish and death,
Look into the heart of the noble day being born,
And know that your dead ones smile beneath the earth
Lifting their clenched fists over the wheatfields.

ANGEL FLORES

WHAT SPAIN WAS LIKE

Spain was taut and dry, diurnal
drum with an opaque tone,
prairie and eagle's nest, silence
of whiplashed weather.

Even with tears, even with my soul
I love your hard soil, your meager bread,
your meager people, even in my deep heart's
core lies the lost flower of your crumpled
villages, moveless in time,
and your mineraled fields
stretched agelong under the moon
and consumed by an empty god.

All you have built, your animal
isolation bound to intelligence,
surrounded by abstract stones of silence,
your sharp wine sweet
wine, your wild
fragile vines.

Solar stone, pure among the regions
of this world, Spain pervaded
by blood and metal, blue and buoyant
worker with petals and bullets, alone
alive and somnolent and sonorous.

Huélamo, Carrascosa,
Alpedrete, Buitrago,
Palencia, Arganda, Galve,
Galapagar, Villalba.

Peñarrubia, Cedrillas,
Alcocer, Tamurejo,
Aguadulce, Pedrera,
Fuente Palmera, Colmenar, Sepúlveda.

Carcabuey, Fuencaliente,
Linares, Solana del Pino,
Carcelén, Alatox,
Mahora, Valdeganda.

Yeste, Riopar, Segorbe,
Orihuela, Montalbo,
Alcaraz, Caravaca,
Almendralejo, Castejón de Monegros.

Palma del Río, Peralta,
Granadella, Quintana
de la Serena, Atienza, Barahona,
Navalmoral, Oropesa.

Alborea, Monóvar,
Almansa, San Benito,
Moratalla, Montesa,
Torre Baja, Aldemuz.

Cevico Navero, Cevico de la Torre,
Albalate de las Nogueras,
Jabaloyas, Teruel,
Camporrobles, La Alberca

Pozo Amargo, Candeleda,
Pedroñeras, Campillo de Altobuey,
Loranca de Tajuña, Puebla de la Mujer Muerta,
Torre la Cárcel, Játiva, Alcoy.

Puebla de Obando, Villar del Rey,
Beloraga, Brihuega,
Cetina, Villacañas, Palomas,
Navalcán, Henarejos, Albatana.

Torredonjimeno, Trasparga,
Agramón, Crevillente,
Poveda de la Sierra, Pedernoso,
Alcolea de Cinca, Matallanos.

Ventosa del Río, Alba de Tormes,
Horcajo Medianero, Piedrahita,
Minglanilla, Navamorcuende, Navalperal,
Navalcarnero, Navalmorales, Jorquera.

Argora, Torremocha, Argecilla,
Ojos Negros, Salvacañete, Utiel,
Laguna Seca, Cañamares, Salorino,
Aldea Quemada, Pesquera de Duero.

Fuenteovejuna, Alpedrete,
Torrejón, Benaguacil,
Valverde de Júcar, Vallanca,
Hiendelaencina, Robledo de Chavela.

Miñogalindo, Ossa de Montiel,
Méntrida, Valdepeñas, Titaguas,
Almodóvar, Gestaldar, Valdemoro,
Almoradiel, Orgaz.

JOHN FELSTINER

BATALLA DEL RÍO JARAMA

Entre la tierra y el platino ahogado
de olivares y muertos españoles,
Jarama, puñal puro, has resistido
　　　la ola de los crueles.

Allí desde Madrid llegaron hombres
de corazón dorado por la pólvora
como un pan de ceniza y resistencia,
　　　allí llegaron.

Jarama, estabas entre hierro y humo
como una rama de cristal caído,
como una larga línea de medallas
　　　para los victoriosos.

Ni socavones de substancia ardiendo,
ni coléricos vuelos explosivos,
ni artillería de tiniebla turbia
        dominaron tus aguas.

Aguas tuyas bebieron los sedientos
de sangre, agua bebieron boca arriba:
agua española y tierra de olivares
        los llenaron de olvido.

Por un segundo de agua y tiempo el cauce
de la sangre de moros y traidores
palpitaba en tu luz como los peces
        de un manantial amargo.

La áspera harina de tu pueblo estaba
toda erizada de metal y huesos,
formidable y trigal como la noble
        tierra que defendían.

Jarama, para hablar de tus regiones
de esplendor y dominio, no es mi boca
suficiente, y es pálida mi mano:
        allí quedan tus muertos.

Allí quedan tu cielo doloroso,
tu paz de piedra, tu estelar corriente,
y los eternos ojos de tu pueblo
        vigilan tus orillas.

BATTLE OF THE JARAMA RIVER

Between the earth and the drowned platinum
of olive orchards and Spanish dead,
Jarama, pure dagger, you have resisted
        the wave of the cruel.

There, from Madrid, came men
with hearts made golden by gunpowder,
like a loaf of ashes and resistance,
            there they came.

Jarama, you were between iron and smoke
like a branch of fallen crystal,
like a long line of medals
            for the victorious.

Neither caverns of burning substance,
nor angry explosive flights,
nor artillery of turbid darkness
            controlled your waters.

The bloodthirsty drank
your waters, face up they drank water:
Spanish water and olive fields
            filled them with oblivion.

For a second of water and time the riverbed
of the blood of Moors and traitors
throbbed in your light like the fish
            of a bitter fountain.

The bitter wheat of your people was
all bristling with metal and bones,
formidable and germinal like the noble
            land that they defended.

Jarama, to speak of your regions
of splendor and dominion, my mouth is not
adequate, and my hand is pale:
            there rest your dead.

There rest your mournful sky,
your flinty peace, your starry stream,
and the eternal eyes of your people
            watch over your shores.

RICHARD SCHAAF

ALMERÍA

A bowl for the bishop, a crushed and bitter bowl,
a bowl with remnants of iron, with ashes, with tears,
a sunken bowl, with sobs and fallen walls,
a bowl for the bishop, a bowl of Almería blood.

A bowl for the banker, a bowl with cheeks
of children from the happy South, a bowl
with explosions, with wild waters and ruins and fright,
a bowl with split axles and trampled heads,
a black bowl, a bowl of Almería blood.

Each morning, each turbid morning of your lives
you will have it steaming and burning at your tables:
you will push it aside a bit with your soft hands
so as not to see it, not to digest it so many times:
you will push it aside a bit between the bread and the grapes,
this bowl of silent blood
that will be there each morning, each
morning.

A bowl for the Colonel and the Colonel's wife
at a garrison party, at each party,
above the oaths and the spittle, with the wine light of early morning
so that you may see it trembling and cold upon the world.

Yes, a bowl for all of you, richmen here and there,
monstrous ambassadors, ministers, table companions,
ladies with cozy tea parties and chairs:
a bowl shattered, overflowing, dirty with the blood of the poor,
for each morning, for each week, forever and ever,
a bowl of Almería blood, facing you, forever.

RICHARD SCHAAF

Evil one, neither fire nor hot vinegar
in a nest of volcanic witches, nor devouring ice,
nor the putrid turtle that barking and weeping with the voice of a
    dead woman scratches your belly
seeking a wedding ring and the toy of a slaughtered child,
will be for you anything but a dark demolished door.

    Indeed.
    From one hell to another, what difference? In the howling
of your legions, in the holy milk
of the mothers of Spain, in the milk and the bosoms trampled
along the roads, there is one more village, one more silence, a broken
    door.

    Here you are. Wretched eyelid, dung
of sinister sepulchral hens, heavy sputum, figure
of treason that blood will not erase. Who, who are you,
oh miserable leaf of salt, oh dog of the earth,
oh ill-born pallor of shadow?

    The flame retreats without ash,
the salty thirst of hell, the circles
of grief turn pale.
    Cursed one, may only humans
pursue you, within the absolute fire of things may
you not be consumed, not be lost
in the scale of time, may you not be pierced by the burning glass or the
    fierce foam.

    Alone, alone, for the tears
all gathered, for an eternity of dead hands
and rotted eyes, alone in a cave
of your hell, eating silent pus and blood
through a cursed and lonely eternity.
    You do not deserve to sleep
even though it be with your eyes fastened with pins:
    you have to be

awake, General, eternally awake
among the putrefaction of the new mothers,
machine-gunned in the autumn. All and all the sad children cut to
     pieces,
rigid, they hang, awaiting in your hell
that day of cold festivity: your arrival.
                         Children blackened by explosions,
red fragments of brain, corridors filled
with gentle intestines, they all await you, all in the very posture
of crossing the street, of kicking the ball,
of swallowing a fruit, of smiling, or being born.

Smiling. There are smiles
now demolished by blood
that wait with scattered exterminated teeth
and masks of muddled matter, hollow faces
of perpetual gunpowder, and the nameless
ghosts, the dark
hidden ones, those who never left
their beds of rubble. They all wait for you
to spend the night. They fill the corridors
like decayed seaweed.

                    They are ours, they were our
flesh, our health, our
bustling peace, our ocean
of air and lungs. Through
them the dry earth flowered. Now, beyond the earth,
turned into destroyed
substance, murdered matter, dead flour,
they await you in your hell.

Since acute terror or sorrow waste away,
neither terror nor sorrow awaits you. May you be alone and accursed,
alone and awake among all the dead,
and let blood fall upon you like rain,
and let a dying river of severed eyes
slide and flow over you staring at you endlessly.

RICHARD SCHAAF

TRIUMPH

Solemn is the triumph of the people.
At its great victorious passage
the eyeless potato and the heavenly
grape glitter in the earth.

RICHARD SCHAAF

LANDSCAPE AFTER A BATTLE

Bitten space, troop crushed
against the grain, broken
horseshoes, frozen between frost and stones,
       harsh moon.

Moon of a wounded mare, charred,
wrapped in exhausted thorns, menacing, sunken
metal or bone, absence, bitter cloth,
       smoke of gravediggers.

Behind the acrid halo of saltpeter,
from substance to substance, from water to water,
swift as threshed wheat,
       burned and eaten.

Accidental crust softly soft,
black ash absent and scattered,
now only echoing cold, abominable
       materials of rain.

May my knees keep it hidden
more than this fugitive territory,
may my eyelids grasp it until they can name and wound,
may my brow keep this taste of shadow
       so that there will be no forgetting.

RICHARD SCHAAF

At this hour I remember everything and everyone,
vigorously, sunkenly in
the regions that—sound and feather—
striking a little, exist
beyond the earth, but on the earth. Today
a new winter begins.
                There is in that city,
where lies what I love,
there is no bread, no light: a cold windowpane falls
upon dry geraniums. By night black dreams
opened by howitzers, like bloody oxen:
no one in the dawn of the ramparts
but a broken cart: now moss, now silence of ages,
instead of swallows, on the burned houses,
drained of blood, empty, their doors open to the sky:
now the market begins to open its poor emeralds,
and the oranges, the fish,
brought each day across the blood,
offer themselves to the hands of the sister and the widow.
City of mourning, undermined, wounded,
broken, beaten, bullet-riddled, covered
with blood and broken glass, city without night, all
night and silence and explosions and heroes,
now a new winter more naked and more alone,
now without flour, without steps, with your moon
of soldiers.
          Everything, everyone.

              Poor sun, our lost
blood, terrible heart
shaken and mourned. Tears like heavy bullets
have fallen on your dark earth sounding
like falling doves, a hand that death
closes forever, blood of each day
and each night and each week and each
month. Without speaking of you, heroes asleep
and awake, without speaking of you who make the water and the earth

tremble with your glorious purpose,
at this hour I listen to the weather on a street,
someone speaks to me, winter
comes again to the hotels
where I have lived,
everything is city that I listen to and distance
surrounded by fire as if by a spume
of vipers assaulted by a
water of hell.

      For more than a year now
the masked ones have been touching your human shore
and dying at the contact of your electric blood:
sacks of Moors, sacks of traitors
have rolled at your feet of stone: neither smoke nor death
has conquered your burning walls.

        Then,
what's happening, then? Yes, they are the exterminators,
they are the devourers: they spy on you, white city,
the bishop of turbid scruff, the fecal and feudal
young masters, the general in whose hand
jingle thirty coins: against your walls are
a circle of women, dripping and devout,
a squadron of putrid ambassadors,
and a sad vomit of military dogs.

Praise to you, praise in cloud, in sunray,
in health, in swords,
bleeding front whose thread of blood
echoes on the deeply wounded stones,
a slipping away of harsh sweetness,
bright cradle armed with lightning,
fortress substance, air of blood
from which bees are born.

      Today you who live, Juan,
today you who watch, Pedro, who conceive, sleep, eat:
today in the lightless night on guard without sleep and without rest,
alone on the cement, across the gashed earth,
from the blackened wire, to the South, in the middle, all around,
without sky, without mystery,

men like a collar of cordons defend
the city surrounded by flames: Madrid hardened
by an astral blow, by the shock of fire:
earth and vigil in the deep silence
of victory: shaken
like a broken rose, surrounded
by infinite laurel.

RICHARD SCHAAF

SOLAR ODE TO THE ARMY OF THE PEOPLE

Arms of the people! Here! The threat, the siege
are still wasting the earth, mixing it with death,
earth rough with goading!
                        Your health,
your health say the mothers of the world,
the schools say your health, the old carpenters,
Army of the People, they say health to you with blossoms,
milk, potatoes, lemon, laurel,
everything that belongs to the earth and to the mouth
of man.
            Everything, like a necklace
of hands, like a
throbbing waist, like a persistence of thunderbolts,
everything prepares itself for you, converges on you!
                              Day of iron.
Fortified blue!
            Brothers, onward,
onward through the plowed lands,
onward in the dry and sleepless night, delirious and threadbare,
onward among the vines, treading the cold color of the rocks,
good health to you, go on. More cutting than winter's voice,
more sensitive than the eyelid, more unfailing than the tip of the
    thunderbolt,
exact as the swift diamond, warlike anew,
warriors according to the biting waters of the central lands,
according to the flower and the wine, according to the spiral heart of the
    earth,

according to the roots of all the leaves, of all the fragrant produce of the
    earth.
Your health, soldiers, your health, red fallow lands,
health, hard clovers, health, towns stopped
in the light of the lightning, your good health,
onward, onward, onward, onward,
over the mines, over the cemeteries, facing the abominable
appetite of death, facing the bristling
terror of the traitors,
people, effective people, hearts and guns,
hearts and guns, onward.
Photographers, miners, railroadmen, brothers
of coal and stone, relatives of the hammer,
woods, festival of gay nonsense, onward,
guerrilla fighters, chiefs, sergeants, political commissars,
people's aviators, night fighters,
sea fighters, onward:
facing you
there is only a mortal chain, a hole
of rotten fish: onward!
there are only dying dead there,
swamps of terrible bloody pus,
there are no enemies; onward, Spain,
onward, people's bells,
onward, apple orchards,
onward, banners of the grain,
onward, giants of the fire,
because in the struggle, in the wave, in the meadow,
in the mountain, in the twilight laden with acrid smell,
you bear a lineage of permanence, a thread
of hard harshness.
                        Meanwhile,
root and garland rise from the silence
to await the mineral victory:
each instrument, each red wheel,
each mountain mango or plume of plow,
each product of the soil, each tremor of blood
wants to follow your steps, Army of the People:
your ordered light reaches poor forgotten

men, your sharp star
sinks its raucous rays into death
and establishes the new eyes of hope.

RICHARD SCHAAF

V

CANTO A STALINGRADO

En la noche el labriego duerme, despierta y hunde
su mano en las tinieblas preguntando a la aurora:
alba, sol de mañana, luz del día que viene,
dime si aún las manos más puras de los hombres
defienden el castillo dei honor, dime, aurora,
si el acero en tu frente rompe su poderío,
si el hombre está en su sitio, si el trueno está en su sitio,
dime, dice el labriego, si no escucha la tierra
cómo cae la sangre de los enrojecidos
héroes, en la grandeza de la noche terrestre,
dime si sobre el árbol todavía está el cielo,
dime si aún la pólvora suena en Stalingrado.

Y el marinero en medio del mar terrible mira
buscando entre las húmedas constelaciones
una, la roja estrella de la ciudad ardiente,
y halla en su corazón esa estrella que quema,
esa estrella de orgullo quieren tocar sus manos,
esa estrella de llanto la construyen sus ojos.

Ciudad, estrella roja, dicen el mar y el hombre,
ciudad, cierra tus rayos, cierra tus puertas duras,
cierra, ciudad, tu ilustre laurel ensangrentado,
y que la noche tiemble con el brillo sombrío
de tus ojos detrás de un planeta de espadas.

Y el español recuerda Madrid y dice: hermana,
resiste, capital de la gloria, resiste:
del suelo se alza toda la sangre derramada
de España, y por España se levanta de nuevo,

y el español pregunta junto al muro
de los fusilamientos, si Stalingrado vive:
y hay en la cárcel una cadena de ojos negros
que horadan las paredes con tu nombre,
y España se sacude con tu sangre y tus muertos,
porque tú le tendiste, Stalingrado, el alma
cuando España paría héroes como los tuyos.

Ella conoce la soledad, España
como hoy, Stalingrado, tú conoces la tuya.
España desgarró la tierra con sus uñas
cuando París estaba más bonita que nunca,
España desangraba su inmenso árbol de sangre
cuando Londres peinaba, como nos cuenta Pedro
Garfias, su césped y sus lagos de cisnes.

Hoy ya conoces eso, recia virgen,
hoy ya conoces, Rusia, la soledad y el frío.
Cuando miles de obuses tu corazón destrozan,
cuando los escorpiones con crimen y veneno,
Stalingrado, acuden a morder tus entrañas,
Nueva York baila, Londres medita, y yo digo "merde,"
porque mi corazón no puede más y nuestros
corazones
no pueden más, no pueden
en un mundo que deja morir solos sus héroes.

Los dejáis solos? Ya vendrán por vosotros!
Los dejáis solos?
                    Queréis que la vida
huya a la tumba, y la sonrisa de los hombres
sea borrada por la letrina y el calvario?
Por qué no respondéis?
Queréis más muertos en el frente del Este
hasta que llenen totalmente el cielo vuestro?
Pero entonces no os va a quedar sino el infierno.
El mundo está cansándose de pequeñas hazañas,
de que en Madagascar los generales
maten con heroísmo cincuenta y cinco monos.

El mundo está cansado de otoñales reuniones
presididas aún por un paraguas.

Ciudad, Stalingrado, no podemos
llegar a tus murallas, estamos lejos.
Somos los mexicanos, somos los araucanos,
somos los patagones, somos los guaraníes,
somos los uruguayos, somos los chilenos,
somos millones de hombres.
Ya tenemos por suerte deudos en la familia,
pero aún no llegamos a defenderte, madre.
Ciudad, ciudad de fuego, resiste hasta que un día
lleguemos, indios náufragos, a tocar tus murallas
como un beso de hijos que esperaban llegar.

Stalingrado, aún no hay Segundo Frente,
pero no caerás aunque el hierro y el fuego
te muerdan día y noche.

Aunque mueras, no mueres!

Porque los hombres ya no tienen muerte
y tienen que seguir luchando desde el sitio en que caen
hasta que la victoria no esté sino en tus manos
aunque estén fatigadas y horadadas y muertas,
porque otras manos rojas, cuando las vuestras caigan,
sembrarán por el mundo los huesos de tus héroes
para que tu semilla llene toda la tierra.

SONG TO STALINGRAD

At night the peasant sleeps, awakes, and sinks
his hand into the darkness asking the dawn:
daybreak, morning sun, light of the coming day,
tell me if the purest hands of men still
defend the castle of honor, tell me, dawn,
if the steel on your brow breaks its might,

if man is in his place, if thunder is in its place,
tell me, says the peasant, if earth does not listen
to how the blood falls from the reddened
heroes in the vastness of earthly night,
tell me if the sky is still above the tree,
tell me if gunpowder still sounds in Stalingrad.

And the sailor in the midst of the terrible sea looks,
seeking amid the watery constellations
one, the red star of the flaming city,
and he finds in his heart that burning star,
his hands seek to touch that star of pride,
his eyes are building that star of tears.

City, red star, say sea and man,
city, close your thunderbolts, close your hard doors,
close, city, your glorious bloodied laurel
and let night tremble with the dark luster
of your eyes behind a planet of swords.

And the Spaniard remembers Madrid and says: sister,
resist, capital of glory, resist:
from the soil rises all the spilt blood
of Spain, and throughout Spain it is rising again,
and the Spaniard asks, next to the
firing-squad wall, if Stalingrad lives:
and there is in prison a chain of black eyes
that riddle the walls with your name,
and Spain shakes herself with your blood and your dead,
because you, Stalingrad, held out to her your heart
when Spain was giving birth to heroes like yours.

She knows loneliness, Spain,
as today, Stalingrad, you know your loneliness.
Spain tore at the earth with her nails
when Paris was prettier than ever,
Spain drained her immense tree of blood
when London was grooming, as Pedro Garfías
tells us, her lawn and her swan lakes.

Today you know that, sturdy virgin,
today you know, Russia, loneliness and cold.
When thousands of howitzers shatter your heart,
when scorpions with crime and venom,
Stalingrad, rush to pierce your heart,
New York dances, London meditates, and I say "merde,"
because my heart can stand no more and our
hearts
can stand no more, cannot live
in a world that lets its heroes die alone.

You leave them alone? They will come for you!
You leave them alone?
                         Do you want life
to flee to the tomb, and the smiles of men
to be erased by cesspools and Calvary?
Why do you not answer?
Do you want more dead on the Eastern Front
until they totally fill your sky?
But then you will have nothing left but hell.
The world is getting bored with little deeds,
bored that in Madagascar the generals
heroically kill fifty-five monkeys.

The world is bored with autumnal meetings
still presided over by an umbrella.

City, Stalingrad, we cannot
reach your walls, we are far away.
We are the Mexicans, we are the Araucanians,
we are the Patagonians, we are the Guaranís,
we are the Uruguayans, we are the Chileans,
we are millions of men.
We now luckily have relatives in the family,
but we still do not come to defend you, mother.
City, city of fire, resist until one day
we come, shipwrecked Indians, to touch your walls
like a kiss from sons who were eager to arrive.

Stalingrad, there is not yet a Second Front,
but you will not fall, even though iron and fire
pierce you day and night.

Even though you die, you do not die!

Because men can no longer die
and must go on struggling from the place where they fall
until victory lies only in your hands
although they are weary and pierced and dead,
because other red hands, when your hands fall,
will sow throughout the world the bones of your heroes
so that your seed may fill all the earth.

DONALD D. WALSH

TINA MODOTTI HA MUERTO

Tina Modotti, hermana, no duermes, no, no duermes.
Tal vez tu corazón oye crecer la rosa
de ayer, la última rosa de ayer, la nueva rosa.
      Descansa dulcemente, hermana.

La nueva rosa es tuya, la nueva tierra es tuya:
te has puesto un nuevo traje de semilla profunda
y tu suave silencio se llena de raíces.
      No dormirás en vano, hermana.

Puro es tu dulce nombre, pura es tu frágil vida.
De abeja, sombra, fuego, nieve, silencio, espuma,
de acero, línea, polen se construyó tu férrea,
      tu delgada estructura.

El chacal a la alhaja de tu cuerpo dormido
aún asoma la pluma y el alma ensangrentada
como si tú pudieras, hermana, levantarte,
      sonriendo sobre el lodo.

A mi patria te llevo para que no te toquen,
a mi patria de nieve para que a tu pureza
no llegue el asesino, ni el chacal, ni el vendido:
        allí estarás tranquila.

Oyes un paso, un paso lleno de pasos, algo
grande desde la estepa, desde el Don, desde el frío?
Oyes un paso firme de soldado en la nieve?
        Hermana, son tus pasos.

Ya pasarán un día por tu pequeña tumba
antes de que las rosas de ayer se desbaraten,
ya pasarán a ver los de un día, mañana,
        donde está ardiendo tu silencio.

Un mundo marcha al sitio donde tú ibas, hermana.
Avanzan cada día los cantos de tu boca
en la boca del pueblo glorioso que tú amabas.
        Tu corazón era valiente.

En las viejas cocinas de tu patria, en las rutas
polvorientas, algo se dice y pasa,
algo vuelve a la llama de tu dorado pueblo,
        algo despierta y canta.

Son los tuyos, hermana: los que hoy dicen tu nombre,
los que de todas partes, del agua y de la tierra,
con tu nombre otros nombres callamos y decimos.
        Porque el fuego no muere.

TINA MODOTTI IS DEAD

Tina Modotti, sister, you do not sleep, no, you do not sleep.
Perhaps your heart hears the rose of yesterday
growing, the last rose of yesterday, the new rose.
        Rest gently, sister.

The new rose is yours, the new earth is yours:
you have put on a new dress of deep seed
and your soft silence is filled with roots.
            You shall not sleep in vain, sister.

Pure is your gentle name, pure is your fragile life.
Of bee, shadow, fire, snow, silence, foam,
of steel, line, pollen was built your tough,
            your slender structure.

The jackal at the jewel of your sleeping body
still shows the white feather and the bloody soul
as if you, sister, could rise up,
            smiling above the mud.

To my country I take you so that they will not touch you,
to my snow country so that your purity
will be far from the assassin, the jackal, the Judas:
            there you will be at peace.

Do you hear a step, a step-filled step, something
huge from the great plain, from the Don, from the cold?
Do you hear the firm step of a soldier upon the snow?
            Sister, they are your steps.

They will pass one day by your little tomb
before yesterday's roses are withered,
the steps of tomorrow will pass by to see
            where your silence is burning.

A world marches to the place where you were going, sister.
The songs of your mouth advance each day
in the mouths of the glorious people that you loved.
            Your heart was brave.

In the old kitchens of your country, on the dusty
roads, something is said and passes on,
something returns to the flame of your golden people,
            something awakes and sings.

They are your people, sister: those who today speak your name,
we who from everywhere, from the water and the land,
with your name leave unspoken and speak other names.
>   Because fire does not die.

SEVENTH OF NOVEMBER:
ODE TO A DAY OF VICTORIES

This double anniversary, this day, this night,
will they find an empty world, will they meet a crude
hollow of desolate hearts?
>   No, more than a day with hours,
it is a procession of mirrors and swords,
it is a double flower that beats upon the night
until it tears daybreak from its night roots!

Day of Spain coming from the
south, valiant day
of iron plumage,
you arrive from there, from the last man that falls with shattered brow
and with your fiery number still in his mouth!

And you go there with our
memory unsubmerged:
you were the day, you are
the struggle, you support
the invisible column, the wing
from which flight, with your number, will be born!

Seven, November, where do you dwell?
Where do the petals burn, where does your whisper
say to the brother: go up! and to the fallen: arise!
Where does your laurel grow from the blood
and cross the frail flesh of man and go up
to fashion the hero?
>   In you, once more, Union,

in you, once more, sister of the peoples of the world,
pure and Soviet fatherland. To you returns your seed
in a leafy flood scattered upon the earth!

There are no tears for you, People, in your struggle!
All must be of iron, all must march and wound,
all, even impalpable silence, even doubt,
even the very doubt that with wintry hand
seeks our hearts to freeze them and sink them,
all, even joy, all must be of iron
to help you, sister and mother, in victory!

May today's renegade be spat upon!
May the wretch today meet his punishment in the hour
of hours, in the total blood,
                              may the coward return
to darkness, may the laurels go to the valiant,
the valiant highway, the valiant ship
of snow and blood that defends the world!

I greet you, Soviet Union, on this day,
with humility: I am a writer and a poet.
My father was a railroad worker: we were always poor.
Yesterday I was with you, far off, in my little
country of great rains. There your name grew
hot, burning in the people's breasts
until it touched my country's lofty sky!

Today I think of them, they are all with you!
From factory to factory, from house to house,
your name flies like a red bird!

Praised be your heroes, and each drop
of your blood, praised
be the overflowing tide of hearts
that defend your pure and proud dwelling!
Praised be the heroic and bitter
bread that nourishes you, while the doors of time open
so that your army of people and iron may march, singing

among ashes and barren plain, against the assassins,
to plant a rose enormous as the moon
upon the fine and divine land of victory!

DONALD D. WALSH

SONG ON THE DEATH AND RESURRECTION OF LUIS COMPANYS

When up the hill where other dead men go on
living, like bloody, buried seeds,
your shadow grew and grew until it blotted out the air
and the shape of the snowy almond shriveled
and your step spread like a cold sound
that fell from a frozen cathedral,
your heart knocked at the most eternal doors:
the house of the dead captains of Spain.

Young father fallen with the flower in your breast,
with the flower in your breast of Catalonian light,
with the carnation drenched in inextinguishable blood,
with the living poppy above the broken light,
your brow has received the eternity of man
among the buried hearts of Spain.

Your soul held the virginal oil of the village
and the harsh dew of your golden earth
and all the roots of wounded Catalonia
received the blood from the fountain of your soul,
the starry grottoes where the militant sea
dashes its blue waves beneath the angry foam,
and man and olive tree sleep in the fragrance
left upon the earth by your spilt blood.

Spreading out from red Catalonia
and from all the stones of Spain,
let them display the carnations of your living wound
and moisten their kerchiefs in your sacred blood,
the sons of Castile that cannot weep for you
because you are forever of Castilian stone,

the girls of Galicia that weep like rivers,
the giant boys of the Asturian mine,
all of them, the Basque fishermen, those from the South, those who have
another dead captain to avenge in Granada,
your warrior land that digs into the earth
finding the ancient springs of Spain.

Guerrilla fighters from all the regions, greetings,
touch, touch the blood under the beloved earth:
it is the same, fallen upon the rainy expanse
of the north and upon the south of burning crust:
attack the same bitter enemies,
raise a single bright banner:
united by the blood of Captain Companys
joined in the earth with the blood of Spain!

DONALD D. WALSH

SONG TO THE RED ARMY ON ITS ARRIVAL
AT THE GATES OF PRUSSIA

This is the song between night and dawn, this is the song
come from the last death rattles as if from the beaten
hide of a bloody drum,
burst forth from the first joys like the flowering
bough in the snow and like the ray of sunlight upon the flowering
    bough.

These are the words that clutched the dying
and that syllable by syllable squeezed the tears like soiled clothes
until they dried up the last bitter drops of sobbing
and made from all the weeping the hardened braid,
the cord, the hard thread that will uphold the dawn.

Brothers, today we can say: daybreak comes,
now we can strike the table with the fist
that until yesterday upheld our tearful brow.
Now we can look at the crystal tower
of our powerful snow-covered range

because in the lofty pride of its snowy wings
shines the stern splendor of a far-off snow
where the invader's claws are buried.

The Red Army at the gates of Prussia. Listen, listen!
dark, humbled, radiant heroes of fallen crown,
listen! villages destroyed and laid waste and broken,
listen! Ukrainian fields where the grain can be reborn with pride.
Listen! martyred ones, hanged ones, listen! dead guerrilla fighters,
rigid beneath the frost with hands still clutching the gun,
listen! girls, homeless children, listen! sacred ashes
of Pushkin and Tolstoy, of Peter and Suvorov,
listen! on this southern height to the sound
that on the gates of Prussia crashes like thunder.

The Red Army at the gates of Prussia. Where are
the angered assassins, the gravediggers,
where are those who hanged mothers from the fir tree,
where are the tigers with a stench of extermination?
They are behind the walls of their own houses trembling,
waiting for the lightningstroke of punishment, and when all the walls fall
they will see the fir tree and the virgin come, the guerrilla fighter and
    the child,
they will see the dead and the living come to judge them.

Listen, Czechoslovaks, prepare the toughest
tongs and the gallows, and the ashes of Lidice
so that they may be swallowed tomorrow by the hangman,
listen, impatient workers of France, prepare your immortal rivers
so that the drowned invaders may navigate them.
Prepare the vengeance, Spaniards, behind the mountain range
and close to the coast of the burning south
clean the little rusted carbine because
the day has come.

This is the song of the dawning day and of the ending night.
Listen to it, and from harsh suffering let the confident voice emerge
that does not forgive, and let the punishing arm not tremble.
Before beginning tomorrow the canticles of human pity

you still have time to know the lands soaked in martyrdom.
Do not raise tomorrow the flag of pardon
over the cursed sons of the wolf and brothers of the serpent,
over those who reached the last edge of the knife and demolished the
    rose.

This is the song of the spring hidden
beneath the earth of Russia, beneath the expanse
of the taiga and the snow, this is the word
that mounts to the throat from the buried root.
From the root covered by so much anguish, from the stalk broken
by the bitterest winter on earth, by the winter
of blood upon the earth.

But things change, and from the depths
of the earth the new spring steps out.
Look at the cannons that flourish in the Prussian mouth.
Look at the machine guns and the tanks that
are landing at this hour in Marseilles.
Listen to the stern heart of Yugoslavia
throbbing again in the blood-drained breast of Europe.
Spanish eyes are looking toward here, toward Mexico and Chile,
because they wait for the return of their wandering brothers.

Something is happening in the world, like a breath that before
we did not sense among the waves of gunpowder.

This is the song of what is happening and of what will be.
This is the song of the rain that fell upon the field
like an immense tear of blood and lead.
Today when the Red Army beats on the gates of Prussia
I have chosen to sing for you, for all the earth,
this song of dark words,
so that we may be worthy of the coming light.

DONALD D. WALSH

from

CANTO GENERAL

CANTO GENERAL

✻

1938–1949

❋

I

AMOR AMERICA (1400)

Before the wig and the dress coat
there were rivers, arterial rivers:
there were cordilleras, jagged waves where
the condor and the snow seemed immutable:
there was dampness and dense growth, the thunder
as yet unnamed, the planetary pampas.

Man was dust, earthen vase, an eyelid
of tremulous loam, the shape of clay—
he was Carib jug, Chibcha stone,
imperial cup of Araucanian silica.
Tender and bloody was he, but on the grip
of his weapon of moist flint,
the initials of the earth were
written.
          No one could
remember them afterward: the wind
forgot them, the language of water
was buried, the keys were lost
or flooded with silence or blood.

Life was not lost, pastoral brothers.
But like a wild rose
a red drop fell into the dense growth,
and a lamp of earth was extinguished.

I am here to tell the story.
From the peace of the buffalo
to the pummeled sands
of the land's end, in the accumulated
spray of the antarctic light,

and through precipitous tunnels
of shady Venezuelan peacefulness
I searched for you, my father,
young warrior of darkness and copper,
or you, nuptial plant, indomitable hair,
mother cayman, metallic dove.
I, Incan of the loam,
touched the stone and said:

Who
awaits me? And I closed my hand
around a fistful of empty flint.
But I walked among Zapotec flowers
and the light was soft like a deer,
and the shade was a green eyelid.

My land without name, without America,
equinoctial stamen, purple lance,
your aroma climbed my roots up to the glass
raised to my lips, up to the slenderest
word as yet unborn in my mouth.

JACK SCHMITT

VEGETATION

To the lands without name
or numbers,
the wind blew down from other domains,
the rain brought celestial threads,
and the god of the impregnated altars
restored flowers and lives.

In fertility time grew.
The jacaranda raised its froth
of transmarine splendor,
the araucaria, bristling with spears,
was magnitude against the snow,

the primordial mahogany tree
distilled blood from its crown,
and to the South of the cypress,
the thunder tree, the red tree,
the thorn tree, the mother tree,
the scarlet ceibo, the rubber tree
were earthly volume, sound,
territorial existence.

A newly propagated aroma
suffused, through the interstices
of the earth, the breaths
transformed into mist and fragrance:
wild tobacco raised
its rosebush of imaginary air.
Like a fire-tipped spear
corn emerged, its stature
was stripped and it gave forth again,
disseminated its flour, had
corpses beneath its roots,
and then, in its cradle, it watched
the vegetable gods grow.
Wrinkle and extension, sown
by the seed of the wind
over the plumes of the cordillera,
dense light of germ and nipples,
blind dawn nursed
by the earthly ointments
of the implacable rainy latitude,
of the enshrouded torrential nights,
of the matinal cisterns.
And still on the prairies,
like laminas of the planet,
beneath a fresh republic of stars,
the ombú, king of the grass, stopped
the free air, the whispering flight,
and mounted the pampa, holding it in
with a bridle of reins and roots.

Arboreal America,
wild bramble between the seas,
from pole to pole you balanced,
green treasure, your dense growth.

The night germinated
in cities of sacred pods,
in sonorous woods,
outstretched leaves covering
the germinal stone, the births.
Green uterus, seminal
American savanna, dense storehouse,
a branch was born like an island,
a leaf was shaped like a sword,
a flower was lightning and medusa,
a cluster rounded off its résumé,
a root descended into the darkness.

JACK SCHMITT

III

THE BIRDS ARRIVE

All was flight in our land.
The cardinal, like drops
of blood and feathers,
bled the dawn of Anáhuac.
The toucan was a lovely
box of shining fruit,
the hummingbird preserved
the original sparks of dawn,
and its minuscule bonfires
burned in the still air.

Illustrious parrots filled
the depths of the foliage,
like ingots of green gold
newly minted from the paste

of sunken swamps,
and from their circular eyes
yellow hoops looked out,
old as minerals.

All the eagles of the sky
nourished their bloody kin
in the uninhabited blue,
and flying over the world
on carnivorous feathers,
the condor, murderous king,
solitary monk of the sky,
black talisman of the snow,
hurricane of falconry.

The ovenbird's engineering
made of the fragrant clay
sonorous little theaters
where it burst forth singing.

The nightjar kept
whistling its wet cry
on the banks of the cenotes.
The Chilean pigeon made
scrubby woodland nests
where it left its regal gift
of dashing eggs.

The southern lark, fragrant,
sweet autumn carpenter,
displayed its breast spangled
with a scarlet constellation,
and the austral sparrow raised
its flute recently fetched
from the eternity of water.

Wet as a water lily,
the flamingo opened the doors
of its rosy cathedral,

and flew like the dawn,
far from the sultry forest
where the jewels dangle
from the quetzal, which suddenly
awakens, stirs, slips off, glows,
and makes its virgin embers fly.

A marine mountain flies
toward the islands, a moon
of birds winging South,
over the fermented islands
of Peru.
It's a living river of shade,
a comet of countless
tiny hearts
that eclipse the world's sun
like a thick-tailed meteor
pulsing toward the archipelago.

And at the end of the enraged
sea, in the ocean rain,
the wings of the albatross rise up
like two systems of salt,
establishing in the silence
with their spacious hierarchy
amid the torrential squalls,
the order of the wilds.

JACK SCHMITT

IV

LOS RÍOS ACUDEN

Amada de los ríos, combatida
por agua azul y gotas transparentes,
como un árbol de venas es tu espectro
de diosa oscura que muerde manzanas:

al despertar desnuda entonces,
eras tatuada por los ríos,
y en la altura mojada tu cabeza
llenaba el mundo con nuevos rocíos.
Te trepidaba el agua en la cintura.
Eras de manantiales construida
y te brillaban lagos en la frente.
De tu espesura madre recogías
el agua como lágrimas vitales,
y arrastrabas los cauces a la arena
a través de la noche planetaria,
cruzando ásperas piedras dilatadas,
rompiendo en el camino
toda la sal de la geología,
apartando los músculos del cuarzo.

THE RIVERS COME FORTH

Lover of the rivers, assailed
by blue water and transparent drops,
like a veined tree your specter
of a dark goddess that eats apples:
when you awakened, naked,
you were tattooed by the rivers,
and in the wet heights your head
filled the world with fresh dew.
Water trembled on your waist.
You were shaped by fountainheads
and lakes glistened on your brow.
From your maternal density you gathered
the water like vital tears,
dredged the sandy riverbeds
through the planetary night,
traversing harsh dilated stones,
shattering on your way
all the salt of geology,

cutting forests of compact walls,
sundering the quartz's muscles.

JACK SCHMITT

ORINOCO

Orinoco, on your banks
of that timeless hour,
let me as then go naked,
let me enter your baptismal darkness.
Scarlet-colored Orinoco,
let me immerse my hands that return
to your maternity, to your flux,
river of races, land of roots,
your spacious murmur, your untamed sheet
come whence I come, from the poor
and imperious wilds, from a secret
like blood, from a silent
mother of clay.

JACK SCHMITT

AMAZON

Amazon,
capital of the water's syllables,
patriarchal father, you're
the secret eternity
of fecundation,
rivers flock to you like birds,
you're shrouded by fire-colored pistils,
the great dead trunks impregnate you with perfume,
the moon can neither watch nor measure you.
You're charged with green sperm
like a nuptial tree, silver-plated
in wild springtime,

you're reddened by woods,
blue between the moon of the stones,
clothed in iron vapor,
leisurely as an orbiting planet.

JACK SCHMITT

V

MINERALS

Mother of metals, they burned you,
bit you, martyred you,
corroded you, then
defiled you, when the idols
could no longer defend you.
Vines climbing toward the hair
of the jungle night, mahogany,
maker of the arrows' shaft,
iron amassed in the flowering loft,
imperious talons of my homcland's
surveillant eagles,
unknown water, malevolent sun,
cruel sea spray,
preying shark, teeth
of the antarctic cordilleras,
serpent goddess dressed in plumes
and rarefied by blue poison,
ancestral fever inoculated
by migrations of wings and ants,
quagmires, butterflies
with acid stingers, woods
approaching the minerals,
why did the hostile chorus
not defend the treasure?

Mother of the dark
stones that would color
your lashes with blood!

Turquoise,
from its epochs, from the larval gloam,
begat for the jewels of the priestly
sun alone, copper slept
in its sulfuric strata,
and antimony advanced layer by layer
to the depths of our star.
Coal glittered with black radiance
like the antithesis of snow,
black ice cysted in the secret
motionless tempest of the earth,
when the flash of a yellow bird
entombed streams of sulfur
at the foot of the glacial cordilleras.
Vanadium clothed in rain
to enter the chamber of gold,
tungsten sharpened knives
and bismuth braided
medicinal hair.

Disoriented glowworms,
still on high, kept
trickling drops of phosphorus
into the seams of abysses
and iron peaks.

They're the vineyards of meteors,
the subways of sapphires.
On the plateaus the toy soldier
sleeps in clothing of tin.

Copper establishes its crimes
in the unburied darkness
charged with green matter,
and in the accumulated silence
the destructive mummies sleep on.
In the Chibcha tranquillity
gold moves slowly from opaque oratories
toward the warriors,

transforms into red stamens,
laminated hearts,
terrestrial phosphorescence,
fabulous teeth.
Then I sleep with the dream
of a seed, of a larva,
and with you I descend
the steps of Querétaro.
Awaiting me were
stones from an indecisive moon,
the fishlike gemstone opal,
the tree petrified in a church
frozen by amethysts.

How, oral Colombia, could you
know that your barefoot stones
concealed a tempest
of enraged gold,
how, homeland
of the emerald, could you foresee
that the jewel of death and the sea,
the chilling splendor,
would climb the throats
of the invading dynasts?

You were pure notion of stone,
rose trained by salt,
malignant buried tear,
siren with dormant arteries,
belladonna, black serpent.
(While the palm dispersed its column
of high ornamental combs,
salt kept stripping
the mountains' splendor,
transforming raindrops on the leaves
into a suit of quartz
and transmuting spruces
into avenues of coal.)

I raced through cyclones to danger
and descended to the emerald light—
I ascended to the tendril of rubies,
but I was silenced forever on the statue
of nitrate stretched out on the desert.
In the ash of the raw-boned
altiplano, I saw how
tin raised
its coral branches of poison
until it spread out, like a jungle,
the equinoctial mist, until it covered
the signet of our cereal monarchies.

JACK SCHMITT

VI
MAN

The mineral race was
like a cup of clay, man
made of stone and atmosphere,
clean as earthen jugs, sonorous.
The moon kneaded the Caribs,
extracted sacred oxygen,
crushed flowers and roots.
Man roamed the islands,
weaving bouquets and garlands
of sulfur-colored seaweed
and trumpeting the conch
on the shore of the sea spray.

The Tarahumara, wearing spurs,
made fire of blood and flint
in the spacious Northeast,
while the universe was being born
again in Tarascan clay:
myths of the amorous lands,
moist exuberance whence

sexual mud and melted fruits
were to be the posture of the gods
or pale walls of vessels.

Like dazzling pheasants
the priests descended
the Aztec steps.
Triangular stones
sustained the infinite
lightning of their vestments.
And the august pyramid,
stone upon stone, agony upon air,
within its domineering structure,
tended like an almond
a sacrificed heart.
In a thundering cry
blood ran down
the sacred stairway.
But thronging multitudes
wove fiber, nurtured
the promise of the crops,
plaited feathered splendor,
coaxed the turquoise,
and in textile vines
expressed the world's light.

Mayas, you had felled
the tree of knowledge.
With the fragrance of granary races
structures of inquiry
and death rose up,
and you scrutinized the cenotes,
casting into them golden brides,
the permanence of germs.

Chichén, your whispers grew
in the jungle dawn.
Toil went on shaping
honeycombed symmetry

in your yellow citadel,
and speculation threatened
the blood of the pedestals,
dismantled the sky in the shade,
directed medicine,
wrote upon the stones.

The South was a golden wonder.
The towering retreats
of Macchu Picchu in the gateway to the sky
were filled with oils and songs,
man had defied the dwelling
of the great birds in the heights,
and in the new dominion among the peaks
the tiller of the soil touched the seed
with fingers wounded by the snow.

Cuzco awakened like a throne
of turrets and granaries,
and the pensive flower of the world
was that race of pale shade
in whose opened hands trembled
diadems of imperial amethysts.
Highland corn
germinated on the terraces,
and over the volcanic pathways
traveled vases and gods.
Agriculture perfumed
the kingdom of kitchens
and spread over the roofs
a mantle of husked sun.

(Sweet race, daughter of the sierras,
lineage of tower and turquoise,
close my eyes now
before we return to the sea,
whence our sorrows come.)

That blue jungle was a grotto,
and in the mystery of tree and darkness
the Guaraní sang like
mist that rises in the afternoon,
water upon the foliage,
rain on a day of love,
sadness beside the rivers.

At the bottom of America without name
was Arauco among the vertiginous
waters, separated
by all the planet's cold.
Behold the great solitary South.
No smoke can be seen in the heights.
Nothing but glaciers
and blizzards repelled
by the bristling araucarias.
Do not seek the song of pottery
beneath the dense green.

All is silence of water and wind.

But in the leaves behold the warrior.
Among the cypress trees a cry.
A jaguar's eyes amid
the snowy heights.

Behold the spears at rest.
Listen to the whispering air
pierced by arrows.
Behold the breasts and legs,
the dark hair
shining in the moonlight.

Behold the warriors' absence.

There's no one. The diuca finch trills
like water in the pure night.

The condor cruises its black flight.

There's no one. Do you hear? It's the puma
stepping in the air and the leaves.

There's no one. Listen. Listen to the tree,
listen to the Araucanian tree.

There's no one. Behold the stones.

Behold the stones of Arauco.

There's no one, it's just the trees.

It's just the stones, Arauco.

JACK SCHMITT

I

From air to air, like an empty net,
dredging through streets and ambient atmosphere, I came
lavish, at autumn's coronation, with the leaves'
proffer of currency and—between spring and wheat ears—
that which a boundless love, caught in a gauntlet fall,
grants us like a long-fingered moon.

(Days of live radiance in discordant
bodies: steels converted
to the silence of acid:
nights disentangled to the ultimate flour,
assaulted stamens of the nuptial land.)

Someone waiting for me among the violins
met with a world like a buried tower
sinking its spiral below the layered leaves
color of raucous sulfur:
and lower yet, in a vein of gold,
like a sword in a scabbard of meteors,
I plunged a turbulent and tender hand
to the most secret organs of the earth.

Leaning my forehead through unfathomed waves
I sank, a single drop, within a sleep of sulfur
where, like a blind man, I retraced the jasmine
of our exhausted human spring.

NATHANIEL TARN

III

El ser como el maíz se desgranaba en el inacabable
granero de los hechos perdidos, de los acontecimientos
miserables, del uno al siete, al ocho,
y no una muerte, sino muchas muertes, llegaba a cada uno:
cada día una muerte pequeña, polvo, gusano, lámpara
que se apaga en el lodo del suburbio, una pequeña muerte de alas gruesas
entraba en cada hombre como una corta lanza
y era el hombre asediado del pan o del cuchillo,
el ganadero: el hijo de los puertos, o el capitán oscuro del arado,
o el roedor de las calles espesas:

todos desfallecieron esperando su muerte, su corta muerte diaria:
y su quebranto aciago de cada día era
como una copa negra que bebían temblando.

III

Being like maize grains fell
in the inexhaustible store of lost deeds, shoddy
occurrences, from nine to five, to six,
and not one death but many came to each,
each day a little death: dust, maggot, lamp,
drenched in the mire of suburbs, a little death with fat wings
entered into each man like a short blade
and siege was laid to him by bread or knife:
the drover, the son of harbors, the dark captain of plows,
the rodent wanderer through dense streets:

all of them weakened waiting for their death, their brief and daily
    death—
and their ominous dwindling each day
was like a black cup they trembled while they drained.

NATHANIEL TARN

V

It was not you, grave death, raptor of iron plumage,
that the drab tenant of such lodgings carried
mixed with his gobbled rations under hollow skin—
rather: a trodden tendril of old rope,
the atom of a courage that gave way
or some harsh dew never distilled to sweat.
This could not be reborn, a particle
of death without a requiem,
bare bone or fading church bell dying from within.

Lifting these bandages reeking of iodine
I plunged my hands in humble aches that would have smothered dying
and nothing did I meet within the wound save wind in gusts
that chilled my cold interstices of soul.

NATHANIEL TARN

VIII

Come up with me, American love.

Kiss these secret stones with me.
The torrential silver of the Urubamba
makes the pollen fly to its golden cup.
The hollow of the bindweed's maze,
the petrified plant, the inflexible garland,
soar above the silence of these mountain coffers.
Come, diminutive life, between the wings
of the earth, while you, cold, crystal in the hammered air,
thrusting embattled emeralds apart,
O savage waters, fall from the hems of snow.

Love, love, until the night collapses
from the singing Andes flint
down to the dawn's red knees,
come out and contemplate the snow's blind son.

O Wilkamayu of the sounding looms,
when you rend your skeins of thunder
in white foam clouds of wounded snow,
when your south wind falls like an avalanche
roaring and belting to arouse the sky,
what language do you wake in an ear
freed but a moment from your Andean spume?

Who caught the lightning of the cold,
abandoned it, chained to the heights,
dealt out among its frozen tears,
brandished upon its nimble swords—
its seasoned stamens pummeled hard—
led to a warrior's bed,
hounded to his rocky conclusions?

What do your harried scintillations whisper?
Did your sly, rebellious flash
go traveling once, populous with words?
Who wanders grinding frozen syllables,
black languages, gold-threaded banners,
fathomless mouths, and trampled cries
in your tenuous arterial waters?

Who goes deadheading blossom eyelids
come to observe us from the far earth?
Who scatters dead seed clusters
dropping from your cascading hands
to bed their own disintegration here
in coal's geology?

Who has flung down the branches of these chains
and buried once again our leave-takings?

Love, love, do not come near the border,
avoid adoring this sunken head:
let time exhaust all measure
in its abode of broken overtures—
here, between cliffs and rushing waters,

take to yourself the air among these passes,
the laminated image of the wind,
the blind canal threading high cordilleras,
dew with its bitter greetings,
and climb, flower by flower, through the thicknesses
trampling the coiling lucifer.

In this steep zone of flint and forest,
green stardust, jungle-clarified,
Mantur, the valley, cracks like a living lake
or a new level of silence.

Come to my very being, to my own dawn,
into crowned solitudes.
The fallen kingdom survives us all this while.
And on this dial the condor's shadow
cruises as ravenous as would a pirate ship.

NATHANIEL TARN

IX

Interstellar eagle, vine-in-a-mist.
Forsaken bastion, blind scimitar.
Orion belt, ceremonial bread.
Torrential stairway, immeasurable eyelid.
Triangular tunic, pollen of stone.
Granite lamp, bread of stone.
Mineral snake, rose of stone.
Ship-burial, source of stone.
Horse in the moon, stone light.
Equinoctial quadrant, vapor of stone.
Ultimate geometry, book of stone.
Iceberg carved among squalls.
Coral of sunken time.

Finger-softened rampart.
Feather-assaulted roof.

Mirror splinters, thunderstorm foundations.
Thrones ruined by the climbing vine.
The blood-flecked talon's law.
Gale at a standstill on a slope.
Still turquoise cataract.
Patriarchal chiming of the sleepers.
Manacle of subjugated snows.
Iron tilting toward statues.
Storm inaccessible and closed.
Puma paws, bloodstone.
Towering shadow, convocation of snows.

Night hoisted upon fingers and roots.
Window of the mists, heartless dove.
Nocturnal foliage, icon of thunderclaps.
Cordillera spine, oceanic roof.
Architecture of stray eagles.
Sky rope, climax of the drone.
Blood level, constructed star.
Mineral bubble, moon of quartz.
Andean serpent, amaranthine brow.
Dome of silence, unsullied home.
Sea bride, cathedral timber.
Branch of salt, black-winged cherry tree.
Snowcapped teeth, chill thunder.

Scarred moon, menacing stone.
Hair of the cold, friction of wind.
Volcano of hands, dark cataract.
Silver wave. Destination of time.

NATHANIEL TARN

X

Stone within stone, and man, where was he?
Air within air, and man, where was he?
Time within time, and man, where was he?

Were you also the shattered fragment
of indecision, of hollow eagle
which, through the streets of today, in the old tracks,
through the leaves of accumulated autumns,
goes pounding at the soul into the tomb?
Poor hand, poor foot, and poor, dear life . . .
The days of unraveled light
in you, familiar rain
falling on feast-day banderillas,
did they grant, petal by petal, their dark nourishment
to such an empty mouth?
                              Famine, coral of mankind,
hunger, secret plant, root of the woodcutters,
famine, did your jagged reef dart up
to those high, side-slipping towers?

I question you, salt of the highways,
show me the trowel; allow me, architecture,
to fret stone stamens with a little stick,
climb all the steps of air into the emptiness,
scrape the intestine until I touch mankind.
Macchu Picchu, did you lift
stone above stone on a groundwork of rags?
coal upon coal and, at the bottom, tears?
fire-crested gold, and in that gold, the bloat
dispenser of this blood?

Let me have back the slave you buried here!
Wrench from these lands the stale bread
of the poor, prove me the tatters
on the serf, point out his window.
Tell me how he slept when alive,
whether he snored,
his mouth agape like a dark scar
worn by fatigue into the wall.
That wall, that wall! If each stone floor
weighed down his sleep, and if he fell
beneath them, as if beneath a moon, with all that sleep!

Ancient America, bride in her veil of sea,
your fingers also,
from the jungle's edges to the rare height of gods,
under the nuptial banners of light and reverence,
blending with thunder from the drums and lances,
your fingers, your fingers also—
that bore the rose in mind and hairline of the cold,
the blood-drenched breast of the new crops translated
into the radiant weave of matter and adamantine hollows—
with them, with them, buried America, were you in that great depth,
the bilious gut, hoarding the eagle hunger?

NATHANIEL TARN

XII

Sube a nacer conmigo, hermano.

Dame la mano desde la profunda
zona de tu dolor diseminado.
No volverás del fondo de las rocas.
No volverás del tiempo subterráneo.
No volverá tu voz endurecida.
No volverán tus ojos taladrados.

Mírame desde el fondo de la tierra,
labrador, tejedor, pastor callado:
domador de guanacos tutelares:
albañil del andamio desafiado:
aguador de las lágrimas andinas:
joyero de los dedos machacados:
agricultor temblando en la semilla:
alfarero en tu greda derramado:
traed a la copa de esta nueva vida
vuestros viejos dolores enterrados.
Mostradme vuestra sangre y vuestro surco,
decidme: aquí fuí castigado,
porque la joya no brilló o la tierra

no entregó a tiempo la piedra o el grano:
señaladme la piedra en que caísteis
y la madera en que os crucificaron,
encendedme los viejos pedernales,
las viejas lámparas, los látigos pegados
a través de los siglos en las llagas
y las hachas de brillo ensangrentado.
Yo vengo a hablar por vuestra boca muerta.
A través de la tierra juntad todos
los silenciosos labios derramados
y desde el fondo habladme toda esta larga noche,
como si yo estuviera con vosotros anclado.
Contadme todo, cadena a cadena,
eslabón a eslabón, y paso a paso,
afilad los cuchillos que guardasteis,
ponedlos en mi pecho y en mi mano,
como un río de rayos amarillos,
como un río de tigres enterrados,
y dejadme llorar, horas, días, años,
edades ciegas, siglos estelares.

Dadme el silencio, el agua, la esperanza.

Dadme la lucha, el hierro, los volcanes.

Apegadme los cuerpos como imanes.

Acudid a mis venas y a mi boca.

Hablad por mis palabras y mi sangre.

XII

Arise to birth with me, my brother.

Give me your hand out of the depths
sown by your sorrows.

You will not return from these stone fastnesses.
You will not emerge from subterranean time.
Your rasping voice will not come back,
nor your pierced eyes rise from their sockets.

Look at me from the depths of the earth,
tiller of fields, weaver, reticent shepherd,
groom of totemic guanacos,
mason high on your treacherous scaffolding,
iceman of Andean tears,
jeweler with crushed fingers,
farmer anxious among his seedlings,
potter wasted among his clays—
bring to the cup of this new life
your ancient buried sorrows.
Show me your blood and your furrow;
say to me: here I was scourged
because a gem was dull or because the earth
failed to give up in time its tithe of corn or stone.
Point out to me the rock on which you stumbled,
the wood they used to crucify your body.
Strike the old flints
to kindle ancient lamps, light up the whips
glued to your wounds throughout the centuries
and light the axes gleaming with your blood.
I come to speak for your dead mouths.
Throughout the earth
let dead lips congregate,
out of the depths spin this long night to me
as if I rode at anchor here with you.
And tell me everything, tell chain by chain,
and link by link, and step by step;
sharpen the knives you kept hidden away,
thrust them into my breast, into my hands,
like a torrent of sunbursts,
an Amazon of buried jaguars,
and leave me cry: hours, days, and years,
blind ages, stellar centuries.

Give me silence, give me water, hope.

Give me the struggle, the iron, the volcanoes.

Let bodies cling like magnets to my body.

Come quickly to my veins and to my mouth.

Speak through my speech, and through my blood.

NATHANIEL TARN

Ccollanan Pachacutec! Ricuy
anceacunac yahuarniy richacaucuta!
TUPAC AMARU I

I

THEY COME THROUGH THE ISLANDS (1493)

The butchers razed the islands.
Guanahaní was first
in this story of martyrdom.
The children of clay saw their smile
shattered, beaten
their fragile stature of deer,
and even in death they did not understand.
They were bound and tortured,
burned and branded,
bitten and buried.
And when time finished its waltzing twirl,
dancing in the palms,
the green salon was empty.

Nothing remained but bones
rigidly arranged
in the form of a cross, to the greater
glory of God and mankind.

From the Greater Clays
and the Branches of Sotavento
to the coralline chains,
Narváez's knife kept cutting away.
Here the cross, there the rosary,
here the Virgin of the Cudgel.
The jewel of Columbus, phosphoric Cuba,

received the flag and knees
on its wet sand.

JACK SCHMITT

IV
CORTÉS

Cortés has no people, is a cold beam,
heart dead in the armor.
    Fruitful lands, my Lord and King,
    mosques that have gold encrusted
    thick by the Indian's hand.

And advances burying daggers, beating
the lowlands, the pawed-up
fragrant cordilleras,
camping his troop among orchids
and crowning pines,
trampling jasmine,
up to the gates of Tlaxcala.

(My downcast brother, make no
friend of the red-flushed vulture:
I speak from the mossy earth to you, from
the roots of our realm.
Tomorrow will rain blood,
will raise tears enough
for mist and fumes and rivers
until your own eyes dissolve.)

Cortés receives a dove,
receives a pheasant, a zither
from the king's musicians,
but he wants the roomful of gold,
wants one thing more, and everything falls
in the plunderers' chests.

The king leans out from a balcony:
"This is my brother," he says. The stones
of the people fly up in answer,
and Cortés whets his daggers
on quisling kisses.

He returns to Tlaxcala, the wind bears
a muted rumor of lament.

JOHN FELSTINER

V

CHOLULA

In Cholula the youths wear
their finest cloth, gold, and plumes.
Adorned for the festival,
they question the invader.

Death has answered them.

Thousands of corpses lie there.
Murdered hearts
laid out, pulsing,
opening the moist pit where
they tend the trickle of that day.
(They entered killing on horseback,
they cut off the hand that offered
its tribute of gold and flowers,
they closed off the plaza, exhausted
their arms until they were numbed,
killing the flower of the kingdom,
plunging up to their elbows in the blood
of my startled brethren.)

JACK SCHMITT

VI

ALVARADO

Alvarado fell upon the huts
with claws and knives, he razed
the patrimony of the goldsmith,
ravished the nuptial rose of the tribe,
assaulted races, properties, religions—
he was the copious coffer of the thieves,
the clandestine falcon of death.
Then he went to the great green river,
the Papaloapan, River of Butterflies,
bearing blood on his standard.

The solemn river saw its children
die or survive as slaves,
it saw race and reason, juvenile heads
burning in the bonfires, beside the water.
But grief, inexhaustible,
continued its cruel advance
toward new captaincies.

JACK SCHMITT

VII

GUATEMALA

Sweet Guatemala, every gravestone
of your mansion bears a drop
of ancient blood devoured
by the jaguars' snouts.
Alvarado crushed your kin,
smashed the astral stele,
wallowed in your martyrdom.
And in Yucatán the bishop
followed upon the pale jaguars.
He gathered up the most
profound wisdom apprehended in the air

since the first day of the world,
when the first Maya recorded
in writing the river's tremor,
the science of pollen, the wrath
of the Gods of the Elements,
the migrations through
the first universes,
the beehive's laws,
the green bird's secret,
the language of the stars,
secrets of day and night
reaped on the shores of
earthly development!

JACK SCHMITT

IX

THE HEAD ON THE SPEAR

Balboa, you brought death and claw
to the corners of the sweet central land,
and among the manhunting dogs,
yours was your soul:
bloody thick-lipped little Leo
brought to bay the fleeing slave,
sank Spanish fangs
into the pulsing throats,
and from the dogs' claws
the flesh went off to martyrdom,
and the treasure fell into the purse.

Accursed be dog and man,
the infamous howl in the primal
jungle, the prowling
step of iron and bandit.

Accursed the thorny
crown of wild brambles
that didn't bristle like a sea urchin
to defend the invaded homeland.

But among the bloodthirsty
captains, the justice of daggers,
the bitter branch of envy
rose out of the shadows.

And when you returned, the name
of Pedrarias stood in the middle
of your road like a noose.

You were tried amid the barks
of Indian-killing dogs.
Now, as you die, do you hear
the pure silence, shattered
by your incited greyhounds?
Now, as you die at the hands
of the fierce captains-general,
do you smell the golden aroma
of the sweet ravaged kingdom?

When they cut off Balboa's
head, it was left impaled
on a spear. His lifeless eyes
released their lightning
and ran down the shaft
in a great drop of filth
that vanished into the earth.

JACK SCHMITT

HOMAGE TO BALBOA

Discoverer, centuries later, the vast sea—
my foam, lunar latitude, empire of the water—
speaks to you through my mouth.
Your plenitude came before your death.
You raised fatigue to the sky,
and from the trees' hard night
toil led you to the sum
of the seashore, the great ocean.
In your gaze the marriage of diffused
light and the little heart of man
was consummated, a chalice never
raised before was filled, a seed
of lightning bolts accompanied you,
and a torrential thunder filled the earth.
Balboa, captain—how diminutive
your hand on your visor—mysterious
marionette of the discovering salt,
bridegroom of the oceanic sweetness,
child of the world's new uterus.

The obscure odor of the ravished
marine majesty entered your eyes
like galloping orange blossoms,
an arrogant aurora fell into your blood
until it filled your soul, possessed man!
When you returned to the taciturn lands,
sleepwalker of the sea, green captain,
the earth awaited your corpse,
eager to embrace your bones.

Mortal bridegroom, betrayal was requited.

Not in vain, throughout history
crime has trampled in, the falcon has devoured
its nest, and the serpents have assembled,
striking one another with tongues of gold.

You entered the frenzied twilight
and the lost steps that you took,
still drenched by the depths,
dressed in splendor and wed
by the greatest foam, brought you
to the shores of another sea: death.

JACK SCHMITT

XV

LA LÍNEA COLORADA

Más tarde levantó la fatigada
mano el monarca, y más arriba
de las frentes de los bandidos,
tocó los muros.
                Allí trazaron
la línea colorada.
                  Tres cámaras
había que llenar de oro y de plata,
hasta esa línea de su sangre.
Rodó la rueda de oro, noche y noche.
La rueda del martirio día y noche.

Arañaron la tierra, descolgaron
alhajas hechas con amor y espuma,
arrancaron la ajorca de la novia,
desampararon a sus dioses.
El labrador entregó su medalla,
el pescador su bota de oro,
y las rejas temblaron respondiendo
mientras mensaje y voz por las alturas
iba la rueda del oro rodando.
Entonces tigre y tigre se reunieron
y repartieron la sangre y las lágrimas.

Atahualpa esperaba levemente
triste en el escarpado día andino.

No se abrieron las puertas. Hasta la última
joya los buitres dividieron:
las turquesas rituales, salpicadas
por la carnicería, el vestido
laminado de plata: las uñas bandoleras
iban midiendo y la carcajada
del fraile entre los verdugos
escuchaba el rey con tristeza.

Era su corazón un vaso lleno
de una congoja amarga como
la esencia amarga de la quina.
Pensó en sus límites, en el alto Cuzco,
en las princesas, en su edad,
en el escalofrío de su reino.
Maduro estaba por dentro, su paz
desesperada era tristeza. Pensó en Huáscar.
Vendrían de él los extranjeros?
Todo era enigma, todo era cuchillo,
todo era soledad, sólo la línea roja
viviente palpitaba,
tragando las entrañas amarillas
del reino enmudecido que moría.

Entró Valverde con la Muerte entonces.
«Te llamarás Juan», le dijo
mientras preparaba la hoguera.
Gravemente respondió: «Juan,
Juan me llamo para morir»,
sin comprender ya ni la muerte.

Le ataron el cuello y un garfio

entró en el alma del Perú.

Later the monarch raised
his weary hand, and above
the bandits' brows
he touched the walls.
                    There they drew
the red line.
                Three chambers
were ordered filled with gold and silver,
up to that line of his blood.
The wheel of gold turned, night after night.
The wheel of martyrdom day and night.

They scored the earth, dismantled
treasures made with love and foam,
tore away the bride's jewels,
disarmed their gods.
The tiller surrendered his medal,
the fisherman his droplet of gold,
and the ingots trembled in response,
while message and voice throughout the
highlands, the wheel of gold kept turning.
Then the jaguars assembled
and divided up the blood and tears.

Atahualpa waited with sad resignation
on the precipitous Andean day.
The doors were not opened. Down to
the last jewel the vultures divided—
ritual turquoise, spattered
by carnage, silver-plated
garments—the plundering claws
kept measuring, and the king
listened sadly to the laughter
of the friar amid the executioners.

His heart was an urn filled
with an anguish bitter

as the bitter essence of quinine.
He thought about his limits, about lofty Cuzco,
the princesses, his age,
the shuddering chill of his kingdom.
He was pensive within, his desperate
tranquillity was sorrow. He thought about Huáscar.
Could he have sent the foreigners?
All was enigma, all was knife,
all solitude, only the vivid red line
kept pulsing on,
swallowing the yellow innards
of the muted moribund kingdom.

Then Valverde entered with Death.
"Your name will be Juan," he told him
as he prepared the bonfire.
Solemnly he replied: "Juan,
my name for death is Juan,"
without understanding even his death.

They put a rope to his neck, and a gaff

plunged into the soul of Peru.

JACK SCHMITT

XVI
ELEGY

Alone, in the wilderness,
I want to weep like the rivers, I want
to grow dark, to sleep
like an ancient mineral night.
Why did the radiant keys
reach the bandit's hands? Rise up,
maternal Oello, rest your secret
upon this night's long fatigue

and infuse my veins with your advice.
I don't ask you yet for the Yupanquis' sun.
I speak to you from my sleep, calling
from land to land, Peruvian
mother, cordilleran matrix.
How did the avalanche of daggers
penetrate your sandy precinct?

Immobile in your hands,
I feel the metals stretching away
in the subterranean channels.

I'm made of your roots
but I don't understand, the earth
doesn't grant me your wisdom,
I see nothing but night upon night
beneath the starry lands.
What senseless serpent's dream
slithered up to the red line?
Bereaved eyes, sinister plant.
How did you come to this vinegar wind,
how did Capac not raise
his tiara of blinding clay
amid the pinnacles of wrath?

Beneath the pavilions, let
me suffer and sink like the lifeless
root that will never beam forth.
Beneath the harsh hard night
I'll descend through the earth until
I reach the jaws of gold.

I want to stretch out on the nocturnal stone.

I want to reach calamity.

JACK SCHMITT

XX
LAND AND MAN UNITE

Araucania, cluster of torrential southland beech,
O merciless Homeland, my dark love,
solitary in your rainy kingdom:
You were only mineral gullets,
hands of cold, fists
accustomed to splitting rocks:
Homeland, you were the peace of hardness
and your men were whisper,
harsh apparition, fierce wind.

My Araucanian ancestors had no
crests of luminous plumes,
they didn't rest on nuptial flowers,
they spun no gold for the priest:
they were stone and tree, roots
of the intractable brambles,
lance-shaped leaves,
heads of militant metal.
Ancestors, you had just raised
your ear to the gallop, just over
the hilltops, when Araucania's
lightning struck.
The forefathers of stone became shadows,
they were bound to the forest, the natural
darkness, they became icy light,
asperities of land and thorns,
and so they waited in the depths
of the indomitable wilds:
one was a red tree that watched,
another a fragment of metal that listened,
another a blasting wind and drill,
another blended in with the trail.
Homeland, ship of snow,
harsh foliage:
you were born there, when your man

asked the earth for his standard
and when land and air and stone and rain,
leaf, root, perfume, howl,
covered the child like a mantle,
they loved him and defended him.
That's how the country was born unanimous:
unity before combat.

JACK SCHMITT

XXII
ERCILLA

Stones of Arauco and unleashed fluvial
roses, territories of roots
engage the man arrived from Spain.
They attack his armor with gigantic lichens.
The fern's shadows invade his sword.
Primal ivy puts blue hands
on the planet's newly arrived silence.
Worthy man, sonorous Ercilla, I hear the pulsing
water of your first dawn, a frenzy of birds
and a thunderclap in the foliage.
Leave, oh, leave your blond
eagle's imprint, crush
your cheek against the wild corn,
everything will be devoured in the dust.
Sonorous, you alone will not drink the chalice
of blood, sonorous, only to the sudden
glow radiating from you
will time's secret mouth arrive in vain
to tell you: in vain.
In vain, in vain
blood in the branches of spattered crystal,
in vain through the puma's nights
the soldier's defiant advance,
the orders,

the footsteps
of the wounded.
All returns to the feather-crowned silence
where a distant king devours vines.

JACK SCHMITT

I

CUAUHTEMOC (1520)

Young brother, never at rest,
unconsoled for time on endless time,
youth shaken in Mexico's
metallic darkness, I read your
naked country's gift on your hand.

On it your smile is born and grows
like a line between the light and the gold.

Your lips sealed by death are
the purest entombed silence.

The fountain submerged
beneath all the earth's mouths.

Did you hear, did you hear, by chance,
from distant Anáhuac,
a waterway, a wind
of shattered springtime?
It was perhaps the cedar's voice.
It was a white wave from Acapulco.

But in the night your heart
fled to the borderlands
like a bewildered deer,
amid the bloody monuments,
beneath the foundering moon.

All the shade prepared shade.
The land was a dark kitchen,
stone and caldron, black steam,

nameless wall, a nightmare
calling you from the nocturnal
metals of your country.

But there is no shade on your standard.

The fateful hour has arrived,
and among your people
you're bread and root, spear and star.
The invader has stopped his advance.
Moctezuma is not extinct
like a fallen chalice,
he's armored lightning,
Quetzal plume, flower of the people,
a flaming crest amid the ships.

But a hand hard as centuries of stone
gripped your throat. They didn't choke
your smile, they didn't make
the secret corn's kernels
fall, but they dragged you,
captive conqueror,
through the far reaches of your kingdom,
amid cascades and chains,
over sandbanks and thorns,
like an incessant column,
like a sorrowful witness,
until a noose snared
the column of purity
and hanged the dangling body
over the hapless land.

JACK SCHMITT

FRAY BARTOLOMÉ DE LAS CASAS

Piensa uno, al llegar a su casa, de noche, fatigado
entre la niebla fría de mayo, a la salida
del sindicato (en la desmenuzada
lucha de cada día, la estación
lluviosa que gotea del alero, el sordo
latido del constante sufrimiento)
esta resurrección enmascarada,
astuta, envilecida,
del encadenador, de la cadena,
y cuando sube la congoja
hasta la cerradura a entrar contigo,
surge una luz antigua, suave y dura
como un metal, como un astro enterrado.
Padre Bartolomé, gracias por este
regalo de la cruda medianoche,

gracias porque tu hilo fue invencible:

pudo morir aplastado, comido
por el perro de fauces iracundas,
pudo quedar en la ceniza
de la casa incendiada,
pudo cortarlo el filo frío
del asesino innumerable
o el odio administrado con sonrisas
(la traición del próximo cruzado),
la mentira arrojada en la ventana.
Pudo morir el hilo cristalino,
la irreductible transparencia
convertida en acción, en combatiente
y despeñado acero de cascada.
Pocas vidas da el hombre como la tuya, pocas
sombras hay en el árbol como tu sombra, en ella
todas las ascuas vivas del continente acuden,
todas las arrasadas condiciones, la herida
del mutilado, las aldeas

exterminadas, todo bajo tu sombra
renace, desde el límite
de la agonía fundas la esperanza.
Padre, fue afortunado para el hombre y su especie
que tú llegaras a la plantación,
que mordieras los negros cereales
del crimen, que bebieras
cada día la copa de la cólera.
Quién te puso, mortal desnudo,
entre los dientes de la furia?
Cómo asomaron otros ojos,
de otro metal, cuando nacías?

Cómo se cruzan los fermentos
en la escondida harina humana
para que tu grano inmutable
se amasara en el pan del mundo?

Eras realidad entre fantasmas
encarnizados, eras
la eternidad de la ternura
sobre la ráfaga del castigo.
De combate en combate tu esperanza
se convirtió en precisas herramientas:
la solitaria lucha se hizo rama,
el llanto inútil se agrupó en partido.

No sirvió la piedad. Cuando mostrabas
tus columnas, tu nave amparadora,
tu mano para bendecir, tu manto,
el enemigo pisoteó las lágrimas
y quebrantó el color de la azucena.
No sirvió la piedad alta y vacía
como una catedral abandonada.
Fue tu invencible decisión, la activa
resistencia, el corazón armado.

Fue la razón tu material titánico.

Fue la flor organizada tu estructura.

Desde arriba quisieron contemplarte
(desde su altura) los conquistadores,
apoyándose como sombras de piedra
sobre sus espadones, abrumando
con sus sarcásticos escupos
las tierras de tu iniciativa,
diciendo: «Ahí va el agitador»,
mintiendo: «Lo pagaron
los extranjeros»,
«No tiene patria», «Traiciona»,
pero tu prédica no era
frágil minuto, peregrina
pauta, reloj del pasajero.
Tu madera era bosque combatido,
hierro en su cepa natural, oculto
a toda luz por la tierra florida,
y más aún, era más hondo:
en la unidad del tiempo, en el transcurso
de la vida, era tu mano adelantada
estrella zodiacal, signo del pueblo.
Hoy a esta casa, Padre, entra conmigo.
Te mostraré las cartas, el tormento
de mi pueblo, del hombre perseguido.
Te mostraré los antiguos dolores.

Y para no caer, para afirmarme
sobre la tierra, continuar luchando,
deja en mi corazón el vino errante
y el implacable pan de tu dulzura.

BROTHER BARTOLOMÉ DE LAS CASAS

On the way home from the union,
at night, exhausted in the cold
May fog (in the grinding

daily struggle, winter
rain dripping from the eaves, the dull
throb of constant suffering), one thinks
about this masked resurrection,
astute, corrupt,
of the enslaver, of enslavement,
and when grief climbs up
to the lock to enter with you,
an ancient light shines forth, smooth
and hard as metal, like a buried star.
Father Bartolomé, thank you for this
gift from a bleak midnight,

thank you, for your thread was invincible:

It could have been crushed to death, devoured
by the dog's angry jaws,
it could have remained in the ashes
of the burned house,
it could have been cut by the countless
assassins' cold blades
or hatred administered with smiles
(the betrayal of the following crusade),
the lie heaved at the window.
The crystalline thread could have died,
the irreducible transparency
transformed into action, into the combatant
and plunging cascade's steel.
Mankind's given few lives like yours,
few shades in the tree like your shade—
all the continent's live coals repair to it,
all the razed conditions, the wound
of the mutilated, the exterminated
villages, everything's reborn
under your shade, from the limits
of agony you engender hope.
Father, it was fortunate for mankind
that you arrived on the plantation,
that you bit into crime's

black grains, drank
the daily cup of wrath.
Naked mortal, who put you
between the fury's teeth?
How did the eyes of another metal
see the light, when you were born?

How are ferments crossed
in the hidden human flour
to knead your immutable kernel
into the world's bread?

You were reality amid bloodthirsty
phantoms, you were
the eternity of tenderness
over the tempest of punishment.
From combat to combat your hope
was transformed into precise tools:
solitary struggle branched,
fruitless tears formed a party.

Piety was useless. When you showed
your columns, your protective nave,
your blessing hand, your mantle,
the enemy trampled the tears
and crushed the lily's color.
Piety, lofty and empty
as an abandoned cathedral, was useless.
It was your invincible decision, active
resistance, an armed heart.

Reason was your titanic material.

Organic flower your structure.

The conquistadors wanted to contemplate you
from above (from their heights),
leaning on their broadswords
like stone shadows, swamping

the lands of your initiative
with their sarcastic spit,
saying: "There goes the agitator";
lying: "The foreigners
paid him,"
"He has no homeland," "He's a traitor";
but your prayer was no
fragile minute, transient
guideline, travel clock.
Your wood was an assailed forest,
iron in its natural stock, hidden
from all light by the flowery land,
and furthermore, it was deeper:
in the unity of time, in the course
of your lifetime, your outstretched hand was
a zodiacal star, a sign of the people.
Today, Father, enter this house with me.
I'll show you the letters, the torment
of my people, of persecuted mankind.
I'll show you the ancient sorrows.

And to keep me from falling, to help me plant my
feet firmly on the ground, to continue fighting,
bequeath to my heart the errant wine
and the implacable bread of your sweetness.

JACK SCHMITT

III

ADVANCING IN THE LANDS OF CHILE

Spain drove into the South of the World.
Overwhelmed, the tall Spaniards explored the snow.
The Bío-Bío, solemn river,
told Spain: "Halt."
The forest of maytens whose green
threads weep like a tremor of rain
told Spain: "Stop here." The southland cypress,

titan of the silent borderlands,
spoke in a thundering voice.
But the invader kept coming, fist and dagger,
down to the bottom of my country.
Near the banks of the Imperial River, where
my heart awakened in the clover,
the hurricane struck in the morning.
The wide riverbed of the egrets stretched
from the islands to the furious sea,
filled like a bottomless wineglass,
between the banks of dark crystal.
On its shores the pollen raised
a carpet of turbulent stamens,
and from the sea the air stirred
all the syllables of springtime.
Araucania's hazel tree
raised bonfires and clusters
where the rain trickled
over the gathering of purity.
Everything was laced with fragrance,
steeped in green and rainy light,
and every pungent thicket
was a deep winter bouquet
or a lost marine formation
still full of oceanic dew.

Towers of birds and feathers
and a gale of sonorous solitude
rose up from the ravines,
while in the moist intimacy
amid the giant fern's
curly down, the flowery topa-topa
was a rosary of yellow kisses.

JACK SCHMITT

VIII
LAUTARO (1550)

The blood touches a gallery of quartz.
The stone grows where the drop falls.
That's how Lautaro is born of the earth.

JACK SCHMITT

XI
LAUTARO AGAINST THE CENTAUR (1554)

Then Lautaro attacked in waves.
He disciplined the Araucanian shadows:
before, the Castilian knife plunged
into the red mass's heart.
Today guerrilla warfare was sown
beneath all the forest eaves,
from stone to stone and ford to ford,
watching from behind the copihues,
lying in wait beneath the rocks.
Valdivia tried to retreat.
It was too late.
Lautaro arrived in a suit of lightning.
He followed the anguished Conquistador.
They made their way through the wet
thickets of the austral twilight.
                    Lautaro arrived
in a black gallop of horses.

Fatigue and death led
Valdivia's troops through the foliage.

Lautaro's spears drew near.

Amid corpses and leaves Pedro de Valdivia
advanced, as in a tunnel.

Lautaro came in the dark.

He thought about stony Extremadura,
about golden olive oil in the kitchen,
the jasmine left beyond the seas.

He recognized Lautaro's war cry.

The sheep, the harsh homesteads,
whitewashed walls, the Extremaduran afternoon.

Lautaro's night fell.

Intoxicated with blood, his captains
staggered homeward, through night and rain.

Lautaro's arrows quivered.

From tumble to tumble, the bleeding
captaincy kept retreating.

Now they touched Lautaro's bosom.

Valdivia saw the light coming, the dawn,
perhaps life, the sea.
    It was Lautaro.

JACK SCHMITT

XVII
COMMONERS FROM SOCORRO (1781)

It was Manuela Beltrán (when she broke the oppressor's
banns and cried, "Down with the despots")
who scattered the new grain
over our land.
It was in New Granada, town
of Socorro. The commoners

shook the viceroyalty
in a precursory eclipse.

They united against the state commissaries,
against stained privilege,
they raised petitions
of the people's rights,
united with firearms and stones,
minutemen and women, the people,
order and fury, marching
on Bogotá and its highborn.

Then the Archbishop stepped down.
"You'll have all your rights,
I promise you in the name of God."

The people assembled in the plaza.

And the Archbishop celebrated
a mass and swore an oath.

He was righteous justice.
"Put down your firearms, repair
to your homes," he pronounced.

The commoners surrendered
their arms. In Bogotá
they feted the Archbishop,
celebrated his betrayal,
his perjury, in the perfidious mass,
and they denied bread and rights.

They executed the leaders,
distributed the recently decapitated
heads among the towns,
with the Prelate's blessings
and dances in the Viceroyalty.

O first, heavy seeds
cast to the regions,
you'll remain, blind statues,
incubating the insurrection
of spikes in the hostile night.

JACK SCHMITT

XVIII

TUPAC AMARU (1781)

Condorcanqui Tupac Amaru,
wise man, just forefather,
you saw the desolate springtime
of the Andean scaffolds
climb up to Tungasuca
with salt and calamity,
iniquities and torments.

Noble Inca, great Chief,
everything was stored in your eyes
as in a coffer burned to dust
by love and sadness.
The Indian showed you his back
on which the new bites
shone over the healed scars
of former punishments,
and it was back after back,
all the highlands shaken
by cascading sobs.

It was sob after sob.
Until you prepared the clay—
colored people's march,
gathered the tears in your cup,
and hardened the trails.
The father of the mountains came,
the gunpowder opened roads,

and the father of combat
came to the humiliated peoples.

They threw their ponchos into the dust,
the old knives united,
and the conch shell
called the scattered bonds.
Against the cruel stone,
against calamitous inertia,
against the metal of the chains.
But they divided your people
and sent brother against
brother, until the stones
of your fortress fell.
They bound your weary members
to four raging horses
and quartered the light
of the implacable dawn.

Tupac Amaru, vanquished sun,
a vanished light rises
from your sundered glory
like the sun over the sea.
The deep tribes of clay,
the sacrificed looms,
the wet sand houses
say in silence: "Tupac,"
and Tupac is a seed,
they say in silence: "Tupac,"
and Tupac is preserved in the furrow,
they say in silence: "Tupac,"
and Tupac germinates in the ground.

JACK SCHMITT

XIX

INSURGENT AMERICA (1800)

Our land—wide land, wilderness—
was filled with murmurs, arms, mouths.
A mute syllable kept burning,
congregating the clandestine rose,
until the meadows shook,
trampled by metals and gallops.

Truth was hard as a plowshare.

It broke the earth, established desire,
sank in its germinal propaganda,
and was born in the secret springtime.
Its flower was silent, its gathering of light
repulsed—the collective yeast,
the hidden banners' kiss
was beaten back,
but it rose up breaking the walls,
uprooting the jails from the soil.

The dark race, its cup,
received the repulsed substance,
dispersed it in the marine limits,
crushed it in indomitable mortars.
And it emerged with its pages hammered
and springtime on the road.
Yesterday's hour, noontime,
today's hour again, hour awaited
between the minute expired and the newborn,
in the bristling age of the lie.

O homeland born of woodcutters,
of unbaptized children, carpenters,
those who gave, like a rare bird,
a drop of winged blood,
today you'll be born harshly,

whence the traitor and the jailer
believe you're submerged forever.

Today, as then, you'll be born of the people.

Today you'll emerge from the coal and the dew.
Today you'll come to shake the doors
with bruised hands, with bits
of surviving soul, with clusters
of expressions that death did not extinguish,
with intractable tools
hidden beneath your tatters.

JACK SCHMITT

XXI
SAN MARTÍN (1810)

San Martín, from so much walking place to place
I discarded your uniform, your spurs,
knowing that someday, walking the roads
made for returning, in the limits
of the cordillera, in the purity
of the elements we inherited from you,
we'd see one another sooner or later.

It's hard to differentiate amid the mahogany's
knots, amid roots,
to see your face amid the footpaths,
to distinguish your gaze amid the birds,
to find your existence in the air.

You're the land you gave us, a branch
of cedrón with an aroma that stuns—we cannot
place it, we don't know where the smell
of the meadows in the homeland comes from.
We gallop you, San Martín, early in the
morning we rise to traverse your body,

to inhale acres of your shade,
to build campfires upon your stature.

You're vast among all the heroes.

Others traveled from table to table,
a cloud of dust on the crossroads—
you were made of remote parts,
and we've begun to see your geography,
your wide open spaces, your territory.

The more time disperses
like eternal water the clumps
of bitterness, the bonfire's
keen disclosures, the more terrain
you'll comprise, the more the seeds
of your tranquillity will cover the hills,
the more you'll extend the springtime.

The man who builds then becomes the smoke of all he built, no one's
    reborn
of his own consumed fire: he turned
his dying flame to vital spark,
he died away and turned to dust.

You embraced more space in your death.

Your death was like a silent granary.
Your life and other lives passed on,
doors were opened, walls were raised,
the spike of grain was sown again.

San Martín, other captains
shine brighter than you, with their
embroidered tendrils of phosphorescent salt,
others still speak like waterfalls,
but there's none like you, clothed
in earth and solitude, in snow and clover.
We meet you returning from the river,

we greet you in the agrarian manner
of flowery Tucumán,
and on the roads we cross you
on horseback, galloping and raising
your vestments, dusty forefather.

Today the sun and the moon, the great wind,
mature your stock, your simple
composition: your truth was
an earthen truth, a gritty mixture,
stable as bread, a fresh sheet
of clay and grain, pure pampa.

To this day you've remained moon and gallop,
a soldier's season, inclemency,
where we're waging war again,
traveling the towns and prairies,
establishing your earthy truth,
disseminating your spacious germ,
winnowing the pages of wheat.

So be it, and let there be
no peace until we've entered
your spirit, after combat,
and you can sleep the measure we've found
in your expanse of germinating peace.

JACK SCHMITT

XXVII
GUAYAQUIL (1822)

When San Martín entered, something nocturnal
of an impalpable road—shade, leather—
entered the room.
                    Bolívar was waiting.
He sensed what was coming.
He was aerial, swift, metallic,

all anticipation, science of flight,
his contained being trembled
there, in the room arrested
in the darkness of history.

He came from the indescribable heights,
from the starry atmosphere,
his army advanced
overcoming night and distance,
captain of an invisible body,
of the snow that trailed behind him.
The lamp flickered, the door
behind San Martín sustained
the night, its baying, the tepid
murmur of a river outlet.
The words blazed a trail
that went between them.
Those two bodies spoke,
repelled each other, hid from one another,
cut one another off, fled from each other.

San Martín brought from the South
a sack of gray numbers,
the solitude of the indefatigable
saddles, galloping horses
pounding ahead, joining
his gritty fortitude.
Chile's tough muleteers
entered with him, a slow
iron army,
the preparatory space,
flags with names
aged in the pampa.

Whatever they said fell body to body
in the silence, in the gaping interstice.
It wasn't words, it was a deep
emanation of adverse lands,
of human stone touching

another inaccessible metal.
The words returned to their source.

Each saw his flags
before his eyes.
One, the time with dazzling flowers,
the other, the corroded past,
the troops in tatters.

Beside Bolívar a white hand
awaited him, dismissed him,
amassed its burning spur,
spread linen on the marriage bed.
San Martín was faithful to his meadow.
His dream was a gallop,
a mesh of leather straps and danger.
His freedom a unanimous pampa.
A cereal order his victory.

Bolívar forged a dream,
an ignored dimension, a fire
of enduring velocity,
so confined that it made him
prisoner, surrendered to its substance.

Words and silence fell.

The door was opened again, again
the entire American night, the wide
many-lipped river pulsed a second.

San Martín returned that night
to the open spaces, to the wheat.
Bolívar continued alone.

JACK SCHMITT

XXXVII
SANDINO (1926)

It was when the crosses
were buried
in our land—they were spent,
invalid, professional.
The dollar came with aggressive teeth
to bite territory,
in America's pastoral throat.
It seized Panama with powerful jaws,
sank its fangs into the fresh earth,
wallowed in mud, whiskey, blood,
and swore in a President with a frock coat:
"Give us this day our
daily bribe."
                    Later, steel came,
and the canal segregated residences,
the masters here, the servants there.

They rushed to Nicaragua.

They disembarked, dressed in white,
firing dollars and bullets.
But there a captain rose forth,
saying: "No, here you're not putting
your concessions, your bottle."
They promised him a portrait
of the President, with gloves,
ribbons, and patent leather
shoes, recently acquired.
Sandino took off his boots,
plunged into the quivering swamps,
wore the wet ribbon
of freedom in the jungle,
and, bullet by bullet, he answered
the "civilizers."

North American fury
was indescribable: documented
ambassadors convinced
the world that their love was
Nicaragua, sooner or later
order must reach
its sleepy intestines.

Sandino hanged the intruders.

The Wall Street heroes
were devoured by the swamp,
a thunderbolt struck them down,
more than one machete followed them,
a noose awakened them
like a serpent in the night,
and hanging from a tree they were
carried off slowly
by blue beetles
and devouring vines.

Sandino was in the silence,
in the Plaza of the People,
everywhere Sandino,
killing North Americans,
executing invaders.
And when the air corps came,
the offensive of the armed
forces, the incision of
pulverizing powers,
Sandino, with his guerrillas,
was a jungle specter,
a coiled tree
or a sleeping tortoise
or a gliding river.
But tree, tortoise, current
were avenging death,
jungle systems,
the spider's mortal symptoms.

(In 1948
a guerrilla
from Greece, Sparta column,
was the urn of light attacked
by the dollar's mercenaries.
From the mountains he fired
on the octupi from Chicago
and, like Sandino, the stalwart man
from Nicaragua, he was named
"the mountain bandit.")

But when fire, blood,
and dollar didn't destroy
Sandino's proud tower,
the Wall Street guerrillas
made peace, invited
the guerrilla to celebrate,

and a newly hired traitor

shot him with his rifle.

His name is Somoza. To this day
he's ruling in Nicaragua:
the thirty dollars grew
and multiplied in his belly.

This is the story of Sandino,
captain from Nicaragua,
heartbreaking incarnation
of our sand betrayed,
divided and assailed,
martyred and sacked.

JACK SCHMITT

XLII

THE TYRANTS AGAIN

Today the hunt spreads
over Brazil again,
the slave traders' cold greed
runs in hot pursuit:
on Wall Street they ordered
their porcine satellites
to bury their fangs
in the people's wounds,
and the hunt began
in Chile, in Brazil, in all
our Americas ravaged
by merchants and executioners.

My people concealed my path,
hid my verses with their hands,
preserved me from death,
and in Brazil the people's
infinite door closes the roads
where Prestes again
resists the oppressor.

Brazil, may your sorrowing
captain be safekept for you,
Brazil, may you not have
to reconstruct his effigy
from memory, tomorrow,
piece by piece,
to erect it in austere stone,
not having allowed your heart
to savor the freedom that he can
still, still conquer for you, Brazil.

JACK SCHMITT

XLIII
LLEGARÁ EL DÍA

Libertadores, en este crepúsculo
de América, en la despoblada
oscuridad de la mañana,
os entrego la hoja infinita
de mis pueblos, el regocijo
de cada hora de la lucha.

Húsares azules, caídos
en la profundidad del tiempo,
soldados en cuyas banderas
recién bordadas amanece,
soldados de hoy, comunistas,
combatientes herederos
de los torrentes metalúrgicos,
escuchad mi voz nacida
en los glaciares, elevada
a la hoguera de cada día
por simple deber amoroso:
somos la misma tierra, el mismo
pueblo perseguido,
la misma lucha ciñe la cintura
de nuestra América:
Habéis visto
por las tardes la cueva sombría
del hermano?
                    Habéis traspasado
su tenebrosa vida?
                    El corazón disperso
del pueblo abandonado y sumergido!

Alguien que recibió la paz del héroe
la guardó en su bodega, alguien robó los frutos
de la cosecha ensangrentada
y dividió la geografía
estableciendo márgenes hostiles,
zonas de desolada sombra ciega.

Recoged de las tierras el confuso
latido del dolor, las soledades,
el trigo de los suelos desgranados:
algo germina bajo las banderas:
la voz antigua nos llama de nuevo.
Bajad a las raíces minerales,
y a las alturas del metal desierto,
tocad la lucha del hombre en la tierra,
a través del martirio que maltrata
las manos destinadas a la luz.

No renunciéis al día que os entregan
los muertos que lucharon. Cada espiga
nace de un grano entregado a la tierra,
y como el trigo, el pueblo innumerable
junta raíces, acumula espigas,
y en la tormenta desencadenada
sube a la claridad del universo.

THE DAY WILL COME

Liberators, in this twilight
of America, in the morning's
forsaken darkness,
I give you my people's
infinite leaf, the exultation
of every hour of struggle.

Blue hussars, fallen
in the depths of time,
soldiers in whose newly
embroidered flags awaken
today's soldiers, communists,
combatant heirs
of the metallurgic torrents,
heed my voice born
of the glaciers, raised

aloft in the daily bonfire
through sheer love of duty.
We're from the same land, the same
persecuted people,
the same struggle encircles the waist
of our America:
                              Have you seen
in the night your brother's
somber cave?
        Have you fathomed
his sinister life?
                              The scattered heart
of the people, abandoned and submerged!
Someone who received the hero's peace
stored it away in his wine cellar, someone
stole the fruits of the bloody harvest
and divided the geography,
establishing hostile shores,
zones of desolate blind shadow.

Glean from the lands the shrouded
throb of sorrow, the solitude,
the wheat of the threshed fields:
something germinates beneath the flags:
the ancient voice calls us again.
Descend to the mineral roots,
and in the desolate metal's veins
reach mankind's struggle on earth,
beyond the martyrdom that mauls
the hands destined for the light.
Don't renounce the day bestowed on you
by those who died struggling. Every spike
is born of a grain seeded in the earth,
and like the wheat, the innumerable people
join roots, accumulate spikes,
and in the tempest unleashed
they rise up to the light of the universe.

JACK SCHMITT

Perhaps, perhaps oblivion on earth, like a mantle
can develop growth and nourish life
(maybe), like dark humus in the forest.

Perhaps, perhaps man, like a blacksmith, seeks
live coals, the hammering of iron on iron,
without entering the coal's blind cities,
without closing his eyes, not sounding
the depths, waters, minerals, catastrophes.
Perhaps, but my plate's another, my food's distinct:
my eyes didn't come to bite oblivion:
my lips open over all time, and all time,
not just part of time has consumed my hands.

That's why I'll tell you these sorrows I'd like to put aside,
I'll oblige you to live among their burns again,
not to mark time as in a terminal, before departing,
or to beat the earth with our brows,
or to fill our hearts with salt water,
but to set forth knowing, to touch rectitude
with decisions infinitely charged with meaning,
that severity may be a condition of happiness, that
we may thus become invincible.

JACK SCHMITT

I

THE HANGMEN

Saurian, scaly America coiled
around vegetable growth, around the flagpole
erected in the swamp:
you nursed terrible children

with poisonous serpent's milk,
torrid cradles incubated
and covered a bloodthirsty
progeny with yellow clay.
The cat and the scorpion fornicated
in the savage land.

The light fled from branch to branch,
but slumbering man did not awaken.

The blanket smelled of sugarcane,
machetes had rolled into
the surliest siesta site,
and in the cantinas' rarefied crest
the shoeless day laborer
spat out his boastful independence.

JACK SCHMITT

DOCTOR FRANCIA

The Paraná in the tangled wet
zones, palpitating with other rivers
where the water network—Yabebiri,
Acaray, Igurey, twin jewels
tinged with quebracho, enveloped
by dense crowns of copal—
runs toward the Atlantic sheets
dredging the delirium of the purple
nazarene tree, the roots
of the curupay in its sandy sleep.

From the hot ooze, from the devouring
alligator's thrones, amid
the wild pestilence
Dr. Francia cruised
toward Paraguay's easy chair.
And he lived amid rose windows

of rose-colored masonry
like a sordid Caesarian statue
shrouded by the dark spider's veils.

Solitary grandeur in the parlor
filled with mirrors, black
bugbear on red felt
and frightened rats in the night.
False column, perverse
academy, agnosticism
of a leprous king surrounded
by extensive maté fields,
drinking platonic numbers
on the gallows of the executed,
counting triangles of stars,
measuring stellar keys,
stalking Paraguay's
orange-colored dusk,
timing the agony
of the man executed at his window,
with his hand on the bolt
of the shackled twilight.

Studies on the table,
eyes on the firmament's
spur, on geometry's
inverted crystalware,
while the intestinal blood
of the man murdered by rifle butts
ran down the steps,
sucked up by green swarms
of glistening flies.

He sealed Paraguay like
his majesty's nest, bound
torture and mud to its borders.
When his silhouette glides
through the streets, the Indians
turn their eyes toward the walls:

his shadow slithers along leaving
two shivering walls.

When death visits
Dr. Francia, he's mute,
motionless, tied up within,
alone in his cave, arrested
by ropes of paralysis,
and he dies alone, without anyone
entering his chamber: no one dares
touch the master's door.

And bound by his serpents,
tongue-tied, stewing in his juice,
he rattles and dies, lost
in the palace's solitude,
while the night, established
like a chair of learning, devours
the miserable capitals
spattered by martyrdom.

JACK SCHMITT

ROSAS (1829–1849)

It is so hard to see through the earth
(not through time, which raises its transparent glass,
illuminating the lofty dew's résumé),
but the dense earth of flour and rancor,
storeroom hardened with corpses and metals,
doesn't let me peer into the depths
where the interwoven solitude rejects me.

But I'll speak to them, to mine, those who one day
fled to my flag, when purity was
a crystal star in its fabric.

Sarmiento, Alberdi, Oro, del Carril:
my pure land, later soiled,
preserved for you
the light of its metallic slenderness,
and among poor agricultural adobes
exiled thoughts
were being spun with hard minerals
and spurs of vineyard sugar.

Chile disseminated them in her fortitude,
gave them salt from her seaboard,
and sowed the exiled seeds.

Meanwhile, the gallop on the prairies.
The hitching ring was split over strands
of celestial hair,
and the pampa bit the horseshoes
of the wet frenzied beasts.

Daggers, government thugs' guffaws
atop martyrdom. From river to river,
the moon crowned atop the whiteness
with a crest of indescribable darkness!

Argentina plundered by rifle butt
in the misty dawn, beaten
and bled to madness, deserted,
ridden roughshod by savage overseers!

You became a procession of red vineyards,
you were a mask, a sealed tremor,
substituted in the air
by a tragic wax hand.
It emerged from you one night—
passageways, slabs of blackened stone,
steps where sound was submerged, carnival
crossroads, with corpses and buffoons,
and an eyelid's silence closing
over all the night's eyes.

Your foamy wheat, where did it flee?
Your fruit-bearing elegance, your wide mouth,
everything that moves your strings
to sing, your vibrant leather
of a great drum, a boundless star,
were silenced beneath the enclosed
cupola's implacable solitude.

Planet, latitude, powerful clarity,
the nocturnal silence that came mounted
on a vertiginous sea was gathered
on your rim, on the ribbon of shared snow,
and wave after wave the naked water reported,
the trembling gray wind unleashed its sand,
the night stirred us with its steppe-land lament.

But people and wheat were kneaded: then
the earthly head was groomed, the buried
light's filaments were combed, agony
tested the free doors, destroyed by the wind,
and from the clouds of dust on the road, one
by one, submerged dignities, schools,
intelligence, faces, ascended in the dust
until they became starry unities,
statues of light, pure meadowlands.

JACK SCHMITT

ESTRADA

Perhaps Estrada's coming, diminutive,
in his ancient dwarf's frock,
and between coughs
Guatemala's walls ferment,
incessantly irrigated
by urine and tears.

JACK SCHMITT

MACHADO

In Cuba Machado harnessed his Island
with machines, imported torments
manufactured in the United States,
machine guns spat,
mowing down phosphorescence,
the marine nectar of Cuba,
and the student with a flesh wound
was cast into the water where
the sharks finished
His Excellency's job.
The assassin's hand reached
Mexico, and Mella spun into the street
like a bloodied discus thrower
while Cuba burned, blue,
papered in lottery,
mortgaged with sugar.

JACK SCHMITT

MARTÍNEZ (1932)

Martínez, the quack
from El Salvador, distributes flasks
of multicolored remedies
which the ministers accept
with deep bows and scraping.
The little vegetarian witch doctor
passes his time prescribing in the palace
while torturous hunger
howls in the cane fields.
Martínez then decrees:
and in a few days twenty thousand
assassinated peasants
decompose in the villages
that Martínez orders burned
with ordinances of hygiene.

Back in the Palace he returns
to his syrups, and receives
the American ambassador's
swift congratulations.
"Western culture
is safe," says he—
"western Christianity,
and besides, good business,
banana concessions
and control of customs."

And together they drink a long
glass of champagne, while hot
rain falls on the putrid
gatherings of the charnel house.

JACK SCHMITT

II

THE OLIGARCHIES

No, the flags had not yet dried,
the soldiers had not yet slept
when freedom changed clothes,
and was turned into a hacienda:
a caste emerged from
the newly sown lands, a quadrille
of nouveaux riches with coats of arms,
with police and with prisons.

They drew a black line:
"Here on our side, Mexico's
Porfiristas, Chile's
"gentlemen," gentry from
the Jockey Club of Buenos Aires,
Uruguay's slicked
freebooters, the Ecuadorian
upper crust, clerical

dandies everywhere."
The poor to the mines, the desert.

Mr. Rodríguez de la Crota
spoke in the Senate with a mellifluous
elegant voice.
               "This law, at long last, establishes
the obligatory hierarchy
and above all the principles
of Christianity.
               It was
necessary as water.
Only the communists, conceived
in hell, as you're well aware,
could object to the Funnel
code, sagacious and severe.
But this Asiatic opposition,
proceeding from subman,
is easy to suppress: to jail with
them all, to the concentration camp,
and that way the distinguished
gentlemen and the obliging
Radical Party lackeys
will stand alone."

There was a round of applause
from the aristocratic benches:
what eloquence, how spiritual,
what a philosopher, what a luminary!
And everyone ran off to fill
his pockets in his business,
one monopolizing milk,
another racketeering in wire,
another stealing in sugar,
and all boisterously proclaiming
themselves patriots, with a monopoly
of patriotism, also accounted for
in the Funnel Law.

JACK SCHMITT

216

ELECTION IN CHIMBORONGO (1947)

In Chimborongo, Chile, long ago
I went to a senatorial election.
I saw how the pillars
of society were elected.
At eleven in the morning
oxcarts crammed with sharecroppers
arrived from the country.
It was winter. Wet,
dirty, hungry, barefoot,
the serfs from Chimborongo
climb down from the oxcarts.
Grim, sunburnt, tattered,
they're packed together, led
ballots in hand,
marshaled in a bunch
to draw their pay and,
herded like horses,
they're led back
to the oxcarts again.

            Then
they're thrown meat and wine
until they're left brutally
debauched and forgotten.

Later I heard the speech
of the senator thus elected:
"We, Christian patriots,
we, defenders of the order,
we, children of the spirit."
And his belly trembled,
his voice of a besotted cow
that seemed to sway
like a mammoth's trunk
in the sinister caverns
of howling prehistory.

JACK SCHMITT

DIPLOMATS (1948)

If you're born a fool in Romania
you pursue the fool's profession,
if you're a fool in Avignon
your quality is known
by France's venerable stones,
by the schools and disrespectful
farm boys.
But if you're born a fool in Chile
you'll soon be appointed Ambassador.
Whether your name is fool John Doe
or fool Joaquín Fernández or fool
So-and-So, keep a well-trimmed
beard if at all possible.
It's all that's required
to "enter into negotiations."

Then you'll send an expert report
on your spectacular
presentation of credentials,
saying: *Etc., the carriage,*
etc., His Excellency, etc.,
clichés, etc., benevolent.

Assume a solemn voice and a
protective cow's tone,
be decorated jointly
with Trujillo's envoy,
discreetly maintain
a "garçonière" ("You know
the convenience of these things
for Border Treaties"),
remit in slightly disguised form
the doctoral newspaper's
editorial that you read over breakfast
the day before yesterday: it's a "report."

Mingle with the "cream"
of "society," with that country's
fools, acquire all
the silver you can buy,
speak at anniversaries
beside bronze horses,
saying: *Ahem, the ties,*
etc., ahem, etc.,
ahem, the descendants,
etc., the race, ahem, the pure,
the sacrosanct, ahem, etc.

And keep a stiff upper lip:
You're a good Chilean
diplomat, you're a decorated
and prodigious fool.

JACK SCHMITT

THE BORDELLOS

The bordello, born of prosperity,
accompanied the banner
of stacked bills:
respected bilge
of capital, ship's hold
of my times.
                    They were mechanized
brothels in the hair
of Buenos Aires, fresh meat
exported, owing to adversity
in remote cities and fields,
where money stalked
the earthen pitchers' movements
and imprisoned the vine.
Rural brothels, of a winter
night, with horses
at the village outskirts

and bewildered girls
falling from sale to sale
in the magnates' hands.
Languorous provincial call houses
in which the town's gentry
—dictators of the wine harvest—
startle the venereal night
with chilling death rattles.
Hidden in the corners,
a flock of whores, inconstant
phantoms, passengers
of the mortal train—now they've taken you,
now you're in the sullied net,
now you can't return to the sea,
now they stalked you and hunted you down,
now you're dead in the void
of the rawest part of life,
now your shadow slinks
along the walls: throughout
the earth these walls
lead to death alone.

JACK SCHMITT

STANDARD OIL CO.

When the drill bored down
toward the stony fissures
and plunged its implacable intestine
into the subterranean estates,
and dead years, eyes
of the ages, imprisoned
plants' roots
and scaly systems
became strata of water,
fire shot up through the tubes
transformed into cold liquid,
in the customs house of the heights,

issuing from its world
of sinister depth,
it encountered a pale engineer
and a title deed.

However entangled the petroleum's
arteries may be, however the layers
may change their silent site
and move their sovereignty
amid the earth's bowels,
when the fountain gushes
its paraffin foliage,
Standard Oil arrived beforehand
with its checks and its guns,
with its governments and its prisoners.

Their obese emperors
from New York are suave
smiling assassins
who buy silk, nylon, cigars,
petty tyrants and dictators.

They buy countries, people, seas,
police, county councils,
distant regions where
the poor hoard their corn
like misers their gold:
Standard Oil awakens them,
clothes them in uniforms, designates
which brother is the enemy.
The Paraguayan fights its war,
and the Bolivian wastes away
in the jungle with its machine gun.

A President assassinated
for a drop of petroleum,
a million-acre
mortgage, a swift
execution on a morning

mortal with light, petrified,
a new prison camp for
subversives, in Patagonia,
a betrayal, scattered shots
beneath a petroliferous moon,
a subtle change of ministers
in the capital, a whisper
like an oil tide,
and zap, you'll see
how Standard Oil's letters
shine above the clouds,
above the seas, in your home,
illuminating their dominions.

JACK SCHMITT

LA UNITED FRUIT CO.

Cuando sonó la trompeta, estuvo
todo preparado en la tierra
y Jehová repartió el mundo
a Coca-Cola Inc., Anaconda,
Ford Motors, y ot ras entidades:
la Compañía Frutera Inc.
se reservó lo más jugoso,
la costa central de mi tierra,
la dulce cintura de América.
Bautizó de nuevo sus tierras
como «Repúblicas Bananas»
y sobre los muertos dormidos,
sobre los héroes inquietos
que conquistaron la grandeza,
la libertad y las banderas,
estableció la ópera bufa:
enajenó los albedríos,
regaló coronas de César,
desenvainó la envidia, atrajo
la dictadura de las moscas,

moscas Trujillo, moscas Tachos,
moscas Carías, moscas Martínez,
moscas Ubico, moscas húmedas
de sangre humilde y mermelada,
moscas borrachas que zumban
sobre las tumbas populares,
moscas de circo, sabias moscas
entendidas en tiranía.

Entre las moscas sanguinarias
la Frutera desembarca,
arrasando el café y las frutas
en sus barcos que deslizaron
como bandejas el tesoro
de nuestras tierras sumergidas.

Mientras tanto, por los abismos
azucarados de los puertos,
caían indios sepultados
en el vapor de la mañana:
un cuerpo rueda, una cosa
sin nombre, un número caído,
un racimo de fruta muerta
derramada en el pudridero.

UNITED FRUIT CO.

When the trumpet blared everything
on earth was prepared
and Jehovah distributed the world
to Coca-Cola Inc., Anaconda,
Ford Motors, and other entities:
United Fruit Inc.
reserved for itself the juiciest,
the central seaboard of my land,
America's sweet waist.
It rebaptized its lands

the "Banana Republics,"
and upon the slumbering corpses,
upon the restless heroes
who conquered renown,
freedom, and flags,
it established the comic opera:
it alienated self-destiny,
regaled Caesar's crowns,
unsheathed envy, drew
the dictatorship of flies:
Trujillo flies, Tacho flies,
Carías flies, Martínez flies,
Ubico flies, flies soaked
in humble blood and jam,
drunk flies that drone
over the common graves,
circus flies, clever flies
versed in tyranny.

Among the bloodthirsty flies
the Fruit Co. disembarks,
ravaging coffee and fruits
for its ships that spirit away
our submerged lands' treasures
like serving trays.

Meanwhile, in the seaports'
sugary abysses,
Indians collapsed, buried
in the morning mist:
a body rolls down, a nameless
thing, a fallen number,
a bunch of lifeless fruit
dumped in the rubbish heap.

JACK SCHMITT

THE BEGGARS

Beside the cathedral, knotted
to the wall, they dragged their feet,
their nondescript shapes, their black stares,
their livid gargoyle growths,
their tattered tins of food,
and from there, from the hard
sanctity of stone,
they became street flora, vagrant
flowers of legal pestilences.

The park has its beggars,
like its trees of tortured
branches and roots:
the slave lives at the foot of the garden,
like the extremity of mankind, reduced to rubbish,
his impure symmetry accepted,
ready for the broom of death.

Charity buries him
in its hole of leprous earth:
he's an object lesson for the man of my times,
who should learn to trample and plunge
the species into the swamps of contempt,
place his foot on the brow of the being
with the uniform of the defeated,
or at least understand him
as the product of nature.
American beggar, child of the year
1948, grandchild
of cathedrals, I don't venerate you,
I'm not going to put ancient ivory
or a regal beard in your written image,
as you're justified in books,
I'm going to expunge you with hope:
you'll not enter my organized love,
you'll not enter my breast with your kind,
with those who created you

spitting on your degraded form:
I'll remove your clay from the earth
until they build you with metals
and you emerge to shine like a sword.

JACK SCHMITT

THE INDIANS

The Indian fled from his skin to
the depths of ancient immensity from which
he rose one day like the islands: defeated,
he turned into invisible atmosphere,
kept expanding in the earth, pouring
his secret sign over the sand.

He who spent the moon and combed
the world's mysterious solitude,
he who didn't transpire without rising up
in lofty air-crowned stones,
he who endured like celestial light
beneath his forest's magnitude,
was suddenly worn threadbare,
transformed into wrinkles,
his torrential towers demolished,
and he received his packet of rags.

I saw him in Amatitlán's
magnetized heights, gnawing the shores
of impenetrable water: one day I walked
the Bolivian altiplano's
stunning majesty, with its remains
of bird and root.
                    I saw Alberti,
my brother of possessed poetry,
weep in the Araucanian precincts
when they surrounded him like Ercilla,

and instead of those red gods, they
were a purple chain of corpses.

Further beyond, in Tierra del Fuego's
network of wild waters,
I saw them clambering, O, squalid
sea dogs, into their battered canoes,
to beg for bread on the Ocean.

They systematically murdered
every fiber of those deserted domains,
and the hunter of Indians received
filthy bounty for bringing back the heads
of those masters of the air, kings
of the snowy antarctic solitude.

Those who paid for crimes sit
today in Parliament, licensing
their marriages in Presidencies,
living with Cardinals and Managers,
and flowers grow above the severed
throats of the masters of the South.

Then Araucania's crests
were dissipated by wine,
ravaged in taverns,
blackened by lawyers
at the service of that kingdom's theft,
and those who shot them down,
those who entered firing and negotiating
on the roads defended
by the dazzling gladiator
of our own seashores,
were called "Pacifiers,"
and their epaulettes were multiplied.

The collapse of the Indian's heritage
was so invisible that he lost without

seeing: he didn't see the banners,
he didn't send his bloody arrow flying,
so he was gnawed, bit by bit:
judges, pickpockets, landowners,
all took his imperial sweetness,
all entangled him in his blanket,
until they threw him bleeding into
America's uttermost swamps.

From the green sheets, from the foliage's
pure and innumerable sky,
from the immortal dwelling made
of heavy granite petals,
he was led to the dilapidated shack,
to the arid dung heap of misery.
From his gleaming nakedness,
his golden breast and pale waist,
or from the mineral ornaments
that joined his skin to all the dew,
they led him by the thread of his rags,
gave him lifeless pants, and that's how
his patched majesty came to parade through
the air of the world that was once his.

That's how this torment was committed.

The deed was invisible like a traitor's
entry, like impalpable cancer,
until our father was overwhelmed,
until they taught him to be a phantom,
and he entered the only door open to him,
the door of the other poor, that
of the entire earth's downtrodden.

JACK SCHMITT

THE JUDGES

In high Peru, in Nicaragua,
throughout Patagonia, in the cities,
you've had no rights, you've nothing:
cup of misery, America's
abandoned child, there's no
law, no judge to protect your land,
your little house with corn.

When your chiefs came,
your masters, by now forgotten
the ancient dream of talons and knives,
the law came to depopulate your sky,
to seize your revered fields,
to debate the rivers' water,
to steal the kingdom of trees.

They testified against you, stamped
your shirts, stuffed your heart
with leaves and papers,
buried you in cold edicts,
and when you awakened on the edge
of the most precipitous calamity,
dispossessed, solitary, vagrant,
they gave you jail, bound you,
shackled you so that swimming
you couldn't escape the water of the poor,
so that you'd drown kicking.

The benign judge reads you clause
number Four Thousand, Third Paragraph,
the same used in the entire
blue geography liberated
by others like you who fell,
and you're instituted by his codicil
without appeal, mangy cur.

Your blood asks, how were the wealthy
and the law interwoven? With what
sulfurous iron fabric? How did the
poor keep falling into the tribunals?

How did the land become so bitter
for poor children, harshly
nourished on stone and grief?
So it was, and so I leave it written.
Their lives wrote it on my brow.

JACK SCHMITT

IV

CHRONICLE OF 1948 (AMERICA)

A bleak year, *year of rats, impure year.*

Your line is lofty and metallic
on the shores of ocean
and air, like a wire
of tempests and tension.
But, America, you're also
nocturnal, blue, and boggy:
swamp and sky, an agony
of hearts broken
like black oranges crushed
in your storeroom silence.

JACK SCHMITT

PARAGUAY

Unbridled Paraguay!
What was the purpose of the pure moon
illuminating golden
geometry's papers?

To what avail was the knowledge
inherited from the columns
and the solemn numbers?

For this hole swamped
with rotten blood, for
this equinoctial liver
seized by death.
For monarchic Moriñigo,
enthroned upon prisons
in his pool of kerosene,
while the electric hummingbirds'
scarlet plumes
hover and glow above
the humble corpses in the jungle.

Bleak year, year of blighted roses,
year of carbines—look down
with your eyes, don't be blinded
by the airplane's aluminum, the music
of its dry sonorous speed—look at
your bread, your land, your torn masses,
your battered lineage!
                    Do you see that green
and ashen valley from the lofty sky?
Pale agriculture, tattered
mining, silence and weeping
like wheat, falling
and rising
            in a malevolent eternity.

JACK SCHMITT

CUBA

In Cuba they're assassinating!

Now they've put Jesús Menéndez
in a newly purchased coffin.
He emerged from the people like a king,
and went forth to examine roots,
stopping passersby,
beating on the breasts of the sleeping,
establishing the ages,
mending broken hearts,
and raising from the sugar
the bloody cane fields,
sweat that rots the stones,
asking in humble kitchens:
"Who are you? How much do you eat?"
touching this arm, this wound,
and accumulating these silences
in a single voice, the hoarse
choked voice of Cuba.

A little captain, a little general
assassinated him: in a train
he told him: "Come," and the little
general shot him in the back
so that the cane fields'
coarse voice would be silent.

                                    JACK SCHMITT

THE TRAITOR

And atop these calamities
a smiling tyrant
spits on the betrayed
miners' hopes.

Every nation has its sorrows,
every struggle its torments,
but come here and tell me
if among the bloodthirsty,
among all the unbridled
despots, crowned with hatred,
with scepters of green whips,
there was ever another like Chile's?
This man betrayed trampling
his promises and smiles,
his scepter was made of filth,
he danced on the poor
affronted people's grief.

And when the black eyes
of the offended and aggrieved
were gathered in the prisons
filled by his disloyal decrees,
he danced in Viña del Mar, surrounded
by jewelry and wineglasses.

But the black eyes stare
through the black night.

What did you do? Did your word ever come
for your brother of the deep mines,
for the grief of the betrayed,
did your fiery syllable ever come
to plead for your people and defend them?

JACK SCHMITT

ACUSO

Acusé entonces al que había
estrangulado la esperanza,
llamé a los rincones de América
y puse su nombre en la cueva

de las deshonras.

Entonces crímenes
me reprocharon, la jauría
de los vendidos y alquilados:
los «secretarios de gobierno»,
los policías, escribieron
con alquitrán su espeso insulto
contra mí, pero las paredes
miraban cuando los traidores
escribían con grandes letras
mi nombre, y la noche borraba,
con sus manos innumerables,
manos del pueblo y de la noche,
la ignominia que vanamente
quieren arrojar a mi canto.

Fueron de noche a quemar entonces
mi casa (el fuego marca ahora
el nombre de quien los enviara),
y los jueces se unieron todos
para condenarme, buscándome,
para crucificar mis palabras
y castigar estas verdades.

Cerraron las cordilleras
de Chile para que no partiera
a contar lo que aquí sucede,
y cuando México abrió sus puertas
para recibirme y guardarme,
Torres Bodet, pobre poeta,
ordenó que se me entregara
a los carceleros furiosos.

Pero mi palabra está viva,
y mi libre corazón acusa.

Qué pasará, qué pasará? En la noche
de Pisagua, la cárcel, las cadenas,
el silencio, la patria envilecida,

y este mal año, año de ratas ciegas,
este mal año de ira y de rencores
qué pasará, preguntas, me preguntas?

I ACCUSE

Then I accused the man
who had strangled hope,
I called out to America's corners
and put his name in the cave
of dishonor.
                    Then they reproached
me for crimes, that pack
of flunkies and hired hoodlums:
the "secretaries of government,"
the police, wrote their murky insult
against me with tar,
but the walls were watching
when the traitors
wrote my name in large letters,
and the night erased,
with its innumerable hands,
hands of the people and the night,
the ignominy that they try
in vain to cast on my song.

Then they went at night to burn
my house (the fire now marks
the name of he who sent them),
and all the judges joined together
to condemn me, to summon me,
to crucify my words
and punish these truths.

They closed Chile's cordilleras
so that I couldn't leave
to tell what's happening here,

and when Mexico opened its doors
to welcome me and protect me,
Torres Bodet, pitiful poet,
demanded that I be delivered
to the furious jailers.

But my word's alive,
and my free heart accuses.

How will it end, how will it end?
In Pisagua's night, jail, chains,
silence, the country debased,
and this bleak year, year of blind rats,
this bleak year of rage and rancor,
you ask, you ask me how it will end?

JACK SCHMITT

THE VICTORIOUS PEOPLE

My heart's in this struggle.
My people will overcome. All the peoples
will overcome, one by one.
                          These sorrows
will be wrung like handkerchiefs until
all the tears shed on the desert's
galleries, on graves, on the steps
of human martyrdom, are squeezed dry.
But the victorious time's nearby.
Let hatred reign so that punishment's
hands won't tremble,
                          let the hour hand
reach its timetable in the pure instant,
and let the people fill the empty streets
with fresh and firm dimensions.

Here's my tenderness for that time.
You'll know it. I have no other flag.

JACK SCHMITT

❋

I

FROM ABOVE (1942)

The journey's end, the indefinable
air, the moon of craters,
dry moon poured
upon scars,
the torn tunic's calcareous hole,
frozen veins of foliage, the panic
of quartz, wheat, the dawn,
keys spread out in secret rocks,
the terrifying line
of the dismembered South,
sulphate asleep in its stature
of long geography,
and turquoise dispositions
rotating round the extinguished light,
the incessantly blossoming pungent bouquet,
the spacious night of density.

JACK SCHMITT

II

AN ASSASSIN SLEEPS

The waist stained by wine
when the vile god steps
on broken wineglasses and dishevels
the unbridled dawn's light:
the rose watered in the little
prostitute's sob, the feverish days' wind
entering the paneless windows
where the victim sleeps with his shoes on,

in an acrid smell of pistols,
in a blue color of lost eyes.

JACK SCHMITT

III

ON THE COAST

In Santos, amid the bittersweet smell of plantains
that, like a river of soft gold opened in the back,
leaves the stupid saliva of
unhinged paradise on the shores,
and the iron clamor of shadows, water, and locomotive,
a current of sweat and feathers,
something that descends and flows from the depths
of burning leaves as from a pulsing armpit:
a crisis of flights, a remote
foam.

JACK SCHMITT

V

WINTER IN THE SOUTH, ON HORSEBACK

I've penetrated the bark a thousand
times assailed by the austral blows:
I've felt the horse's neck grow numb
beneath the cold stone of the South's night,
quiver in the naked mountain's compass,
ascend in the pale cheek that begins:
I know the end of the gallop in the mist,
the poor transient's tatters:
and for me there's no god but dark sand,
the interminable spine of stone and night,
the unsociable day
with an advent
of miserable clothes, of exterminated soul.

JACK SCHMITT

V

LOS CRÍMENES

Tal vez tú, de las noches oscuras has recorrido
el grito con puñal, la pisada en la sangre:
el solitario filo de nuestra cruz mil veces
pisoteada,
los grandes golpes en la callada puerta,
el abismo o el rayo que tragó al asesino
cuando ladran los perros y la violenta policía
llega entre los dormidos
a torcer fuertemente los hilos de la lágrima
tirándolos del párpado aterrado.

CRIMES

On dark nights, perhaps you've traced
the stabbing cry, footsteps in the blood:
the solitary edge of our cross a thousand times
trampled,
heavy blows on the silent door,
the abyss or thunderbolt that swallowed the assassin
when dogs bark and the violent police
enter among the sleeping
to forcefully twist the tear's threads
plucking them from the terrified eyelid.

JACK SCHMITT

VI

YOUTH

A perfume like an acid plum
sword on a road,
sugary kisses on the teeth,

vital drops trickling down the fingers,
sweet erotic pulp,
threshing floors, haystacks, inciting
secret hideaways in spacious houses,
mattresses asleep in the past, the pungent green valley
seen from above, from the hidden window:
all adolescence becoming wet and burning
like a lantern tipped in the rain.

JACK SCHMITT

VII
CLIMATES

In autumn, high arrows, renewed
oblivion, fall from the poplar:
feet plunge into the pure blanket:
the aroused leaves' coldness
is a dense fountain of gold,
a spiny splendor sets the dry
candelabras of bristling stature near the sky,
and the yellow jaguar scents a live droplet
between its claws.

JACK SCHMITT

VIII
VARADERO EN CUBA

Fulgor de Varadero desde la costa eléctrica
cuando, despedazándose, recibe en la cadera
la Antilla, el mayor golpe de luciérnaga y agua,
el sinfín fulgurario del fósforo y la luna,
el intenso cadáver de la turquesa muerta:
y el pescador oscuro saca de los metales
una cola erizada de violetas marinas.

VARADERO IN CUBA

From the electric coast Varadero glows
when, shattering, it receives on its hip the Antilles,
the greatest blow of glowworm and water,
the radiant infinity of phosphorus and moon,
the intense cadaver of dead turquoise:
and the dark fisherman extracts from the metals
a tail bristling with marine violets.

JACK SCHMITT

XI
HUNGER IN THE SOUTH

I see the sob in Lota's coal
and the humiliated Chilean's wrinkled shadow
picking the innards' bitter vein, dying,
living, born stooped
in the hard ash, fallen as if the world
entered and departed so,
amid black dust, amid flames,
and just the winter cough, a horse
moving through black water, where a eucalyptus
leaf has fallen like a dead knife.

JACK SCHMITT

XIII
A ROSE

I see a rose beside the water, a little cup
of red eyelids
sustained aloft by an ethereal sound:
a green-leaved light touches the headsprings
and transfigures the forest with solitary beings

with transparent feet:
the air's full of bright vestments
and the tree establishes its dormant magnitude.

JACK SCHMITT

XIV

LIFE AND DEATH OF A BUTTERFLY

The butterfly from Muzo flies in the tempest:
all the equinoctial threads,
the emeralds' frozen paste,
everything flies in the thunderbolt,
the air's ultimate consequences are shaken,
then a rain of green stamens
and the emerald's startled pollen rises:
its great velvets of wet fragrance
fall on the cyclone's blue shores,
merge with the fallen terrestrial leavens,
return to the homeland of leaves.

JACK SCHMITT

XV

THE MAN BURIED IN THE PAMPA

From tango to tango, if I could
circumscribe the dominion, the grasslands,
if now asleep
the wild wheat rising from my mouth,
if on the prairies I heard
a thunderclap of horses,
a furious tempest of hooves
passing over my buried fingers,
lipless I'd kiss the seed
and bind to it the vestiges

of my eyes
to see the gallop that my turbulence loved:
O kill me, Vidalita,
kill me and let my substance flow
like the harsh metal of the guitars.

JACK SCHMITT

XVIII
AMERICA

I am, I am surrounded
by honeysuckle and wasteland, by jackal and lightning,
by the enchained perfume of lilacs:
I am, I am surrounded
by days, months, waters that I alone know,
by fingernails, fish, months that I alone establish,
I am, I am surrounded
by the slender combatant foam
of the seaboard full of bells.
The scarlet shirt of Indian and volcano,
the road, which the naked foot raised amid the leaves
and thorns amid the roots,
comes to my feet at night that I may walk it.
Dark blood like autumn
poured on the ground,
the dreadful banner of death in the jungle,
invading footsteps dissolving, the warriors'
cry, the dormant spear twilight,
the soldiers' startled sleep, the great
rivers in which the alligator's peace splashes,
your recent cities of unforeseen mayors,
the chorus of birds of indomitable custom,
in the jungle's rank day, the firefly's
tutelary glow,
when I exist in your womb, in your beaconed
evening, in your repose, in the uterus of your births, in the

earthquake, in the peasants' oxcart, in the ash
that falls from the glaciers, in space,
in pure space, inapprehensible trajectory,
in the condors' bloody talons, in Guatemala's
humiliated peace, in the blacks,
on Trinidad's docks, in La Guayra:
all is my night, all is
my day, all is
my air, all is
whatever I live, suffer, raise, and agonize.
America, the syllables that
I sing aren't made of night or light.
The empowered matter of my victory's
radiance and bread is made of earth,
and my dream's not dream but earth.
I sleep surrounded by spacious clay
and when I live a fountain of boundless
lands flows through my hands.
And what I drink is not wine but earth,
hidden earth, my mouth's earth,
earth of agriculture with dew,
a gale of luminous vegetables,
cereal stock, granary of gold.

JACK SCHMITT

XIX

AMERICA, I DO NOT INVOKE YOUR NAME IN VAIN

America, I do not invoke your name in vain.
When I hold the sword to my heart,
when I endure the leaks in my soul,
when your new day
penetrates me through the windows,
I'm of and I'm in the light that produces me,
I live in the shade that determines me,
I sleep and rise in your essential dawn,

sweet as grapes and terrible,
conductor of sugar and punishment,
soaked in the sperm of your species,
nursed on the blood of your legacy.

JACK SCHMITT

ETERNITY

I write for a land recently dried, recently
fresh with flowers, pollen, mortar,
I write for some craters whose chalk cupolas
repeat the round void beside the pure snow,
I suddenly decree for that which barely
conveys the iron vapor recently emerged from the abyss,
I speak for meadows that know no name
other than the lichen's little bell or the burned stamen
or the harsh density where the mare burns.

Where am I from, but these seedlings, blue
matter that entangles or curls or uproots
or clamorously sows or somnolently spreads,
or climbs and forms the tree's bulwark,
or sinks and binds the copper's cell,
or springs to the rivers' branch, or succumbs
in the coal's buried stock, or gleams
in the grape's green darkness?

At night I sleep like the rivers, incessantly
on the move, surging ahead, overtaking
the swimming night, raising hours
to the light, groping for secret
images unearthed by lime, rising through bronze
to the recently disciplined cascades, and I touch
in a river network all that it doesn't distribute
except the unborn rose, the drowned hemisphere.
The earth's a cathedral of pale eyelids,
eternally bound and gathered in a
tempest of segments, in salt domes,
in a final color of forgiven autumn.

You've never, you've never touched
what the naked stalactite determines,
the fiesta amid the glacial lamps,
the black leaves' lofty coldness,
you've never entered with me the fibers
hidden by the earth,
after death you've never again climbed
the steps of sand grain by grain
until the crowns of dew
cover a blooming rose again,
you cannot exist with the hand-me-downs
of happiness without dying a slow death.

But I'm the metallic nimbus, the ring
chained to space, clouds, spheres,
that touches hurtling mute waters,
and again defies the infinite inclemency.

JACK SCHMITT

II

I WANT TO RETURN TO THE SOUTH (1941)

Ill in Veracruz, I remember a day,
in the South, my land, a day silvery
as a darting fish in the water of the sky.
Loncoche, Lonquimay, Carahue, sown
from above, surrounded by silence and roots,
seated on their thrones of leather and wood.
The South's a shipwrecked horse
crowned with slow trees and dew,
when it raises its green muzzle raindrops fall,
the shade from its tail soaks the great archipelago
and venerated coal grows in its intestine.
Will you never again—tell me, shade, never again, tell me,
hand, never again, tell me, foot, door, leg, combat—
disturb the forest, roads, spikes of grain,
mist, the cold, whatever, blue, determined

every one of your footprints, incessantly consumed?
Sky, someday let me go from star to star
treading light and gunpowder, destroying my blood,
until I reach the rain's nest!
                              I want to
follow the wood down the fragrant
River Toltén, I want to leave the sawmills,
enter the cantinas with wet feet,
be guided by the electric hazel tree's light,
stretch out beside the cowpies,
die and revive chewing wheat.
                              Ocean, bring me
a day from the South, a day embracing your waves,
a wet-tree day, bring a polar–
blue wind to my cold flag!

JACK SCHMITT

V

SADDLERY

For me this saddle designed
like a heavy rose in silver and leather,
gently sloped, smooth and durable.
Every cut is a hand, every
stitch a life in which the unity
of forest lives, a chain of eyes
and horses, lives on.
Grains of wheat shaped it,
woodlands and water hardened it,
the opulent harvest gave it pride,
metal and wrought morocco leather:
and so from misfortune and dominion,
this throne set forth through the meadowlands.

JACK SCHMITT

POTTERY SHOP

Crude dove, clay piggy bank,
on your grieving back a sign, something
that barely deciphers you. My people,
how—shouldering your sorrows,
beaten and subdued—how did you manage
to accumulate naked science?
Black prodigy, magic matter
raised to the light by blind fingers,
minute statue in which the earth's most
secret essence unlocks its languages for us,
Pomaire's earthen pitcher in whose kiss
earth and skin congregate, infinite
forms of clay, vessels' light,
shape of a hand that was mine,
movement of a shadow that calls me,
you're a gathering of hidden dreams,
indestructible, ceramic dove!

JACK SCHMITT

VII
ATACAMA

Insufferable voice, disseminated
salt, substituted
ash, black bouquet
on whose extreme dewdrop the blind moon
rises, through grieving galleries of copper.
What matter, what hollow swan
plunges its naked agony into the sand
and hardens its slow liquid light?
What hard thunderbolt shatters its emerald
amid the indomitable stones until
the lost salt congeals?
Land, land
above the sea, above the air, above the gallop

of the horsewoman full of coral:
heaping granary where wheat
sleeps in the bells' tremulous root:
O mother of the ocean!, maker
of blind jasper and golden silica:
upon your pure skin of bread, far from the forest,
nothing but your secret lines,
nothing but your sandy brow,
nothing but mankind's days and nights,
but beside the thistle's thirst, where
there's a submerged and forgotten paper, a stone
marks the deep cradles of sword and cup,
indicates the calcium's sleeping feet.

JACK SCHMITT

X

UNTILLED ZONES

Forsaken limit! Frenzied line
on which wildfire or enraged thistle
form layers of electrified blue.

Stones hammered by
the copper's needles, roads
of silent matter, branches submerged
in the stones' salt.

Here I am, here am I,
a human mouth abandoned to the pale passage
of a time arrested like a wineglass or hip,
a central penitentiary of impounded water,
tree of a demolished corporal flower,
nothing but deaf and brusque sand.
My country, earthly and blind as
newborn spurs of sand, for you all
my soul's foundation, for you my blood's

perpetual eyelids, for you my
plate of poppies home again.

Give me at night, amid the earthly plants,
the sullen rose of dew that sleeps in your flag,
give me of moon or earth your bread dusted
with your frightful dark blood:
beneath your sandy light
there are no corpses, but long cycles of salt, blue
branches of mysterious dead metal.

JACK SCHMITT

XII
BOTÁNICA

El sanguinario litre y el benéfico boldo
diseminan su estilo
en irritantes besos de animal esmeralda
o antologías de agua oscura entre las piedras.

El chupón en la cima del árbol establece
su dentadura nívea
y el salvaje avellano construye su castillo
de páginas y gotas.
La altamisa y la chépica rodean
los ojos del orégano
y el radiante laurel de la frontera
perfuma las lejanas intendencias.

Quila y quelenquelén de las mañanas.
Idioma frío de las fucsias,
que se va por las piedras tricolores
gritando viva Chile con la espuma!

El dedal de oro espera
los dedos de la nieve

y rueda el tiempo sin su matrimonio
que uniría a los ángeles del fuego y del azúcar.

El mágico canelo
lava en la lluvia su racial ramaje,
y precipita sus lingotes verdes
bajo la vegetal agua del Sur.

La dulce aspa del ulmo
con fanegas de flores
sube las gotas del copihue rojo
a conocer el sol de las guitarras.

La agreste delgadilla
y el celestial poleo
bailan en las praderas con el joven rocío
recientemente armado por el río Toltén.

La indescifrable doca
decapita su púrpura en la arena
y conduce sus triángulos marinos
hacia las secas lunas litorales.

La bruñida amapola,
relámpago y herida, dardo y boca,
sobre el quemante trigo
pone sus puntuaciones escarlata.

La patagua evidente
condecora sus muertos
y teje sus familias
con manantiales aguas y medallas de río.

El paico arregla lámparas
en el clima del Sur, desamparado,
cuando viene la noche
del mar nunca dormido.

El roble duerme solo,
muy vertical, muy pobre, muy mordido,
muy decisivo en la pradera pura
con su traje de roto maltratado
y su cabeza llena de solemnes estrellas.

BOTANY

The sanguinary liter and the beneficent
boldo tree disseminate their style
in irritating emerald animal kisses or
anthologies of dark water around the stones.

Mistletoe establishes its white teeth
in the treetops
and the wild hazel tree builds its castle
of pages and raindrops.
Mugwort and grama grass circle
the oregano's eyes
and radiant borderlands laurel
perfumes the distant intendencies.

Quila and quelenquelén in the morning.
Cold language of fuchsias
wending its way through the tricolored stones
shouting "Viva Chile" with the foam!

Golden foxglove waits for
the snow's fingers
and time rolls on without its matrimony
that would join the angels of fire and sugar.

The magic Winter's bark
bathes its family branches in the rain
and hurtles its green ingots
beneath the vegetable water of the South.

Laden with flowers,
the ulmo's sweet limb
raises the droplets of the red copihue
to meet the sun of the guitars.

Wild delgadilla
and celestial spearmint
dance on meadows with young dew,
recently arranged by the River Toltén.

The indecipherable doca
decapitates its purple in the sand
and conducts its marine triangles
toward the dry littoral moons.

The burnished poppy,
lightning and wound, dart and mouth,
puts its scarlet punctuations
upon the burning wheat.

The evident patagua
decorates its dead
and weaves its families
with springwater and river medallions.

Paico arranges lanterns
in the climate of the South, forsaken,
when the ever sleepless
sea night falls.

The southland beech sleeps alone,
very vertical, very poor, very frazzled,
very decisive in the pure meadow
with its shabby down-and-outer's suit
and its head full of solemn stars.

JACK SCHMITT

Elemental waters, walls of water, clover
and battered oats,
cordage bound in the net of a damp
sopping night, savagely spun,
earth-rending drops drummed into lament,
slant anger slashing sky.
Soaked in aroma the horses gallop
underneath water, walloping the water, their red
branchwork cleaving it, hair stone and water:
and steam like some wild milk clings to
a water ridden with fleeting doves.
No daylight is there but deep pools
in this hard tropic, this green career
and the hooves knit swift earth to swift
in the bestial aura of horse-and-rain.
Ponchos, saddles, saddle rugs massed
in russet mounds above
blazing sulfur loins that pound
the forest binding it down.
         On and on, and on, go on and on,
and on, and on, and on, and o-o-o-on,
the riders hurl down the rain, the riders
pace beneath bitter nut-trees, the rain
twists its everlasting wheat into trembling rays.
There is light from the water, a vague flash
spilled on the leaves, and the sounding gallop
spawns a flightless earth-wounded water.
Damp bridle, branched arch,
pacing on pacing, nighttime plant
of fractured stars like ice or moon, cyclone horse
spattered with arrows like an icy ghost,
bristling with new hands born in the furor,
throbbing fruit surrounded by fear
and its monarch dreadful banner.

JOHN FELSTINER

XVI
CHILE'S SEAS

In faraway regions I bathed
your foamy feet, your scattered shore,
with furious exiled tears.

Today I come to your mouth, today to your brow.

I didn't disclose your respectful secret
or syllable to the sanguinary coral,
to the burned star
or the incandescent and battered waters.
I safeguarded your enraged voice, a petal
of tutelary sand
amid the furniture and old clothes.

A dust of bells, a wet rose.

And it was often Arauco's
selfsame water, hard water:
but I preserved my submerged stone
and in it, the pulsing sound of your shadow.

O, Chilean sea, O, water
soaring and encircling like a raging wildfire,
pressure and dream and sapphire fingernails,
O, earthquake of salt and lions!
Fountainhead, source, planet's
seashore, your eyelids
open the earth's noontide
attacking the stars' blue.
Salt and movement are released from you,
distributing ocean to mankind's grottoes
until your weight breaks beyond the islands
and extends a bouquet of total substances.
Sea of the northern desert, sea that hammers the copper
and advances the foam toward the hand
of the harsh solitary inhabitant,

amid pelicans, rocks with cold sun and dung,
coast burned by the passage of an inhuman dawn!

Sea of Valparaíso, wave
of lonely nocturnal light,
window of the ocean
from which my country's
statue looks out,
gazing with eyes still blind.

Sea of the South, sea ocean,
sea, mysterious moon,
in Imperial, terror of the southland beech,
in Chiloé anchored to blood,
and from Magellan to the limit
all the whistling salt, all the mad moon,
and the stellar streaking horse of the ice.

JACK SCHMITT

I

CRISTÓBAL MIRANDA (SHOVELER, TOCOPILLA)

I met you, Cristóbal, on the barges
in the bay, when the saltpeter
comes down, to the sea, in the scorching
attire of a November day.
I remember that static bearing,
the metal hills, the still water.
And the bargeman alone, bathed
in sweat, moving snow.
Nitrate snow, poured
on the shoulders of sorrow, falling
into the ships' blind bellies.
There, shovelers, heroes of an
acid-etched dawn, subject
to the fates of death, firm,
receiving the torrential nitrate.
Cristóbal, this keepsake for you.
For the shovel comrades,
in whose breasts acid enters,
and murderous emanations,
bloating hearts like vanquished
eagles, until man falls,
until man tumbles into the streets,
into the pampa's broken crosses.
Enough said, Cristóbal, now this
paper remembers you, all of you—
bargemen in the bay, man
blackened by the ships—my eyes
accompany you on this shift
and my soul's a shovel that rises

loading and unloading blood and snow,
beside you, desert lives.

JACK SCHMITT

VII

ANTONIO BERNALES (FISHERMAN, COLOMBIA)

The Magdalena River moves like the moon,
leisurely through the planet of green leaves,
a red bird wails, the whirring sound
of aged black wings, the riverbanks
tinge the coursing of waters upon waters.
Everything is river, every life river,
and Antonio Bernales was river.
Fisherman, carpenter, oarsman, netting
needle, nail for the planks,
hammer and song, Antonio was everything
while the Magdalena dredged the torrent
of river lives like a leisurely moon.
Higher up in Bogotá, flames, fire,
blood, Gaitán is dead, or so
it's rumored. Amid the leaves,
like a jackal, Laureano's laughter
fans the flames, the people's
tremor penetrates the Magdalena
like a shiver.
Antonio Bernales is the culprit.
He never left his shack.
He spent those days sleeping.
But the lawyers so decree,
Enrique Santos wants blood.
They all join beneath their frock coats.
Antonio Bernales has fallen
murdered in revenge,
he fell open-armed into the river,
returned to his river as to mother water.
The Magdalena washes his corpse to sea

and from the sea to other rivers, to other waters
and other seas and other little rivers
spinning round the earth.
                    Again
he enters the Magdalena, they're the riverbanks
that he loves, he opens arms of red water,
passes amid shadows, amid dense light,
and again continues his waterway.
Antonio Bernales, no one can
distinguish you in the riverbed, but I remember you
and hear the tow of your name that cannot
die, that envelops the earth,
just a name, people, amid names.

JACK SCHMITT

XII

MAESTRO HUERTA

(FROM THE "LA DESPRECIADA" MINE, ANTOFAGASTA)

When you visit the North, sir,
go to the mine "La Despreciada,"
and ask for maestro Huerta.
From afar you'll see nothing
but gray sandbanks.
Then you'll see structures,
the cableway, mounds of rubble.
Fatigue, suffering,
aren't visible, they're moving
underground, crushing beings,
or they're at rest, stretched out,
silently transforming themselves.
Maestro Huerta was a "pickman."
He measured 6' 5".
Pickmen are the people who break
the earth down to the lower ground
when the vein's level decreases.
1600 feet below,

with water up to the waist,
the pickman keeps picking away.
He only leaves the inferno
once every forty-eight hours,
after the drilling
in the rock, in the darkness,
in the mud, leaves the pulp
wherever the mine meanders.
Maestro Huerta, a great pickman,
seemed to fill the shaft
with his shoulders. He entered
singing like a captain.
He emerged pocked, yellow,
hunchbacked, withered, and his eyes
were those of a corpse.
Then he shuffled through the mine.
He could no longer descend the shaft.
Antimony consumed his innards.
He grew so thin that it was frightening.
He couldn't even walk.
His legs seemed pierced
by knifepoint, and since he was
so tall he looked
like a starving ghost
begging without begging, you know.
He didn't reach his thirtieth birthday.
Ask where he's buried.
No one can tell you,
because the sand and wind batter
and bury the crosses, afterward.
It's up in "La Despreciada,"
where maestro Huerta worked.

JACK SCHMITT

CATASTROPHE IN SEWELL

Sánchez, Reyes, Ramírez, Núñez, Álvarez.
These names are like Chile's foundations.
The people are the country's foundation.
If you let them die, the country keeps collapsing,
keeps bleeding until it is drained.
Ocampo has told us: every minute
there's a wound, and every hour a corpse.
Every minute and every hour
our blood falls, Chile dies.
Today it's smoke from the fire, yesterday firedamp,
the day before the cave-in, tomorrow the sea or the cold,
machinery and hunger, the unforeseen or acid.
But there where the seaman dies,
but there where people from the pampa die,
but there in Sewell where they disappeared,
everything is maintained—machinery, glass,
iron, papers—
except man, woman, or child.
It's not the gas: it's greed that kills in Sewell.
That tap turned off in Sewell so that not even a drop
of water for the miners' poor coffee would fall,
there's the crime, the fire's not to blame.
Everywhere they turn off the people's tap
so that the water of life won't be distributed.
But the hunger and cold and fire that consume
our race (the flower, Chile's foundations),
the tatters, the miserable house,
they're not rationed, there's always enough
so that every minute there's a casualty
and every hour a corpse.
We have no gods to turn to.
Poor mothers dressed in black
already wept all their tears while they prayed.

We don't pray.
Stalin said: "Our best treasure

is mankind,"
the foundations, the people.
Stalin erects, cleans, builds, fortifies,
preserves, ponders, protects, nourishes,
but he punishes too.
And that's what I wanted to tell you, comrades:
punishment is needed.
This human cave-in cannot be,
this bleeding of the beloved country,
this blood that falls from the people's heart
every minute, this death
of every hour.
My name's the same as theirs, as the ones who died.
I, too, am Ramírez, Muñoz, Pérez, Fernández.
My name's Álvarez, Núñez, Tapia, López, Contreras.
I'm related to all those who die, I'm people,
and I mourn for all the blood that falls.
Compatriots, dead brothers, from Sewell, Chile's
dead, workers, brothers and sisters, comrades,
as you're silent today, we're going to speak.
And may your martyrdom help us
to build a severe nation
that will know how to flower and punish.

JACK SCHMITT

XVII

THE EARTH'S NAME IS JUAN

Juan followed upon the liberators
working, fishing and fighting,
in his carpentry work or in his damp mine.
His hands have plowed the earth and measured the roads.
                    His bones are everywhere.
But he's alive. He returned from the earth. He was born.
He was born again like an eternal plant.
All the impure night tried to submerge him
and today he affirms his indomitable lips in the dawn.

263

They bound him, and he's now a determined soldier.
They wounded him, and he's still hearty as an apple.
They cut off his hands, and today he pounds with them.
They buried him, and he sings along with us.

Juan, the door and the road are yours.
                                        The earth
is yours, people, truth was born
with you, with your blood.
                    They couldn't exterminate you.
        Your roots,
tree of humanity,
tree of eternity,
are today defended with steel,
are today defended with your own grandeur
in the Soviet land, armored
against the snaps of the moribund wolf.

People, order was born of suffering.

Your victorious flag was born of order.

Hoist it with all the hands that fell,
defend it with all the hands that are joined:
and let the unity of your invisible faces
advance to the final struggle, to the star.

JACK SCHMITT

. . . And thou, Capernaum, which art
exalted to heaven, shalt be thrust down to hell . . .
SAINT LUKE, 10:15

III

BEYOND YOUR LANDS, AMERICA

Beyond your lands, America, I also wend my way
and make my wandering house: I fly about, pass through,
sing and chat for days on end.
And in Asia, in the USSR, in the Urals I stop
and stretch out my soul drenched in wilds and resin.

In the open spaces I love whatever
man has created by dint of love and struggle.
The pines' ancient night
still surrounds my house in the Urals,
and silence like a towering column.
Here wheat and steel were born
of mankind's hand and breast.
And a song of hammers cheers the ancient forest
like a new blue phenomenon.
From here I see extensive zones of humanity,
geography of children and women, love,
factories and songs, schools
that glow like gillyflowers in the forest
where only yesterday the wild fox thrived.
From this point my hand on the map embraces
the meadowlands' green, smoke
from a thousand workshops, textile
aromas, the wonder
of harnessed energy.
In the afternoon I return
on recently charted new roads
and enter kitchens

where cabbage simmers and a new
fountainhead rises for the world.

Here, too, the boys returned,
but countless millions remained behind,
strung up, hanging from the gallows,
burned in special ovens,
savaged until nothing was left of them
except a name in memory.
Their towns were annihilated too:
the Soviet land was annihilated:
millions of glass shards and bones fused,
cows and factories, until springtime
vanished, engulfed by the war.
But the boys returned,
and love for the homeland founded
had mingled in them with so much blood
that they say *Motherland* with their veins,
sing Soviet Union with their blood.
The voice of the conquerors of Prussia and
Berlin was loud when they returned
so that the cities, animals,
and springtime would be reborn.
Walt Whitman, raise your beard of grass,
look with me from the forest,
from these perfumed magnitudes.
What do you see there, Walt Whitman?
I see, my deep brother tells me,
I see how the factories run,
in the city that the dead remember,
in the pure capital,
in resplendent Stalingrad.
From the field contested
through suffering and fire,
I see, rising in the morning moisture,
a tractor whirring toward the prairies.
Give me your voice and the weight of your buried breast,
Walt Whitman, and the solemn
roots of your face

to sing these reconstructions!
Let's sing together whatever arises
from all the sorrows, whatever surges
from the great silence, from the solemn
victory:
        Stalingrad, your steely voice surges,
floor by floor hope's reborn
like a collective house,
and there's a new tremor on the march
teaching,
singing
and building.

From the blood Stalingrad surges
like an orchestra of water, stone, and iron,
and bread's reborn in the bakeries,
springtime in the schools,
it raises new scaffolds, new trees,
while the old iron Volga pulses on.
                These books,
in fresh pine and cedar boxes,
are gathered over
the dead executioners' grave:
these theaters made in the ruins
blanket martyrdom and resistance:
books transparent as monuments:
a book above each hero,
above each millimeter of death,
above each petal of this immutable glory.
Soviet Union, if we joined
all the blood spilt in your struggle,
all that you gave like a mother to the world
that moribund freedom might live,
we'd have a new ocean,
greater than any,
deeper than any,
alive as all the rivers,
active as the Araucanian volcanoes' fire.
Plunge your hand into that sea,

mankind from every land,
then raise it to drown
the one who forgot, the one who defiled,
the one who lied and the one who soiled,
the one who joined a hundred little curs
from the rubbish heap of the West
to insult your blood, Mother of the free!

From the fragrant smell of the Ural pines
I see the library born
in the heart of Russia,
the laboratory where silence
labors, I see trains that transport
wood and songs to the new cities,
and in this balmy peace a throbbing swells
as in a new breast:
girls and doves return
to the steppeland waving whiteness,
orange groves are filled with gold:
today the market has
a new aroma
every dawn,
a new aroma that comes from the high lands
where martyrdom was unmatched:
engineers make the map of the prairies
tremble with their numbers
and the pipelines are wrapped like long serpents
in the lands of the new vaporous winter.

In three rooms of the old Kremlin
lives a man named Joseph Stalin.
His bedroom light is turned off late.
The world and his country allow him no rest.
Other heroes have given birth to a nation,
he helped to conceive his as well,
to build it
and defend it.
His immense country is, then, part of himself
and he cannot rest because it's never at rest.

In times past snow and gunpowder
found him facing the old bandits
who wanted (then as now) to revive
the *knut*, and misery, the slaves' anguish,
the slumbering sorrow of millions of poor.
He opposed those who, like Wrangel and Deniken,
were sent from the West to "defend Culture."
There those defenders of executioners
left their hides behind, and in the USSR's
spacious terrain, Stalin worked night and day.
But later the Germans fattened by Chamberlain
advanced in a wave of lead.
Stalin confronted them on all the vast frontiers,
on all the retreats, on all the advances,
and entered Berlin with his children like a hurricane
of peoples and brought Russia's spacious peace.

Molotov and Voroshilov
are there, I see them
with the others, the high generals,
the indomitable.
Firm as snowy oak groves.
None of them has palaces.
None has regiments of slaves.
None became rich in the war
selling blood.
None struts like a peacock
to Rio de Janeiro or Bogotá
to direct the little satraps stained with torture:
none has two hundred suits:
none has stocks in weapons factories,
and all have
stocks
in the happiness and construction
of the vast country where the dawn risen
on the night of death resounds.
They said "Comrade" to the world.
They made a king of the carpenter.
A camel won't be threaded through that needle.

They washed the villages.
They distributed land.
They raised the serf.
They expunged the beggar.
They annihilated the cruel.
They gave light to the spacious night.

That's why I address you, young lady from Arkansas, or
you, golden youth from West Point or best
you mechanic from Detroit or rather
you stevedore from old Orleans, to all
I speak and say: steady your step,
open your ears to the vast human world,
it's not the State Department dandies
or the ferocious owners of steel
speaking to you
but a poet from the far South of America,
son of a railwayman from Patagonia,
American as the Andean air,
today fugitive of a country where
prison, torment, anguish prevail
while copper and petroleum are slowly
turned into gold for foreign kings.
                            You're not
the idol that bears gold in one hand
and in the other a bomb.
                    You're
what I am, what I was, what we should
shelter, purest America's
fraternal subsoil, humble
humanity of the roads and streets.
My brother Juan sells shoes
like your brother John,
my sister Juana peels potatoes,
like your cousin Jane,
and my blood's miner and mariner
like your blood, Peter.

You and I are going to open the doors
so that air from the Urals
can breach the ink curtain,
you and I are going to tell the enraged:
"My dear guy, you've reached the limit,"
on this side the land belongs to us
so that we won't be hearing the hiss
of a machine gun but rather a
song, and song after song.

JACK SCHMITT

❋

I

Through the dead of night, through my entire life,
from tear to paper, from clothes to clothes,
I paced these trying days.
I was the fugitive from justice:
and in the crystal hour, in the fastness
of solitary stars,
I crossed cities, forests,
small farms, seaports,
from the door of one human being to another,
from the hand of one being to another being, and another.
Solemn's the night, but man
has disposed his fraternal signs,
and groping my way along roads and shadows
I reached the lit doorway, the little
point of star that was mine,
the bread crumb that the wolves in the forest
had not devoured.

Once, in the countryside,
at night, I reached a house, where
I'd never seen anyone before that night
or even imagined those lives.
Whatever they did, their hours
were new in my consciousness.
I entered, they were a family of five:
all had arisen as on the night
of a fire.
              I shook
hand after hand, saw face after face,
that said nothing to me: they were doors
that I didn't see before in the street,
eyes that didn't know my face,

and in the dead of night, after
welcoming me, I succumbed to fatigue,
to sleep my country's anguish.

As sleep approached,
the innumerable echo of the earth
with its hoarse barking and filaments
of solitude, the night advanced,
and I thought: "Where am I? Who
are they? Why are they sheltering me today?
Why do they, who never saw me before today,
open their doors and defend my song?"
And no one answered
except the rustling of a leafless night,
a fabric of crickets building up:
the entire night barely
seemed to tremble in the foliage.
Nocturnal land, you came
to my window with your lips
that I might sleep peacefully,
like falling on thousands of leaves,
from season to season, from nest to nest,
from branch to branch, until I suddenly
slumbered like a corpse in your roots.

                                        JACK SCHMITT

IV

A young couple opened a door
that I didn't know before either.
                          She was
golden as the month of June,
he an engineer with lofty eyes.
From then on I shared bread and wine
with them,
               little by little
I reached their unknown intimacy.

They told me: "We were
separated,
our dissension was now eternal:
today we joined to welcome you,
today we awaited you together."
There, united
in the little room,
we embodied silent fortitude.
I kept silence even in my sleep.
I was in the dead
center of the city, I almost heard
the Traitor's footsteps, beside the walls
that separated me, I heard
the jailors' filthy voices,
their crooked laughter, their drunk
syllables inserted amid bullets
in my homeland's waist.
The belches of Holgers and Pobletes
almost brushed my silent skin,
their footsteps, shuffling along, almost
touched my heart and its bonfires:
they, consigning my people to torment,
I preserving my swordlike health.
And again, in the night, goodbye, Irene,
goodbye, Andrés, goodbye, new friend,
goodbye to the scaffolds, to the star,
goodbye perhaps to the unfinished house
which in front of my window seemed
to become filled with linear phantoms.
Goodbye to the minute speck of mountain
that gathered in my eyes every afternoon,
goodbye to the green neon light that opened
every new night with its lightning.

JACK SCHMITT

X

And so, from night to night,
that long hour, the entire Chilean
seaboard engulfed in darkness,
I fled from door to door.
Other humble homes, other hands
in every crease of the country
awaited my footsteps.
               You passed
a thousand times by that door that said nothing to you,
by that unpainted wall, by those
windows with wilted flowers.
The secret was for me:
it was pulsing for me,
it was the zones of coal
soaked in martyrdom,
it was in the coastal seaports
beside the antarctic archipelago,
perhaps it was (listen) in that
sonorous street, amid the midday
music of the streets,
or beside the park, that window
that no one distinguished amid the other
windows, and that awaited me
with a bowl of clear soup
and its heart on the table.
All the doors were mine,
they all said: "It's my brother,
bring him to this humble home,"
while my country stained itself
with so much punishment,
like a press of bitter wine.
The little tinsmith came,
the mother of those girls,
the ungainly farmer,
the man who made soap,
the sweet lady novelist, the young man
pinned like an insect

to the desolate office
came, and there was a secret sign
on their doorway, a key
defended like a tower
that I might enter abruptly
at night, afternoon, or day
and not knowing anyone
I could say: "Brother, you know who I am,
I think you were expecting me."

JACK SCHMITT

XII

To all, to you
silent beings of the night
who took my hand in the darkness, to you,
lamps
of immortal light, star lines,
staff of life, secret brethren,
to all, to you,
I say: there's no giving thanks,
nothing can fill the wineglasses
of purity,
nothing can
contain all the sun in the invincible
springtime's flags,
like your quiet dignity.
I only
think
that I've perhaps been worthy of so much
simplicity, of a flower so pure,
that perhaps I'm you, that's right,
that bit of earth, flour, and song,
that natural batch that knows
whence it comes and where it belongs.
I'm not such a distant bell
or a crystal buried so deep

that you can't decipher, I'm just
people, hidden door, dark bread,
and when you welcome me, you welcome
yourself; that guest
repeatedly beaten
and repeatedly
reborn.
                    To all, to all,
to whomever I don't know, to whomever never
heard this name, to those who dwell
all along our long rivers,
at the foot of the volcanoes, in the sulfuric
shadow of copper, to fishermen and farmhands,
to blue Indians on the shores
of lakes sparkling like glass,
to the shoemaker who at this very hour questions,
nailing leather with ancient hands,
to you, to the one who unknowingly has awaited me,
I belong and acknowledge and sing.

JACK SCHMITT

XIII

American sand, solemn
plantation, red cordillera,
children, brothers and sisters stripped
by the old storms,
let's join each living kernel
before it returns to the earth,
and may the new corn that comes forth
have heard your words
and repeat them and multiply.
And may they sing to one another day and night,
and bite and consume one another,
and be scattered throughout the earth,
and become, suddenly, silence,
plunge beneath the stones,

find the nocturnal doors,
and again rise to be born,
to be sown, to perform
like bread, like hope,
like the ships' air.
The corn brings you my song,
risen from my people's
roots, to be born,
to build, to sing,
and to be seed again,
more numerous in the storm.

Here are my lost hands.
They're invisible, but you
see them through the night,
through the invisible wind.
Give me your hands, I see them
through the rasping sands
of our American night,
and I choose yours and yours,
that hand and that other hand,
the one that rises to struggle
and the one that's sown again.

I don't feel alone in the night,
in the darkness of the land.
I'm people, innumerable people.
I have in my voice the pure strength
to penetrate silence
and germinate in the dark.
Death, martyrdom, shadow, ice,
suddenly shroud the seed.
And the people seem to be buried.
But the corn returns to the earth.
Its implacable red hands
pierced the silence.
From death we're reborn.

JACK SCHMITT

※

II

BROTHER PABLO

But today peasants come to see me: "Brother, there's
no water, brother Pablo, there's no water, it hasn't rained.

And the river's
scant current
circulates seven days, runs dry seven days.

Our cattle died in the cordillera.

And the drought begins to kill children.
Up above, many have nothing to eat.
Brother Pablo, speak to the Minister."

(Yes, brother Pablo will speak to the Minister, but they don't know
how those armchairs of ignominious leather
receive me,
and then the ministerial wood, rubbed
and polished by servile saliva.)
The Minister will lie, he'll wash his hands,
and the livestock of the poor commoner,
with his burro and his dog, will fall,
from hunger to hunger, amid threadbare rocks.

JACK SCHMITT

GOLD

Gold had that day of purity.
Before plunging its structure again
into the dirty debut that awaits it,
recently arrived, recently extracted
from the solemn statue of the earth,
it was purged by fire, enveloped
by man's sweat and hands.

There the gold's people said goodbye.
And their contact was earthy, pure
as the gray mother of emerald.
The sweaty hand that scoured
the snarled ingot was like
the stock of soil reduced
by the infinite dimension of time,
the earthly color of seeds,
the ground charged with secrets,
the earth that fashions clusters.

Lands of unstained gold, human
stock, immaculate metal
of the people, virginal veinstones
that touch without seeing one another in
the implacable junction of their two roads:
man will keep biting the dust,
he'll keep being flinty soil,
and gold will rise above his blood
until it wounds and rules over the wounded.

JACK SCHMITT

X

EL POETA

Antes anduve por la vida, en medio
de un amor doloroso: antes retuve
una pequeña página de cuarzo
clavándome los ojos en la vida.
Compré bondad, esruve en el mercado
de la codicia, respiré las aguas
más sordas de la envidia, la inhumana
hostilidad de máscaras y seres.
Viví un mundo de ciénaga marina
en que la flor, de pronto, la azucena
me devoraba en su temblor de espuma,
y donde puse el pie resbaló mi alma
hacia las dentaduras del abismo.
Así nació mi poesía, apenas
rescatada de ortigas, empuñada
sobre la soledad como un castigo,
o apartó en el jardín de la impudicia
su más secreta flor hasta enterrarla.
Aislado así como el agua sombría
que vive en sus profundos corredores,
corrí de mano en mano, al aislamiento
de cada ser, al odio cuotidiano.
Supe que así vivían, escondiendo
la mitad de los seres, como peces
del más extraño mar, y en las fangosas
inmensidades encontré la muerte.
La muerte abriendo puertas y caminos.
La muerte deslizándose en los muros.

THE POET

I used to wander through life amid
an ill-starred love: I used to keep
a little page of quartz

to rivet my eyes to life.
I bought kindness, I was in the market
of greed, I inhaled envy's
most sordid waters, the inhuman
hostility of masks and beings,
I lived a sea-swamp world
in which the flower, the lily, suddenly
consumed me in their foamy tremor,
and wherever I stepped my soul slid
toward the teeth of the abyss.
That's how my poetry was born, barely
freed from the nettles, clutched
above solitude like a punishment,
or its most secret flower sequestered
in the garden of immodesty until it was buried.
And so isolated like the dark water
that inhabits its deep corridors,
I fled from hand to hand, to each
being's alienation, to daily hatred.
I knew that was how they lived, hiding
half of their beings, like fish
from the strangest sea, and in the murky
immensities I encountered death.
Death opening doors and roads.
Death gliding along the walls.

JACK SCHMITT

XI

DEATH IN THE WORLD

Death kept dispatching and reaping
its tribute in sites and tombs:
man with dagger or with pocket,
at noon or in the nocturnal light,
hoped to kill, kept killing,
kept burying beings and branches,
murdering and devouring corpses.

He prepared his nets, wrung dry,
bled white, departed in the morning
smelling blood from the hunt,
and upon returning from his triumph he was shrouded
by fragments of death and abandonment,
and killing himself, he then buried
his tracks with sepulchral ceremony.

The homes of the living were dead.
Slag, broken roofs, urinals,
wormy alleyways, hovels
awash with human tears.
"You must live like this," said the decree.
"Rot in your substance," said the Foreman.
"You're filthy," reasoned the Church.
"Sleep in the mud," they told you.
And some of them armed the ash
to govern and decide,
while the flower of mankind beat
against the walls built for them.

The Cemetery possessed pomp and stone.
Silence for all the stature
of lofty tapered vegetation.

At last you're here, at last you leave
us a hollow in the heart of the bitter jungle,
at last you lie stiff between walls
that you won't breach. And every day
the flowers, like a river of perfume,
joined the river of the dead.
The flowers untouched by life
fell on the hollow that you left.

JACK SCHMITT

XII

MANKIND

Here I found love. It was born in the sand,
it grew without voice, touched the flintstones
of hardness, and resisted death.
Here mankind was life that joined
the intact light, the surviving sea,
and attacked and sang and fought
with the same unity of metals.
Here cemeteries were nothing but
turned soil, dissolved sticks
of broken crosses over which
the sandy winds advanced.

JACK SCHMITT

✳

I

CARTA A MIGUEL OTERO SILVA, EN CARACAS (1949)

Un viajero me trajo tu carta escrita
con palabras invisibles, sobre su traje, en sus ojos.
Qué alegre eres, Miguel, qué alegres somos!
Ya no queda en un mundo de úlceras estucadas
sino nosotros, indefinidamente alegres.
Veo pasar al cuervo y no me puede hacer daño.
Tú observas el escorpión y limpias tu guitarra.
Vivimos entre las fieras, cantando, y cuando tocamos
un hombre, la materia de alguien en quien creíamos,
y éste se desmorona como un pastel podrido,
tú en tu venezolano patrimonio recoges
lo que puede salvarse, mientras que yo defiendo
la brasa de la vida.
        Qué alegría, Miguel!
Tú me preguntas dónde estoy? Te contaré
—dando sólo detalles *útiles* al Gobierno—
que en esta costa llena de piedras salvajes
se unen el mar y el campo, olas y pinos,
águilas y petreles, espumas y praderas.
Has visto desde muy cerca y todo el día
cómo vuelan los pájaros del mar? Parece
que llevaran las cartas del mundo a sus destinos.
Pasan los alcatraces como barcos del viento,
otras aves que vuelan como flechas y traen
los mensajes de los reyes difuntos, de los príncipes
enterrados con hilos de turquesa en las costas andinas,
y las gaviotas hechas de blancura redonda,
que olvidan continuamente sus mensajes.
Qué azul es la vida, Miguel, cuando hemos puesto en ella
amor y lucha, palabras que son el pan y el vino,

palabras que ellos no pueden deshonrar todavía,
porque nosotros salimos a la calle con escopeta y cantos.
Están perdidos con nosotros, Miguel.
Qué pueden hacer sino matarnos y aun así
les resulta un mal negocio, sólo pueden
tratar de alquilar un piso frente a nosotros y seguirnos
para aprender a reír y a llorar como nosotros.
Cuando yo escribía versos de amor, que me brotaban
por todas partes, y me moría de tristeza,
errante, abandonado, royendo el alfabeto,
me decían: «Qué grande eres, oh Teócrito!».
Yo no soy Teócrito: tomé a la vida,
me puse frente a ella, la besé hasta vencerla,
y luego me fui por los callejones de las minas
a ver cómo vivían otros hombres.
Y cuando salí con las manos teñidas de basura y dolores,
las levanté mostrándolas en las cuerdas de oro,
y dije: «Yo no comparto el crimen».
Tosieron, se disgustaron mucho, me quitaron el saludo,
me dejaron de llamar Teócrito, y terminaron
por insultarme y mandar toda la policía a encarcelarme,
porque no seguía preocupado exclusivamente de asuntos metafísicos.
Pero yo había conquistado la alegría.
Desde entonces me levanté leyendo las cartas
que traen las aves del mar desde tan lejos,
cartas que vienen mojadas, mensajes que poco a poco
voy traduciendo con lentitud y seguridad: soy meticuloso
como un ingeniero en este extraño oficio.
Y salgo de repente a la ventana. Es un cuadrado
de transparencia, es pura la distancia
de hierbas y peñascos, y así voy trabajando
entre las cosas que amo: olas, piedras, avispas,
con una embriagadora felicidad marina.
Pero a nadie le gusta que estemos alegres, a ti te asignaron
un papel bonachón: «Pero no exagere, no se preocupe»,
y a mí me quisieron clavar en un insectario, entre las lágrimas,
para que éstas me ahogaran y ellos pudieran decir sus discursos en mi
    tumba.

Yo recuerdo un día en la pampa arenosa
del salitre, había quinientos hombres
en huelga. Era la tarde abrasadora
de Tarapacá. Y cuando los rostros habían recogido
toda la arena y el desangrado sol seco del desierto,
yo vi llegar a mi corazón, como una copa que odio,
la vieja melancolía. Aquella hora de crisis,
en la desolación de los salares, en ese minuto débil de
la lucha, en que podríamos haber sido vencidos,
una niña pequeñita y pálida venida de las minas
dijo con una voz valiente en que se juntaban el cristal y el acero
un poema tuyo, un viejo poema tuyo que rueda entre los ojos arrugados
de todos los obreros y labradores de mi patria, de América.
Y aquel trozo de canto tuyo refulgió de repente
en mi boca como una flor purpúrea
y bajó hacia mi sangre, llenándola de nuevo
con una alegría desbordante nacida de tu canto.
Y yo pensé no sólo en ti, sino en tu Venezuela amarga.
Hace años vi un estudiante que tenía en los tobillos
la señal de las cadenas que un general le había impuesto,
y me contó cómo los encadenados trabajaban en los caminos
y los calabozos donde la gente se perdía. Porque así ha sido nuestra
   América:
una llanura con ríos devorantes y constelaciones
de mariposas (en algunos sitios, las esmeraldas son espesas como
   manzanas),
pero siempre a lo largo de la noche y de los ríos
hay tobillos que sangran, antes cerca del petróleo,
hoy cerca del nitrato, en Pisagua, donde un déspota sucio
ha enterrado la flor de mi patria para que muera, y él pueda comerciar
   con los huesos.
Por eso cantas, por eso, para que América deshonrada y herida
haga temblar sus mariposas y recoja sus esmeraldas
sin la espantosa sangre del castigo, coagulada
en las manos de los verdugos y de los mercaderes.
Yo comprendí qué alegre estarías, cerca del Orinoco, cantando,
seguramente, o bien comprando vino para tu casa,
ocupando tu puesto en la lucha y en la alegría,
ancho de hombros, como son los poetas de este tiempo

—con trajes claros y zapatos de camino—.
Desde entonces, he ido pensando que alguna vez te escribiría,
y cuando el amigo llegó, todo lleno de historias tuyas
que se le desprendían de todo el traje
y que bajo los castaños de mi casa se derramaron,
me dije: «Ahora», y tampoco comencé a escribirte.
Pero hoy ha sido demasiado: pasó por mi ventana
no sólo un ave del mar, sino millares,
y recogí las cartas que nadie lee y que ellas llevan
por las orillas del mundo hasta perderlas.
Y entonces en cada una leía palabras tuyas
y eran como las que yo escribo y sueño y canto,
y entonces decidí enviarte esta carta, que termino aquí
para mirar por la ventana el mundo que nos pertenece.

LETTER TO MIGUEL OTERO SILVA, IN CARACAS (1949)

A friend delivered me your letter written
with invisible words, on his suit, in his eyes.
How happy you are, Miguel, how happy we are!
No one's left in a world of stuccoed ulcers
except us, indefinably happy.
I see the crow pass by and it can't harm me.
You observe the scorpion and clean your guitar.
We live among wild beasts, singing, and when we touch
a man, the substance of someone in whom we believed,
and he crumbles like rotten pastry,
you in your Venezuelan patrimony rescue
whatever can be salvaged, while I defend
the live coal of life.
                    What happiness, Miguel!
You wonder where I am? I'll tell you
—giving only details *useful* to the government—
that on this coast full of wild stones,
sea and countryside merge: waves and pines,
eagles and petrels, foam and meadows.
Have you seen from very close up and all day long

how the seabirds fly? It seems as if
they carried the world's letters to their destinations.
Pelicans cruise by like windships,
other birds that fly like arrows and bring
the messages of deceased kings, of princes
entombed with turquoise threads on the Andean coasts,
and gulls made of round whiteness,
that constantly forget their messages.
How blue life is, Miguel, when we've put into it
love and struggle, words that are bread and wine,
words that they cannot yet dishonor,
because we take to the streets with shotgun and songs.
They're lost with us, Miguel.
What can they do but kill us, and even so
it's a poor bargain for them, they can only
try to rent a flat in front of us and shadow us
to learn to laugh and weep like us.
When I wrote love lyrics, which sprouted
from all my pores, and I pined away,
aimless, forlorn, gnawing the alphabet,
they told me: "How great you are, O Theocritus!"
I'm not Theocritus: I took life,
stood before it, kissed it until I conquered it,
and then I went through the mine galleries
to see how other men lived.
And when I emerged with my hands stained with filth and grief
I raised and displayed them on gold chains,
and I said: "I'm not an accomplice to this crime."
They coughed, became very annoyed, withdrew their welcome,
stopped calling me Theocritus, and ended up
insulting me and sending all the police to imprison me,
because I didn't continue to be preoccupied exclusively with
    metaphysical matters.
But I had conquered happiness.
Ever since I've awakened to read letters
that seabirds bring from afar,
letters delivered wet, messages that little by little
I keep translating leisurely and confidently: I'm
meticulous as an engineer in this strange craft.

And suddenly I go to the window. It's a square
of transparency, the distance of grasses
and pinnacles is pure, so I keep working
amid things that I love—waves, stones, wasps—
with an intoxicating marine cheerfulness.
But no one likes us to be happy, to you they assigned
a fool's role: "But don't overdo it, relax,"
and they tried to pin me in an insect collection amid the tears,
so that I'd drown and they could make their speeches on my grave.
I remember a day on the sandy nitrate
pampa, there were five hundred men
on strike. It was the scorching afternoon
of Tarapacá. And when their faces had drawn
all the sand and the dry bloodless desert sun,
I saw old melancholy approach my heart,
like a wineglass of hatred. That critical hour,
in the desolate salt marshes, in that frail minute
of struggle, in which we could have been defeated,
a pale little girl from the mines
recited with a plaintive voice composed of crystal and steel
one of your poems, one of your old poems that rolls between the
     wrinkled eyes
of all the workers and farmhands of my country, of America.
And that fragment of your song suddenly beamed
on my mouth like a purple flower
and ran down to my blood, filling it again
with a surging happiness born of your song.
And I thought not only of you but of your bitter Venezuela.
Years ago, I saw a student whose ankles bore
the scar of the chains that a general had put on him,
and he told me how chain gangs worked on the roads
and people disappeared in the prisons. Because that's how our America
     has been:
a prairie with devouring rivers and constellations
of butterflies (in some places, emeralds are thick as apples),
but always, all night long and along the rivers
there are bleeding ankles, near the petroleum before,
today near the nitrate, in Pisagua, where a dirty despot

has buried the flower of my country so that it will perish, and he can
    market the bones.
That's why you sing, that's why, so that dishonored and wounded
    America
will make its butterflies flutter and will harvest its emeralds
without punishment's ghastly blood, clotted
on the hands of hangmen and merchants.
I realized how happy you'd be, beside the Orinoco, singing,
for sure, or perhaps buying wine for your home,
occupying your place in the struggle or in happiness,
broad shouldered, like the poets of our times
—with light-colored suits and walking shoes.
Ever since, I've been thinking that sometime I'd write you,
and when the friend arrived, chock-full of your stories
that fell from his entire suit and were
scattered under the chestnut trees in my garden,
I told myself: "Now," yet I still didn't sit down to write you.
But today has been too much: not just one but thousands
of seabirds passed by my window, and I collected
the letters which no one reads and which they carry
around the world's sea coasts, until they lose them.
And then, in each one I read your words
and they were like those that I write and dream and sing,
and so I decided to send you this letter, which I sign off now
in order to gaze through the window at the world that is ours.

JACK SCHMITT

V

TO MIGUEL HERNÁNDEZ, MURDERED IN THE PRISONS OF SPAIN

You came to me directly from the Levant. You brought me,
goatherder, your wrinkled innocence,
the scholasticism of old pages, an aroma
of Fray Luis, of citrus blossoms, of manure burned
on the mountains, and on your mask
the cereal asperity of reaped oats
and a honey that measured the earth with your eyes.

You also brought the nightingale in your mouth.
A nightingale spotted with oranges, a thread
of incorruptible song, of naked force.
Ah, youth, gunpowder supervened in the light
and you, with nightingale and rifle, strolling
beneath the moon and the sun of combat.

Now you know, dear friend, how much I couldn't do, now you
know that for me, of all poetry, you were the bluest fire.
Today I put my face on the earth and I hear you,
I hear you, blood, music, moribund honeycomb.

I haven't seen a dazzling race like yours,
or roots so hard, or soldier's hands,
nor have I seen anything alive as your heart
burning in the purple of my own flag.

You live, eternal youth, commoner of yesteryear,
inundated by germs of wheat and springtime,
wrinkled and dark as innate metal,
waiting for the minute that will elevate your armor.

I'm not alone since you died. I'm with those who seek you.
I'm with those who'll come someday to avenge you.
You'll recognize my footsteps among those
that will hurtle over Spain's breast,
crushing Cain so that he'll return
the buried faces to us.

Let those who murdered you know that they'll pay with blood.
Let those who tormented you know that they'll see me someday.
Let the wretches who today include your name
in their books—the Dámasos, the Gerardos, the sons
of bitches, silent accomplices of the executioner—
know that your martyrdom won't be expunged, that your death
will fall on their entire moon of cowards.
And to those who denied you in their rotten laurel,
on American soil, the space that you mantle
with your fluvial crown of bled lightning,

let me give them contemptuous oblivion
for they tried to mutilate me with your absence.

Miguel, far away from the Osuna prison, far away
from cruelty, Mao Tse-tung directs
your poetry dismembered in combat
toward our victory.
                    And humming Prague
building the sweet hive that you sang,
green Hungary cleans its granaries
and dances beside the river that awakens from slumber.
And rising from Varsovia, the naked siren that edifies
brandishes its crystalline sword.
And further beyond the earth becomes gigantic,
                              the earth,
which your song visited, and the steel
that defended your country are secure,
spreading over the firmness
of Stalin and his children.
                    Now the light
approaches your dwelling.
                    Miguel from Spain, star
from razed lands, I won't forget you, dear friend,
I won't forget you, dear friend!
                    But I learned life
with your death: my eyes were slightly blurred,
and within myself I found
not tears but
inexorable arms!
                    Wait for them! Wait for me!

JACK SCHMITT

VIII

CHILE'S VOICES

Before, Chile's voice was the metallic voice
of freedom, of wind and silver,
before, it resounded in the heights
of the newly scarred planet,
of our America assailed
by thickets and centaurs.
Even the intact snow, in vigil,
raised your chorus of honorable leaves,
your rivers' song of free waters,
the blue majesty of your decorum.
It was Isidoro Errázuriz pouring
his combatant crystalline star,
upon obscure and fettered towns,
it was Bilbao with his tumultuous
little planet's brow,
it was Vicuña Mackenna transporting
his innumerable germinal foliage
impregnated with signs and seeds
through other towns where the window
was closed to the light. They entered
and lit the lamp in the night,
and in the bitter day of other towns
they were the snow's loftiest light.

JACK SCHMITT

XIV
I RECALL THE SEA

Chilean, have you gone to the sea lately?
Go in my name, wet your hands and raise them
and from other lands I'll adore those drops
that fall on your face from the infinite water.
I know, I've lived all my sea coast,
the heavy sea of the North, of the barrens, to
the tempestuous weight of foam in the islands.
I recall the sea, the pocked iron coasts
of Coquimbo, the imperious waters of Tralca,
the solitary waves of the South, that formed me.
I recall in Puerto Montt or in the islands, at night,
or returning along the beach, the boat waiting,
and our feet left fire in their tracks,
the mysterious flames of a phosphorescent god.
Each footstep was a streak of phosphorus.
We were writing the earth with stars.
And the boat, skimming the sea, shook
a branch of marine fire, of glowworms,
an innumerable wave of eyes that awakened
once and slept again in their abyss.

JACK SCHMITT

XV
THERE'S NO FORGIVING

I want land, fire, bread, sugar, flour,
sea, books, homeland for all, that's why
I wander about: the traitor's judges pursue me
and his thurifers, like trained monkeys,
try to muddy my reputation.
And I went with *him*, the man who presides,
to the mine shaft, to the desert of the forgotten dawn,
I went with him and told my poor brothers:
"You won't save the threads of tattered clothes,

you won't have this breadless day, you'll be treated
as if you were the country's children." "Now
we're going to distribute beauty, and women's
eyes won't weep for their children."
And when instead of distributing love, in the night
they took that same man off to hunger and martyrdom,
that one who heeded *him* and surrendered
his powerful tree's strength and tenderness,
then I wasn't with the little satrap,
but with that nameless man, with my people.
I want my country for mine own, I want
equal light above
my fiery country's hair,
I want the day's and plow's love,
I want to erase the line they draw
with hatred to segregate the people's bread,
and the man who switched the country's line
until (like a jailer) he delivered it,
handcuffed, to those who pay to hurt it,
I'm not going to sing or silence this,
I'm going to leave their numbers and names
nailed to the wall of dishonor.

JACK SCHMITT

XVII

HAPPY YEAR TO MY COUNTRY IN DARKNESS

Happy year to you, this year, to all
mankind and lands, beloved Araucania.
Between you and my existence a new night
separates us, and forests and rivers and roads.
But my heart gallops toward you
like a dark horse, my little land:
I enter deserts of pure geography,
pass green valleys where the grape accumulates
its green alcohols, the sea of its clusters.
I enter your communities of enclosed gardens,

white as camellias, the pungent smell
of your sawmills, and like a log,
I penetrate the water of rivers that tremble,
quivering and singing with bursting lips.

I remember, on the roads, perhaps at this time,
or else in autumn, they set golden
ears of corn to dry on roofs,
and how many times I was like an enraptured child
seeing gold on the roofs of the poor.

I embrace you, now I must
return to my hideaway. I embrace you
without knowing you: tell me who you are, do you recognize
my voice in the chorus of all that's being born?
Among all the things that surround you, do you hear
my voice, don't you feel yourself surrounded by my accent,
emanating from the earth like natural water?

It's me embracing the entire sweet surface,
my homeland's flowery waist, and I call you
so that we can talk when happiness expires
and to hand you this hour like a closed flower.
Happy New Year to the country in darkness.
Let's walk together, the world is crowned with wheat,
the lofty sky races along, bowling and dashing
its pure towering stones against the night: the new
wineglass has just been filled with a minute
bound to join the river of time that bears us.
This time, this wineglass, this land are yours:
conquer them and hark the dawning of the day.

JACK SCHMITT

IV

THE MEN AND THE ISLANDS

The oceanic men awakened, waters
sang in the islands, from stone to green stone:
textile maidens crossed the enclosure
in which the entwined fire and rain
procreated diadems and drums.
                              The Melanesian moon
was a hard madrepore, sulfurous flowers
came from the ocean, the earth's
daughters trembled like waves
in the nuptial wind of the palms
and harpoons penetrated flesh
in pursuit of the foam's lives.

Canoes rocked on the deserted day,
from the islands like specks of pollen to
the metallic mass of nocturnal America:
diminutive unnamed stars, perfumed
like secret fountains, brimming
with feathers and coral, when
oceanic eyes discovered the dark
heights of the copper coast, the steep
tower of snow, and the men of clay
saw the wet banners
and the remote marine solitude's
atmospheric children dance,
                              the lost branch
of orange blossoms arrived, the wind
of oceanic magnolias came up, the sweetness
of the blue spur on hips,
the kiss of the metal-free islands,

pure as wild honey,
sonorous as sheets from the sky.

JACK SCHMITT

V

RAPA NUI

Tepito-te-henua, navel of the great sea,
workshop of the sea, extinguished diadem.
From your volcanic ash man's
brow rose above the Ocean,
the cracked stone eyes
measured the cyclonic universe,
and the hand that erected the pure
magnitude of your statues was central.

Your religious rock was cut
toward all the Ocean's lines
and the faces of man appeared,
surging from the island's womb,
rising from the empty craters
with their feet entwined to silence.

They were the sentinels and they closed
the cycle of waters that came
from all the wet dominions,
and the sea facing the masks arrested
its tempestuous blue trees.
No one but the faces inhabited
the kingdom's circle. The thread
which enveloped the island's mouth
was silent as the entry of a planet.

And so, in the light of the marine apsis
the stone fable decorates
the immensity with its dead medals,
and the little kings who raise

this entire solitary monarchy
for the eternity of the foam,
return to sea in the invisible night,
return to their sarcophagi of salt.

Only the moonfish that perished in the sand.

Only time that erodes the carved heads.

Only eternity in the sands
know the words:
the sealed light, the dead labyrinth,
the keys of the submerged cup.

JACK SCHMITT

VIII

THE OCEANICS

With no gods but rotten seal hides,
honor of the sea, Yámanas lashed
by the antarctic whip, Alakalufs
smeared with oils and detritus:
amid the walls of crystal and abyss
the little canoe, in the bristling
enmity of icebergs and rain,
carried the sea lions' roving love
and the fire's coals borne
above the endmost mortal waters.

Man, if extermination
did not descend from the rivers of snow
or from the moon hardened
above the glacial vapor of the glaciers,
but from man who, even in the substance
of lost snow and the Ocean's
uttermost waters,
speculated with exiled bones

until he drove you beyond everything,
and today, beyond everything and the snow
and the unleashed tempest of ice
your dugout plies the wild salt
and furious solitude seeking
the haunts of bread, you're Ocean,
a droplet from the sea and its furious blue,
and your frazzled heart calls me
like an incredible fire that refuses to die.

I love the icy plant assailed
by the howling foamy wind,
and at the base of the gorges,
diminutive lucernarian hosts
burn above crustacean lamps
of water stirred by the cold,
and the antarctic dawn in its castle
of pale imaginary splendor.

I love even the turbulent roots
of plants burned by the dawn
of transparent hands,
but this wave
born in ruptures, driven
like love wounded beneath the wind,
rolls to you, seashade, child
of the glacial plumes, tattered oceanic.

JACK SCHMITT

IX
ANTARCTICA

Antarctica, austral crown, cluster
of cold lamps, cinerarium
of ice sundered
from the earthly skin, church rent
by purity, nave opening

over the cathedral of whiteness,
immolator of shattered glass,
hurricane dashed on the walls
of nocturnal snow,
grant me your double breast stirred
by the invading solitude, the channel
of terrifying wind masked
by all the corollas of an ermine,
with all the shipwreck's horns
and the white sinking of worlds,
or your peaceful breast that cleans the cold
like a pure rectangle of quartz,
and everything that's not breathed, the infinite
transparent matter, the open air,
the solitude without land or poverty.
Kingdom of the harshest meridian,
whispery, motionless ice harp,
beside the enemy stars.

All seas are your round sea.
All the Ocean's resistances
concentrated their transparency in you,
and the salt filled you with its castles,
the ice made cities raised
on a crystal spire, the wind
ranged your salty paroxysm
like a jaguar burned by snow.

Your cupolas birthed danger
from the glaciers' vessel,
and in your desolate dorsal, life is
like a vineyard beneath the sea, burning
unconsumed, reserving fire
for the snow's springtime.

JACK SCHMITT

XI

LA MUERTE

Escualos parecidos a las ovas,
al naval terciopelo del abismo,
y que de pronto como angostas lunas
aparecéis con filo empurpurado:
aletas aceitadas en tiniebla,
luto y velocidad, naves del miedo
a las que asciende como una corola
el crimen con su luz vertiginosa,
sin una voz, en una hoguera verde,
en la cuchillería de un relámpago.

Puras formas sombrías que resbalan
bajo la piel del mar, como el amor,
como el amor que invade la garganta,
como la noche que brilla en las uvas,
como el fulgor del vino en los puñales:
anchas sombras de cuero desmedido
como estandartes de amenaza: ramos
de brazos, bocas, lenguas que rodean
con ondulante flor lo que devoran.

En la mínima gota de la vida
aguarda una indecisa primavera
que cerrará con su sistema inmóvil
la cinta ultravioleta que desliza
lo que tembló al caer en el vacío:
un cinturón de fósforo perverso
en la agonía negra del perdido,
y el tapiz del ahogado recubierto
por un bosque de lanzas y murenas
temblorosas y activas como el telar que teje
en la profundidad devoradora.

DEATH

Ulva-like dogfish,
naval velvet of the abyss,
like slivery moons you appear
suddenly with a purple blade:
fins oiled in darkness,
mourning, and speed, vessels of fear
to which crime with its vertiginous light
ascends like a corolla,
voiceless, in a green bonfire,
in the cutlery of lightning.

Pure dark forms that glide
beneath the sea's skin, like love,
like love invading the throat,
like night shining in grapes,
like the flash of wine in daggers:
wide shadows of boundless hide
like foreboding banners: clusters
of arms, mouths, tongues that envelop
whatever they consume with an undulating flower.

In the slightest droplet of life
awaits an indecisive springtime
that will close whatever fell into the void
with its motionless system:
the ultraviolet ribbon that slips
a perverse phosphorous belt
onto the black agony of the lost
and the tapestry of the drowned man covered
by a forest of lances and lampreys
trembling and busy as a loom that weaves
in the devouring depths.

JACK SCHMITT

XII
THE WAVE

The wave rises from the bottom with roots,
offspring of the submerged firmament.
Its elastic invasion was heaved
by the pure potency of the Ocean.
Its eternity appeared flooding
the pavilions of deep power
and each being resisted it,
shed cold fire on its waist
until its snowy might broke away
from the branches of strength.

It rises like a flower from the earth
when it advanced with resolute aroma
to the magnitude of the magnolia,
but this flower that has erupted from the sea floor
brings all the abolished light,
brings all the unburned branches
and the entire fountain of whiteness.

And so when its round eyelids,
its volume, its cups, its corals
swell the sea's skin this entire
being of submarine beings appears:
it is the unity of the sea building itself:
the sea's column rising forth:
all its births and defeats.

The school of salt opened its doors,
all the light exploded striking the sky,
the yeast of wet metal
rose from night to dawn,
all clarity became corolla,
the flower grew until it eroded the stone,
the river of foam ascended to death,
the procellous plants attacked,
the rose poured onto the steel:

the bulwarks of water buckled,
and the sea collapsed without spilling
its tower of crystal and chills.

JACK SCHMITT

XVII
THE ENIGMAS

You've asked me what the crustacean spins
between its gold claws
and I reply: the sea knows.
You wonder what the sea squirt waits for in its transparent bell? What
    does it wait for?
I'll tell you: it's waiting for time like you.
You ask me whom the embrace of the alga Macrocystis reaches?
Inquire, inquire at a certain hour, in a certain sea that I know.
You'll doubtlessly ask me about the accursed ivory of the narwhal, so that
    I'll tell you
how the sea unicorn dies harpooned.
You'll perhaps ask me about the halcyonic feathers that tremble
in the pure origins of the austral sea?
And about the polyp's crystalline construction you're no doubt
    pondering
another problem, trying to unriddle it now?
Do you want to know the electric matter of the sea floor's barbs?
The armed stalactite that breaks as it walks?
The hook of the fisher fish, music stretched out
in the depths like a thread in the water?

I want to tell you that the sea knows this,
that life in its coffers
is wide as the sand, countless and pure,
and amid sanguinary grapes time has polished
the hardness of a petal, the medusa's light,
and it has plucked the bouquet of its coral fibers
from a cornucopia of infinite mother-of-pearl.

I'm nothing but the empty net that advances
human eyes, lifeless in that darkness,
fingers accustomed to the triangle, measurements
of an orange's shy hemisphere.

I lived like you probing
the interminable star,
and in my net, at night, I awakened naked,
the only catch, a fish trapped in the wind.

JACK SCHMITT

XXI
LEVIATHAN

Ark, wrathful peace, slippery
bestial night, antarctic alien,
you won't pass by me displacing
your shadowy floe without my
one day entering your walls and raising
your armor of submarine winter.

Your black fire of an exiled planet
crackled South, the territory
of your silence that moved algae
shook the age of density.

It was just form, magnitude closed
by a tremor of the world in which
his leathery majesty glides by startled
by his own potency and tenderness.

Angry ark lit
with torches of black snow,
when your blind blood was founded
the sea's age slept in gardens,
and in its extension the moon dismantled
the tail of its phosphorescent magnet.

Life crackled
like a blue bonfire, mother medusa,
multiplied tempest of ovaries,
and all growth was purity,
pulsing of a marine tendril.

And so your gigantic rigging was
disposed amid the waters like the passage
of maternity over blood,
and your power was immaculate night
that slipped down engulfing the roots.
Deviance and terror shook
the solitude, and your continent fled
beyond the awaited isles:
but terror passed over the globes
of the glacial moon, and entered your flesh,
assailing wilds that harbored
your terrifying extinguished lamp.
The night went with you: it enveloped you,
bonded a tempestuous ooze to you
and your cyclonic tail churned
ice in which the stars slumbered.

O great wound, hot fountain
churning its thunder vanquished
in the region of the harpoon, stained
by the sea of blood, bled white,
sweet slumbering beast conveyed
like a cyclone of broken hemispheres
to the black longboats of grease
filled with wrath and pestilence.

O great statue murdered in the crystals
of the polar moon, brimming the sky
like a cloud of terror that weeps
and covers the oceans with blood.

JACK SCHMITT

XXIII
NOT ONLY THE ALBATROSS

You're not expected, not by
springtime, not in the corolla's thirst,
not in the purple honey woven
fiber by fiber in vine stocks and clusters,
but in the tempest, in the tattered
torrential cupola of the reef,
in the crevice drilled by dawn,
and even more, on the green spears
of defiance, in the crumbling
solitude of marine wastelands.

Brides of salt, procellarian pigeons,
you lent your back wet by the sea
to every impure aroma of the earth,
and into the wild purity you plunged
the celestial geometry of flight.

You're sacred, not only the one that rode
the gale of the bough like a cyclonic
droplet: not only the one that nests
on the slopes of fury, but
the gull rounded off with snow,
the form of the cormorant upon the foam,
the silver-plated bundle of platinum.

When the pelican fell like a
clenched fist, plunging its volume,
when prophecy soared
on the vast wings of the albatross,
and when the petrel's wind flew
over eternity in motion,
beyond the old cormorants,
my heart took refuge in its cup
and extended the mouth of its song
to the seas and feathers.

Grant me the icy tin that you bear
in your breast to the tempestuous stones,
grant me the condition that collects
in the talons of the osprey,
or the motionless stature that resists
all growth and ruptures,
the abandoned orange-blossom wind
and the taste of the boundless homeland.

JACK SCHMITT

XV: I AM

✳

I

THE FRONTIER (1904)

I first saw trees, ravines
adorned with flowers of wild beauty,
moist territory, forests aflame
and winter behind the world, in flood.
My childhood is wet shoes, broken trunks
fallen in the forest, devoured by vines
and beetles, sweet days upon the oats,
and the golden beard of my father leaving
for the majesty of the railways.

In front of my house the austral water dug
deep defeats, swamps of mournful clays
which in summer were yellow atmosphere
through which the oxcarts creaked and wept,
heavy with nine months of wheat.
Rapid sun of the South:

                 stubble, clouds of smoke
on roads of scarlet earth, banks of rivers
of round lineage, corrals and pastures
in which the high noon honey reverberated.

The dusty world gradually inched into
the sheds, around barrels and twine,
into the storerooms stacked with the red résumé
of hazel trees, all the forest's eyelids.

I seemed to ascend the torrid dress
of summer, with the threshing machines,
over boldu tree slopes, on the varnished earth,
indelible, raised amid the southland beeches,
sticking to the wheels like mangled flesh.

My childhood journeyed the stations: amid
the rails, the stacks of fresh wood,
the house, with no city, protected only
by cattle and apple trees of indescribable perfume
I went, a slender child whose pale form
was impregnated with pristine forests and storerooms.

JACK SCHMITT

III

THE HOUSE

My house, the walls whose fresh,
recently cut wood still smells: dilapidated
homestead that creaked
with every step, and whistled with the warrior wind
of austral weather, becoming stormy
element, strange bird
beneath whose frozen feathers my song grew.
I saw shadows, faces that grew
around my roots like plants, kin
who sang songs in the shade of a tree
and shot amid the wet horses,
women hidden in the shadow
cast by masculine towers,
gallops that lashed the light,
                              rarefied
nights of wrath, barking dogs.
To what lost archipelagoes
did my father slip away, with the land's
dark daybreak, in his howling trains?
Later I loved the smell of coal in smoke,
oils, axles of frozen precision,
and the solemn train crossing winter stretched
over the earth, like a proud caterpillar.
Suddenly the doors trembled.
                              It's my father.
The centurions of the road surround him:

railwaymen wrapped in wet ponchos,
steam and rain cloaked the house
with them, the dining room was filled with
hoarse stories, glasses were drained,
and from those beings to me, like a separate
barrier, inhabited by sorrow,
anguish arrived, sullen
scars, men without money,
the mineral claw of poverty.

JACK SCHMITT

VI

THE TRAVELER (1927)

I plied the seas to the seaports.
The world amid cranes
and storerooms of the sordid shore
revealed stiffs and beggars in its chasm,
companies of the spectral hungry
alongside the ships.
                        Recumbent,
parched countries, in the sand,
resplendent robes, flaming mantles
emerged from the desert, armed
like scorpions, guarding the hole
of petroleum, in the dusty
network of calcined wealth.

I lived in Burma, amid cupolas
of powerful metal, and thickets
where the tiger burned its rings
of bloody gold. From my windows
on Dalhousie Street, the indefinable
odor, moss in the pagodas,
perfumes and excrement, pollen, gunpowder,
of a world saturated with human moisture,
rose up to me.

The streets summoned me
with their countless movements
of saffron fabrics and red spittle,
beside the filthy waves of the Irrawaddy,
soupy water whose blood and oil
ran down discharging its lineage
from the high lands whose gods
at least slept enveloped by its clay.

JACK SCHMITT

VII

FAR FROM HERE

India, I didn't love your tattered clothes,
your dismantled community of rags.
For years I walked with eyes that wanted
to scale the promontories of contempt,
amid cities like green wax,
amid talismans, pagodas
whose bloody pastry
sowed terrible spines.
I saw the miserable wretch heaped
atop the suffering of his brother,
streets like rivers of anguish,
tiny villages crushed
between the flowers' thick fingernails,
and I went in the throngs, a sentry
of time, separating blackened
scars, tribulations of slaves.
I entered temples, steps of stucco
and gemstones, dirty blood and death,
and bestial priests, inebriated
by the burning stupor, quarreling over
coins rolling on the floor,
while, O minuscule human being,
great idols with phosphoric feet
stuck out vindictive tongues,

or crushed flowers slipped over
a phallus of scarlet stone.

JACK SCHMITT

X

THE WAR (1936)

Spain, shrouded in dreams, awakening
like a head of hair with spikes of wheat,
I saw you being born, perhaps amid brambles
and darkness, industrious,
rising amid oak trees and mountains,
traversing the air with open veins.
But I saw you attacked on street corners
by the ancient bandoliers. They
were masked, with their crosses made
of vipers, their feet mired
in the glacial swamp of corpses.
Then I saw your body extricated
from brushlands, broken
on the sand, bloody, opened,
without world, spurred in agony.
To this very day water from your crags
runs amid dungeons, and you bear
your barbed crown in silence,
to see who will last longer, your grief
or the faces that pass without looking at you.
I lived with your dawn of rifles,
and I want people and gunpowder
to shake the dishonored branches
until the dream trembles and the earth's
divided fruits are gathered again.

JACK SCHMITT

You gave me firm love, Spain, with your gifts.
The tenderness that I waited for joined me
and the one who brings the deepest kiss
to my mouth accompanies me.
                             Storms could not
separate her from me,
nor did distances add ground
to the space of love we conquered.
When before the fire, your clothing appeared
amid Spain's fields of grain,
I was double notion, duplicated light,
and bitterness rolled down your face
until it fell on lost stones.
From great sorrow, from bristling harpoons
I rushed into your waters, my love,
like a horse galloping amid
rage and death, and suddenly
a morning apple receives it,
waterfalls of wild tremors.
Since then, love, the wastelands
that created my conduct knew you,
the dark ocean that pursues me,
and chestnuts of the immense Autumn.

Who didn't see you, my sweet love,
struggling beside me, like a
vision, with all the signs
of the star? Who, if he walked
amid the multitudes to seek me
(for I'm a kernel from the human granary),
didn't find you, pressed to my roots,
raised in the song of my blood?

I don't know, my love, if I'll have the time
and place to write once more your fine shade
cast over my pages, my bride:

these days are hard and radiant
and from them we harvest sweetness
kneaded with eyelids and spines.
I no longer recall when you begin:
you were before love,
                    you came
with all the essences of destiny,
and before you, solitude was yours,
perhaps it was your slumbering hair.
Today, wineglass of my love, I only name you,
title of my days, adorable,
and in space you occupy like the day
all the light that the universe possesses.

JACK SCHMITT

from

THE CAPTAIN'S
VERSES

LOS VERSOS

DEL CAPITÁN

1951–1952

IN YOU THE EARTH

Little
rose,
roselet,
at times,
tiny and naked,
it seems
as though you would fit
in one of my hands,
as though I'll clasp you like this
and carry you to my mouth,
but
suddenly
my feet touch your feet and my mouth your lips:
you have grown,
your shoulders rise like two hills,
your breasts wander over my breast,
my arm scarcely manages to encircle the thin
new-moon line of your waist:
in love you have loosened yourself like seawater:
I can scarcely measure the sky's most spacious eyes
and I lean down to your mouth to kiss the earth.

DONALD D. WALSH

THE QUEEN

I have named you queen.
There are taller ones than you, taller.
There are purer ones than you, purer.
There are lovelier than you, lovelier.

But you are the queen.

When you go through the streets
no one recognizes you.
No one sees your crystal crown, no one looks
at the carpet of red gold
that you tread as you pass,
the nonexistent carpet.

And when you appear
all the rivers sound
in my body, bells
shake the sky,
and a hymn fills the world.

Only you and I,
only you and I, my love,
listen to it.

DONALD D. WALSH

THE POTTER

Your whole body holds
a stemmed glass or gentle sweetness destined for me.

When I let my hand climb,
in each place I find a dove
that was looking for me, as if
my love, they had made you of clay
for my very own potter's hands.

Your knees, your breasts,
your waist,
are missing in me, like in the hollow
of a thirsting earth
where they relinquished
a form,

and together
we are complete like one single river,
like one single grain of sand.

MARK EISNER

SEPTEMBER 8

Today, the day was a full glass,
Today, the day was an immense wave,
Today, it was all the earth.

Today the tempestuous sea
lifted us in a kiss
so high that we trembled
in the flash of lightning
and, tied together, descended
and submerged without unraveling.

Today our bodies became immense,
they grew up to the edge of the world
and rolled melting themselves
into one single drop
of wax or meteor.

A new door opened between you and me
and someone, still without a face,
was waiting for us there.

MARK EISNER

TUS MANOS

Cuando tus manos salen,
amor, hacia las mías,
qué me traen volando?
Por qué se detuvieron

en mi boca, de pronto,
por qué las reconozco
como si entonces, antes,
las hubiera tocado,
como si antes de ser
hubieran recorrido
mi frente, mi cintura?

Su suavidad venía
volando sobre el tiempo,
sobre el mar, sobre el humo,
sobre la primavera,
y cuando tú pusiste
tus manos en mi pecho,
reconocí esas alas
de paloma dorada,
reconocí esa greda
y ese color de trigo.

Los años de mi vida
yo caminé buscándolas.
Subí las escaleras,
crucé los arrecifes,
me llevaron los trenes,
las aguas me trajeron,
y en la piel de las uvas
me pareció tocarte.
La madera de pronto
me trajo tu contacto,
la almendra me anunciaba
tu suavidad secreta,
hasta que se cerraron
tus manos en mi pecho
y allí como dos alas
terminaron su viaje.

YOUR HANDS

When your hands go out,
love, toward mine,
what do they bring me flying?
Why did they stop
at my mouth, suddenly,
why do I recognize them
as if then, before,
I had touched them,
as if before they existed
they had passed over
my forehead, my waist?

Their softness came
flying over time,
over the sea, over the smoke,
over the spring,
and when you placed
your hands on my chest,
I recognized those golden
dove wings,
I recognized that clay
and that color of wheat.

All the years of my life
I walked around looking for them.
I went up the stairs,
I crossed the roads,
trains carried me,
waters brought me,
and in the skin of the grapes
I thought I touched you.
The wood suddenly
brought me your touch,
the almond announced to me
your secret softness,
until your hands
closed on my chest

and there like two wings
they ended their journey.

DONALD D. WALSH

TU RISA

Quítame el pan, si quieres,
quítame el aire, pero
no me quites tu risa.

No me quites la rosa,
la lanza que desgranas,
el agua que de pronto
estalla en tu alegría,
la repentina ola
de plata que te nace.

Mi lucha es dura y vuelvo
con los ojos cansados
a veces de haber visto
la tierra que no cambia,
pero al entrar tu risa
sube al cielo buscándome
y abre para mí todas
las puertas de la vida.

Amor mío, en la hora
más oscura desgrana
tu risa, y si de pronto
ves que mi sangre mancha
las piedras de la calle,
ríe, porque tu risa
será para mis manos
como una espada fresca.

Junto al mar en otoño,
tu risa debe alzar

su cascada de espuma,
y en primavera, amor,
quiero tu risa como
la flor que yo esperaba,
la flor azul, la rosa
de mi patria sonora.

Ríete de la noche,
del día, de la luna,
ríete de las calles
torcidas de la isla,
ríete de este torpe
muchacho que te quiere,
pero cuando yo abro
los ojos y los cierro,
cuando mis pasos van,
cuando vuelven mis pasos,
niégame el pan, el aire,
la luz, la primavera,
pero tu risa nunca
porque me moriría.

YOUR LAUGHTER

Take bread away from me, if you wish,
take air away, but
do not take from me your laughter.

Do not take away the rose,
the lanceflower that you pluck,
the water that suddenly
bursts forth in your joy,
the sudden wave
of silver born in you.

My struggle is harsh and I come back
with eyes tired
at times from having seen

the unchanging earth,
but when your laughter enters
it rises to the sky seeking me
and it opens for me all
the doors of life.

My love, in the darkest
hour your laughter
opens, and if suddenly
you see my blood staining
the stones of the street,
laugh, because your laughter
will be for my hands
like a fresh sword.

Next to the sea in the autumn,
your laughter must raise
its foamy cascade,
and in the spring, love,
I want your laughter like
the flower I was waiting for,
the blue flower, the rose
of my echoing country.

Laugh at the night,
at the day, at the moon,
laugh at the twisted
streets of the island,
laugh at this clumsy
boy who loves you,
but when I open
my eyes and close them,
when my steps go,
when my steps return,
deny me bread, air,
light, spring,
but never your laughter
for I would die.

DONALD D. WALSH

THE FICKLE ONE

My eyes went away from me
following a dark girl who went by.

She was made of black mother-of-pearl,
made of dark purple grapes,
and she lashed my blood
with her tail of fire.

After them all
I go.

A pale blonde went by
like a golden plant
swaying her gifts.
And my mouth went
like a wave
discharging on her breast
lightning bolts of blood.

After them all
I go.

But to you, without my moving,
without seeing you, distant you,
go my blood and my kisses,
my dark one and my fair one,
my tall one and my little one,
my broad one and my slender one,
my ugly one, my beauty,
made of all the gold
and of all the silver,
made of all the wheat
and of all the earth,
made of all the water
of the sea waves,
made for my arms,

made for my kisses,
made for my soul.

DONALD D. WALSH

THE SON

Ah son, do you know, do you know
where you come from?

From a lake with white
and hungry gulls.

Next to the water of winter
she and I raised
a red bonfire
wearing out our lips
from kissing each other's souls,
casting all into the fire,
burning our lives.

That's how you came into the world.

But she, to see me
and to see you, one day
crossed the seas
and I, to clasp
her tiny waist,
walked all the earth,
with wars and mountains,
with sands and thorns.

That's how you came into the world.

You come from so many places,
from the water and the earth,
from the fire and the snow,
from so far away you journey

toward the two of us,
from the terrible love
that has enchained us,
that we want to know
what you're like, what you say to us,
because you know more
about the world we gave you.

Like a great storm
we shook
the tree of life
down to the hiddenmost
fibers of the roots
and you appear now
singing in the foliage,
in the highest branch
that with you we reach.

DONALD D. WALSH

THE HURT

I have hurt you, my dear,
I have torn your soul.

Understand me.
Everyone knows who I am,
but that "I am"
is besides a man
for you.

In you I waver, fall
and rise up burning.
You among all beings
have the right
to see me weak.
And your little hand
of bread and guitar
must touch my breast
when it goes off to fight.

That's why I seek in you the firm stone.
Harsh hands I sink in your blood
seeking your firmness
and the depth that I need,
and if I find
only your metallic laughter, if I find
nothing on which to support my harsh steps
adored one, accept
my sadness and my anger,
my enemy hands
destroying you a little
so that you may rise from the clay
refashioned for my struggles.

DONALD D. WALSH

EL SUEÑO

Andando en las arenas
yo decidí dejarte.

Pisaba un barro oscuro
que temblaba,
y hundiéndome y saliendo,
decidí que salieras
de mí, que me pesabas
como piedra cortante,
y elaboré tu pérdida
paso a paso:
cortarte las raíces,
soltarte sola al viento.

Ay en ese minuto,
corazón mío, un sueño
con sus alas terribles
te cubría.

Te sentías tragada por el barro,
y me llamabas y yo no acudía,
te ibas, inmóvil,
sin defenderte
hasta ahogarte en la boca de arena.

Después
mi decisión se encontró con tu sueño,
y desde la ruptura
que nos quebraba el alma
surgimos limpios otra vez, desnudos,
amándonos
sin sueño, sin arena,
completos y radiantes,
sellados por el fuego.

Walking on the sands
I decided to leave you.

I was treading a dark clay
that trembled
and I, sinking and coming out,
decided that you should come out
of me, that you were weighing me down
like a cutting stone,
and I worked out your loss
step by step:
to cut off your roots,
to release you alone into the wind.

Ah in that minute,
my dear, a dream
with its terrible wings
was covering you.

You felt yourself swallowed by the clay,
and you called to me and I did not come,
you were going, motionless,
without defending yourself
until you were smothered in the quicksand.

Afterwards
my decision encountered your dream,
and from the rupture
that was breaking our hearts
we came forth clean again, naked,
loving each other
without dream, without sand,
complete and radiant,
sealed by fire.

DONALD D. WALSH

OBLIVION

All of love in a goblet
as wide as the earth, all
of love with stars and thorns
I gave you, but you walked
with little feet, with dirty heels
upon the fire, putting it out.

Ah great love, small beloved!

I did not stop in the struggle.
I did not stop marching toward life,
toward peace, toward bread for all,
but I lifted you in my arms
and I nailed you to my kisses
and I looked at you as never
again will human eyes look at you.

Ah great love, small beloved!

You did not then measure my stature,
and the man who for you put aside
blood, wheat, water,
you confused him
with the little insect that fell into your skirt.

Ah great love, small beloved!

Do not expect that I will look back at you
in the distance, stay
with what I left you, walk about
with my betrayed photograph,
I shall go on marching,
opening broad roads against the shadow, making
the earth smooth, spreading
the star for those who come.

Stay on the road.
Night has fallen for you.
Perhaps at dawn
we shall see each other again.

Ah great love, small beloved!

DONALD D. WALSH

YOU WOULD COME

You have not made me suffer,
merely wait.

Those tangled
hours, filled
with serpents,
when
my heart stopped and I stifled,
you would come along,
you would come naked and scratched,
bleeding you would reach my bed,
my bride,
and then
all night we walked
sleeping
and when we woke up
you were intact and new,
as if the dark wind of dreams
had newly given
fire to your tresses
and in wheat and silver had submerged
your body and left it dazzling.

I did not suffer, my love,
I was only waiting for you.
You had to change heart
and vision

after having touched the deep
sea zone that my breast gave to you.
You had to leave the water
pure as a drop raised
by a night wave.

My bride, you had
to die and be born, I was waiting for you.
I did not suffer looking for you,
I knew that you would come,
a new woman with what I adore
out of the one that I did not adore,
with your eyes, your hands, and your mouth
but with another heart,
who was beside me at dawn
as if she had always been there
to go on with me forever.

DONALD D. WALSH

THE MOUNTAIN AND THE RIVER

In my country there is a mountain.
In my country there is a river.

Come with me.

Night climbs up to the mountain.
Hunger goes down to the river.

Come with me.

Who are those who suffer?
I do not know, but they are my people.

Come with me.

I do not know, but they call to me
and they say to me: "We suffer."

Come with me.

And they say to me: "Your people,
your luckless people,
between the mountain and the river,
with hunger and grief,
they do not want to struggle alone,
they are waiting for you, friend."

Oh you, the one I love,
little one, red grain
of wheat,

the struggle will be hard,
life will be hard,
but you will come with me.

DONALD D. WALSH

THE FLAG

Stand up with me.

No one would like
more than I to stay
on the pillow where your eyelids
try to shut out the world for me.
There too I would like
to let my blood sleep
surrounding your sweetness.

But stand up,
you, stand up,
but stand up with me
and let us go off together
to fight face to face
against the devil's webs,
against the system that distributes hunger,
against organized misery.

Let's go,
and you, my star, next to me,
newborn from my own clay,
you will have found the hidden spring
and in the midst of the fire you will be
next to me,
with your wild eyes,
raising my flag.

DONALD D. WALSH

LITTLE AMERICA

When I look at the shape
of America on the map,
my love, it is you I see:
the heights of copper on your head,
your breasts, wheat and snow,
your slender waist,
swift throbbing rivers, sweet
hills and meadows
and in the cold of the south your feet end
its geography of duplicated gold.

Love, when I touch you
not only have my hands
explored your delight
but boughs and lands, fruits and water,
the springtime that I love,
the desert moon, the breast
of the wild dove,
the smoothness of stones worn away
by the waters of the sea or the rivers
and the red thickness
of the bush where
thirst and hunger lie in wait.
And thus my spacious country welcomes me,
little America, in your body.

Still more, when I see you lying down
I see in your skin, in your oaten color,
the nationality of my affection.
Because from your shoulders
the cane cutter
of blazing Cuba
looks at me, covered with dark sweat,
and from your throat
fishermen who tremble
in the damp houses of the shore
sing to me their secret.

And so along your body,
little adored America,
the lands and the peoples
interrupt my kisses
and your beauty then
not only lights the fire
that burns unquenched among us
but with your love it is calling to me
and across your life
it is giving me the life that I lack
and to the taste of your love is added the clay,
the kiss of the earth that waits for me.

DONALD D. WALSH

EPITHALAMIUM

Do you remember when
in winter
we reached the island?
The sea raised toward us
a crown of cold.
On the walls the climbing vines
murmured letting
dark leaves fall
as we passed.
You too were a little leaf
that trembled on my chest.
Life's wind put you there.
At first I did not see you: I did not know
that you were walking with me,
until your roots
pierced my chest,
joined the threads of my blood,
spoke through my mouth,
flourished with me.
Thus was your inadvertent presence,
invisible leaf or branch,

and suddenly my heart
was filled with fruits and sounds.
You occupied the house
that darkly awaited you
and then you lit the lamps.
Do you remember, my love,
our first steps on the island?
The gray stones knew us,
the rain squalls,
the shouts of the wind in the shadow.
But the fire was
our only friend,
next to it we hugged
the sweet winter love
with four arms.
The fire saw our naked kiss grow
until it touched hidden stars,
and it saw grief be born and die
like a broken sword
against invincible love.
Do you remember,
oh sleeper in my shadow,
how sleep would grow
in you,
from your bare breast
open with its twin domes
toward the sea, toward the wind of the island,
and how I in your dream sailed
free, in the sea and in the wind
yet tied and sunken
in the blue volume of your sweetness?
Oh sweet, my sweet,
spring changed
the island's walls.
A flower appeared like a drop
of orange blood,
and then the colors discharged
all their pure weight.
The sea reconquered its transparency,

night in the sky
outlined its clusters
and now all things murmured
our name of love, stone by stone
they said our name and our kiss.
The island of stone and moss
echoed in the secret of its grottoes
like the song in your mouth,
and the flower that was born
between the crevices of the stone
with its secret syllable
spoke, as it passed, your name
of blazing plant
and the steep rock, raised
like the wall of the world,
knew my song, well beloved,
and all things spoke of
your love, my love, beloved,
because earth, time, sea, island,
life, tide,
the seed that half opens
its lips in the earth,
the devouring flower,
the movement of spring,
everything recognizes us.
Our love was born
outside the walls,
in the wind,
in the night,
in the earth,
and that's why the clay and the flower,
the mud and the roots
know your name,
and know that my mouth
joined yours
because we were sown together in the earth
and we alone did not know it
and that we grow together
and flower together

and therefore
when we pass,
your name is on the petals
of the rose that grows on the stone,
my name is in the grottoes.
They know it all,
we have no secrets,
we have grown together
but we did not know it.
The sea knows our love, the stones
of the rocky height
know that our kisses flowered
with infinite purity,
as in their crevices a scarlet
mouth dawns:
just as our love and the kiss
that joins your mouth and mine
in an eternal flower.
My love,
sweet spring,
flower and sea, surround us.
We did not change it
for our winter,
when the wind
began to decipher your name
that today at all hours it repeats,
when
the leaves did not know
that you were a leaf,
when
the roots
did not know that you were seeking me
in my breast.
Love, love,
spring
offers us the sky,
but the dark earth
is our name,
our love belongs

to all time and the earth.
Loving each other, my arm
beneath your neck of sand,
we shall wait
as earth and time change
on the island,
as the leaves fall
from the silent climbing vines,
as autumn departs
through the broken window.
But we
are going to wait for
our friend,
our red-eyed friend,
the fire,
when the wind again
shakes the frontiers of the island
and does not know the names
of everyone,
winter
will seek us, my love,
always
it will seek us, because we know it,
because we do not fear it,
because we have
with us
fire
forever,
we have
earth with us
forever,
spring with us
forever,
and when a leaf
falls
from the climbing vines,
you know, my love,
what name is written
on that leaf,

a name that is yours and mine,
our love name, a single
being, the arrow
that pierced winter,
the invincible love,
the fire of the days,
a leaf
that dropped upon my breast,
a leaf from the tree
of life
that made a nest and sang,
that put out roots,
that gave flowers and fruits.
And so you see, my love,
how I move
around the island,
around the world,
safe in the midst of spring,
crazy with light in the cold,
walking tranquil in the fire,
lifting your petal
weight in my arms
as if I had never walked
except with you, my heart,
as if I could not walk
except with you,
as if I could not sing
except when you sing.

DONALD D. WALSH

LA CARTA EN EL CAMINO

Adiós, pero conmigo
serás, irás adentro
de una gota de sangre que circule en mis venas
o fuera, beso que me abraza el rostro
o cinturón de fuego en mi cintura.

Dulce mía, recibe
el gran amor que salió de mi vida
y que en ti no encontraba territorio
como el explorador perdido
en las islas del pan y de la miel.
Yo te encontré después
de la tormenta,
la lluvia lavó el aire
y en el agua
tus dulces pies brillaron como peces.

Adorada, me voy a mis combates.

Arañaré la tierra para hacerte una cueva
y allí tu Capitán
te esperará con flores en el lecho.
No pienses más, mi dulce,
en el tormento
que pasó entre nosotros
como un rayo de fósforo
dejándonos tal vez su quemadura.
La paz llegó también porque regreso
a luchar a mi tierra,
y como tengo el corazón completo
con la parte de sangre que me diste
para siempre,
y como
llevo
las manos llenas de tu ser desnudo,
mírame,
mírame,
mírame por el mar, que voy radiante,
mírame por la noche que navego,
y mar y noche son los ojos tuyos.
No he salido de ti cuando me alejo.
Ahora voy a contarte:
mi tierra será tuya,
yo voy a conquistarla,
no sólo para dártela,

sino que para todos,
para todo mi pueblo.
Saldrá el ladrón de su torre algún día.
Y el invasor será expulsado.
Todos los frutos de la vida
crecerán en mis manos
acostumbrados antes a la pólvora.
Y sabré acariciar las nuevas flores
porque tú me enseñaste la ternura.
Dulce mía, adorada,
vendrás conmigo a luchar cuerpo a cuerpo
porque en mi corazón viven tus besos
como banderas rojas,
y si caigo, no sólo
me cubrirá la tierra
sino este gran amor que me trajiste
y que vivió circulando en mi sangre.
Vendrás conmigo,
en esa hora te espero,
en esa hora y en todas las horas,
en todas las horas te espero.
Y cuando venga la tristeza que odio
a golpear a tu puerta,
dile que yo te espero
y cuando la soledad quiera que cambies
la sortija en que está mi nombre escrito,
dile a la soledad que hable conmigo,
que yo debí marcharme
porque soy un soldado,
y que allí donde estoy,
bajo la lluvia o bajo
el fuego,
amor mío, te espero.
Te espero en el desierto más duro
y junto al limonero florecido,
en todas las partes donde esté la vida,
donde la primavera está naciendo,
amor mío, te espero.

Cuando te digan: "Ese hombre
no te quiere," recuerda
que mis pies están solos en esa noche, y buscan
los dulces y pequeños pies que adoro.
Amor, cuando te digan
que te olvidé, y aun cuando
sea yo quien lo dice,
cuando yo te lo diga,
no me creas,
quién y cómo podrían
cortarte de mi pecho
y quién recibiría
mi sangre
cuando hacia ti me fuera desangrando?
Pero tampoco puedo
olvidar a mi pueblo.
Voy a luchar en cada calle,
detrás de cada piedra.
Tu amor también me ayuda:
es una flor cerrada
que cada vez me llena con su aroma
y que se abre de pronto
dentro de mí como una gran estrella.

Amor mío, es de noche.

El agua negra, el mundo
dormido me rodean.
Vendrá luego la aurora,
y yo mientras tanto te escribo
under rain or under
fire,
para decirte: "Te amo."
Para decirte "Te amo," cuida,
limpia, levanta,
defiende
nuestro amor, alma mía.
Yo te lo dejo como si dejara

un puñado de tierra con semillas.
De nuestro amor nacerán vidas.
En nuestro amor beberán agua.
Tal vez llegará un día
en que un hombre
y una mujer, iguales
a nosotros,
tocarán este amor y aún tendrá fuerza
para quemar las manos que lo toquen.
Quiénes fuimos? Qué importa?
Tocarán este fuego
y el fuego, dulce mía, dirá tu simple nombre
y el mío, el nombre
que tú sola supiste porque tú sola
sobre la tierra sabes
quién soy, y porque nadie me conoció como una,
como una sola de tus manos,
porque nadie
supo cómo ni cuándo
mi corazón estuvo ardiendo:
tan sólo
tus grandes ojos pardos lo supieron,
tu ancha boca,
tu piel, tus pechos,
tu vientre, tus entrañas
y el alma tuya que yo desperté
para que se quedara
cantando hasta el fin de la vida.

Amor, te espero.

Adiós, amor, te espero.

Amor, amor, te espero.

Y así esta carta se termina
sin ninguna tristeza:
están firmes mis pies sobre la tierra,
mi mano escribe esta carta en el camino,

y en medio de la vida estaré
siempre
junto al amigo, frente al enemigo,
con tu nombre en la boca
y un beso que jamás
se apartó de la tuya.

LETTER ON THE ROAD

Farewell, but you will be
with me, you will go within
a drop of blood circulating in my veins
or outside, a kiss that burns my face
or a belt of fire at my waist.
My sweet, accept
the great love that came out of my life
and that in you found no territory
like the explorer lost
in the isles of bread and honey.
I found you after
the storm,
the rain washed the air
and in the water
your sweet feet gleamed like fishes.

Adored one, I am off to my fighting.

I shall scratch the earth to make you a cave
and there your Captain
will wait for you with flowers in the bed.
Think no more, my sweet,
about the anguish
that went on between us
like a bolt of phosphorus
leaving us perhaps its burning.
Peace arrived too because I return
to my land to fight,

and as I have a whole heart
with the share of blood that you gave me
forever,
and as
I have
my hands filled with your naked being,
look at me,
look at me,
look at me across the sea, for I go radiant,
look at me across the night through which I sail,
and sea and night are those eyes of yours.
I have not left you when I go away.
Now I am going to tell you:
my land will be yours,
I am going to conquer it,
not just to give it to you,
but for everyone,
for all my people.
The thief will come out of his tower someday.
And the invader will be expelled.
All the fruits of life
will grow in my hands
accustomed once to powder.
And I shall know how to touch the new flowers gently
because you taught me tenderness.
My sweet, adored one,
you will come with me to fight face-to-face
because your kisses live in my heart
like red banners,
and if I fall, not only
will earth cover me
but also this great love that you brought me
and that lived circulating in my blood.
You will come with me,
at that hour I wait for you,
at that hour and at every hour,
at every hour I wait for you.
And when the sadness that I hate comes
to knock at your door,

tell her that I am waiting for you
and when loneliness wants you to change
the ring in which my name is written,
tell loneliness to talk with me,
that I had to go away
because I am a soldier,
and that there where I am,
my love, I wait for you.
I wait for you in the harshest desert
and next to the flowering lemon tree,
in every place where there is life,
where spring is being born,
my love, I wait for you.
When they tell you: "That man
does not love you," remember
that my feet are alone in that night, and they seek
the sweet and tiny feet that I adore.
Love, when they tell you
that I have forgotten you, and even when
it is I who say it,
when I say it to you,
do not believe me,
who could and how could anyone
cut you from my heart
and who would receive
my blood
when I went bleeding toward you?
But still I cannot
forget my people.
I am going to fight in each street,
behind each stone.
Your love also helps me:
it is a closed flower
that constantly fills me with its aroma
and that opens suddenly
within me like a great star.

My love, it is night.

The black water, the sleeping
world surround me.
Soon dawn will come,
and meanwhile I write you
to tell you: "I love you."
To tell you "I love you," care for,
clean, lift up,
defend
our love, my darling.
I leave it with you as if I left
a handful of earth with seeds.
From our love lives will be born.
In our love they will drink water.
Perhaps a day will come
when a man
and a woman, like
us,
will touch this love and it will still have the strength
to burn the hands that touch it.
Who were we? What does it matter?
They will touch this fire
and the fire, my sweet, will say your simple name
and mine, the name
that only you knew, because you alone
upon earth know
who I am, and because nobody knew me like one,
like just one hand of yours,
because nobody
knew how or when
my heart was burning:
only
your great dark eyes knew,
your wide mouth,
your skin, your breasts,
your belly, your insides,
and your soul that I awoke
so that it would go on
singing until the end of life.

Love, I am waiting for you.

Farewell, love, I am waiting for you.

Love, love, I am waiting for you.

And so this letter ends
with no sadness:
my feet are firm upon the earth,
my hand writes this letter on the road,
and in the midst of life I shall be
always
beside the friend, facing the enemy,
with your name on my mouth
and a kiss that never
broke away from yours.

DONALD D. WALSH

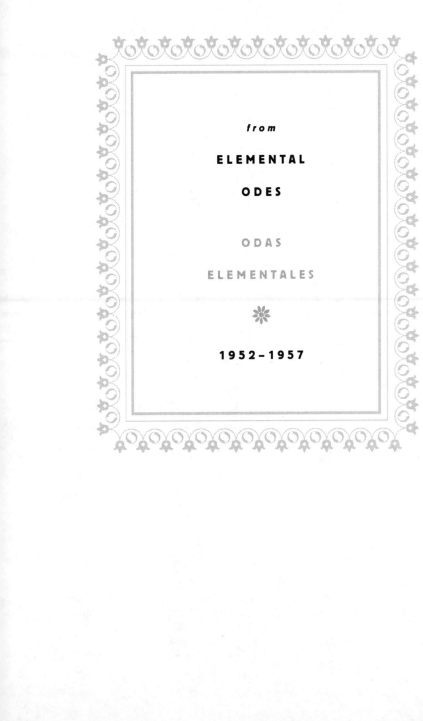

from

ELEMENTAL

ODES

ODAS

ELEMENTALES

1952–1957

THE INVISIBLE MAN

I laugh,
I smile
at the old poets,
and love all the
poetry they wrote,
all the dew,
moon, diamond, drops
of submerged silver
with which my elder brother
adorned the rose;
but
I smile;
they always say "I,"
at every turn
something happens,
it's always "I,"
only they or
the dear heart they love
walk through the streets,
only they,
no fishermen pass by,
or booksellers,
no masons pass by,
no one falls
from a scaffolding,
no one suffers,
no one loves,
except my poor brother,
the poet,
everything happens
to him
and to his dear beloved,

no one lives
but him, him alone,
no one weeps from hunger
or from anger,
in his poems no one suffers
because he can't
pay the rent,
in poetry no one
is ever thrown into the street
with all his furniture,
and nothing happens
in the factories,
no, nothing,
umbrellas and goblets are manufactured,
weapons and locomotives,
ores are mined
by scraping hell,
there is a strike,
soldiers come
and fire,
they fire against the people,
which is to say,
against poetry,
but my brother
the poet
was in love,
or was suffering
because all his emotion
is for the sea,
he loves remote ports
for their names,
and he writes about oceans
he doesn't know,
when life is as full
as an ear of corn with grain
he passes by, never knowing
how to harvest it,
he rides the waves
without ever touching land,

and, occasionally,
he is profoundly moved
and melancholy,
he is too big
to fit inside his skin,
he gets tangled and untangles himself,
he declares he is maudit,
with great difficulty he carries the cross
of darkness,
he believes that he is different from
anyone else in the world,
he eats bread every day
but he's never seen a
baker
or gone to a meeting
of a bakers' union,
and so my poor brother
is deliberately dark,
he twists and writhes
and finds himself
interesting,
interesting,
that's the word,
I am no better
than my brother,
but I smile,
because when I walk through the streets
—the only one who does not exist—
life flows around me
like rivers,
I am the only one
who is invisible,
no mysterious shadows,
no gloom and darkness,
everyone speaks to me,
everyone wants to tell me things,
to talk about their relatives,
their misery and
their joy,

everyone passes by, and everyone
tells me something,
look at all the things they do!
They cut wood,
string electric lines,
bake bread late into the night,
our daily bread,
with an iron pick
they pierce the entrails
of the earth
and convert the iron
into locks,
they climb into the sky and
carry letters and sobs and kisses,
someone is standing
in every doorway,
someone is being born,
or the one I love is waiting for me,
and as I walk by, things
ask me to sing them,
but I haven't time,
I must think about everything,
I must go home,
go by the Party office;
what can I do,
everything asks me
to speak,
everything asks me
to sing, sing forever,
everything is saturated with
dreams and sound,
life is a box
filled with songs, the box opens
and a flock
of birds
flies out
and wants to tell me something,
perching on my shoulders,
life is a struggle,

like an advancing river,
and men
want to tell me,
tell you,
why they struggle,
and, if they die,
why they die,
and I walk by and I haven't
time for so many lives,
I want
them all to live
through my life,
to sing through my song,
I am not important,
I have no time
for my own affairs,
night and day
I must write down what's happening,
not forgetting anyone.
It's true that suddenly
I get tired,
I look at the stars,
I lie down in the grass, an insect
the color of a violin goes by,
I place my arm across
a small breast
or beneath the waist
of the woman I love,
and I look at the hard
velvet
of the night trembling
with frozen constellations,
then
I feel a wave of mysteries
rising in my soul,
childhood,
weeping in corners,
melancholy adolescence,
I feel sleepy

and I sleep
like a log,
I am immediately
asleep,
with or without the stars,
with or without my love,
and when I get up
the night is gone,
the street has awakened before me,
the poor girls of the neighborhood
are on their way to work,
fishermen are returning
from the sea,
miners
in new shoes
are going down into the mines,
everything's alive,
everyone's
hurrying to and fro,
and I scarcely have time
to get into my clothes,
I must run:
no one must
pass by without my knowing
where he's going,
what he's doing.
I cannot live
without life,
without man's being man,
and I run and look and listen
and sing,
stars have nothing
to do with me,
solitude bears no flowers,
no fruit.
For my life, give me
all lives,
give me all the sorrow
of all the world

and I will transform it
into hope.
Give me
all the joys,
even the most secret,
for if not,
how will they be known?
I must tell of them,
give me
the daily
struggle,
because these things are my song,
and so we will go together,
shoulder to shoulder,
all men,
my song unites them:
the song of the invisible man
who sings with all men.

MARGARET SAYERS PEDEN

ODA A LA ALCACHOFA

La alcachofa
de tierno corazón
se vistió de guerrero,
erecta, construyó
una pequeña cúpula,
se mantuvo
impermeable
bajo
sus escamas,
a su lado,
los vegetales locos
se encresparon,
se hicieron
zarcillos, espadañas,
bulbos conmovedores,

en el subsuelo
durmió la zanahoria
de bigotes rojos,
la viña
resecó los sarmientos
por donde sube el vino,
la col
se dedicó
a probarse faldas,
el orégano
a perfumar el mundo,
y la dulce
alcachofa
allí en el huerto,
vestida de guerrero,
bruñida
como una granada,
orgullosa,
y un día
una con otra
en grandes cestos
de mimbre, caminó
por el mercado
a realizar su sueño:
la milicia.
En hileras
nunca fue tan marcial
como en la feria,
los hombres
entre las legumbres
con sus camisas blancas
eran
mariscales
de las alcachofas,
las filas apretadas,
las voces de comando,
y la detonación
de una caja que cae,
pero

entonces
viene
María
con su cesto,
escoge
una alcachofa,
no le teme,
la examina, la observa
contra la luz como si fuera un huevo,
la compra,
la confunde
en su bolsa
con un par de zapatos,
con un repollo y una
botella
de vinagre
hasta
que entrando a la cocina
la sumerge en la olla.
Así termina
en paz
esta carrera
del vegetal armado
que se llama alcachofa,
luego
escama por escama
desvestimos
la delicia
y comemos
la pacífica pasta
de su corazón verde.

ODE TO THE ARTICHOKE

The tender-
hearted artichoke
dressed in its armor,

built its modest cupola
and stood
erect,
impenetrable
beneath
a lamina of leaves.
Around it,
maddened vegetables,
ruffling their leaves,
contrived
creepers, cattails,
bulbs, and tubers to astound;
beneath the ground
slept
the red-whiskered carrot;
above, the grapevine
dried its runners,
bearers of the wine;
the cabbage
preened itself,
arranging its flounces;
oregano
perfumed the world,
while the gentle
artichoke
stood proudly in the garden,
clad in armor
burnished
to a pomegranate
glow.
And then one day,
with all the other artichokes
in willow baskets,
our artichoke
set out to market
to realize its dream:
life as a soldier.
Amid the ranks
never was it so martial

as in the fair,
white-shirted
men
among the greens
marshaled
the field
of artichokes;
close formations,
shouted commands,
and the detonation
of a falling crate.
But
look,
here comes
Maria
with her shopping basket.
Unintimidated,
she selects
our artichoke,
examines it, holds it to
the light as if it were an egg;
she buys it,
she drops it
in a shopping bag
that holds a pair of shoes,
a cabbage head, and one
bottle
of vinegar.
Once home
and in the kitchen
she drowns it in a pot.
And thus ends
in peace
the saga
of the armored vegetable
we call the artichoke,
as
leaf by leaf
we unsheathe

its delights
and eat
the peaceable flesh
of its green heart.

MARGARET SAYERS PEDEN

ODE TO THE ARTICHOKE

The tender-hearted
artichoke
got dressed as a warrior,
erect, built
a little cupola,
stood
impermeable
under
its scales,
around it
the crazy vegetables
bristled,
grew
astonishing tendrils,
cattails, bulbs,
in the subsoil
slept the carrot
with its red whiskers,
the grapevine
dried the runners
through which it carries the wine,
the cabbage
devoted itself
to trying on skirts,
oregano
to perfuming the world,
and the gentle
artichoke
stood there in the garden,

dressed as a warrior,
burnished
like a pomegranate,
proud,
and one day
along with the others
in large willow
baskets, it traveled
to the market
to realize its dream:
the army.
Amid the rows
never was it so military
as at the fair,
men
among the vegetables
with their white shirts
were
marshals
of the artichokes,
the tight ranks,
the voices of command,
and the detonation
of a falling crate,
but
then
comes
Maria
with her basket,
picks
an artichoke,
isn't afraid of it,
examines it, holds it
to the light as if it were an egg,
buys it,
mixes it up
in her bag
with a pair of shoes,
with a head of cabbage and a

bottle
of vinegar
until
entering the kitchen
she submerges it in a pot.
Thus ends
in peace
the career
of the armored vegetable
which is called artichoke,
then
scale by scale
we undress
its delight
and we eat
the peaceful flesh
of its green heart.

STEPHEN MITCHELL

ODA AL ÁTOMO

Pequeñísima
estrella,
parecías
para siempre
enterrada
en el metal: oculto,
tu diabólico
fuego.
Un día
golpearon
en la puerta
minúscula:
era el hombre.
Con una
descarga
te desencadenaron,

viste el mundo,
saliste
por el día,
recorriste
ciudades,
tu gran fulgor llegaba
a iluminar las vidas,
eras
una fruta terrible,
de eléctrica hermosura,
venías
a apresurar las llamas
del estío,
y entonces
llegó
armado
con anteojos de tigre
y armadura,
con camisa cuadrada,
sulfúricos bigotes,
cola de puerco espín,
llegó el guerrero
y te sedujo:
duerme,
te dijo,
enróllate,
átomo, te pareces
a un dios griego,
a una primaveral
modista de París,
acuéstate
en mi uña,
entra en esta cajita,
y entonces
el guerrero
te guardó en su chaleco
como si fueras sólo
píldora
norteamericana,

y viajó por el mundo
dejándote caer
en Hiroshima.

Despertamos.

La aurora
se había consumido.
Todos los pájaros
cayeron calcinados.
Un olor
de ataúd,
gas de las tumbas,
tronó por los espacios.
Subió horrenda
la forma del castigo
sobrehumano,
hongo sangriento, cúpula,
humareda,
espada
del infierno.
Subió quemante el aire
y se esparció la muerte
en ondas paralelas,
alcanzando
a la madre dormida
con su niño,
al pescador del río
y a los peces,
a la panadería
y a los panes,
al ingeniero
y a sus edificios,
todo
fue polvo
que mordía,
aire
asesino.

La ciudad
desmoronó sus últimos alvéolos,
cayó, cayó de pronto,
derribada,
podrida,
los hombres
fueron súbitos leprosos,
tomaban
la mano de sus hijos
y la pequeña mano
se quedaba en sus manos.
Así, de tu refugio,
del secreto
manto de piedra
en que el fuego dormía
te sacaron,
chispa enceguecedora,
luz rabiosa,
a destruir las vidas,
a perseguir lejanas existencias,
bajo el mar,
en el aire,
en las arenas,
en en último
recodo de los puertos,
a borrar
las semillas,
a asesinar los gérmenes,
a impedir la corola,
te destinaron, átomo,
a dejar arrasadas
las naciones,
a convertir el amor en negra pústula,
a quemar amontonados corazones
y aniquilar la sangre.

Oh chispa loca,
vuelve
a tu mortaja,

entiérrate
en tus mantos minerales,
vuelve a ser piedra ciega,
desoye a los bandidos,
colabora
tú, con la vida, con la agricultura,
suplanta los motores,
eleva la energía,
fecunda los planetas.
Ya no tienes
secreto,
camina
entre los hombres
sin máscara
terrible,
apresurando el paso
y extendiendo
los pasos de los frutos,
separando
montañas,
enderezando ríos,
fecundando,
átomo,
desbordada
copa
cósmica,
vuelve
a la paz del racimo,
a la velocidad de la alegría,
vuelve al recinto
de la naturaleza,
ponte a nuestro servicio,
y en vez de las cenizas
mortales
de tu máscara,
en vez de los infiernos desatados
de tu cólera,
en vez de la amenaza
de tu terrible claridad, entréganos

tu sobrecogedora
rebeldía
para los cereales,
tu magnetismo desencadenado
para fundar la paz entre los hombres,
y así no será infierno
tu luz deslumbradora,
sino felicidad,
matutina esperanza,
contribución terrestre.

ODE TO THE ATOM

Infinitesimal
star,
you seemed
forever
buried
in metal, hidden,
your diabolic
fire.
One day
someone knocked
at your tiny
door:
it was man.
With one
explosion
he unchained you,
you saw the world,
you came out
into the daylight,
you traveled through
cities,
your great brilliance
illuminated lives,
you were a

terrible fruit
of electric beauty,
you came to
hasten the flames
of summer,
and then
wearing
a predator's eyeglasses,
armor,
and a checked shirt,
sporting sulfuric mustaches
and a prehensile tail,
came
the warrior
and seduced you:
sleep,
he told you,
curl up,
atom, you resemble
a Greek god,
a Parisian modiste
in springtime,
lie down here
on my fingernail,
climb into this little box,
and then
the warrior
put you in his jacket
as if you were nothing but
a North American
pill,
and he traveled through the world
and dropped you
on Hiroshima.

We awakened.

The dawn
had been consumed.

All the birds
burned to ashes.
An odor
of coffins,
gas from tombs,
thundered through space.
The shape of punishment arose,
hideous,
superhuman,
bloody mushroom, dome,
cloud of smoke,
sword
of hell.
Burning air arose,
spreading death
on parallel waves,
reaching
the mother sleeping
with her child,
the river fisherman
and the fish,
the bakery
and the bread,
the engineer
and his buildings;
everything
was acid
dust,
assassin
air.

The city
crumbled its last honeycombs
and fell, fell suddenly,
demolished,
rotten;
men
were instant lepers,
they took

their children's hand
and the little hand
fell off in theirs.
So, from your refuge
in the secret
mantle of stone
in which fire slept
they took you,
blinding spark,
raging light,
to destroy lives,
to threaten distant existences,
beneath the sea,
in the air,
on the sands,
in every twist and turn
of the ports,
to destroy
seeds,
to kill cells,
to stunt the corolla,
they destined you, atom,
to level
nations,
to turn love into a black pustule,
to burn heaped-up hearts
and annihilate blood.

Mad spark,
go back
to your shroud,
bury yourself
in your mineral mantle,
be blind stone once again,
ignore the outlaws,
and collaborate
with life, with growing things,
replace motors,
elevate energy,

fertilize planets.
You have no secret
now,
walk
among men
without your terrible
mask,
pick up your pace
and pace
the picking of the fruit,
parting
mountains,
straightening rivers,
making fertile,
atom,
overflowing
cosmic
cup,
return
to the peace of the vine,
to the velocity of joy,
return to the province
of nature,
place yourself at our service,
and instead of the fatal
ashes
of your mask,
instead of the unleashed infernos
of your wrath,
instead of the menace
of your terrible light, deliver to us
your amazing
rebelliousness
for our grain,
your unchained magnetism
to found peace among men,
and then your dazzling light
will be happiness,
not hell,

hope of morning,
gift to earth.

MARGARET SAYERS PEDEN

ODA A LA CRÍTICA

Yo escribí cinco versos:
uno verde,
otro era un pan redondo,
el tercero una casa levantándose,
el cuarto era un anillo,
el quinto verso era
corto como un relámpago
y al escribirlo
me dejó en la razón su quemadura.

Y bien, los hombres,
las mujeres,
vinieron y tomaron
la sencilla materia,
brizna, viento, fulgor, barro, madera,
y con tan poca cosa
construyeron
paredes, pisos, sueños.
En una línea de mi poesía
secaron ropa al viento.
Comieron
mis palabras,
las guardaron
junto a la cabecera,
vivieron con un verso,
con la luz que salió de mi costado.
Entonces,
llegó un crítico mudo
y otro lleno de lenguas,
y otros, otros llegaron

ciegos o llenos de ojos,
elegantes algunos
como claveles con zapatos rojos,
otros estrictamente
vestidos de cadáveres,
algunos partidarios
del rey y su elevada monarquía,
otros se habían
enredado en la frente
de Marx y pataleaban en su barba,
otros eran ingleses,
sencillamente ingleses,
y entre todos
se lanzaron
con dientes y cuchillos,
con diccionarios y otras armas negras,
con citas respetables,
se lanzaron
a disputar mi pobre poesía
a las sencillas gentes
que la amaban:
y la hicieron embudos,
la enrollaron,
la sujetaron con cien alfileres,
la cubrieron con polvo de esqueleto,
la llenaron de tinta,
la escupieron con suave
benignidad de gatos,
la destinaron a envolver relojes,
la protegieron y la condenaron,
le arrimaron petróleo,
le dedicaron húmedos tratados,
la cocieron con leche,
le agregaron pequeñas piedrecitas,
fueron borrándole vocales,
fueron matándole
sílabas y suspiros,
la arrugaron e hicieron
un pequeño paquete

que destinaron cuidadosamente
a sus desvanes, a sus cementerios,
luego
se retiraron uno a uno
enfurecidos hasta la locura
porque no fui bastante
popular para ellos
o impregnados de dulce menosprecio
por mi ordinaria falta de tinieblas
se retiraron
todos
y entonces,
otra vez,
junto a mi poesía
volvieron a vivir
mujeres y hombres,
de nuevo
hicieron fuego,
construyeron casas,
comieron pan,
se repartieron la luz
y en el amor unieron
relámpago y anillo.
Y ahora,
perdonadme, señores,
que interrumpa este cuento
que les estoy contando
y me vaya a vivir
para siempre
con la gente sencilla.

ODE TO CRITICISM

I wrote five poems:
one was green,
another a round wheaten loaf,

the third was a house, abuilding,
the fourth a ring,
and the fifth was
brief as a lightning flash,
and as I wrote it,
it branded my reason.

Well, then, men
and women
came and took
my simple materials,
breeze, wind, radiance, clay, wood,
and with such ordinary things
constructed
walls, floors, and dreams.
On one line of my poetry
they hung out the wash to dry.
They ate my words
for dinner,
they kept them
by the head of their beds,
they lived with poetry,
with the light that escaped from my side.
Then
came a mute critic,
then another babbling tongues,
and others, many others, came,
some blind, some all-seeing,
some of them as elegant
as carnations with bright red shoes,
others as severely
clothed as corpses,
some were partisans
of the king and his exalted monarchy,
others had been snared
in Marx's brow
and were kicking their feet in his beard,
some were English,
plain and simply English,

and among them
they set out
with tooth and knife,
with dictionaries and other dark weapons,
with venerable quotes,
they set out
to take my poor poetry
from the simple folk
who loved it.
They trapped and tricked it,
they rolled it in a scroll,
they secured it with a hundred pins,
they covered it with skeleton dust,
they drowned it in ink,
they spit on it with the suave
benignity of a cat,
they used it to wrap clocks,
they protected it and condemned it,
they stored it with crude oil,
they dedicated damp treatises to it,
they boiled it with milk,
they showered it with pebbles,
and in the process erased vowels from it,
their syllables and sighs
nearly killed it,
they crumbled it and tied it up in a
little package
they scrupulously addressed
to their attics and cemeteries,
then,
one by one, they retired,
enraged to the point of madness
because I wasn't
popular enough for them,
or saturated with mild contempt
for my customary lack of shadows,
they left,
all of them,
and then,

once again,
men and women
came to live
with my poetry,
once again
they lighted fires,
built houses,
broke bread,
they shared the light
and in love joined
the lightning flash and the ring.
And now,
gentlemen, if you will excuse me
for interrupting this story
I'm telling,
I am leaving to live
forever
with simple people.

MARGARET SAYERS PEDEN

ODE TO NUMBERS

Oh, the thirst to know
how many!
The hunger
to know
how many
stars in the sky!

We spent
our childhood counting
stones and plants, fingers and
toes, grains of sand, and teeth,
our youth we passed counting
petals and comets' tails.
We counted
colors, years,

lives, and kisses;
in the country,
oxen; by the sea,
the waves. Ships
became proliferating ciphers.
Numbers multiplied.
The cities
were thousands, millions,
wheat hundreds
of units that held
within them smaller numbers,
smaller than a single grain.
Time became a number.
Light was numbered
and no matter how it raced with sound
its velocity was 37.
Numbers surrounded us.
When we closed the door
at night, exhausted,
an 800 slipped
beneath the door
and crept with us into bed,
and in our dreams
4000s and 77s
pounded at our foreheads
with hammers and tongs.
5s
added to 5s
until they sank into the sea or madness,
until the sun greeted us with its zero
and we went running
to the office,
to the workshop,
to the factory,
to begin again the infinite
1 of each new day.

We had time, as men,
for our thirst slowly

to be sated,
the ancestral desire
to give things a number,
to add them up,
to reduce them
to powder,
wastelands of numbers.
We
papered the world
with numbers and names,
but
things survived,
they fled
from numbers,
went mad in their quantities,
evaporated,
leaving
an odor or a memory,
leaving the numbers empty.

That's why
for you
I want *things*.
Let numbers
go to jail,
let them march
in perfect columns
procreating
until they give the sum
total of infinity.
For you I want only
for the numbers
along the road
to protect you
and for you to protect them.
May the weekly figure of your salary
expand until it spans your chest.
And from the 2 of you, embraced,
your body and that of your beloved,

may pairs of children's eyes be born
that will count again
the ancient stars
and countless
heads of grain
that will cover a transformed earth.

MARGARET SAYERS PEDEN

ODE TO THE PAST

Today, in conversation,
the past
cropped up,
my past.
Sleazy
incidents
indulged,
vacuous
episodes,
spoiled flour,
dust.
You crouch down,
gently
sink
into yourself,
you smile,
congratulate yourself,
but
when it's a matter
of someone else, some friend,
some enemy,
then
you are merciless,
you frown:
What a terrible life he had!
That woman, what a life
she led!

You hold
your nose,
visibly
you disapprove of pasts
other than your own.
Looking back, we view
our worst days
with nostalgia,
cautiously
we open the coffer
and run up the ensign
of our feats
to be admired.
Let's forget the rest.
Just a bad memory.
Listen and learn.
Time
is divided
into two rivers:
one
flows backward, devouring
life already lived;
the other
moves forward with you
exposing
your life.
For a single second
they may be joined.
Now.
This is that moment,
the drop of an instant
that washes away the past.
It is the present.
It is in your hands.
Racing, slipping,
tumbling like a waterfall.
But it is yours.
Help it grow
with love, with firmness,

with stone and flight,
with resounding
rectitude,
with purest grains,
the most brilliant metal
from your heart,
walking
in the full light of day
without fear
of truth, goodness, justice,
companions of song,
time that flows
will have the shape
and sound
of a guitar,
and when you want
to bow to the past,
the singing spring of
transparent time
will reveal your wholeness.
Time is joy.

MARGARET SAYERS PEDEN

ODE TO LAZINESS

Yesterday I felt as if my ode
was never going to sprout.
At least it should
have been showing
a green leaf.
I scratched the soil: "Come up,
sister ode,"
I said,
"I promised to produce you,
don't be afraid of me,
I'll not step on your
four leaves, your

four hands, ode,
we'll have tea together.
Come up
and I'll crown you first among my odes,
we'll go to the seashore
on our bicycles."
It was useless.

Then,
high amid the pines,
I saw lovely
naked laziness,
she led me off bedazzled
and bemused,
she showed me on the sand
small broken bits
of marine matter,
driftwood, seaweed, stones,
seabirds' feathers.
I hunted but did not find
yellow agates.
The sea
surged higher,
crumbling towers,
invading
the shoreline of my homeland,
sending forth
successive catastrophes of foam.
A solitary corolla
cast a ray
against the sand.
I saw silvery petrels cruising
and, like black crosses,
cormorants
clinging to the rocks.
I freed a bee from
its death throes in a spiderweb,
I put a pebble
in my pocket,

it was smooth, as smooth
as a bird's breast,
meanwhile along the coast,
all afternoon,
sun and fog waged war.
At times
the fog glowed
with
a topaz light,
other times
a moist sun cast
rays dripping yellow drops.

That night,
thinking of the duties of my
elusive ode,
I took off my shoes
beside the fire,
sand spilled from them
and soon I was falling
fast asleep.

MARGARET SAYERS PEDEN

ODE TO THE EARTH

I do not sing to the prodigal
earth,
the profligate
mother of roots,
the squanderer
choked with fruits and birds,
with mud and flowing springs,
homeland of the caiman,
full-breasted sultana
with spiky diadem,
not to the birthplace
of the jungle cat,

to the tilled and gravid earth,
its every seed a
tiny nest ready
to greet the dawn with song,
no, I praise
mineral earth, Andean rock,
the severe scar
of the lunar desert, the spacious
nitrate sands,
I sing
to iron,
to the rippling of veins
of copper and its clusters
as it emerges,
blasted and dusty,
newly unearthed
from its geography.
Oh, earth, harsh mother,
here is where you hid
your buried metals, and
here we scratched them out,
and then with fire,
men,
a Pedro,
a Rodríguez or Ramírez,
restored them
to primeval light, to liquid lava,
and then
hard like you, earth,
choleric metal,
you willed yourself
in the small strong hands of my uncle
into wire or horseshoe,
ship or locomotive,
the skeleton of a school,
the speed of a bullet.
Arid earth, palm
without a lifeline,
I sing to you,

here barren of birdsong,
bereft of the rose
of the current that runs
dry and hard and silent,
enemy fist, black
star,
I sing to you
because man
will make you yield, will make you bear,
he will expose your ovaries,
he will spill his special rays
into your secret cup,
desert land,
lineal purity,
to you the lines of my song,
and though you lie dormant now,
the dynamite's scourge
will shake you,
and as metals leap toward the sky,
a plume of bloody smoke
will signal birth.
Earth, I like you
as clay and sand,
I hold you and shape you
as you shaped me,
you slip from my fingers
as I, freed, will return
to your encompassing womb.
Earth, suddenly
I seem to embrace you
in all your contours,
porous medallion,
common clay jug,
I run my hand
over your body
tracing the hips of the woman I love,
the small breasts,
wind like a grain
of smooth, sun-warmed oats,

and I cling to you, earth,
I sleep beside you,
my arms and lips caress your waist,
I lie beside you, sowing my warmest kisses.

MARGARET SAYERS PEDEN

ODE TO MY SUIT

Every morning, suit,
you are waiting on a chair
to be filled
by my vanity, my love,
my hope, my body.
Still
only half awake
I leave the shower
to shrug into your sleeves,
my legs seek
the hollow of your legs,
and thus embraced
by your unfailing loyalty
I take my morning walk,
work my way into my poetry;
from my windows I see
the things,
men, women,
events, and struggles
constantly shaping me,
constantly confronting me,
setting my hands to the task,
opening my eyes,
creasing my lips,
and in the same way,
suit,
I am shaping you,
poking out your elbows,
wearing you threadbare,

and so your life grows
in the image of my own.
In the wind
you flap and hum
as if you were my soul,
in bad moments
you cling
to my bones,
abandoned, at nighttime
darkness and dream
people with their phantoms
your wings and mine.
I wonder
whether someday
an enemy
bullet
will stain you with my blood,
for then
you would die with me,
but perhaps
it will be
less dramatic,
simple,
and you will grow ill,
suit,
with me,
grow older
with me, with my body,
and together
we will be lowered
into the earth.
That's why
every day
I greet you
with respect and then
you embrace me and I forget you,
because we are one being
and shall be always
in the wind, through the night,

the streets and the struggle,
one body,
maybe, maybe, one day, still.

MARGARET SAYERS PEDEN

ODE TO SADNESS

Sadness, scarab
with seven crippled feet,
spiderweb egg,
scramble-brained rat,
bitch's skeleton:
No entry here.
Don't come in.
Go away.
Go back
south with your umbrella,
go back
north with your serpent's teeth.
A poet lives here.
No sadness may
cross this threshold.
Through these windows
comes the breath of the world,
fresh red roses,
flags embroidered with
the victories of the people.
No.
No entry.
Flap
your bat's wings,
I will trample the feathers
that fall from your mantle,
I will sweep the bits and pieces
of your carcass to
the four corners of the wind,
I will wring your neck,

I will stitch your eyelids shut,
I will sew your shroud,
sadness, and bury your rodent bones
beneath the springtime of an apple tree.

MARGARET SAYERS PEDEN

ODE TO WINE

Wine color of day
wine color of night
wine with your feet of purple
or topaz blood,
wine,
starry child
of the earth,
wine, smooth
as a golden sword,
soft
as ruffled velvet,
wine spiral-shelled
and suspended,
loving,
of the sea,
you've never been contained in one glass,
in one song, in one man,
choral, you are gregarious
and, at least, mutual.
Sometimes
you feed on mortal
memories,
on your wave
we go from tomb to tomb,
stonecutter of icy graves,
and we weep
transitory tears,
but
your beautiful

spring suit
is different,
the heart climbs to the branches,
the wind moves the day,
nothing remains
in your motionless soul.
Wine
stirs the spring,
joy grows like a plant,
walls, large rocks
fall,
abysses close up,
song is born.
Oh thou, jug of wine, in the desert
with the woman I love,
said the old poet.
Let the pitcher of wine
add its kiss to the kiss of love.

My love, suddenly
your hip
is the curve of the wineglass
filled to the brim,
your breast is the cluster,
your hair the light of alcohol
your nipples, the grapes
your navel pure seal
stamped on your belly of a barrel,
and your love the cascade
of unquenchable wine,
the brightness that falls on my senses
the earthen splendor of life.

But not only love,
burning kiss,
or ignited heart—
vino de vida,
you are also
fellowship, transparency,

chorus of discipline,
abundance of flowers.
I love the light of a bottle
of intelligent wine
upon a table
when people are talking,
that they drink it,
that in each drop of gold
or ladle of purple,
they remember
that autumn worked
until the barrels were filled with wine
and let the obscure man learn,
in the ceremony of his business,
to remember the earth and his duties,
to propagate the canticle of the fruit.

                                        MARK EISNER

ODA A LA CRÍTICA (II)

Toqué mi libro:
era
compacto,
firme,
arqueado
como una nave blanca,
entreabierto
como una nueva rosa,
era
para mis ojos
un molino,
de cada hoja
la flor del pan crecía
sobre mi libro:
me cegué con mis rayos,
me sentí demasiado
satisfecho,
perdí tierra,
comencé a caminar
en nubes
y entonces,
camarada,
me bajaste
a la vida,
una sola palabra
me mostró de repente
cuanto dejé de hacer
y cuanto pude
avanzar con mi fuerza y mi ternura,
navegar con la nave de mi canto.

Volví más verdadero,
enriquecido,
tomé cuanto tenía
y cuanto tienes,
cuanto anduviste tú
sobre la tierra,
cuanto vieron
tus ojos,
cuanto
luchó tu corazón día tras día
se dispuso a mi lado,
numeroso,
y levanté la harina
de mi canto,
la flor del pan acrecentó su aroma.

Gracias te digo,
crítica,
motor claro del mundo,
ciencia pura,
signo
de la velocidad, aceite
de la eterna rueda humana,
espada de oro,
piedra
de la estructura.
Crítica, tú no traes
la espesa gota
sucia
de la envidia,
la personal guadaña
o el ambiguo, encrespado
gusanillo
del café rencoroso,
no eres tampoco el juego
del viejo tragasables y su tribu,
ni la pérfida
cola

de la feudal serpiente
siempre enroscada en su exquisita rama.

Crítica, eres
mano
constructora,
burbuja del nivel, línea de acero,
palpitación de clase.

Con una sola vida
no aprenderé bastante.

Con la luz de otras vidas
vivirán otras vidas en mi canto.

ODE TO CRITICISM (II)

I touched my book:
it was
compact,
solid,
arched
like a white ship,
half open
like a new rose,
it was
to my eyes
a mill,
from each page
of my book
sprouted the flower of bread;
I was blinded by my own rays,
I was insufferably
self-satisfied,
my feet left the ground
and I was walking
on clouds,

and then,
comrade criticism,
you brought me down
to earth,
a single word
showed me suddenly
how much I had left undone,
how far I could go
with my strength and tenderness,
sail with the ship of my song.

I came back a more genuine man,
enriched,
I took what I had
and all you have,
all your travels
across the earth,
everything your eyes
had seen;
all the battles
your heart had fought day after day
aligned themselves
beside me,
and as I held high the flour
of my song,
the flower of the bread smelled sweeter.

I say, thank you,
criticism,
bright mover of the world,
pure science,
sign
of speed, oil
for the eternal human wheel,
golden sword,
cornerstone
of the structure.
Criticism, you're not the bearer
of the thick, foul

drop
of envy,
the personal scythe,
or ambiguous, curled-up
worm
in the bitter coffee bean,
nor are you part of the scheme
of the old sword swallower and his tribe,
nor the treacherous
tail
of the feudal serpent
always twined around its exquisite branch.

Criticism, you are
a helping
hand,
bubble in the level, mark on the steel,
notable pulsation.

With a single life
I will not learn enough.

With the light of other lives,
many lives will live in my song.

MARGARET SAYERS PEDEN

ODA AL DICCIONARIO

Lomo de buey, pesado
cargador, sistemático
libro espeso:
de joven
te ignoré, me vistió
la suficiencia
y me creí repleto,
y orondo como un
melancólico sapo

dictaminé: "Recibo
las palabras
directamente
del Sinaí bramante.
Reduciré
las formas a la alquimia.
Soy mago."

El gran mago callaba.

El Diccionario,
viejo y pesado, con su chaquetón
de pellejo gastado,
se quedó silencioso
sin mostrar sus probetas.

Pero un día,
después de haberlo usado
y desusado,
después
de declararlo
inútil y anacrónico camello,
cuando por largos meses, sin protesta,
me sirvió de sillón
y de almohada,
se rebeló y plantándose
en mi puerta
creció, movió sus hojas
y sus nidos,
movió la elevación de su follaje:
árbol
era,
natural,
generoso
manzano, manzanar o manzanero,
y las palabras
brillaban en su copa inagotable,
opacas o sonoras,

fecundas en la fronda del lenguaje,
cargadas de verdad y de sonido.

Aparto una
sola de
sus
páginas:
Caporal
Capuchón
qué maravilla

pronunciar estas sílabas
con aire,
y más abajo
Cápsula
hueca, esperando aceite o ambrosía,
y junto a ellas
Captura Capucete Capuchina
Caprario Captatorio
palabras
que se deslizan como suaves uvas
o que a la luz estallan
como gérmenes ciegos que esperaron
en las bodegas del vocabulario
y viven otra vez y dan la vida:
una vez más el corazón las quema.

Diccionario, no eres
tumba, sepulcro, féretro,
túmulo, mausoleo,
sino preservación,
fuego escondido,
plantación de rubíes,
perpetuidad viviente
de la esencia,
granero del idioma.
Y es hermoso
recoger en tus filas

la palabra
de estirpe,
la severa
y olvidada
sentencia,
hija de España,
endurecida
como reja de arado,
fija en su límite
de anticuada herramienta,
preservada
con su hermosura exacta
y su dureza de medalla.
O la otra
palabra
que allí vimos perdida
entre renglones
y que de pronto
se hizo sabrosa y lisa en nuestra boca
como una almendra
o tierna como un higo.

Diccionario, una mano
de tus mil manos, una
de tus mil esmeraldas,
una
sola
gota
de tus vertientes virginales,
un grano
de
tus
magnánimos graneros
en el momento
justo
a mis labios conduce,
al hilo de mi pluma,
a mi tintero.
De tu espesa y sonora

profundidad de selva,
dame,
cuando lo necesite,
un solo trino, el lujo
de una abeja,
un fragmento caído
de tu antigua madera perfumada
por una eternidad de jazmineros,
una
sílaba,
un temblor, un sonido,
una semilla:
de tierra soy y con palabras canto.

ODE TO THE DICTIONARY

Back like an ox, beast of
burden, orderly
thick book:
as a youth
I ignored you,
wrapped in my smugness,
I thought I knew it all,
and as puffed up as a
melancholy toad
I proclaimed: "I receive
my words
in a loud, clear voice
directly from Mt. Sinai.
I shall convert
forms to alchemy.
I am the Magus."

The Great Magus said nothing.

The Dictionary,
old and heavy in its scruffy

leather jacket,
sat in silence,
its resources unrevealed.

But one day,
after I'd used it
and abused it,
after
I'd called it
useless, an anachronistic camel,
when for months, without protest,
it had served me as a chair
and a pillow,
it rebelled and planting its feet
firmly in my doorway,
expanded, shook its leaves
and nests,
and spread its foliage:
it was
a tree,
a natural,
bountiful
apple blossom, apple orchard, apple tree,
and words
glittered in its infinite branches,
opaque or sonorous,
fertile in the fronds of language,
charged with truth and sound.

I
turn
its
pages:
caporal,
capote,
what a marvel
to pronounce these plosive
syllables,
and further on,

capsule,
unfilled, awaiting ambrosia or oil
and others,
capsicum, caption, capture,
comparison, capricorn,
words
as slippery as smooth grapes,
words exploding in the light
like dormant seeds waiting
in the vaults of vocabulary,
alive again, and giving life:
once again the heart distills them.

Dictionary, you are not a
tomb, sepulcher, grave,
tumulus, mausoleum,
but guard and keeper,
hidden fire,
groves of rubies,
living eternity
of essence,
depository of language.
How wonderful
to read in your columns
ancestral
words,
the severe and
long-forgotten
maxim,
daughter of Spain,
petrified
as a plow blade,
as limited in use
as an antiquated tool,
but preserved
in the precise beauty and
immutability of a medallion.
Or another
word

we find hiding
between the lines
that suddenly seems
as delicious and smooth on the tongue
as an almond,
or tender as a fig.

Dictionary, let one hand
of your thousand hands, one
of your thousand emeralds,
a
single
drop
of your virginal springs,
one grain
from
your
magnanimous granaries,
fall
at the perfect moment
upon my lips,
onto the tip of my pen,
into my inkwell.
From the depths of your
dense and reverberating jungle
grant me,
at the moment it is needed,
a single birdsong, the luxury
of one bee,
one splinter
of your ancient wood perfumed
by an eternity of jasmine,
one
syllable,
one tremor, one sound,
one seed:
I am of the earth and with words I sing.

MARGARET SAYERS PEDEN

ODE TO THE SEAGULL

To the seagull
high above
the pinewoods
of the coast,
on the wind
the sibilant
syllable of my ode.

Sail,
bright boat,
winged banner,
in my verse,
stitch,
body of silver,
your emblem
across the shirt
of the icy firmament,
oh, aviator,
gentle
serenade of flight,
snow arrow, serene
ship in the transparent storm,
steady, you soar
while
the hoarse wind sweeps
the meadows of the sky.

After your long voyage,
feathered magnolia,
triangle borne
aloft on the air,
slowly you regain
your form,
arranging
your silvery robes, shaping
your bright treasure in an oval,
again a

white bud of flight,
a round
seed,
egg of beauty.

Another
poet
would end here
his triumphant ode.
I cannot
limit myself
to
the luxurious whiteness
of useless froth.
Forgive me,
seagull,
I am
a realist
poet,
photographer of the sky.
You eat,
and eat,
and eat,
there is nothing
you don't devour,
on the waters of the bay
you bark
like a beggar's dog,
you pursue
the last
scrap of
fish gut,
you peck
at your white sisters,
you steal
your despicable prize,
a rotting clump
of floating garbage,
you stalk

decayed
tomatoes,
the discarded
rubbish of the cove.
But
in you
it is transformed
into clean wing,
white geometry,
the ecstatic line of flight.

That is why,
snowy anchor,
aviator,
I celebrate you as you are:
your insatiable voraciousness,
your screech in the rain,
or at rest
a snowflake blown
from the storm,
at peace or in flight,
seagull,
I consecrate to you
my earthbound words,
my clumsy attempt at flight;
let's see whether you scatter
your birdseed in my ode.

MARGARET SAYERS PEDEN

ODE TO FIREFOOT

You have
two little
feet
no bigger than
bees,
but oh, what

you do
to shoes!
I know,
all that coming and going,
up and down ladders,
you outstrip the wind.
Before
I can
call you,
you're there;
you walk the
forbidding coastline,
sand, stone, thorns,
by my side,
in the woods
you tramp through trees and
still green water,
in the suburbs
you stride along
unnavigable
streets,
across pavements
of dejected tar,
and at that hour
when the light
of the world
unravels
like a flag,
in streets or woods,
you walk
beside me,
a dauntless, tireless
companion,
but
oh, my God!
What you do
to shoes!

It seems
only yesterday
you brought them home
in a box,
you opened it
and they emerged
gleaming
like
two army
pistols,
two
gold
coins
in mint
condition,
two little bells,
but today
what do I see?
On your feet
two trodden
chestnut burrs,
two relaxed fists,
two shapeless
cucumbers,
two toads
of faded
leather,
that,
that's
what's
become of
two bright stars that
a month ago, only a month ago,
left
the store.

You are
a beautiful yellow flower
perfuming the ravine,

a vine flowering in the treetops,
calceolaria,
copihue,
vibrant amaranth,
crystalline,
fragrant,
blooming,
with me always,
the chorus of an aviary,
a waterfall
in southern
mountains,
your heart
sings
with mine,
but oh,
Firefoot,
how you
burn up
shoes!

MARGARET SAYERS PEDEN

ODA A WALT WHITMAN

Yo no recuerdo
a qué edad,
ni dónde,
si en el gran Sur mojado
o en la costa
temible, bajo el breve
grito de las gaviotas,
toqué una mano y era
la mano de Walt Whitman:
pisé la tierra
con los pies desnudos,
anduve sobre el pasto,

sobre el firme rocío
de Walt Whitman.

Durante
mi juventud
toda
me acompañó esa mano,
ese rocío,
su firmeza de pino patriarca, su extensión de pradera,
y su misión de paz circulatoria.

Sin
desdeñar
los dones
de la tierra,
la copiosa
curva del capitel,
ni la inicial
purpúrea
de la sabiduría,
tú
me enseñaste
a ser americano,
levantaste
mis ojos
a los libros,
hacia
el tesoro
de los cereales:
ancho,
en la claridad
de las llanuras,
me hiciste ver
el alto
monte
tutelar. Del eco
subterráneo,
para mí

recogiste
todo,
todo lo que nacía,
cosechaste
galopando en la alfalfa,
cortando para mí las amapolas,
visitando
los ríos,
acudiendo en la tarde
a las cocinas.

Pero no sólo
tierra
sacó a la luz
tu pala;
desenterraste
al hombre,
y el
esclavo
humillado
contigo, balanceando
la negra dignidad de su estatura,
caminó conquistando
la alegría.

Al fogonero,
abajo,
en la caldera,
mandaste
un canastito
de frutillas,
a todas las esquinas de tu pueblo
un verso
tuyo llegó de visita
y era como un trozo
de cuerpo limpio
el verso que llegaba,
como

tu propia barba pescadora
o el solemne camino de tus piernas de acacia.

Pasó entre los soldados
tu silueta
de bardo, de enfermero,
de cuidador nocturno
que conoce
el sonido
de la respiración en la agonía
y espera con la aurora
el silencioso
regreso
de la vida.

Buen panadero!
Primo hermano mayor
de mis raíces,
cúpula
de araucaria,
hace
ya
cien
años
que sobre el pasto tuyo
y sus germinaciones,
el viento
pasa
sin gastar tus ojos.

Nuevos
y crueles años en tu patria:
persecuciones,
lágrimas,
prisiones,
armas envenenadas
y guerras iracundas,
no han aplastado

la hierba de tu libro,
el manantial vital
de su frescura.
Y, ay!
los
que asesinaron
a Lincoln
ahora
se acuestan en su cama,
derribaron
su sitial
de olorosa madera
y erigieron un trono
por desventura y sangre
salpicado.

Pero
canta en
las estaciones
suburbanas
tu voz,
en
los
desembarcaderos
vespertinos
chapotea
como
un agua oscura
tu palabra,
tu pueblo
blanco
y negro,
pueblo
de pobres,
pueblo simple
como
todos
los pueblos,
no olvida

tu campana:
se congrega cantando
bajo
la magnitud
de tu espaciosa vida:
entre los pueblos con tu amor camina
acariciando
el desarrollo puro
de la fraternidad sobre la tierra.

ODE TO WALT WHITMAN

I can't recall my age, or if
I was in the vast streaming South,
or on some forbidding coastline
where seagulls wheeled & cried . . .
But I touched a hand that day,
& it was Walt Whitman's hand.
And barefoot I walk the earth,
I wade through tenacious dew
in the grasslands of Whitman.

Throughout my entire childhood,
my companion was that hand
with dew on it, the timber
of its patriarchal pine,
the expanse of its prairie,
its mission of articulate peace.

And Walt did not disdain
all the gifts of the earth,
the capital's surfeit of curves,
the purple initial of learning,
but taught me to be americano,
& raised my eyes to books,
toward the treasure that we find
inside a kernel of wheat.

Engirthed by the clarity
of the plains, he made me see
how the high mountain tutors us.
From the subterranean echo
he fetched it all in for me,
whatever he could harvest
gallivanting through the alfalfa,
on the days he passed in the kitchen
or at the bend of the river.

But not just earth by itself
was brought into the light
by the work of his shovel:
he disinterred humanity.
And the slaves who were abased
along with him, balancing
the black dignity of their stature,
went on to conquer happiness.

To the stoker, down below
in the boiler room, Walt sent
a basket of strawberries,
& each corner of his city
was visited by his verse,
verse like a strip of clean flesh,
the beard of a true fisherman,
the solemn supple gait
of his acacian legs.

Passing among the soldiers—
his bardic silhouette.
Night nurse, camerado,
he knew painful, rasping breath,
& he waited with the dawn
for life's silent return.

Breadmaker supreme!
Prime old brother of my roots!
Cupola of the conifers!

For the last hundred years
the wind has passed over
your germinating grassland
without consuming your vision.

But now your country is cruel—
full of persecution, tears,
prisons & lethal weapons,
uncivil wars that nonetheless
haven't crushed the grass of your book,
living source of originality.

And ay!, those who murdered Lincoln,
who now lie in that bed,
have dismantled the fragrant
lilac of his memorial
& put a throne in its place,
splattered with blood & misfortune.

Your voice, that's still singing
in the suburban stations, on
the unloading docks at night . . .
Your word, that's still splashing
like dark water . . .
And your people, black, white,
poor & simple, like all people
still not forgetting
the tolling of your bell . . .

They congregate & sing
beneath the magnitude
of your spacious life.
They walk among the people
with your love. They caress
the pure development
of fraternity on earth.

GREG SIMON

ODE TO BEES

Multitude of bees!
In and out of the
crimson, the blue,
the yellow,
of the softest
softness in the world;
you tumble
headlong
into a corolla
to conduct your business,
and emerge
wearing a golden suit
and quantities of
yellow boots.

The waist,
perfect,
the abdomen striped
with dark bars,
the tiny,
ever-busy
head,
the
wings,
newly made of water;
you enter
every sweet-scented window,
open
silken doors,
penetrate the bridal chamber
of the most fragrant
love,

discover
a
drop
of diamond
dew,
and from every house
you visit
you remove
honey,
mysterious,
rich and heavy
honey, thick aroma,
liquid, guttering light,
until you return
to your
communal
palace
and on its gothic parapets
deposit
the product
of flower and flight,
the seraphic and secret nuptial sun!
Multitude of bees!
Sacred
elevation
of unity,
seething
schoolhouse.

Buzzing,
noisy
workers
process
the nectar,
swiftly
exchanging
drops
of ambrosia;
it is summer

siesta in the green
solitudes
of Osorno. High above,
the sun casts its spears
into the snow,
volcanoes glisten,
land
stretches
endless
as the sea,
space is blue,
but
something
trembles, it is
the fiery
heart
of summer,
the honeyed heart
multiplied,
the buzzing
bee,
the crackling
honeycomb
of flight and gold!

Bees,
purest laborers,
ogival
workers,
fine, flashing
proletariat,
perfect,
daring militia
that in combat attack
with suicidal sting;
buzz,
buzz above
the earth's endowments,
family of gold,

multitude of the wind,
shake the fire
from the flowers,
thirst from the stamens,
the sharp,
aromatic
thread
that stiches together the days,
and propagate
honey,
passing over
humid continents, the most
distant islands of the
western sky.

Yes:
let the wax erect
green statues,
let honey
spill in
infinite
tongues,
let the ocean be
a
beehive,
the earth
tower and tunic
of flowers,
and the world
a waterfall,
a comet's tail, a
never-ending
wealth
of honeycombs!

MARGARET SAYERS PEDEN

ODE TO BICYCLES

I was walking
down
a sizzling road:
the sun popped like
a field of blazing maize,
the
earth
was hot,
an infinite circle
with an empty
blue sky overhead.

A few bicycles
passed
me by,
the only
insects
in
that dry
moment of summer,
silent,
swift,
translucent;
they
barely stirred
the air.

Workers and girls
were riding to their
factories,
giving
their eyes
to summer,
their heads to the sky,
sitting on the
hard
beetle backs

of the whirling
bicycles
that whirred
as they rode by
bridges, rosebushes, brambles
and midday.

I thought about evening when
the boys
wash up,
sing, eat, raise
a cup
of wine
in honor
of love
and life,
and waiting
at the door,
the bicycle,
stilled,
because
only moving
does it have a soul,
and fallen there
it isn't
a translucent insect
humming
through summer
but
a cold
skeleton
that will return to
life
only
when it's needed,
when it's light,
that is,
with
the

resurrection
of each day.

MARGARET SAYERS PEDEN

ODE TO A VILLAGE MOVIE THEATER

Come, my love,
let's go to the movies
in the village.

Transparent night
turns
like a silent
mill, grinding out
stars.
We enter the
tiny theater, you and I,
a ferment of children
and the strong smell of apples.
Old movies
are
secondhand dreams.
The screen is the color
of stone, or rain.
The beautiful victim
of the villain
has eyes like pools
and a voice like a swan;
the fleetest
horses in the world
careen
at breakneck speed.

Cowboys
make
Swiss cheese of
the dangerous Arizona

moon.
Our hearts
in our mouths,
we thread our way
through
these
cyclones
of violence,
the death-defying
duel of the swordsmen in the tower,
unerring as wasps
the feathered avalanche
of Indians,
a spreading fan on the prairie.

Many of the
village
boys and girls
have fallen asleep,
tired after a day in the shop,
weary of scrubbing kitchens.

Not we,
my love,
we'll not lose
even this one
dream;
as long
as we
live
we will claim
every minute
of reality,
but claim
dreams as well:
we
will dream
all the dreams.

MARGARET SAYERS PEDEN

ODE TO AGE

I don't believe in age.

All old people
carry
in their eyes
a child,
and children
at times
observe us with the
eyes of wise ancients.

Shall we measure
life
in meters or kilometers
or months?
How far since you were born?
How long
must you wander
until
like all men
instead of walking on its surface
we rest below the earth?

To the man, to the woman
who utilized their
energies, goodness, strength,
anger, love, tenderness,
to those who truly
alive
flowered,
and in their sensuality matured,
let us not apply
the measure
of a time
that may be
something else, a mineral
mantle, a solar

bird, a flower,
something, maybe,
but not a measure.

Time, metal
or bird, long
petiolate flower,
stretch
through
man's life,
shower him
with blossoms
and with
bright
water
or with hidden sun.
I proclaim you
road,
not shroud,
a pristine
ladder
with treads
of air,
a suit lovingly
renewed
through springtimes
around the world.

Now,
time, I roll you up,
I deposit you in my
bait box
and I am off to fish
with your long line
the fishes of the dawn!

MARGARET SAYERS PEDEN

Album of perfect stamps!

Butterflies,
ships,
sea shapes, corollas,
leaning towers,
dark eyes, moist and
round as grapes,
album
smooth
as
a
slippery
fish,
with thousands
of glistening
scales,
each page
a
racing
charger
in search of
distant pleasures, forgotten
flowers!

Other pages are
bonfires or carnations,
red clusters of stones
set afire
by a secret ruby,
some display
the snow,
the doves
of Norway,
the architectural clarity of the dew.

How was it possible
to bring
to paper
such beauty,
so many
expeditions
into infinity?

How
possible
to capture
the ineffable
glow
of
the Sambuca
butterfly
and its phosphorescent
caterpillar colonies,
and,
as well,
that
gentle
locomotive
puffing through pastures
like an
iron
bull,
small
but fiery,
and that
fauna from a distant sun,
elegant
wasps,
sea serpents,
incredible
camels?

World of miracles!

Insatiable
spiral,
comet's tail
of all earth's
highways,
dictionary
of the wind,
starstruck album
bulging
with noble
fruits and territories,
treasure keeper
sailing
on its treasure,
garnet
pomegranate,
nomadic
stamp album!

MARGARET SAYERS PEDEN

ODE TO MAIZE

America, from a grain
of maize you grew
to crown
with spacious lands
the ocean
foam.
A grain of maize was your geography.
From the grain
a green lance rose,
was covered with gold,
to grace the heights
of Peru with its yellow tassels.

But, poet, let
history rest in its shroud;

praise with your lyre
the grain in its granaries:
sing to the simple maize in the kitchen.

First, a fine beard
fluttered in the field
above the tender teeth
of the young ear.
Then the husks parted
and fruitfulness burst its veils
of pale papyrus
that grains of laughter
might fall upon the earth.

To the stone,
in your journey, you returned.
Not to the terrible stone,
the bloody
triangle of Mexican death,
but to the grinding stone,
sacred
stone of our kitchens.
There, milk and matter,
strength-giving, nutritious
cornmeal pulp,
you were worked and patted
by the wondrous hands
of dark-skinned women.

Wherever you fall, maize,
whether into the
splendid pot of partridge, or among
country beans, you light up
the meal and lend it
your virginal flavor.

Oh, to bite into
the steaming ear beside the sea
of distant song and deepest waltz.

To boil you
as your aroma
spreads through
blue sierras.

But is there
no end
to your treasure?

In chalky, barren lands
bordered
by the sea, along
the rocky Chilean coast,
at times
only your radiance
reaches the empty
table of the miner.

Your light, your cornmeal, your hope
pervades America's solitudes,
and to hunger
your lances
are enemy legions.

Within your husks,
like gentle kernels,
our sober provincial
children's hearts were nurtured,
until life began
to shuck us from the ear.

MARGARET SAYERS PEDEN

ODE TO THE DOUBLE AUTUMN

The sea is alive while the land
does not move:
the grave autumn

of the coast
covers
the still light
of the land
with its death,
but
the roaming sea, the sea
keeps living.

There is not
one
single
drop
of
sleep,
death,
or
night
in her
combat:
all
the machines
of water, the blue
cauldrons,
the crackling factories
of wind
crowning
the waves
with
its violent flowers,
all
alive
as
the viscera
of the bull,
as
the fire
in music,
as

the act
of amorous union.

The works of autumn
on the land
have always
been obscure;
immobile
roots, seeds
submerged
in time
and above
only
the corolla of the cold,
a vague
aroma of leaves
dissolving itself
in gold:
nothing.
An ax
in the forest
breaks
a trunk of crystals,
later,
evening
falls
and the land
places a black
mask
upon her face.

But
the sea
does not rest, doesn't sleep, has not died.
Its belly
grows by night
which warped
the wet
stars, like wheat in the dawn,

it grows,
throbs,
and cries
like a lost
child
that only with the beat
of daybreak
like a drum, wakes
gigantic
and grows rough.
All its hands move,
its incessant organism,
its extensive teeth,
its business
with salt, with sun, with silver,
all
is moved, is stirred
with its leveling
springs,
with the combat
of its movement,
while
the sad
autumn
passes
over the land.

MARK EISNER

ODA AL VIEJO POETA

Me dio la mano
como si un árbol viejo
alargara un gancho
sin
hojas y sin frutos.
Su
mano

que escribió desenlazando
los hilos y las hebras
del
destino
ahora estaba
minuciosamente
rayada
por los días, los meses y los años.
Seca en su rostro
era
la escritura
del tiempo,
diminuta
y errante
como
si allí estuvieran
dispuestos
las líneas y los signos
desde su nacimiento
y poco a poco
el aire
las hubiera erigido.

Largas líneas profundas,
capítulos cortados
por la edad en su cara,
signos interrogantes,
fábulas misteriosas,
asteriscos,
todo lo que olvidaron las sirenas
en la extendida
soledad de su alma,
lo que cayó del
estrellado cielo,
allí estaba en su rostro
dibujado.
Nunca el antiguo
bardo
recogió

con pluma y papel duro
el río derramado
de la vida
o el dios desconocido
que cortejó su verso,
y ahora,
en sus mejillas,
todo
el misterio
diseño
con frío
el álgebra
de sus revelaciones
y las pequeñas,
invariables
cosas
menospreciadas
dejaron
en su frente
profundísimas
páginas
y
hasta
en su
nariz
delgada,
como pico
de cormorán errante,
los viajes y las olas
depositaron
su letra
ultramarina.
Sólo
dos piedrecitas
intratables,
dos ágatas
marinas
en aquel
combate,

eran
sus ojos
y sólo a través de ellos
vi la apagada
hoguera,
una rosa
en las manos
del poeta.

Ahora
el traje
le quedaba grande
como si ya viviera
en una
casa
vacía,
y los huesos
de todo
su cuerpo se acercaban
a la piel
levantándola
y era
de hueso,
de hueso que advertía
y enseñaba,
un pequeño
árbol, al fin, de hueso,
era el poeta
apagado
por la caligrafía
de la lluvia,
por los inagotables
manantiales del tiempo.
Allí le dejé andando
presuroso a su muerte
como
si lo esperara
también casi desnuda
en un parque sombrío

y de la mano
fueran
hasta
un desmantelado dormitorio,
y en él durmieran
como dormiremos
todos
los hombres:
con
una rosa
seca
en
una
mano
que también cae
convertida en polvo.

ODE TO AN AGED POET

He offered me his hand
the way an old tree might
extend a broken branch
stripped
of leaves and fruit.
The
hand
that once wrote, spinning
the thread and strands
of
destiny,
now was
intricately
scored
by days, months, and years.
Sere on his face
was
the writing

of time,
minute
and meandering
as if
the lines
and signs
had been ordained
at birth
and little by little
air
had etched them.

Long deep lines,
chapters carved
in his face by age,
question marks,
mysterious tales,
asterisks,
all that the sirens had forgot
in the far-reaching
solitude of his soul,
all that fell from the
starry sky,
was traced in his
face.
Never had the ancient
bard
captured
with pen and unyielding paper
the overflowing river
of life
or the unidentified god
that flirted with his verse,
and now,
on his cheeks,
all that
mystery
coldly
drafted

the algebra
of its revelations,
and the humble,
unchanging
things
he had scorned
imprinted
on his brow
their most profound
pages,
and
even
on his
nose
thin
as the beak
of the errant cormorant,
voyages and waves
had sketched
their ultramarine
scrawl.
Two
unfriendly
pebbles,
two
ocean agates
in that
combat,
were
his eyes,
and only through them
did I see the extinguished
fire,
a rose
in the poet's
hands.

Now
his suit

was much too large,
as if he were already living
in an
empty
house,
and all
the bones
of his body were visible
beneath his skin,
skin draped on bone,
he was nothing but
bone,
alert and instructive
bone,
a tiny
tree, finally, of bone,
was the poet
quenched
by the calligraphy
of the rain,
by the inexhaustible
springs of time.

There I left him
hurrying toward death
as if
death awaited,
she too, almost naked,
in a somber park,
and hand in hand
they would make
their way to
a decaying resting place
where they would sleep
as every man
of us
will sleep:
with
a dry

rose
in
a
hand
that will also
crumble into dust.

MARGARET SAYERS PEDEN

from

EXTRAVAGARIA

ESTRAVAGARIO

❋

1957–1958

                              need
                        you
                  sky
            the
        to
    rise
To

two wings,
a violin,
and so many things,
incalculable things, things without names,
a license for a large slow-moving eye,
the inscription on the nails of the almond tree,
the titles of the grass in the morning.

ALASTAIR REID

PIDO SILENCIO

Ahora me dejen tranquilo.
Ahora se acostumbren sin mí.

Yo voy a cerrar los ojos.

Y sólo quiero cinco cosas,
cinco raíces preferidas.

Una es el amor sin fin.

Lo segundo es ver el otoño.
No puedo ser sin que las hojas
vuelen y vuelvan a la tierra.

Lo tercero es el grave invierno,
la lluvia que amé, la caricia
del fuego en el frío silvestre.

En cuarto lugar el verano
redondo como una sandía.

La quinta cosa son tus ojos.
Matilde mía, bienamada,
no quiero dormir sin tus ojos,
no quiero ser sin que me mires:
yo cambio la primavera
por que tú me sigas mirando.

Amigos, eso es cuanto quiero.
Es casi nada y casi todo.

Ahora si quieren se vayan.

He vivido tanto que un día
tendrán que olvidarme por fuerza,
borrándome de la pizarra:
mi corazón fue interminable.

Pero porque pido silencio
no crean que voy a morirme:
me pasa todo lo contrario:
sucede que voy a vivirme.

Sucede que soy y que sigo.

No será, pues, sino que adentro
de mí crecerán cereales,
primero los granos que rompen
la tierra para ver la luz,
pero la madre tierra es oscura:
y dentro de mí soy oscuro:
soy como un pozo en cuyas aguas
la noche deja sus estrellas
y sigue sola por el campo.

Se trata de que tanto he vivido
que quiero vivir otro tanto.

Nunca me sentí tan sonoro,
nunca he tenido tantos besos.

Ahora, como siempre, es temprano.
Vuela la luz con sus abejas.

Déjenme solo con el día.
Pido permiso para nacer.

I ASK FOR SILENCE

Now they can leave me in peace,
and grow used to my absence.

I am going to close my eyes.

I only want five things,
five chosen roots.

One is an endless love.

Two is to see the autumn.
I cannot exist without leaves
flying and falling to earth.

The third is the solemn winter,
the rain I loved, the caress
of fire in the rough cold.

My fourth is the summer,
plump as a watermelon.

And fifthly, your eyes.
Matilde, my dear love,
I will not sleep without your eyes,
I will not exist but in your gaze.
I adjust the spring
for you to follow me with your eyes.

That, friends, is all I want.
Next to nothing, close to everything.

Now they can go if they wish.

I have lived so much that someday
they will have to forget me forcibly,
rubbing me off the blackboard.
My heart was inexhaustible.

But because I ask for silence,
don't think I'm going to die.
The opposite is true;
it happens I'm going to live.

To be, and to go on being.

I will not be, however, if, inside me,
the crop does not keep sprouting,

the shoots first, breaking through the earth
to reach the light;
but the mothering earth is dark,
and, deep inside me, I am dark.
I am a well in the water of which
the night leaves stars behind
and goes on alone across fields.

It's a question of having lived so much
that I want to live that much more.

I never felt my voice so clear,
never have been so rich in kisses.

Now, as always, it is early.
The light is a swarm of bees.

Let me alone with the day.
I ask leave to be born.

ALASTAIR REID

I'M ASKING FOR SILENCE

Now leave me alone.
Now learn to do without me.

I'm going to close my eyes.

And I want five things only,
five favorite roots.

One is endless love.

The second is to see autumn.
I cannot be if the leaves
don't fly and fall to earth.

The third is solemn winter,
the rain I loved, the caress
of fire on the wild coldness.

In fourth place, summer
round as a watermelon.

The fifth thing is your eyes.
Matilde mine, beloved,
I don't want to sleep without your eyes,
I don't want to be if you're not looking at me:
I'd give up spring
for you to keep on looking at me.

That, friends, is all I want.
Nearly nothing and almost everything.

Now you can go if you wish.

I've lived so much that one day
you will have to forget me
erasing me from the blackboard:
my heart went on forever.

But because I'm asking for silence
don't think I'm going to die.
On the contrary:
It happens that I'm going to live.

It happens that I am, and I'm going on.

So it will only be inside me
that grains will grow,
first the sprouts thrusting through
the earth to see the light,
but mother earth is dark:
and inside I am dark:
I am like a well on whose waters

night leaves its stars
to go on alone across the fields.

It's that I've lived so much
that I want to live as much more.

Never have I felt so sonorous,
never have I had so many kisses.

Now, as always, it is early.
Light flies with its bees.

Let me alone with the day.
I ask leave to be born.

BETTY FERBER

AND THE CITY NOW HAS GONE

How the clock moves on, relentlessly,
with such assurance that it eats the years.
The days are small and transitory grapes,
the months grow faded, taken out of time.

It fades, it falls away, the moment, fired
by that implacable artillery—
and suddenly, only a year is left to us,
a month, a day, and death turns up in the diary.

No one could ever stop the water's flowing;
nor thought nor love has ever held it back.
It has run on through suns and other beings,
its passing rhythm signifying our death.

Until, in the end, we fall in time, exhausted,
and it takes us, and that's it. Then we are dead,
dragged off with no being left, no life, no darkness,

no dust, no words. That is what it comes to;
and in the city where we'll live no more,
all is left empty, our clothing and our pride.

ALASTAIR REID

REPERTOIRE

I will find someone for you to love
before you stop being a child—
then it will be your turn to open your box
and swallow your own sufferings.

I have at my command
queen bees in boxes
and you'll see how, one by one,
they smooth out the honey,
dressing up as apples,
climbing the cherry trees,
quivering in the smoke.

For you I'm keeping these wild loves
who will weave the spring,
who are strangers to weeping.

Hide yourself in the clock
in the belfry while they pass,
girls bright as amaranth,
the last girls of the snow,
the lost ones, the lucky ones,
the ones crowned in yellow,
the infinitely mysterious;
and some, gentle and loving,
will perform their limpid dance,
while others pass on fire,
swift as meteors.

Tell me which ones you want for now;
later is too late.

Today you believe what I'm telling you.

Tomorrow you'll be contradicting the light.

I am one who keeps turning out dreams,
and in my house of feather and stone,
with a knife and a watch,
I cut up clouds and waves,
and with all these elements
I shape my own handwriting;
and I make these beings grow quietly
who could not have been born till now.

What I want is for them to love you
and for you to know nothing of death.

ALASTAIR REID

WITH HER

This time is difficult. Wait for me.
We will live it out vividly.
Give me your small hand:
we will rise and suffer,
we will feel, we will rejoice.

We are once more the pair
who lived in bristling places,
in harsh nests in the rock.
This time is difficult. Wait for me
with a basket, with a shovel,
with your shoes and your clothes.

Now we need each other,
not only for the carnations' sake,
not only to look for honey—
we need our hands
to wash with, to make fire.

So let our difficult time
stand up to infinity
with four hands and four eyes.

ALASTAIR REID

POINT

There is no space wider than that of grief,
there is no universe like that which bleeds.

ALASTAIR REID

FEAR

Everyone is after me to exercise,
get in shape, play football,
rush about, even go swimming and flying.
Fair enough.

Everyone is after me to take it easy.
They all make doctor's appointments for me,
eyeing me in that quizzical way.
What is it?

Everyone is after me to take a trip,
to come in, to leave, not to travel,
to die and, alternatively, not to die.
It doesn't matter.

Everyone is spotting oddnesses
in my innards, suddenly shocked
by radio-awful diagrams.
I don't agree with them.

Everyone is picking at my poetry
with their relentless knives and forks,

trying, no doubt, to find a fly.
I am afraid.

I am afraid of the whole world,
afraid of cold water, afraid of death.
I am as all mortals are,
unable to be patient.

And so, in these brief, passing days,
I shall put them out of my mind.
I shall open up and imprison myself
with my most treacherous enemy,
Pablo Neruda.

ALASTAIR REID

CUÁNTO PASA EN UN DÍA

Dentro de un día nos veremos.

Pero en un día crecen cosas,
se venden uvas en la calle,
cambia la piel de los tomates,
la muchacha que te gustaba
no volvió más a la oficina.

Cambiaron de pronto el cartero.
Las cartas ya no son las mismas.
Varias hojas de oro y es otro:
este árbol es ahora un rico.

Quién nos diría que la tierra
con su vieja piel cambia tanto?
Tiene más volcanes que ayer,
el cielo tiene nuevas nubes,
los ríos van de otra manera.
Además cuánto se construye!
Yo he inaugurado centenares

de carreteras, de edificios,
de puentes puros y delgados
como navíos o violines.

Por eso cuando te saludo
y beso tu boca florida
nuestros besos son otros besos
y nuestras bocas otras bocas.

Salud, amor, salud por todo
lo que cae y lo que florece.

Salud por ayer y por hoy,
por anteayer y por mañana.

Salud por el pan y la piedra,
salud por el fuego y la lluvia.

Por lo que cambia, nace, crece,
se consume y vuelve a ser beso.

Salud por lo que tenemos de aire
y lo que tenemos de tierra.

Cuando se seca nuestra vida
nos quedan sólo las raíces
y el viento es frío como el odio.

Entonces cambiamos de piel,
de uñas, de sangre, de mirada,
y tú me besas y yo salgo
a vender luz por los caminos.

Salud por la noche y el día
y las cuatro estaciones del alma.

HOW MUCH HAPPENS IN A DAY

In the course of a day we shall meet one another.

But, in one day, things spring to life—
they sell grapes in the street,
tomatoes change their skin,
the young girl you wanted
never came back to the office.

They changed the postman suddenly.
The letters now are not the same.
A few golden leaves and it's different;
this tree is now well off.

Who would have said that the earth
with its ancient skin would change so much?
It has more volcanoes than yesterday,
the sky has brand-new clouds,
the rivers are flowing differently.
Besides, so much has come into being!
I have inaugurated hundreds
of highways and buildings,
delicate, clean bridges
like ships or violins.

And so, when I greet you
and kiss your flowering mouth,
our kisses are other kisses,
our mouths are other mouths.

Joy, my love, joy in all things,
in what falls and what flourishes.

Joy in today and yesterday,
the day before and tomorrow.

Joy in bread and stone,
joy in fire and rain.

In what changes, is born, grows,
consumes itself, and becomes a kiss again.

Joy in the air we have,
and in what we have of earth.

When our life dries up,
only the roots remain to us,
and the wind is cold like hate.

Then let us change our skin,
our nails, our blood, our gazing;
and you kiss me and I go out
to sell light on the roads.

Joy in the night and the day,
and the four stations of the soul.

ALASTAIR REID

SOLILOQUY AT TWILIGHT

Given that now perhaps
we are seriously alone,
I mean to ask some questions—
we'll speak man to man.

With you, with that passerby,
with those born yesterday,
with all those who died,
and with those to be born tomorrow,
I want to speak without being overheard,
without them always whispering,
without things getting changed
in ears along the way.

Well then, where from, where to?
What made you decide to be born?
Do you know that the world is small,

scarcely the size of an apple,
like a little hard stone,
and that brothers kill each other
for a fistful of dust?

For the dead there's land enough!

You know by now, or you will,
that time is scarcely one day
and a day is a single drop?

How will you be, how have you been?
Sociable, talkative, silent?
Are you going to outdistance
those who were born with you?
Or will you be sticking a pistol
grimly into their kidneys?

What will you do with so many days
left over, and even more,
with so many missing days?

Do you know there's nobody in the streets
and nobody in the houses?

There are only eyes in the windows.

If you don't have somewhere to sleep,
knock on a door and it will open,
open up to a certain point
and you'll see it's cold inside,
and that that house is empty
and wants nothing to do with you;
your stories are worth nothing,
and if you insist on being gentle,
the dog and cat will bite you.

Until later, till you forget me—

I'm going, since I don't have time
to ask the wind more questions.

I can scarcely walk properly,
I'm in such a hurry.
Somewhere they're waiting
to accuse me of something
and I have to defend myself;
nobody knows what it's about
except that it's urgent,
and if I don't go, it will close,
and how can I hold my own
if I knock and nobody opens the door?

Until later, we'll speak before then.
Or speak after, I don't remember,
or perhaps we haven't even met
or cannot communicate.
I have these crazy habits—
I speak, there is no one and I don't listen,
I ask myself questions and never answer.

ALASTAIR REID

V

I suffer for that friend who died
and who like me was a good carpenter.
Together we worked our way through tables and streets,
through wars, through sorrows, through stones.
How his awareness grew along with mine!
He was dazzling, that bony one,
and his smile was bread to me.
We stopped meeting and V. went on burying himself
till he was forced into the ground.

From then on, the same people
who cornered him while he lived

dress him up, shake him,
bemedal him, refuse him his death,
and they arm the poor sleeping one
with their own sharp thorns
and aim them at me, to kill me,
to see who measures more: my poor dead one,
or I, his living brother.

And I look now for someone to tell this to
and there is no one to understand these miseries,
this consuming bitterness.
It would take someone generous
and that one no longer smiles.
He's dead, and I find no one to whom I can say
that they cannot and will not accomplish anything—
he, in the country of his death,
with his work fulfilled
and I with my labors.
We are only two poor carpenters
who deserve respect among ourselves,
with a right to death and a right to life.

ALASTAIR REID

HORSES

From the window I saw the horses.

I was in Berlin, in winter. The light
was without light, the sky skyless.

The air white like a moistened loaf.

From my window, I could see a deserted arena,
a circle bitten out by the teeth of winter.

All at once, led out by a single man,
ten horses were stepping, stepping into the snow.

Scarcely had they rippled into existence
like flame, than they filled the whole world of my eyes,
empty till now. Faultless, flaming,
they stepped like ten gods on broad, clean hoofs,
their manes recalling a dream of salt spray.

Their rumps were globes, were oranges.

Their color was amber and honey, was on fire.

Their necks were towers
carved from the stone of pride,
and in their furious eyes, sheer energy
showed itself, a prisoner inside them.

And there, in the silence, at the mid-
point of the day, in a dirty, disgruntled winter,
the horses' intense presence was blood,
was rhythm, was the beckoning light of all being.

I saw, I saw, and seeing, I came to life.
There was the unwitting fountain, the dance of gold, the sky,
the fire that sprang to life in beautiful things.

I have obliterated that gloomy Berlin winter.

I shall not forget the light from these horses.

ALASTAIR REID

WE ARE MANY

Of the many men who I am, who we are,
I can't find a single one;
they disappear among my clothes,
they've left for another city.

When everything seems to be set
to show me off as intelligent,
the fool I always keep hidden
takes over all that I say.

At other times, I'm asleep
among distinguished people,
and when I look for my brave self,
a coward unknown to me
rushes to cover my skeleton
with a thousand fine excuses.

When a decent house catches fire,
instead of the fireman I summon,
an arsonist bursts on the scene,
and that's me. What can I do?
What can I do to distinguish myself?
How can I pull myself together?

All the books I read
are full of dazzling heroes,
always sure of themselves.
I die with envy of them;
and in films full of wind and bullets,
I goggle at the cowboys,
I even admire the horses.

But when I call for a hero,
out comes my lazy old self;
so I never know who I am,
nor how many I am or will be.
I'd love to be able to touch a bell
and summon the real me,
because if I really need myself,
I mustn't disappear.

While I am writing, I'm far away;
and when I come back, I've gone.
I would like to know if others

go through the same things that I do,
have as many selves as I have,
and see themselves similarly;
and when I've exhausted this problem,
I'm going to study so hard
that when I explain myself,
I'll be talking geography.

ALASTAIR REID

TO THE FOOT FROM ITS CHILD

The child's foot is not yet aware it's a foot,
and would like to be a butterfly or an apple.

But in time, stones and bits of glass,
streets, ladders,
and the paths in the rough earth
go on teaching the foot that it cannot fly,
cannot be a fruit bulging on the branch.
Then, the child's foot
is defeated, falls
in the battle,
is a prisoner
condemned to live in a shoe.

Bit by bit, in that dark,
it grows to know the world in its own way,
out of touch with its fellow, enclosed,
feeling out life like a blind man.

These soft nails
of quartz, bunched together,
grow hard, and change themselves
into opaque substance, hard as horn,
and the tiny, petaled toes of the child
grow bunched and out of trim,
take on the form of eyeless reptiles

with triangular heads, like worms.
Later, they grow callused
and are covered
with the faint volcanoes of death,
a coarsening hard to accept.

But this blind thing walks
without respite, never stopping
for hour after hour,
the one foot, the other,
now the man's,
now the woman's,
up above,
down below,
through fields, mines,
markets, and ministries,
backwards,
far afield, inward,
forward,
this foot toils in its shoe,
scarcely taking time
to bare itself in love or sleep;
it walks, they walk,
until the whole man chooses to stop.

And then it descended
underground, unaware,
for there, everything, everything was dark.
It never knew it had ceased to be a foot
or if they were burying it so that it could fly
or so that it could become
an apple.

ALASTAIR REID

AQUÍ VIVIMOS

Yo soy de los que viven
a medio mar y cerca del crepúsculo,
más allá de esas piedras.

Cuando yo vine
y vi lo que pasaba
me decidí de pronto.

El día ya se había repartido,
ya era todo de luz
y el mar peleaba
como un león de sal,
con muchas manos.

La soledad abierta allí cantaba,
y yo, perdido y puro,
mirando hacia el silencio
abrí la boca, dije:
'Oh madre de la espuma,
soledad espaciosa,
fundaré aquí mi propio regocijo,
mi singular lamento.'

Desde entonces jamás
me defraudó una ola,
siempre encontré sabor central de cielo
en el agua, en la tierra,
y la leña y el mar ardieron juntos
durante los solitarios inviernos.

Gracias doy a la tierra
por haberme
esperado
a la hora en que el cielo y el océano
se unen como dos labios,
porque no es poco, no es así? haber vivido

en una soledad y haber llegado a otra,
sentirse multitud y revivirse solo.

Amo todas las cosas,
y entre todos los fuegos
sólo el amor no gasta,
por eso voy de vida en vida,
de guitarra en guitarra,
y no le tengo miedo
a la luz ni a la sombra,
y porque casi soy de tierra pura
tengo cucharas para el infinito.

Así, pues, nadie puede equivocarse,
no hallar mi casa sin puertas ni número,
allí entre las piedras oscuras
frente al destello
de la sal violenta,
allí vivimos mi mujer y yo,
allí nos quedaremos.
Auxilio, auxilio! Ayuden!
Ayúdennos a ser más tierra cada día!
Ayúdennos a ser
más espuma sagrada, más aire de la ola!

THIS IS WHERE WE LIVE

I am one of those who live
in the middle of the sea and close to the twilight,
a little beyond those stones.

When I came
and saw what was happening
I decided on the spot.

The day had spread itself
and everything was light
and the sea was beating
like a salty lion,
many-handed.

All that deserted space was singing
and I, lost and awed,
looking toward the silence,
opened my mouth and said:
"Mother of the foam,
expansive solitude,
here I will begin my own rejoicing,
my particular poetry."

From then on I was never
let down by a single wave.
I always found the flavor of the sky
in the water, in the earth,
and the wood and the sea burned together
through the lonely winters.

I am grateful to the earth
for having waited
for me
when sky and sea came together
like two lips touching;
for that's no small thing, no?—
to have lived
through one solitude to arrive at another,
to feel oneself many things and recover wholeness.

I love all the things there are,
and of all fires
love is the only inexhaustible one;
and that's why I go from life to life,
from guitar to guitar,
and I have no fear
of light or of shade,

and almost being earth myself,
I spoon away at infinity.

So no one can ever fail
to find my doorless numberless house—
there between dark stones,
facing the flash
of the violent salt,
there we live, my woman and I,
there we take root.
Grant us help then.
Help us to be more of the earth each day!
Help us to be
more the sacred foam,
more the swish of the wave!

ALASTAIR REID

GETAWAY

I almost thought in my sleep.
I almost dreamed in the dust,
in the falling rain of the dream.
I felt I had old teeth
as I fell asleep; perhaps
little by little I'm changing,
changing into a horse.

I caught the smell of the rough
grass, of the mountain ranges,
and I galloped toward water,
toward the four stormy
stations of the wind.

Good to be a horse
loose in the June light
close to Selva Negra
where the rivers run

tunneling under the turf—
the air there runs a comb
along a horse's flanks
and the language of leaves
moves in the blood.

I galloped that night
without end or country, alone,
coursing through mud and wheat,
dreams and springwater.
I left behind like centuries
the corrugated forests,
the conversations of trees,
the greening capitals,
the families of the soil.

I went back to my own region,
went back to not dreaming
on the street, to being
this grayish traveler
in the world of barbershops,
this me wearing shoes,
with hunger and spectacles,
who doesn't know where
he came from, who is lost,
who gets up in the morning
missing the meadow grass,
who goes to bed sightless
to dream without rain.

The minute they're not looking,
I leave for Renaico.

ALASTAIR REID

THE UNHAPPY ONE

I left her in the doorway waiting
and I went away, away.

She didn't know I would not come back.

A dog passed, a nun passed,
a week and a year passed.

The rains washed out my footprints
and the grass grew in the street,
and one after another, like stones,
like gradual stones, the years
came down on her head.

Then the war came
like a volcano of blood.
Children and houses died.

And that woman didn't die.

The whole plain caught fire.
The gentle yellow gods
who for a thousand years
had gone on meditating
were cast from the temple in pieces.
They could not go on dreaming.

The sweet houses, the veranda
where I slept in a hammock,
the rosy plants, the leaves
in the shape of huge hands,
the chimneys, the marimbas,
all were crushed and burned.

And where the city had been
only cinders were left,
twisted iron, grotesque

heads of dead statues
and a black stain of blood.

And that woman waiting.

ALASTAIR REID

PASTORAL

I copy out mountains, rivers, clouds.
I take my pen from my pocket. I note down
a bird in its rising
or a spider in its little silkworks.
Nothing else crosses my mind. I am air,
clear air, where the wheat is waving,
where a bird's flight moves me, the uncertain
fall of a leaf, the globular
eye of a fish unmoving in the lake,
the statues sailing in the clouds,
the intricate variations of the rain.

Nothing else crosses my mind except
the transparency of summer. I sing only of the wind,
and history passes in its carriage,
collecting its shrouds and medals,
and passes, and all I feel is rivers.
I stay alone with the spring.

Shepherd, shepherd, don't you know
they are all waiting for you?

I know, I know, but here beside the water
while the locusts chitter and sparkle,
although they are waiting, I want to wait for myself.
I too want to watch myself.
I want to discover at last my own feelings.
And when I reach the place where I am waiting,
I expect to fall asleep, dying of laughter.

ALASTAIR REID

BESTIARY

If I could speak with birds,
with oysters and with little lizards,
with the foxes of the Dark Forest,
with the exemplary penguins;
if the sheep,
the languid woolly lapdogs,
the cart horses would understand me;
if I could discuss things with cats,
if hens would listen to me!

It has never occurred to me to speak
with elegant animals:
I am not curious
about the opinion of wasps
or of racing mares.
Let them settle matters while flying,
let them win decorations by running!
I want to speak with flies,
with the bitch that has recently littered,
and to converse with snakes.

When I had feet for walking
in triple nights now past,
I followed the nocturnal dogs,
those squalid travelers
that trot in silence
with great haste traveling nowhere,
and I followed them for many hours.
They mistrusted me,
ah, poor stupid dogs,
they lost their opportunity
to pour out their sorrows,
to run through streets of ghosts
with grief and tail.

I have always been curious
about the erotic rabbit.

Who excites them and whispers
in their genital ears?
They procreate endlessly
and pay no attention to Saint Francis,
they hear no nonsense:
the rabbit mounts and remounts
with an inexhaustible organism.
I wish to speak with the rabbit,
I like his flighty habits.

Spiders are wasted
on exasperating naturalists who
in their foolish pages
see them with a fly's eyes,
describe them as devouring,
carnal, unfaithful, sexual, lascivious.
For me this reputation
provides a portrait of those who
impute it to them:
the spider is an engineer,
a divine watchmaker,
that the idiots detest
for a fly more or less.
I want to converse with a spider:
I want her to weave me a star.

Fleas interest me so much
that I let them bite me for hours.
They are perfect, ancient, Sanskrit,
machines that admit of no appeal.
They do not bite to eat,
they bite only to jump;
they are the dancers of the celestial sphere,
delicate acrobats
in the softest and most profound circus;
let them gallop on my skin,
divulge their emotions,
amuse themselves with my blood,
but someone should introduce them to me.

I want to know them closely,
I want to know what to rely on.

I have never been able to become
intimate with ruminants in any deep way,
yet I am a ruminant;
I do not understand their not understanding me.
I must take up this subject
grazing with cows and oxen,
and working out plans with bulls.
In some manner I will know
so many intestinal things
which were hidden within
like clandestine passions.

What does the pig think of the dawn?
They do not sing but they hold it up
with their great rosy bodies,
with their hard little feet.

The pigs hold up the dawn.

The birds consume the night.

And in the morning the world is deserted:
the spiders, men, dogs, the wind sleep,
pigs grunt and day breaks.

I want to speak with pigs.

Sweet, sonorous, husky-voiced frogs!
I always wanted to be a frog for a day,
always loved the pool, the leaves
fine as filaments,
the green world of the watercress
where the frogs are masters of the sky.

The frogs' serenade
rises into my dream and excites it,

rises like a twisting vine
to the balconies of my childhood,
to my cousin's breasts,
to the astronomical jasmines
in the black night of the South,
and now that the time has passed
let them not ask the sky of me.
I think that I have not yet learned
the hoarse idiom of the frogs.

If this is so, how am I a poet?
What do I know of the multiplied
geography of the night?

In this world which runs and is silent,
I want more communications,
other languages, other signs,
I want to know this world.

Everyone has been contented
with the sinister presentations
of shrewd capitalists
and systematic women.
I want to speak with many things
and I will not leave this planet
without knowing what I came to seek,
without investigating this matter,
and people do not suffice for me,
I have to go much further
and I have to go much closer.

Therefore, gentlemen, I am going
to converse with a horse.
May the poetess excuse me,
and the professor forgive me.
My whole week is taken up,
I have to listen to a confusion of talk.

What was the name of that cat?

ELSA NEUBERGER

AUTUMN TESTAMENT

*The poet
talks of his
state and his
predilections*

Between dying and not dying
I picked on the guitar
and in that dedication
my heart takes no respite,
for where I'm least expected
I turn up with my stuff
to gather the first wine
in the sombreros of autumn.

If they close the door, I'll go in;
if they greet me, I'll be off.
I'm not one of those sailors
who flounder about on the ice.
I'm adaptable as the wind is,
with the yellowest leaves,
with the fallen histories
in the eyes of statues,
and if I come to rest anywhere,
it's in the nub of the fire,
the throbbing crackling part
that flies off to nowhere.

Along the margins
you'll have come across your name;
I don't apologize,
it had to do with nothing
except almost everything,
for you do and you don't exist—
that happens to everybody—
nobody realizes,
and when they add up the figures,
we're not rich at all—
now we're the new poor.

*He speaks of
his enemies
and divides
up his
possessions*
I've been ripped apart
by a set of spitting rodents
who seemed too much for me.
In the sea I would often eat
dark sea cucumbers,
strange kinds of amber,
and storm lost cities
in my shirt and my armor
in ways that would kill you—
you would die of laughter.

So I leave to all who snarled at me
my traveler's eyelashes,
my passion for salt,
the slant of my smile—
let them take it all away
discreetly, if that's possible;
since they weren't able to kill me
I can hardly stop them
from dressing in my clothes
or appearing on Sundays
convincingly disguised.
I left no one in peace
so they'll grant me no peace.
That's clear, but it doesn't matter—
they'll be publishing my socks.

*He turns to
other matters*
I've left my worldly goods
to my party and my people—
we're talking here of other things,
things both obscure and clear
which all add up to one thing.
It's the same with the grapes
and their two powerful children,
white wine, red wine.
All life is red and white,
all clarity is cloudy.

It's not all earth and adobe—
I inherited shadows and dreams.

He replies to   Once they asked me
some well-   why my writing was so obscure.
meaning   They might ask the night that,
people   or minerals, or roots.
I didn't know what to answer,
then, some time after,
two crazy men attacked me,
saying I was simple—
the answer's in running water
and I went off, running and singing.

He parcels out   Has anyone been granted
his sufferings   as much joy as I have
(it flows through my veins)
and this fruitful unfruitful mixture
that is my nature?
I've been a great flowing river
with hard ringing stones,
with clear night-noises,
with dark day-songs.
To whom can I leave so much,
so much and so little,
joy beyond its objects,
a lone horse by the sea,
a loom weaving the wind?

And hands on   My own sorrows I leave to
his joys   all those who made me suffer
but by now I've forgotten them
and I don't know where I lost them—
if they turn up in the forest
they're like tangleweed.
They grow from the ground up
and end where you end,
at your head, at the air—

to keep them from growing,
spring has to be changed.

*He comes out
against hate*
I've come within range of hate.
Terrifying, its tremors,
its dizzying obsessions.
Hate's like a swordfish
invisible in the water,
knifing suddenly into sight
with blood on its blade—
clear water misleads you.

Why, why do we hate so much
those who hate us?
There they are underwater,
hunters lying in wait,
swords and oilcans ready,
spiderwebs and mousetraps.
It has nothing to do with being Christian,
or with prayer or with tailoring;
it's just that hate is a loser.
Scales fell from eyes
in the poison market;
meanwhile the sun comes out
and I start to work
and to buy bread and wine.

*But deals
with it in
his will*
To hate I'll leave
my own horseshoes,
my sailor's shirt,
my traveler's shoes,
my carpenter's heart,
all things I did well,
and which helped me to suffer,
the strong clear things I had,
permanent and passing,
so that it dawns on the world
that those who have trees and water

can carve ships, set sail,
can go away and come back,
suffer and love,
have fears, do work,
be and go on being,
be fruitful and die,
be simple and complex,
not have ears,
turn misery to account,
wait for a flower's coming—
in a word, live;
although there are always some shitheads
who will not accept our lives.

At last he Matilde Urrutia, I'm leaving you here
turns in all I had, all I didn't have,
ecstasy to all I am, all I am not.
his love My love is a child crying,
reluctant to leave your arms,
I leave it to you forever—
you are my chosen one.

You are my chosen one,
more tempered by winds
than thin trees in the south,
a hazel in August;
for me you are as delicious
as a great bakery.
You have an earth heart
but your hands are from heaven.

You are red and spicy,
you are white and salty
like pickled onions,
you are a laughing piano
with every human note;
and music runs over me
from your eyelashes and your hair.
I wallow in your gold shadow,

I'm enchanted by your ears
as though I had seen them before
in underwater coral.
In the sea for your nails' sake,
I took on terrifying fish.

Your eyes widen from south to south,
your smile goes east and west;
your feet can hardly be seen,
and the sun takes pleasure
in dawning in your hair.
Your face and your body come from
hard places, as I do,
from rain-washed rituals,
ancient lands and martyrs.
The Bío-Bío still sings
in our bloodstained clay,
but you brought from the forest
every secret scent,
and the way your profile has of shining
like a lost arrow,
an old warrior's medal.
You overcame me
with love and origins,
because your mouth brought back
ancient beginnings,
forest meetings from another time,
dark ancestral drums.
I suddenly heard myself summoned—
it was far away, vague.
I moved close to ancient foliage.
I touched my blood in your mouth,
dear love, my Araucana.

What can I leave you, Matilde,
when you have at your touch
that aura of burning leaves,
that fragrance of strawberries,
and between your sea-breasts

the half-light of Cauquenes,
and the laurel-smell of Chile?

It is high autumn at sea,
full of mists and hidden places;
the land stretches and breathes,
leaves fall by the month.
And you, bent over my work,
with both passion and patience,
deciphering the green prints,
the spiderwebs, the insects
of my fateful handwriting.
Lioness on your little feet,
what would I do without
the neat ways of your hands?
Where would I be wandering
with no heart, with no end?
On what faraway buses,
flushed with fire or snow?

I owe you marine autumn
with dankness at its roots
and fog like a grape
and the graceful sun of the country;
and the silent space
in which sorrows lose themselves
and only the bright crown
of joy comes to the surface.
I owe you it all,
my unchained dove,
my crested quail,
my mountain finch,
my peasant from Coihueco.

Sometime when we've stopped being,
stopped coming and going,
under seven blankets of dust
and the dry feet of death,
we'll be close again, love,

curious and puzzled.
Our different feathers,
our bumbling eyes,
our feet which didn't meet
and our printed kisses,
all will be back together,
but what good will it do us,
the closeness of a grave?
Let life not separate us;
and who cares about death?

Last remarks   So I'm saying goodbye, gentlemen,
after so many farewells;
and since I'm leaving nothing,
I want everyone to have something;
the stormiest thing I had,
the craziest and most seething
comes back to earth, comes back to life.
The petals of well-wishing
fell like bells
in the green mouth of the wind.

But I've had in abundance
the bounty of friends and strangers.
I've found generosity
wherever my ways took me
and I found it everywhere
like a shared-out heart.

Nor did medicinal frontiers
ever upset my exile—
they shared bread with me,
danger, shelter, wine.
The world threw open its orchards
and I went in, like Jack to his house,
between two rows of tenderness.
I have as many friends in the South
as I have in the North,
the sun could never set

on my friends in the East—
and how many in the West?
I can't count the wheat.
I can't number or count
my friends among the Oyarzunes.
In America, shaken by
so much night-fear,
there's not a moon doesn't know me,
no roads that don't expect me,
in the poor clay villages
or the concrete cities
there's some remote Arce
whom I don't know yet
except we were born brothers.

Everywhere I gathered
the honey that bears devour,
the secret stirrings of spring,
the treasure of the elephants,
and that I leave to my own ones,
the clear stream of my family.
The people defined me
and I never stopped being one of them.
I held in the palm of my hand
the world with its archipelagoes
and since I can't be denied,
I never denied my heart,
or oysters, or stars.

The poets ends his book by talking about his transformations and confirms his faith in poetry

From having been born so often
I have salty experience
like creatures of the sea
with a passion for stars
and an earthy destination.
And so I move without knowing
to which world I'll be returning
or if I'll go on living.
While things are settling down,
here I've left my testament,

my shifting extravagaria,
so whoever goes on reading it
will never take in anything
except the constant moving
of a clear and bewildered man,
a man rainy and happy,
lively and autumn–minded.

And now I'm going behind
this page, but not disappearing.
I'll dive into clear air
like a swimmer in the sky,
and then get back to growing
till one day I'm so small
that the wind will take me away
and I won't know my own name
and I won't be there when I wake.

Then I will sing in the silence.

ALASTAIR REID

from

VOYAGES AND
HOMECOMINGS

NAVEGACIONES Y

REGRESOS

❋

1957–1959

ODE TO THINGS

I love things with a wild passion,
extravagantly.
I cherish tongs,
and scissors;
I adore
cups,
hoops,
soup tureens,
not to mention
of course—the hat.
I love
all things,
not only the
grand,
but also
the infinite-
ly
small:
the thimble,
spurs,
dishes,
vases.

Oh, my soul,
the planet
is radiant,
teeming with
pipes
in hand,
conductors
of smoke;
with keys,
saltshakers, and
well,
things crafted
by the human hand, everything—
the curves of a shoe,

fabric,
the new bloodless
birth
of gold,
the eyeglasses,
nails,
brooms,
watches, compasses,
coins, the silken
plushness of chairs.

Oh
humans
have constructed
a multitude of pure things:
objects of wood,
crystal,
cord,
wondrous
tables,
ships, staircases.

I love
all
things,
not because they
might be warm
or fragrant,
but rather because—
I don't know why,
because
this ocean is yours,
and mine:
the buttons,
the wheels,
the little
forgotten
treasures,
the fans

of feathery
love spreading
orange blossoms,
the cups, the knives,
the shears,
everything rests
in the handle, the contour,
the traces
of fingers,
of a remote hand
lost
in the most forgotten regions of the ordinary obscured.

I pass through houses,
streets,
elevators,
touching things;
I glimpse objects
and secretly desire
something because it chimes,
and something else because
because it is as yielding
as gentle hips,
something else I adore for its deepwater hue,
something else for its velvety depths.

Oh irrevocable
river
of things.
People will not
say that I only
loved
fish
or plants of the rain forest or meadow,
that I only
loved
things that leap, rise, sigh, and survive.
It is not true:
many things gave me completeness.

They did not only touch me.
My hand did not merely touch them,
but rather,
they befriended
my existence
in such a way
that with me, they indeed existed,
and they were for me so full of life,
that they lived with me half-alive,
and they will die with me half-dead.

KEN KRABBENHOFT

ODE TO THE CHAIR

A chair in the jungle:
under the severe lianas
a sacred tree trunk creaks,
tangles of vines press high,
in the shadows
bloody beasts cry out,
majestic leaves descend from the green sky,
the rattles of snakes
quiver like bells.
A bird spanned the sprawling greenness,
like an arrow shot through a flag,
and branches hoisted high their violins.
Insects
pray in stillness,
seated on their wild bouquets.
Feet sink into
the black sargasso
of the watery jungle,
into the rain forest's tumbled clouds.
I only request one thing
for the stranger,
for the desperate

explorer,
a chair in the tree of chairs,
a throne,
disheveled and plush,
the velvet of a deep easy chair,
eaten away by creepers.
Yes,
a chair,
loving the universe,
for the walkabout man,
the sure
foundation,
the supreme
dignity
of rest!

Behind thirsty tigers,
bands of bloodthirsty flies,
behind the black expanse
of ghost-ridden leaves,
behind the low waters,
the thicket like iron,
perpetual snakes,
in the middle
of the thunder,
a chair,
a chair,
for me,
for everyone,
a chair not
only for the weary body's
rescue,
but also for everything,
and for everybody,
to renew lost strength,
and for meditation.

War is wide like the light–starved jungle.
Peace
begins
in
a
single
chair.

KEN KRABBENHOFT

from

ONE HUNDRED
LOVE SONNETS

CIEN SONETOS
DE AMOR

1957–1959

❋

III

Bitter love, a violet with its crown
of thorns in a thicket of spiky passions,
spear of sorrow, corolla of rage: how did you come
to conquer my soul? What via dolorosa brought you?

Why did you pour your tender fire
so quickly, over my life's cool leaves?
Who pointed the way to you? What flower,
what rock, what smoke showed you where I live?

Because the earth shook—it did—, that awful night;
then dawn filled all the goblets with its wine;
the heavenly sun declared itself;

while inside, a ferocious love wound around
and around me—till it pierced me with its thorns, its sword,
slashing a seared road through my heart.

STEPHEN TAPSCOTT

IV

Recordarás aquella quebrada caprichosa
a donde los aromas palpitantes treparon,
de cuando en cuando un pájaro vestido
con agua y lentitud: traje de invierno.

Recordarás los dones de la tierra:
irascible fragancia, barro de oro,
hierbas del matorral, locas raíces,
sortílegas espinas como espadas.

Recordarás el ramo que trajiste,
ramo de sombra y agua con silencio,
ramo como una piedra con espuma.

Y aquella vez fue como nunca y siempre:
vamos allí donde no espera nada
y hallamos todo lo que está esperando.

IV

You will remember that leaping stream
where sweet aromas rose and trembled,
and sometimes a bird, wearing water
and slowness, its winter feathers.

You will remember those gifts from the earth:
indelible scents, gold clay,
weeds in the thicket and crazy roots,
magical thorns like swords.

You'll remember the bouquet you picked,
shadows and silent water,
bouquet like a foam-covered stone.

That time was like never, and like always.
So we go there, where nothing is waiting;
we find everything waiting there.

STEPHEN TAPSCOTT

VI

In the forests, lost, I cut a dark stick
and lifted its whisper to my thirsty lips:
perhaps it was the voice of crying rain,
a broken bell, or a torn heart.

Something that from so far away seemed
seriously hidden to me, covered by the earth,
a cry deafened by immense autumns,
by the darkness of the leaves, humid and ajar.

But there, waking from the dreams of the forest,
the hazel branch sung below my mouth
and its roaming odor climbed to my view

as if the roots which I had abandoned, the land
lost with my childhood, suddenly came searching for me,
and I stopped, wounded by the wandering aroma.

MARK EISNER

IX

Al golpe de la ola contra la piedra indócil
la claridad estalla y establece su rosa
y el círculo del mar se reduce a un racimo,
a una sola gota de sal azul que cae.

Oh radiante magnolia desatada en la espuma,
magnética viajera cuya muerte florece
y eternamente vuelve a ser y a no ser nada:
sal rota, deslumbrante movimiento marino.

Juntos tú y yo, amor mío, sellamos el silencio,
mientras destruye el mar sus constantes estatuas
y derrumba sus torres de arrebato y blancura,

porque en la trama de estos tejidos invisibles
del agua desbocada, de la incesante arena,
sostenemos la única y acosada ternura.

IX

There where the waves shatter on the restless rocks
the clear light bursts and enacts its rose,
and the sea-circle shrinks to a cluster of buds,
to one drop of blue salt, falling.

O bright magnolia bursting in the foam,
magnetic transient whose death blooms
and vanishes—being, nothingness—forever:
broken salt, dazzling lurch of the sea.

You and I, Love, together we ratify the silence,
while the sea destroys its perpetual statues,
collapses its towers of wild speed and whiteness:

because in the weavings of those invisible fabrics,
galloping water, incessant sand,
we make the only permanent tenderness.

STEPHEN TAPSCOTT

XI

I crave your mouth, your voice, your hair.
Silent and starving, I prowl through the streets.
Bread does not nourish me, dawn disrupts me, all day
I hunt for the liquid measure of your steps.

I hunger for your sleek laugh,
your hands the color of a savage harvest,
hunger for the pale stones of your fingernails,
I want to eat your skin like a whole almond.

I want to eat the sunbeam flaring in your lovely body,
the sovereign nose of your arrogant face,
I want to eat the fleeting shade of your lashes,

and I pace around hungry, sniffing the twilight,
hunting for you, for your hot heart,
like a puma in the barrens of Quitratúe.

STEPHEN TAPSCOTT

XVI

I love the handful of the earth you are.
Because of its meadows, vast as a planet,
I have no other star. You are my replica
of the multiplying universe.

Your wide eyes are the only light I know
from extinguished constellations;
your skin throbs like the streak
of a meteor through rain.

Your hips were that much of the moon for me;
your deep mouth and its delights, that much sun;
your heart, fiery with its long red rays,

was that much ardent light, like honey in the shade.
So I pass across your burning form, kissing
you—compact and planetary, my dove, my globe.

STEPHEN TAPSCOTT

XVII

I don't love you as if you were a rose of salt, topaz,
or arrow of carnations that propagate fire:
I love you as one loves certain dark things,
secretly, between the shadow and the soul.

I love you as the plant that doesn't bloom and carries
the light of those flowers, hidden, within itself,

and thanks to your love the tight aroma that rose
from the earth lives in my body in darkness.

I love you without knowing how, or when, or from where
I love you directly without problems or pride:
I love you like this because I don't know any other way to love

except in this form in which I am not nor are you,
so close that your hand upon my chest is mine,
so close that your eyes close with my dreams.

MARK EISNER

XXVII

Naked, you are as simple as one of your hands,
smooth, earthen, minimal, round, transparent,
you have moon lines, apple paths,
naked, you are slender as naked wheat.

Naked you are blue as the night in Cuba,
you have vines and stars in your hair,
naked you are as enormous and yellow
as summer in a church of gold.

Naked you are as small as one of your nails,
curved, subtle, rose until day is born
and you withdraw into the world's subterrane

as if in a long tunnel of clothes and chores:
your clarity flickers out, dresses, looses its leaves—
and once more returns to being a naked hand.

MARK EISNER

XXXIV

Eres hija del mar y prima del orégano,
nadadora, tu cuerpo es de agua pura,
cocinera, tu sangre es tierra viva
y tus costumbres son floridas y terrestres.

Al agua van tus ojos y levantan las olas,
a la tierra tus manos y saltan las semillas,
en agua y tierra tienes propiedades profundas
que en ti se juntan como las leyes de la greda.

Náyade, corta tu cuerpo la turquesa
y luego resurrecto florece en la cocina
de tal modo que asumes cuanto existe

y al fin duermes rodeada por mis brazos que apartan
de la sombra sombría, para que tú descanses,
legumbres, algas, hierbas: la espuma de tus sueños.

XXXIV

You are the daughter of the sea, oregano's first cousin.
Swimmer, your body is pure as the water;
cook, your blood is quick as the soil.
Everything you do is full of flowers, rich with the earth.

Your eyes go out toward the water, and the waves rise;
your hands go out to the earth, and the seeds swell;
you know the deep essence of water and the earth,
conjoined in you like a formula for clay.

Naiad: cut your body into turquoise pieces,
they will bloom resurrected in the kitchen.
This is how you become everything that lives.

And so, at last, you sleep, in the circle of my arms
that push back the shadows so that you can rest—
vegetables, seaweed, herbs: the foam of your dreams.

STEPHEN TAPSCOTT

XXXIX

But I forgot that your hands fed the roots,
watering the tangled roses,
till your fingerprints bloomed
full, in a natural peace.

Like pets, your hoe and your sprinkling can
follow you around, biting and licking the earth.
That work is how you let this richness loose,
the carnations' fiery freshness.

I wish the love and dignity of bees for your hands,
mixing and spreading their transparent brood
in the earth: they cultivate even my heart,

so that I am like a scorched rock
that suddenly sings when you are near, because it drinks
the water you carry from the forest, in your voice.

STEPHEN TAPSCOTT

XL

It was green, the silence; the light was moist;
the month of June trembled like a butterfly;
and you, Matilde, passed through noon,
through the regions of the South, the sea, and the stones.

You went carrying your cargo of iron flowers,
seaweed battered and abandoned by the South wind,
but your hands, still white, cracked by corrosive salt,
gathered the blooming stalks that grew in the sand.

I love your pure gifts, your skin like whole stones,
your nails, offerings, in the suns of your fingers,
your mouth brimming with all joys.

Oh, in my house beside the abyss, give me
the tormenting structure of that silence,
pavilion of the sea, forgotten in the sand.

STEPHEN TAPSCOTT

XLVII

I want to look back and see you in the branches.
Little by little you turned into fruit.
It was easy for you to rise from the roots,
singing your syllable of sap.

Here you will be a fragrant flower first,
changed to the statuesque form of a kiss,
till the sun and the earth, blood and the sky, fulfill
their promises of sweetness and pleasure, in you.

There in the branches I will recognize your hair,
your image ripening in the leaves,
bringing the petals nearer my thirst,

and my mouth will fill with the taste of you,
the kiss that rose from the earth
with your blood, the blood of a lover's fruit.

STEPHEN TAPSCOTT

XLVIII

Dos amantes dichosos hacen un solo pan,
una sola gota de luna en la hierba,
dejan andando dos sombras que se reúnen,
dejan un solo sol vacío en una cama.

De todas las verdades escogieron el día:
no se ataron con hilos sino con un aroma,
y no despedazaron la paz ni las palabras.
La dicha es una torre transparente.

El aire, el vino van con los dos amantes,
la noche les regala sus pétalos dichosos,
tienen derecho a todos los claveles.

Dos amantes dichosos no tienen fin ni muerte,
nacen y mueren muchas veces mientras viven,
tienen la eternidad de la naturaleza.

XLVIII

Two happy lovers make one bread,
a single moon drop in the grass.
Walking, they cast two shadows that flow together;
waking, they leave one sun empty in their bed.

Of all the possible truths, they chose the day;
they held it, not with ropes but with an aroma.
They did not shred the peace; they did not shatter words;
their happiness is a transparent tower.

The air and wine accompany the lovers.
The night delights them with its joyous petals.
They have a right to all the carnations.

Two happy lovers, without an ending, with no death,
they are born, they die, many times while they live:
they have the eternal life of the Natural.

STEPHEN TAPSCOTT

L

Cotapos says your laughter drops
like a hawk from a stony tower. It's true:
daughter of the sky, you slit the world
and its green leaves, with one bolt of your lightning:

it falls, it thunders: the tongues of the dew,
the waters of a diamond, the light with its bees
leap. And there where a long-bearded silence had lived,
little bombs of light explode, the sun and the stars,

down comes the sky, with its thick-shadowed night,
bells and carnations glow in the full moon,
the saddlemakers' horses gallop.

Because you are small as you are, let it
rip: let the meteor of your laughter
fly: electrify the natural names of things!

STEPHEN TAPSCOTT

LIII

Here are the bread—the wine—the table—the house:
a man's needs, and a woman's, and a life's.
Peace whirled through and settled in this place:
the common fire burned, to make this light.

Hail to your two hands, which fly and make
their white creations, the singing and the food:
salve! the wholesomeness of your busy feet;
viva! the ballerina who dances with the broom.

Those rugged rivers of water and of threat,
torturous pavilions of the foam,
incendiary hives and reefs: today

they are this respite, your blood in mine,
this path, starry and blue as the night,
this never-ending simple tenderness.

STEPHEN TAPSCOTT

✳

LV

Thorns, shattered glass, sickness, crying: all day
they attack the honeyed contentment. And neither the tower,
nor the walls, nor secret passageways are of much help.
Trouble seeps through, into the sleepers' peace.

Sorrow rises and falls, comes near with its deep spoons,
and no one can live without this endless motion;
without it there would be no birth, no roof, no fence.
It happens: we have to account for it.

Eyes squeezed shut in love don't help,
nor soft beds far from the pestilent sick,
from the conqueror who advances, pace by pace, with his flag.

For life throbs like a bile, like a river: it opens
a bloody tunnel where eyes stare through at us,
the eyes of a huge and sorrowful family.

STEPHEN TAPSCOTT

LIX

(G. M.)

Poor unlucky poets: whom both life and death
harass, with the same dark stubbornness,
who then are smothered in mindless pomp, committed
to rituals, to a funeral like a craw full of teeth.

Obscure as pebbles now, they are dragged
behind the arrogant horses, to sleep
without silence, overcome in the end
by the invaders, among their minions—

who, then, certain the dead one *is* dead, once and for all,
celebrate their sniveling feast at his funeral
with turkeys, and pigs, and other orators.

They sabotaged his death, and now they defame it—
but only because his mouth is shut:
he can no longer protest with his song.

STEPHEN TAPSCOTT

LXIII

I walked: not only through the wasteland where the salted rock is
like the only rose, a flower buried in the sea—
but also on the banks of rivers gouging through the snow;
the high bitter mountain ranges felt my footsteps too.

Tangled, whistling realms of my savage homeland,
liana vines whose deadly kiss is chained to the jungle,
wet cry of the bird that rises, throwing off its shivers:
O realm of lost sorrow and inclement tears!

The poisonous skin of the copper, the nitrate salt spread out
like a statue, crumbled and snowy: they're mine, but not
only them: also the vineyards, the cherries the spring rewards,

they are mine too, and I belong to them, like a black atom
in the arid land, in the autumn light on the grapes,
in this metallic homeland lifted by towers of snow.

STEPHEN TAPSCOTT

LXXVI

Diego Rivera con la paciencia del oso
buscaba la esmeralda del bosque en la pintura

o el bermellón, la flor súbita de la sangre,
recogía la luz del mundo en tu retrato.

Pintaba el imperioso traje de tu nariz,
la centella de tus pupilas desbocadas,
tus uñas que alimentan la envidia de la luna,
y en tu piel estival, tu boca de sandía.

Te puso dos cabezas de volcán encendidas
por fuego, por amor, por estirpe araucana,
y sobre los dos rostros dorados de la greda

te cubrió con el casco de un incendio bravío
y allí secretamente quedaron enredados
mis ojos en su torre total: tu cabellera.

LXXVI

With the patience of a bear, Diego Rivera
hunted through paint for the forest's emerald,
or vermilion, the blood's sudden flower;
in your picture he gathered the light of the world.

He painted the imperious clothing of your nose,
the spark of your cantering eyes,
your nails that fuel the moon's envy,
and, in your summery skin, the melon of your mouth.

He gave you two heads of molten volcanoes,
for fire, for love, for your Araucan lineage,
and over the two golden faces of clay

he covered you with a helmet of noble fire:
there my eyes lingered, in secret,
tangled in your full and towering hair.

STEPHEN TAPSCOTT

LXXX

My love, I returned from travel and sorrow
to your voice, to your hand flying on the guitar,
to the fire interrupting the autumn with kisses,
to the night that circles through the sky.

I ask for bread and dominion for all;
for the worker with no future I ask for land.
May no one expect my blood or my song to rest!
But I cannot give up your love, not without dying.

So: play the waltz of the tranquil moon,
the barcarole, on the fluid guitar,
till my head lolls, dreaming:

for all my life's sleeplessness has woven
this shelter in the grove where your hand lives and flies,
watching over the night of the sleeping traveler.

STEPHEN TAPSCOTT

XC

I thought I was dying, I felt the cold up close
and knew that from all my life I left only you behind:
my earthly day and night were your mouth,
your skin the republic my kisses founded.

In that instant the books stopped,
and friendship, treasures restlessly amassed,
the transparent house that you and I built:
everything dropped away, except your eyes.

Because while life harasses us, love is
only a wave taller than the other waves:
but oh, when death comes knocking at the gate,

there is only your glance against so much emptiness,
only your light against extinction,
only your love to shut out the shadows.

STEPHEN TAPSCOTT

XCI

Age covers us like drizzle;
time is interminable and sad;
a salt feather touches your face;
a trickle ate through my shirt.

Time does not distinguish between my hands
and a flock of oranges in yours:
with snow and picks life chips away
at your life, which is my life.

My life, which I gave you, fills
with years like a swelling cluster of fruit.
The grapes will return to the earth.

And even down there time
continues, waiting, raining
on the dust, eager to erase even absence.

STEPHEN TAPSCOTT

XCV

Whoever loved as we did? Let us hunt
for the ancient cinders of a heart that burned
and make our kisses fall one by one,
till that empty flower rises again.

Let us love the love that consumed its fruit and went
down, its image and its power, into the earth:
you and I are the light that endures,
its irrevocable delicate thorn.

Bring to that love, entombed by so much cold time,
by snow and spring, by oblivion and autumn,
the light of a new apple, light

of a freshness opened by a new wound,
like that ancient love that passes in silence
through an eternity of buried mouths.

STEPHEN TAPSCOTT

XCVII

These days, one must fly—but where to?
without wings, without an airplane, fly—without a doubt:
the footsteps have passed on, to no avail;
they didn't move the feet of the traveler along.

At every instant, one must fly—like
eagles, like houseflies, like days:
must conquer the rings of Saturn
and build new carillons there.

Shoes and pathways are no longer enough,
the earth is no use anymore to the wanderer:
the roots have already crossed through the night,

and you will appear on another planet,
stubbornly transient,
transformed in the end into poppies.

STEPHEN TAPSCOTT

C

In the center of the earth I will push aside
the emeralds so that I can see you—
you like an amanuensis, with a pen
of water, copying the green sprigs of plants.

What a world! What deep parsley!
What a ship sailing through the sweetness!
And you, maybe—and me, maybe—a topaz.
There'll be no more dissensions in the bells.

There won't be anything but all the fresh air,
apples carried on the wind,
the succulent book in the woods:

and there where the carnations breathe, we will begin
to make ourselves a clothing, something to last
through the eternity of a victorious kiss.

STEPHEN TAPSCOTT

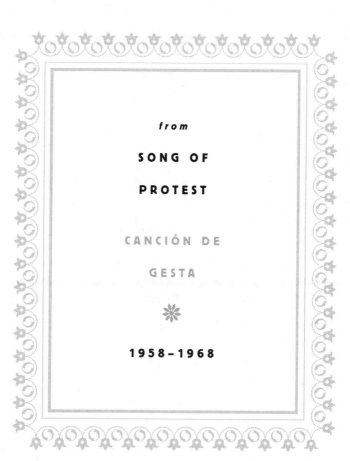

from

SONG OF

PROTEST

CANCIÓN DE

GESTA

❋

1958–1968

IV

CUBA APPEARS

But when tortures and darkness
seem to extinguish the free air
and it is not the spume of the waves
but the blood among the reefs that you see,
Fidel's hand comes forth and in it
Cuba, the pure rose of the Caribbean.
And so History teaches with her light
that man can change that which exists
and if he takes purity into battle
in his honor blooms a noble spring:
behind is left the tyrant's night,
his cruelty and his insensible eyes,
the gold snatched by his claws,
his mercenaries, his cannibal judges,
his high monuments sustained
by torment, dishonor, and crime:
everything falls in the dust of the dead
when the people set their violins
and looking forward interrupt and sing,
interrupt the hatred of shadows and watchdogs,
sing and wake the stars with their song
and pierce the darkness with guns.
And so Fidel came forth cutting shadows
so that the jasmine tree could dawn.

MIGUEL ALGARÍN

VI

ANCIENT HISTORY

Now I open my eyes and I remember:
it sparkles and dims, electric and dark,
with joys and suffering
the bitter and magic history of Cuba.
Years passed as fish pass

through the blue of the sea and its sweetness,
the island lived in liberty and dance,
the palm trees danced with the foam,
Blacks and Whites were a single loaf of bread
because Martí kneaded their ferment,
peace fulfilled its destiny of gold
and the sun crackled in the sugar,
while ripened by the sun fell
a beam of honey over the fruit:
man was content with his reign
and family with its agriculture,
when from the North arrived a seed
threatening, covetous, unjust,
that like a spider spread her threads
extending a metallic structure
that drove bloodied nails into the land
raising over the dead a vault.
It was the dollar with its yellow teeth,
commandant of blood and grave.

MIGUEL ALGARÍN

XI
TREASON

For peace, on a sad night
General Sandino was invited
to dine, to celebrate his courage,
with the "American" Ambassador
(for the name of the whole continent
these pirates have usurped).
General Sandino was joyous:
wine and drinks raised to his health:
the Yankees were returning to their land
desolately defeated
and the banquet sealed with honors
the struggle of Sandino and his brothers.
The assassin waited at the table.

He was a mysterious spineless being
raising his cup time and again
while in his pockets resounded
the thirty horrendous dollars of the crime.
O feast of bloodied wine!
O night, O false moonlit paths!
O pale stars that did not speak!
O land mute and blind by night!
Earth that did not restrain his horse!
O treasonous night that betrayed
the tower of honor into evil hands!
O banquet of silver and agony!
O shadow of premeditated treason!
O pavilion of light that flourished,
since then defeated and mourned!

MIGUEL ALGARÍN

XII
DEATH

Sandino stood up not knowing
that his victory had ended
as the Ambassador pointed him out
thus fulfilling his part of the pact:
everything was arranged for the crime
between the assassin and the North American.
And at the door as they embraced him
they bade him farewell condemning him.
Congratulations! And Sandino took his leave
walking with the executioner and death.

MIGUEL ALGARÍN

XIX
TO FIDEL CASTRO

Fidel, Fidel, the people are grateful
for words in action and deeds that sing,
that is why I bring from far
a cup of my country's wine:
it is the blood of a subterranean people
that from the shadows reaches your throat,
they are miners who have lived for centuries
extracting fire from the frozen land.
They go beneath the sea for coal
but on returning they are like ghosts:
they grew accustomed to eternal night,
the working-day light was robbed from them,
nevertheless here is the cup
of so much suffering and distances:
the happiness of imprisoned men
possessed by darkness and illusions
who from the inside of mines perceive
the arrival of spring and its fragrances
because they know that Man is struggling
to reach the amplest clarity.
And Cuba is seen by the southern miners,
the lonely sons of la pampa,
the shepherds of cold in Patagonia,
the fathers of tin and silver,
the ones who marry cordilleras
extract the copper from Chuquicamata,
men hidden in buses
in populations of pure nostalgia,
women of the fields and workshops,
children who cried away their childhoods:
this is the cup, take it, Fidel.
It is full of so much hope
that upon drinking you will know your victory
is like the aged wine of my country
made not by one man but by many men
and not by one grape but many plants:

it is not one drop but many rivers:
not one captain but many battles.
And they support you because you represent
the collective honor of our long struggle,
and if Cuba were to fall we would all fall,
and we would come to lift her,
and if she blooms with all her flowers
she will flourish with our own nectar.
And if they dare touch Cuba's
forehead, by your own hands liberated,
they will find the people's fists,
we will take out our buried weapons:
blood and pride will come to rescue,
to defend our beloved Cuba.

MIGUEL ALGARÍN

XXII
SO IS MY LIFE

My duty moves along with my song:
I am I am not: that is my destiny.
I exist not if I do not attend to the pain
of those who suffer: they are my pains.
For I cannot be without existing for all,
for all who are silent and oppressed,
I come from the people and I sing for them:
my poetry is song and punishment.
I am told: you belong to darkness.
Perhaps, perhaps, but I walk toward the light.
I am the man of bread and fish
and you will not find me among books,
but with women and men:
they have taught me the infinite.

MIGUEL ALGARÍN

XXVII
CARIBBEAN BIRDS

In this brief gust of wind without men
I invite you to celebrate birds,
the martin, swift sail of the wind,
the dazzling light of the hummingbird
housecleaner that divides the sky
for the gloomy crane
until the substance of dawn
weaves the color of the "aguaitacaminos."
O birds precious stones of the Caribbean,
quetzal, nuptial beam of Paradise,
airborne jewelry of the foliage
birds of yellow lightning
kneaded with drops of turquoise
and the fire of naked catastrophes:
come to my small human song,
water troupial, simple partridge,
thrushes of miraculous forms,
earthbound "chocorocay,"
light dancers of gold and air,
spear-tailed ultraviolet "tintora,"
rock roosters, waterbirds,
companions, mysterious friends,
how did feathers surpass flowers?
Golden Mask, invincible woodpecker,
what can I do to sing in the midst
of Venezuela, next to your nests,
brilliant, celestial semaphore,
martins fishermen of dew
from the Far South my voice is
opaque, the voice of a somber heart,
am I nothing on Caribbean sand
but a rock that comes from the cold?
How am I to sing the melody,
the plumage, the light, the power
of what I saw without believing
or heard without believing I heard?

because the red heron went by me:
they were flying like a red river
against the Venezuelan brilliance,
the burning blue sun in sapphire
surged like an eclipse of beauty:
these birds flew from the ceremony itself.
If you did not see the crimson of the "corocoro"
flying like a suspended hive
cutting the air like a scythe,
the whole sky beating in flight
as the scarlet plumage passes
leaving a burning lightning bolt,
if you did not see the Caribbean air
flowing with blood without being wounded,
you do not know the beauty of this world,
you are not aware of the world you've lived in.
And that is why I speak and sing
and see and live for all men:
it is my duty to tell what you don't know
and what you do know I'll sing with you:
your eyes accompany my words
and my words flourish in the wheat
and they fly with the wings of the Caribbean
or they fight against your enemies.
I have so many duties, friends, that I am
moving on to another theme, so I take my leave.

MIGUEL ALGARÍN

XXIX
NO ME LO PIDAN

Piden algunos que este asunto humano
con nombres, apellidos y lamentos
no lo trate en las hojas de mis libros,
no le dé la escritura de mis versos:
dicen que aquí murió la poesía,
dicen algunos que no debo hacerlo:

la verdad es que siento no agradarles,
los saludo y les saco mi sombrero
y los dejo viajando en el Parnaso
como ratas alegres en el queso.
Yo pertenezco a otra categoría
y sólo un hombre soy de carne y hueso,
por eso si apalean a mi hermano
con lo que tengo a mano lo defiendo
y cada una de mis líneas lleva
un peligro de pólvora o de hierro,
que caerá sobre los inhumanos,
sobre los crueles, sobre los soberbios.
Pero el castigo de mi paz furiosa
no amenaza a los pobres ni a los buenos:
con mi lámpara busco a los que caen,
alivio sus heridas y las cierro:
y éstos son los oficios del poeta
del aviador y del picapedrero:
debemos hacer algo en esta tierra
porque en este planeta nos parieron
y hay que arreglar las cosas de los hombres
porque no somos pájaros ni perros.
Y bien, si cuando ataco lo que odio,
o cuando canto a todos los que quiero,
la poesía quiere abandonar
las esperanzas de mi manifiesto
yo sigo con las tablas de mi ley
acumulando estrellas y armamentos
y en el duro deber americano
no me importa una rosa más o menos:
tengo un pacto de amor con la hermosura:
tengo un pacto de sangre con mi pueblo.

DO NOT ASK ME

Some people ask me that human affairs
with names, surnames, and laments

not be dealt with in the pages of my books,
not to give them space in my verses:
they say poetry died here,
some say I should not do it:
the truth is I do not want to please them.
I greet them, I tip my hat to them,
and I leave them voyaging in Parnassus
like happy rats in cheese.
I belong to another category,
I am only a man of flesh and bones,
therefore if they beat my brother
I defend him with what I have in hand
and each one of my lines carries
the threat of gunpowder or steel,
that will fall over the inhuman,
over the cruel and over the arrogant.
But the punishment of my furious peace
menaces neither the poor nor the good:
with my lamp I search for those who fall:
I soothe and close their wounds:
these are the chores of the poet
of the aviator and of the stonecutter:
we should do something on this earth
because we were born on this planet
and we must arrange man's society
because we are neither birds nor dogs.
And so, if when I attack what I hate,
or when I sing to those I love,
poetry wants to abandon
the hopes of my manifesto,
I'll follow the letter of my law
accumulating stars and armaments
and in my steadfast duty to America
one more rose does not matter:
I have a pact of love with beauty:
I have a pact of blood with my people.

MIGUEL ALGARÍN

XXXV
THE "FREE" PRESS

While briefly chilled, I want to tell
without vengeance and what's more with joy
how from my bed in Buenos Aires
the police took me to prison.
It was late, we had just arrived from Chile,
and without saying anything to us
they plundered my friend's papers,
they offended the house in which I slept.
My wife vented her disdain
but there were orders to be executed
and in a moving car we roved about
the tyrannous black night.
Then it was not Perón, it was another,
a new tyrant for Argentina
and by his orders doors opened,
bolt after bolt was unlocked
in order to swallow me, the patios passed,
forty bars and the infirmary,
but still they took me up into a cell,
the most impenetrable and hidden:
only there did they feel protected
from the exhalations of my poetry.
I discovered through that broken night
that three thousand were imprisoned that day:
jail, penitentiary, and as if not enough,
boats were set adrift
filled with men and women,
the pride of Argentinean souls.
My tale comes only to this:
the rest is collective history:
I wanted to read it in newspapers,
in *La Prensa* (which is so informative),
yet Mr. Gaínza Paz does not know
if Argentinean prisons are being filled.
He is the champion of our "free" press

but if communist journals are closed
this grandee acts dumb without reporting it,
his feet ache and he has eye trouble,
and if the workers go to jail
everybody knows it except Gaínza,
everybody resorts to newspapers,
but "large" journals do not publish
anything about these stupid tales:
La Prensa is preoccupied
with the last divorce taking place
with motion picture asses in Hollywood
and while press syndicates cloister themselves
La Prensa and *La Nación* are metaphysical.
Oh what silence from the fat press
when the people are beaten,
but if one of Batista's jackals
is assassinated in Cuba
the presses of our poor America
confess and print their sensational stories,
they lift their hands to their temples,
it is then that they know and publish,
the Sip, Sop, Sep meets
to save the virgins in trouble
and running to their purse in New York
they hurriedly solicit
the constant inducement of money
for the "liberty" they patronize.
And these web-footed men
swarm over Latin America,
they kiss Chamudes in Santiago,
Judas Ravines waits for them in Lima
later enriched and enthused
by that liberty exhaled
from Washington where rock and roll plays,
they dance with Dubois and Gaínza.

MIGUEL ALGARÍN

XL
TOMORROW THROUGHOUT THE CARIBBEAN

Unsullied youth of this bloody sea,
young communists of the day:
there will be more of you to clean
this territory of tyrannies,
one day we shall be able to meet,
and in freedom my poetry
will sing once again among you.
Comrades, I await this rejoicing.

MIGUEL ALGARÍN

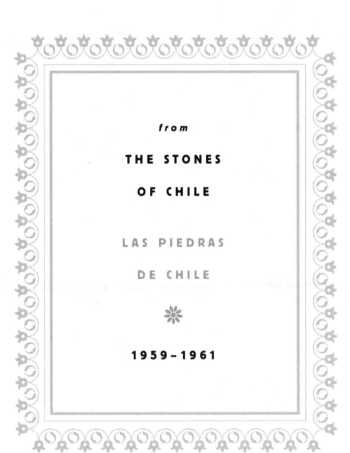

from

THE STONES
OF CHILE

LAS PIEDRAS

DE CHILE

❄

1959–1961

For stone was the blood,
for stone the weeping,
the prayer, the procession:
stone was free will.

Because in sweat and in fire
the gods of stone were born
and then the saint of rain grew,
the lord of the struggles
for the corn, for the earth,
bird gods, serpent gods,
the fertile, the unfortunate,
all were born of stone:
America raised them
with a thousand small golden hands,
with eyes lost already,
clouded with blood and neglect.

But my country was of light,
a man alone came and went,
without other gods than thunder:

and there my heart grew:
I came from Araucania.

It was plant and seashore,
diurnal like the hummingbirds,
red like the crab,
green as water in October,
silvery as small fish,
wild as a partridge,
and thinner than an arrow
was the southern land, worn away
by the great winds of the sky,
by the stars of the sea.

In Chile gods are not born,
Chile is the home of quarries.

So, in the rock grew
arms and mouths, feet and hands,
the stone became a monument:
it cut open the cold, the month of June
added petals and feathers
and then time came and arrived,
left and returned, returned and left,
until it deserted,
the kingdom without blood and without gods,
filled with pure figures:

Stone illuminated my country
with its natural statues.

DENNIS MALONEY

THE BULL

The oldest bull crossed the day.
His legs scratched the planet.
He continued, traveling to where the sea lives.
He reached the shore, the oldest bull.
On the edge of time, the ocean.
He closed his eyes and grass covered him.
He breathed the whole green distance.
And silence built the rest.

DENNIS MALONEY

SOLITUDES

Among the stones of the coast, walking,
by the shore of Chile,
farther off

sea and sea, moon and sea grass,
the lonely expanse of the planet.

The coast broken
by thunder,
consumed
by the teeth of every dawn,
worn by great stirrings
of weather and waves:
slow birds circle,
with iron-colored feathers
and they know that here the world ends.
No one said why,
no one exists,
it isn't written, there are no numbers or letters,
no one trampled the obscure sand
like lead pollen:
here desolate flowers were born,
plants that expressed themselves with thorns
and sudden blossoms
of furious petals.
No one said there wasn't any territory,
that here the void begins,
the ancient emptiness that guides
with catastrophe, darkness
and shadow, darkness, shadows:
so it is the rough coast, that road
of south to north to west, to solitude.

Beautiful virtue, that of conflict,
that water and sea foam erect
along this long border:
the wave reconstructing itself like a flower,
repeating its castlelike form,
its tower that decays and crumbles
only to grow beating anew
like it sought
to populate the darkness with its beauty,
to fill the abyss with light.

Walking
from the final Antarctic
by stone and sea, hardly
saying a word,
only the eyes speak and rest.

Innumerable solitude swept
by wind and salt, by cold,
by chains,
by moon and tides:
I must recall the toothless star
that here collapsed,
to gather the fragments
of stone, to hear
no one and speak with no one,
to be and not be a solitary motion of the heart:
I am the sentinel
of a barracks without soldiers,
of a great solitude filled with stones.

DENNIS MALONEY

THE STONES OF CHILE

Mad stones of Chile, pouring
from mountain ranges,
full of rocks
black, blind, opaque,
that joined
roads to the earth,
that placed time and stone
by the day's journey,
white rocks
that interrupt the rivers
and are kissed
smooth
by a seismic
ribbon of sea foam,

granite
of the glimmering
high seas
beneath
the snow
like a monastery,
backbone
of the
strongest
country
or unmovable
ship,
prow
of the terrible earth,
stone, infinitely pure stone,
sealed
like
a cosmic dove,
stiff from sun, from wind, from energy,
from mineral dream, from dark time,
crazy stones,
stars
and pavilion
slept,
rolling peaks, cliffs:
knew the stillness
around
your lasting silence,
beneath the Antarctic
mantle of Chile,
beneath
your iron clarity.

DENNIS MALONEY

THE BLIND STATUE

It's been thousands and thousands of
years of stone.
I was a stonecutter
and this is what I did
striking
without hands
or hammer,
piercing
without chisel,
staring into the sun without eyes,
without being,
without existence but in the wind,
with only a wave for my thought,
without tools other
than time,
the time,
the passing time.

I sculptured the statue blind
so that she wouldn't see,
that there
in the desolate
sand
she would keep her mass
like my monument:
the blind
statue
which the first man
that departed from stone,
the son of power,
the first
that dug, touched and imposed on
its lost creation,
searching for fire.

And I was born, naked
and blue, a stonecutter,

lengthwise from shores in darkness
from rivers still unknown,
in caves lashed by the tails
of somber lizards,
and it was hard to encounter myself,
to become hands,
eyes, fingers, seeking
my own blood,
and then my joy
became a statue:
my own form that I had copied
striking across the centuries in stone.

DENNIS MALONEY

BUEY

Animal de la espuma
caminando
por noche, día,
arena.
Animal
del otoño
andando
hacia el antiguo
olor del musgo,
buey dulce
en cuya barba
florecieron las rocas
del subsuelo
y se armó el terremoto
de truenos y pisadas,
rumiando las tinieblas,
perdido
entre relámpagos,
mientras vive la espuma,
mientras el día
saca

las horas de su torre,
y desploma la noche
sobre el tiempo
su oscuro saco frío,
tembloroso.

OX

Creature of sea foam
traveling
by night, day,
sand.
Animal
of autumn
walking
towards the ancient
scent of moss,
sweet ox
in whose beard
flowered rocks
of the subsoil,
and where the earthquake armed itself
with thunder and footsteps,
ruminating the darkness,
lost
between lightning flashes,
while sea foam lives,
while the day
extracts
the hours from its tower
and the night collapses,
over time
her dark cold sack,
trembling.

DENNIS MALONEY

THEATER OF THE GODS

It is like this on the coast.
Suddenly, contorted,
harsh, piled up,
static,
collapsing,
either tenacious theaters,
or ships and corridors
or rolling
severed limbs:
it is like this on the coast,
the rocky lunar slope,
the grapes of granite.

Orange stains
of oxide, green seams,
above the calcareous peace,
that the sea foam strikes with its keys
or dawn with its rose
these stones are like this:
no one knows
if they came from the sea or will return to the sea,
something
astonished them
while they lived,
and they faltered in the stillness
and constructed a dead city.

A city without cries,
without kitchens,
a solemn ring
of purity,
tumbling pure shapes
in a confusion without resurrection,
in a crowd that lost its vision,
in a gray monastery condemned
to the naked truth of its gods.

DENNIS MALONEY

YO VOLVERÉ

Alguna vez, hombre o mujer, viajero,
después, cuando no viva,
aquí buscad, buscadme
entre piedra y océano,
a la luz proceleria
de la espuma.
Aquí buscad, buscadme,
porque aquí volveré sin decir nada,
sin voz, sin boca, puro,
aquí volveré a ser el movimiento
del agua, de
su corazón salvaje,
aquí estaré perdido y encontrado:
aquí seré tal vez piedra y silencio.

I WILL RETURN

Some other time, man or woman, traveler,
later, when I am not alive,
look here, look for me
between stone and ocean,
in the light storming
through the foam.
Look here, look for me,
for here I will return, without saying a thing,
without voice, without mouth, pure,
here I will return to be the churning
of the water, of
its unbroken heart,
here, I will be discovered and lost:
here, I will, perhaps, be stone and silence.

DENNIS MALONEY

THE SHIP

We walked and climbed: the world
was a parched noon,
the air didn't tremble, the leaves didn't exist,
the water was far away.

The boat or prow then
rose from the deserts
and sailed towards the sky:
a point of stone guided
towards the unbearable infinity,
a closed palace
for the lost gods.
And there was the prow, the arrow, the ship
or dreadful tower,
and for the toiling,
the thirsty, the dusty,
the sweating race
of man that climbed
the difficult hills,
neither water nor bread nor pasture,
only a large rock that rose,
only a stubborn boat of stone and music.

For how long? I cried out, we shouted.
Finally mother earth killed us
with its harsh cactus,
with its ironous maternity,
with all this desert,
sweat, wind, and sand,
and when we finally arrived
to rest, wrapped in void,
a boat of stone
still wanted to ship us
toward where, without wings,
we couldn't fly
without dying.

This we endured when we were tired
and the mountain range was hard,
heavy as a chain.

Only then, my journey ended, here:
beyond, where death began.

DENNIS MALONEY

THE CREATION

That happened in the great silence
when grass was born,
when light had just detached itself
and created the vermilion and the statues,
then
in the great solitude
a howl began,
something rolled crying,
the shadows half-opened, rising alone
as if the planets sobbed
and then the echo
rolled, tumbling and tumbling
until what was born was silent.

But stone preserved the memory.

It guarded the opened snout of the shadows,
the trembling sword of the howl,
and there is in the stone an animal without name
that still howls without voice toward the emptiness.

DENNIS MALONEY

THE TURTLE

The turtle that
has walked
so long
and seen so much
with
his
ancient
eyes,
the turtle
that fed on
olives
of the deep
sea,
the turtle that has swum
for seven centuries
and known
seven
thousand
springs,
the turtle
shielded
against
the heat
and cold,
against
the rays and waves,
the turtle
of yellow
and silver,
with stern
lunar
amber
and rapine feet,
the turtle
remains
here

asleep,
and doesn't know it.

The old man
assumed
a hardness,
abandoned
the love of waves
and became rigid
as an iron plate.

Closing
the eyes that
have dared
so much
ocean, sky, time, and earth,
and now, he sleeps
among the other
rocks.

DENNIS MALONEY

LAS PIEDRAS Y LOS PÁJAROS

Aves del Sur del Mar,
descansad,
es la hora
de la gran soledad, la hora de piedra.
Conocí cada nido,
la habitación huraña
del errante,
amé su vuelo antártico,
la rectitud sombría de las remotas aves.

Ahora, descansad
en el anfiteatro
de las islas:
no más, no puedo

conversar con vosotras,
no hay
      cartas, no hay
           telégrafo
entre poeta y pájaro:
hay música secreta,
sólo secretas alas,
plumaje y poderío.

Cuánta distancia y ávidos
los ojos de oro cruel
acechando la plata fugitiva!

Con las alas cerradas
desciende un meteoro,
salta en su luz la espuma,
y el vuelo otra vez sube,
sube a la altura con un pez sangriento.

Desde los archipiélagos de Chile,
allí donde la lluvia
estableció su patria,
vienen cortando el cielo
las grandes alas negras,
y dominando
territorio y distancias
del invierno,
aquí en el continente
de piedra solitaria,
amor, estiércol, vida,
habéis dejado,
aves aventureras
de piedra y mar y de imposible cielo.

THE STONES AND THE BIRDS

Birds of the South Sea,
resting,
it is the hour
of great solitude, the hour of stone.
I knew every nest,
the unsociable lodging
of the nomadic,
I loved your Antarctic flight,
the somber accuracy of the remote birds.

Now, rest
in the amphitheater
of the islands:
no longer can I
talk with you,
there are no
      letters, there is no
              telegraph
between poet and bird:
there is secret music,
only hidden wings,
plumage and power.

How much distance and greed
awaited the cruel gold eyes
of the silver fugitive!

With closed wings
a meteor descended,
exploding in your sea-foam light,
and the flight again ascended,
climbing to the heights with a bloody fish.

From the Chilean Archipelago,
there, where rain
established its home,
great black wings

came cutting the sky,
and dominating
the territories and distances
of winter,
here on the continent
of solitary stone,
love, manure, life,
all that is left,
adventurous birds
of stone, sea and impossible sky.

DENNIS MALONEY

AL CAMINANTE

No son tan tristes estas piedras.
Adentro de ellas vive el oro,
tienen semillas de planetas,
tienen campanas en el fondo,
guantes de hierro, matrimonios
del tiempo con las amatistas:
por dentro ríen con rubíes,
se alimentaron de relámpagos.

Por eso, viajero, cuidado
con las tristezas del camino,
con los misterios en los muros.

Me ha costado mucho saber
que no todo vive por fuera
y no todo muere por dentro,
y que la edad escribe letras
con agua y piedra para nadie,
para que nadie sepa dónde,
para que nadie entienda nada.

TO THE TRAVELER

These stones aren't sad.
Within them lives gold,
they have the seeds of planets,
they have bells in their depths,
gloves of iron, marriages
of time with the amethysts:
on the inside laughing with rubies,
nourishing themselves from lightning.

Because of this, traveler, pay attention
to the hardships of the road,
to mysteries on the walls.

I know this at great cost,
that all life is not outward
nor all death within,
and that the age writes letters
with water and stone for no one,
so that no one knows,
so that no one understands anything.

DENNIS MALONEY

STONES FOR MARÍA

The pure pebbles,
oval olives,
were once
inhabitants
of the ocean's
vines,
clusters
of grapes
in submerged honeycombs:
The waves picked them,
felled by wind,

rolling in the abyss
among slow-moving fish
and sleepwalking jellyfish,
tails of lacerated sharks,
eels like bullets!
Transparent stones,
smooth stones,
pebbles,
sliding towards
the bottom of humid regions,
far below, near where
the sky reemerges
and the sea dies above its artichokes.
Rolling and rolling
among the fingers and lips underwater
down to the smooth interminable,
until they were only touch,
curve of the smooth cup,
petal of the hip.
Then the surf grew stronger
and a beat of hard wave,
a hand of stone
winnowed cobbles
sifted them along the coast
and then disappeared in silence.
Small amber teeth,
raisins of honey and salt, beans of water,
blue olives of the wave,
forgotten almonds in the sand.

Stones for María!
Stones of honor for her labyrinth!

She, like a spider
of transparent stone,
will weave her embroidery,
make her banner of pure stone,
fabricate, with silvery stones,
the structure of the day;

with sulfurous stones,
the root of a lost lightning flash,
and one by one will climb to her wall,
to the pattern, to the honesty, to the motion,
the fugitive stone,
the grape of the sea has returned to the clusters,
wearing the light of her sea foam full of wonder.

Stones for María!

Wrinkled agates of Isla Negra,
sulfurous stones
of Tocopilla, like shattered stars,
descending from hellish mineral,
stones of La Serenta that the ocean
smoothed and then settled in the heights,
and from Coquimbo the black power,
the rolling basalt
of Maitencillo, of Toltén, of Niebla,
the wet dress
of the Chiloé seashore,
round stones, stones like eggs
of southern birds, translucent fingers
of the secret salt, of frozen
quartz, or enduring heritage
of the Andes, boats
and monasteries
of granite.

Praise
the stones
of María,
those that she arranged like a crystal bee
in the honeycomb of her wisdom:
the stones
of its walls,
of the book that is built
letter by letter,
leaf by leaf,

and stone by stone!
It is necessary to see and read this beauty
and I love its hands
from whose power
appears, gently,
a
lesson
of stone.

DENNIS MALONEY

NADA MÁS

De la verdad fui solidario:
de instaurar luz en la tierra.

Quise ser común como el pan:
la lucha no me encontró ausente.

Pero aquí estoy con lo que amé,
con la soledad que perdí:
junto a esta piedra no reposo.

Trabaja el mar en mi silencio.

NOTHING MORE

I stood by truth:
to establish light in the land.

I wanted to be common like bread:
so when the struggle came she wouldn't find me missing.

But here I am with what I loved,
with the solitude I lost:
but by this stone I don't rest.

The sea works in my silence.

DENNIS MALONEY

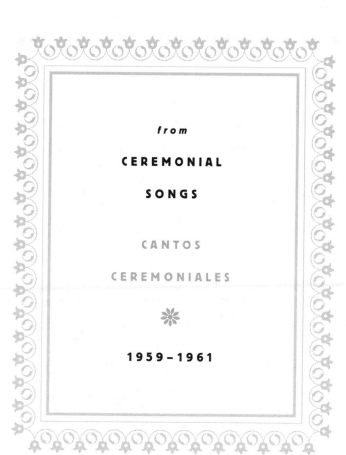

from

CEREMONIAL

SONGS

CANTOS

CEREMONIALES

❋

1959 – 1961

THE UNBURIED WOMAN OF PAITA

Elegy dedicated to the memory of Manuela Sáenz,
lover of Simón Bolívar

PROLOGUE

From Valparaíso through the sea.
The Pacific, hard road of knives.
The dying sun, a guiding sky.
And the ship, an arid insect over the ocean.
Each day gives birth to a blaze, a crown.
The night is quenched: it thins out, it scatters.
Oh day, oh night,
oh ships
of shadow and illumination, twin ships!
Oh time, broken wake of the ship.
Slowly, we cut a path to Panama—the air is guiding.
Oh sea, extended flower of stillness!
We do not go, return, or know.
With eyes closed, we simply exist.

I

THE PERUVIAN COAST

It surged like a dagger
between two blue enemies,
fallow hills, the hush.
A convoy of
suspended shadows,
the day there, again the same,
mute, a mouth
forever sealed with its secret

in stubborn solitude
with no other threats—
just the silence.

Oh long
cordillera
of sand and toothless
isolation, naked
and sleepy
intractable statue,
whom,
whom
did you escort
to the sea?
Whose return
from the sea
do you await?

What flower perished?
Which vessel laden with bouquets voyaged
to establish oceanic springtime?
You were abandoned
with the cemetery's relics,
the cave
of metallic death,
the hill, eaten away
by stormy salt.
And neither root nor springtime returned!
Everything perished in the waves and wind!

When
through
long hours,
you persist,
deserted, united with the sea,
sandy loneliness, iron death,
the traveler uses up
his wandering heart.
You did not bestow upon him

a single green branch
for refreshment,
or songs or slopes,
or a roof to shelter
a man and woman making love—
only the salty flight
of the seabird
splashing the rocks
with foam.
The departing gesture went away—
far from the planet's shivering.

Into the past, goodbye,
I am leaving you,
bitter
coast.
In each man,
a seed
trembles
in search of heavenly waters,
or a porous foundation.

When he sees only a long cup
of mineral mountains
and the extended blueness
against an inexorable
citadel,
man changes his course;
he continues his journey,
leaving behind the abandoned coast,
leaving behind
the oblivion.

II

THE UNBURIED WOMAN

In Paita, we asked
about her, the Dead Woman,
so that we could touch, could feel the earth
of the Buried Woman's radiance.

They did not know.

The old balustrades,
the balconies in the sky,
an aged city of vines
with an intrepid aroma
like a basket of
invincible mangoes,
pineapples,
deep chirimoyas.
The market
flies
buzz over
the neglect and abandon,
among the severed
fish heads,
and the Indian women, seated,
selling
uncertain spoils
with ferocious majesty—
queens from a realm
of subterranean copper—
the day was enshrouded in clouds,
the day was weary,
the day was a lost traveler
on foot, on a road
of dust and bewilderment.

I stopped the boy, the man,

the old man—

they did not know where

Manuela had perished,

or where her home once existed,

or where the powder of her bones

now rested.

Above, the burnished hills traveled,
dry as camels,
on a motionless journey,
on a trip with the dead,
and because water
is movement,
the spring runs without rest,
the river grows and sings.
There the hard mountains
walked with time;
the ages, the quiescent travels
of plush hills.
I asked them about Manuelita,
but they did not know,
they did not remember the names of flowers.

We asked the sea,
the ancient ocean.
In the foam of breaking waves,
the Peruvian sea opened old Incan eyes,
and the toothless turquoise mouth
began to speak.

THE SEA AND MANUELITA

She brought me here, the womanly sailor,
Colan's shipper, the brave one.
The ravishing lady guided me, I remember her,
a siren of rifles,
a widow of nets,
a little Creole merchant
of honey, doves, pineapples, and pistols.
She slept among the casks,
familiar with the insurgent gunpowder,
with the fish just caught
shivering on the ship,
with the gold of the most fugitive days,
with the phosphorescent dream of earth for an anchor.
Yes, I recall her dark tuberose skin,
her turbulent eyes, her short hands like iron.

I remember the lost commander;
she lived here
gliding over these same waves,
but I don't know where she vanished.

I don't know

where she left her last kiss for love,

or where the last wave reached her.

IV

WE WILL NOT FIND HER

No, the earthy woman does not rest at sea.
Manuela doesn't exist without a pathway, without a star,
without a ship, only among the tempests.
Her heart was bread, and then it became

flour and sand.
It spread through the burning hills,
her silence, transformed through space.
The solitary woman is not here—
but she is here.

Her hand doesn't rest; it is not possible
to find her rings or her bosom,
or her mouth which the ray guided
with its long whip of lemon blossoms.
The traveler will not find
Paita's sleeping lady
in this crypt—not surrounded by
wormy lances, by useless marble
in the intractable graveyard
which protects its dead against
dust and the sea.
In this promontory, there is
no tomb for Manuelita.
There is no burial for the flower.
There is no sepulchre for the scattered beauty.
Her name is not preserved in wood
or on the brutal temple stone.

She went away. Her essence spread
out among the hard cordilleras,
and she was lost amid salt and boulders,
the saddest eyes of the world.
Her braids became water
in Peruvian rivers,
and her kisses thinned out
in the mountain air.
Here, we find the earth, the dreams,
the quivering flags,
and she is here—but it's too late
for anyone to piece together her beauty.

THE ABSENT LOVER

Lover, why speak your name?
In these mountains
only she lingers.
She embodies only silence,
rough, enduring solitude.

Love and earth established
the solar amalgam,
this last sun,
the mortuary sun
searches for the integrity
of her lost light.
It searches
and its ray,
sometimes flickering near death,
slices while searching, cuts like a sword
and halts in the sand.
The lover's hand is not there.
It does not stroke the shattered hilt.

Your name is absent,
Dead Lover,
but the silence knows that your name
vanished on horseback through the sierra,
vanished on horseback in the wind.

VI

PORTRAIT

Who lived? Who was living? Who was loving?

Damn Spanish spiderwebs!

During the night, the blaze of equatorial eyes,
your heart burning in the vast emptiness,
and so your mouth was mistaken for the dawn.

Manuela, radiant coal and water, column
of sustenance, not a restless ceiling, but rather a wild star.

Today, we still inhale that wounded love,
the dagger of sun in the distance.

VII

IN VAIN WE SEARCH FOR YOU

No. *No one will reunite your firm body.*
No one will resuscitate your feverish sands.
Never again will your mouth open its double petals.
White garments will not swell above your breasts.

Loneliness commanded salt, silence, gulfweeds,
and your silhouette was devoured by the sand.
Your wild waist was lost in the distance,
alone, without contact with the imperious horseman,
galloping through the flames until death.

VIII

MATERIAL MANUELA

You don't just rest here in the desolate hills.
You didn't choose the still universe of dust.
You aren't a soul's projection in the void.
Your memory is material, flesh, fire, oranges.

Your footsteps won't startle the silent hall.
At midnight, you won't return with the moon.

You won't enter, transparent, without a whisper.
Your hands won't seek out the dreaming zither.

You won't transport a green halo from tower to tower
like orange blossoms, extinguished and abandoned.
Your ankles won't stir crystalline melodies at night.
Only death unchained you.

No, not a ghost, shadow, moon above the iciness,
not tears, not lamentation, not a fugue of fluttering garments,
but rather that body, that body wrapped in love,
those eyes sundering the earth.

The legs nestling the hussar's urgent fire,
that wandering road captain, the legs
mounting a horse in the lush forest,
descending in flight the alabaster ladder.

The embracing arms, the fingers, the cheeks,
the breasts (two dark hemispheres of magnolia),
the bird of her long hair (two great black wings),
her round hips of equatorial bread.

So perhaps naked, you travel with the wind
and it continues being your stormy lover.
And so you exist now as before: as matter
and truth: you are life,
never to be lost in death's translation.

IX

THE GAME

Your small dark hand,
your slim Spanish feet,
your clear hips of plenty—
ancient rivers of green fire traveled
through your veins:

and you put everything on the table
like a flaming treasure,
like dead orange blossoms of abandonment
in the blazing cards:
in the game of life or extinction.

X
RIDDLE

Who *is kissing her now?*
It is not he. It is not she.
They are not themselves.
It is the wind bearing a flag.

XI
EPITAPH

This was the wounded lover:
during the night, woven with pathways,
she dreamed of victory,
she embraced the grief.
Her lover was a sword.

XII
SHE

You were freedom,
a liberator in love.

You handed over gifts and debts,
an idol, challenging respect.

The shadowy owl became frightened
when your rich hair grazed the darkness.

And housetops remained clear;
umbrellas shimmered.

The houses changed their clothing.
Winter was transparent.

It was Manuela crossing
the tired streets of Lima,
Bogotá's night,
Guayaquil's darkness,
the black suit of Caracas.

And since then, daytime has prevailed.

XIII

QUESTIONS

Why? *Why didn't you return?*
Oh infinite lover, a woman crowned
not only with lemon flowers,
not only with immense love,
not only with yellow brilliance
and crimson silks on the dais,
not only with sheets and honeysuckle
in deep beds,
but also
you were a woman crowned
with our blood and our war.

XIV

OF ALL SILENCE

Now let's be alone.
Alone with the proud woman.
Alone with the woman who dressed herself

in purple lightning.
With the empress of three colors.
With Quito's whirling vine.

Of all the silence in the world,
she chose this sad inlet,
Paita's pale waters.

XV
WHO KNOWS

I cannot speak to you about that brilliance.
Today I only want to find the lost
rose, hidden in the sand.
I want to share the oblivion.

I want to see the long minutes
displayed like flags,
hidden in the silence.

I want to behold the concealed lover.

I want to know.

XVI
EXILES

There are biting exiles;
others are like hungry fire.

There are pains of the extinct homeland
rising from below,
from feet and roots—
and man quickly drowns.
He no longer recognizes the thorns.

The guitar no longer makes music.
Air no longer exists for that mouth.
He can no longer live without earth,
and then he falls headlong,
not onto Earth, but into death.

I knew the exile of song,
and that one, yes, holds an elixir,
because one bleeds into the song.
The blood escapes and becomes song.

And the one who lost mother and father,
the one who also lost his children,
the one who lost the door to his house—
he has nothing—not even a flag.
That man travels like a nomad.
I give a name to his pain
and keep it in my dark box.

And the exile he battles,
even in dreams, and while he eats,
while he neither eats nor sleeps,
while he walks and when he doesn't walk—
it is not the exiled pain,
but rather the hand which strikes
until the stones of the wall
listen and fall—and then
there is bloodshed; this happens:
such is man's victory.

I DON'T UNDERSTAND

But I don't understand this exile.
This bitter honor, Manuela.

XVII
THE LONELINESS

I want to walk with you and know,
know the reasons why; I want to walk
inside of your shattered heart,
to ask the lost dust,
the shy, dispersed jasmine.

Why? Why this miserable dirt?

Why this forsaken light?

Why this shadow without stars?

Why doom in Paita?

XVIII
THE FLOWER

Oh love, heart of sand!

Oh woman, buried in life's full flower,

resting without a tomb,

hellfiery little girl in memories,

sword-tinted angel.

Oh invincible victor

of war and sun and cruel dew.

Oh supreme flower seized

by tenderness and austerity.

Oh puma, gifted sky blue claws,

oh bloody palm tree,

tell me why the lips that kissed fire
remained mute,
and the hands that caressed
the diamond's secret powers,
the strings of the wind's violin,
God's scimitar—
drew near the dark coast.
And those eyes, opening and closing
in all brilliance,
remained here, staring
at the way the waves came and went,
at how oblivion came and went,
and at how time did not return:
only loneliness without a way out,
and these rocks with terrible soul,
smeared by pelicans.

Oh comrade lady, I don't understand!

XIX
GOODBYE

Goodbye. *Beneath the fog, your slow boat cruises,*
transparent as an X ray.
It is mute surrounded by the shadows of shadows.
It goes alone, rises alone, without a route or ferryman.

Goodbye, Manuela Sáenz, pure smuggler,
guerrilla. Perhaps your love has compensated
the parched loneliness and the empty night.
Your love scattered its wild ashes.

Liberator, you have no tomb.
Take this crown made bloody with your bones.
Receive a kiss of love over the oblivion.
Goodbye, goodbye, Juliet of storms.

Return to the electric prow of your fishing boat.
Aim the net and gun over the sea.
Let your long hair come together with your eyes.
May your heart terrify the waters of death.
May you be witnessed again, parting tides,
the ship, propelled by your intrepid love.

XX

THE RESURRECTED WOMAN

In the tomb or sea or earth, battalion or window,
let us return to the ray of your unfaithful beauty.
Call your body, seek your broken form.

Once again be the guiding statue on the ship's prow.

(And the lover in his tomb will tremble like a river.)

XXI

INVOCATION

Goodbye. Goodbye. Goodbye. Ferocious unburied woman,
wounded rose, rose tree even in errant death.
Goodbye, body penetrated by Paita's dust,
flower head demolished by the sand and gales.

Here I invoke you so that you return to become
a flickering ancient, a rose still radiant.
May whatever survives of you unite
until your adored bones are named.

The Lover in his dream will sense the call.
Someone, at last, she, the lost one approaches.
The sailor lady will voyage in a singular ship
again with the dream and the dreaming Lover,
the two now reunited in the nakedness of the truth;
cruel ashes of a ray that did not bury death,
or devour the salt, or swallow the dunes.

XXII

NOW WE ARE LEAVING PAITA

Paita, over the coast,
rotten wharves,
shattered
staircases,
the gloomy pelicans,
exhausted,
sitting
on dead wood,
the cotton bales,
the vendors' booths at Piura.
Full of dreams and empty,
Paita moves
to the rhythm
of the small waves of the ocean's road,
against the calcified wall.

It seems
that here
some huge absence shook and demolished
the rooftops and the streets.
Empty houses, dense
broken walls,
a bougainvillea shoots up
into the light: a jet of
purple blood,
the desert's dry abandon.

The ship has long
cut its path into the distance.

Paita remained asleep
in the sand.

Unburied Manuela,
shattered,
in the atrocities, harsh
loneliness.

The ships returned. In full sunlight,
they unloaded black merchandise.

Great bald birds
remain
still
over
burning stones.

The ship leaves.
The Earth no longer
has a name.

Between the twin blueness
of the sky and the ocean,
there exists a sandy line.
It is dry, lonely, the product of shadows.

Then night caves in.

And the ship and coast and sea
and land and song
set a course for oblivion.

MARÍA JACKETTI

THE BULL

*

I

Between northern and southern seas,
Spain was dry,
thirsty, devoured, tense as a drum.
Spain was dry as the moon,
and water was needed to end the burning.
Everything withered, sick and yellow
exhausted and brown.
Everything withered and became dirt—
even eyes would not give up their tears
(the time for weeping will come),
from eternity not a drop of time fell,
a thousand rainless years transpired,
the earth cracked,
the dead lay in fissures:
and it did not rain—
it did not rain.

II

And then the bull was sacrificed.
A red light broke free,
swift, like the assassin's knife;
this shine extended from Alicante,
and was made flesh in Somosierra.
The domes shone like geraniums.
Everyone stared at the sky.
"What is this?" they asked.
And in the middle of the fear,
between whispers and silence,

someone who knew answered:
"That is the bull's light."

III

They dressed a pale worker
in blue fire, in amber ashes,
in silvery tongues, in clouds and vermilion,
in emerald eyes, in sapphire tails,
and the pale man advanced against the fury,
the poor man, so richly dressed,
advanced for the killing.
He came adorned in lightning—to die.

IV

Then the first drop of blood fell and flowered.
Like a terrible unknown beast, incapable of satiation,
the earth received blood and consumed it.
It did not crave water.
It changed the name of its thirst.
And everything was bathed in scarlet.
The cathedrals heaved with walls of fire.
Rubies trembled in Góngora.
The plaza of bulls flowed with carnation-blood.
The rite was repeated in furious silence,
and the drops flowed, face down,
toward bloody founts.
And so it happened—the ceremony endured:
the pale man, the sweeping shadow
of the beast and the game
between death and existence,
below the wounded day.

V

The compact was chosen among all,
purity rippled by fresh waves,
bestial purity, the green bull,
at home with the lush, rough dew,
the moon designed his place in the herd
just as an Indian chief was elected.
Here is the bull: mountainous, opulent.
His face, beneath the sharp-horn of the half moon,
does not know, does not understand
if the new silence covering him is a genital blanket
of ecstasy, or eternal shadow, the catastrophe's jaws,
until, at last, light opens like a door,
and a shine harder than pain enters,
a new sound like stone sacks, rolling,
and in the infinite plaza of priestly eyes,
a man condemned to die,
wears for the meeting,
his own turquoise chill,
a suit of the rainbow—and a small sword.

VI

A small sword with his suit,
a small death with his manhood,
a complete circus, under the sun's
implacable orange, facing the unseeing eyes
in the sand, lost as a newborn,
preparing his long dance, his geometry.
Then like the shadow and like the sea,
the bull's angry hooves are untied.
(The bull already knows; already he is only pure force),
and the pale doll becomes reason,
intelligence is a quest under his golden raiment:
to find the way to dance, the way to wound.

The silken soldier should dance, dying.

But when he escapes, he is invited to the palace.

He raises a cup in remembrance of his sword.

Again the night of fear and its stars are glowing.

The cup is empty—like the circus at night.

The men want to touch the one who agonizes.

VII

The feminine one is smooth like a tender almond.
The shape is flesh and bone and hair,
coral and honey gathered in its immense nudity.
And man and hunger gallop to devour the rose.
Oh flower! The flesh rises in a wave,
whiteness cascades.
In white combat, the horseman is disarmed,
finally falling, covered in floral chastity.

VIII

The horse that escaped the fire,
the smoky horse
arrives at the Plaza.
It traveled like a shadow
and awaits the bull.
The horseman is a dark,
clumsy insect.
He raises his thorny spear
above the ebony horse.
The black lance gleams.

He attacks and leaps,
netted in the shadow, in the blood.

IX

Soft horns sound from the bestial shadow,
returning an empty dream to a bitter pasture.
Just a drop penetrated the sand,
a drop of the bull's essence, a thick seed,
a different blood, the pale soldier's blood:
a silkless splendor pierced the twilight,
the night, dawn's metallic coldness.

Everything was ready. Everything was devoured.

The towers of Spain are red blazes.

MARÍA JACKETTI

CORDILLERAS

✻

I

I was traveling by air from Copiapó,
from the Northern Hemisphere, through the atmosphere,
fixed in my thoughts like a thousand-fingered glove,
I felt the airplane shake and slip through an invisible tunnel,
and vacillate suddenly ready to hold back its power,
to continue an invisible line, sleeping and flying.

I was voyaging from the north, the Chilean wilderness,
copper and stone, silence, tools, motors,
and I didn't look outside during hours with the sky,
I looked inside of myself—my own
stormy journeys.

II

It was true, surely, we existed,
that secret energy,
people tangled in their personal nets,
passengers of so many things-to-do, ears
listening to God's money falling,
the divine money—and so, they arranged things
with hardly the space for a day to die,
without time, without doubt, to heed
the distant rain, the violin of suffocated winter.

III

Suddenly I witnessed the last light—
daytime's banner shipwrecked and spreading out;
sky and light battling moon and twilight
crimson roosters in a fleshy quarrel.
And I beheld, close to me, near my face,
how Mt. Aconcagua created a kingdom of order
with the solitude of its stature—
and over all the snowy nakedness:
a bloody sombrero was girded by the night.

IV

But I lowered my eyes and looked,
I witnessed the body of iron, the great still river
in its bed, in its day of drowsy stone,
and the sum of round breasts was soft,
domes crafted by the wind's mouth,
churches sustained in the tranquillity of topaz,
ships of sand, pure material forms.
It was a dry courtyard, without gods, without a calendar.
Looking down from my flight
I had, at last, beneath me the ship of solitude,
the airship's sky, pure and newborn,
like a bubble or circle united with a fish in the cold,
and then not earth, not foam,
not autumn, not summer, not lusty springtime
unweaving and weaving like oceanic lovers,
but rather the planet's pure stone.
Everything there made great hands resting
on the hard secret of power.
The great vast silence was smooth and dry,
the dignity of sleeping cordilleras.

V

Well, I'll say, the color
did not come from a single petal,
not from a single feather of an iron bird,
not from a single angry and quiet fruit,
not from a single wave of salt and crystal,
not from the skin of a celestial beast.
It was more, it was everything: fireworks and grapes.
It was the golden volcano and the golden spring.
It was the color of bread kneaded on the moon.
It was the shimmering of zinc and apples,
the forgotten smoke of the weeping amethyst,
death's brilliance within the emerald,
geology's purple coffin.

VI

It was my country, and it was naked.
The impalpable March night spilled
a new mineral, vast as tin,
and everything in the sky stirred to life again:
all the celestial minerals awakened,
while my cordillera, with ashes, quenched
that fire ardent with all the universe.
At my side, I saw Orion's three stones,
falling, like a clover leaf, in the shadow,
and then four thorns, four cold diamonds,
four snowy kisses in the distance,
four blazing cups on the table
of the solitary sky.
The Southern Cross was calling me.
I fell asleep, voyaging with my destiny.

MARÍA JACKETTI

CATACLYSM

※

I

The night of a thousand and one nights,
the shadow of a thousand shadows and a heartbeat,
the water of a thousand waters falling,
fire uncovering funnels,
ashes dressed up like Medusa,
the Earth's lamentation.

I am a man. Why was I born on Earth?

Where is the shroud?

Is this death?

II

During the last forty days,
no one witnessed or understood that something changed.
Winter presents itself like a traveler,
like a typical bird following the sky's tour.
Forty rainy suns over the mountains.
And then light, gloved fingers of light,
the winter night is dark like a dreaming hand,
and then with the dawn, the justice
of trees, a world of trees,
and the wars of trees in the deep, tenacious forest,
ringlike, never-ending, dressed
in immense perfume.

III

I am the man submerged in those latitudes.
There I left my hands, my first jewels,
empty treasures, more precious than money,
the fire of that world of leaves, roots, syllables
with a language, ragged leaves,
which one by one made me understand
my youth, quivering blessings, and because
of this,
when smoke and lava tumbled into the sea,
fear also fell there, making a net in a knot of thorns,
surrounding the day with tremors,
with a tail of furry water and biting rocks,
the Earth giving birth and dying, a tormented delivery,
and again calling herself Earth, with night cascading,
and again erasing her name with fright,
oh, oh, absent brothers, as if the pain
were an unbroken system,
a cup of bitter air between the whole of invisible atmosphere and sky.
Death arrived at my lips where I waited.
The Earth quaked where I traveled and searched.
And my heart split into flames with a single bolt of lightning.

IV

Tell me, poor Pedro, poor Juan,
you, poor, silent, inhabitant of the islands,
Augustine Fisherman, husband of María Forest,
or you, Martín, minus your oblivion, your amnesia dissolved forever,
child of stony memory,
tell me, tell me, without day, without night, without words,
tell me only with your injuries, the nets, the plows,
the little house and the pigs, the Singer sewing machine bargained for in
    Temuco,
in exchange for so much cloth, so much work raining down,
raining, always burdened by the rain,

and the shoes of the entire family
awaiting with patience the winter to break apart and rot.
Oh now maybe the lost wages mean nothing,
that stolen horse which later appeared in Nehuentúe means nothing.
Now life's great debt was paid with terror,
churned with the earth like a harvest
of that thing which everyone escaped from
with prayers, weeping, and extinguishing their lives,
without understanding why we were born, not understanding
why the earth, she who waited so long for the wheat to mature,
now, without patience, like a fierce widow,
drunk and quivering, calls for sudden payment:
love for love, life for life, and death for death.

V

The Andwanter cemetery on the Island,
facing Valdivia, cast a shroud over one hundred years,
the last drop of pure forgetfulness. Just
a handful of dead founders, a blond aristocrat
and his wife, the cook, and children, devourers of winter.
The lianas, ivy, chains of the forest,
threads extending from the *drimis winterey* and the *notofagus*
towering like vanquished cathedrals,
gothic like ferocious birthday dreams.
With a needle and silence, they fashioned a verdant homeland—
the vegetal church of their bones' desire.
And now, what did those dead ones accomplish?
Where do they live on?
From that faraway glass of water and oblivion, from that secret, whispering
shadow in the distance, did fear, dressed in a cloudburst,
also step out to stroll through Valdivia's loneliness?
Or did the volcano's tongue also stretch to touch there—
the interminable waters of death's appetite,
the sharp shout, the sea's arrows launched against oblivion?

VI

From Puerto Saavedra, a patio of poppies,
the negated life of Indians, summer's tower,
like a lantern whipped by waves of wheat,
the melancholic sky, hard and blue,
and a root, heavy with dust and perfume,
inside of me, giving birth, sundering the moon.

The old yellow-bearded poet, shepherd of the cold swan,
the nomadic swan, dome, snowy monarchy,
clear capsule, ship of solemn lakes,
the ancient poet extended his hand to me, with fugitive
urgency, before going to his grave—
now then, what could be done with the small skeleton
when everything trembled without swans, when everything flowed in the
    downpour,
and the sea from the other side devoured Malecón,
entering through the windows wrath and enemy waters,
bottomless ill will, nature's sword.
And my friend, reduced to seed—what could he do?—
returned to grain, perhaps a new birth,
when the sea's malice demolished wood
and solitude became the sacrifice?

VII

Volcanoes! Lost gods, renegades,
substitute gods, carnivorous flower heads,
I grew accustomed to setting my eyes at water's level,
at a bug or pebble's pinnacle,
your intact silence of snowy horses,
volcano necks, the snouts, the teeth,
only gnawing on the cold, the necklaces
of the great god Chillán, of Puntiagudo, of Osorno,
the plumes of Villarica, spread out by the stormy winds
in the distance, and reconcentrated water,

oh Tronador, bread of new creation from the cold oven
at the lush forest's heart, sealed like a church,
Llaima, with your tufts of gold and smoke,
Aconcagua, heavy father of the world's silence,
Calbuco, pristine volcano, apple-saint.

In this volcano and within other cradles of the earth's race,
your being and nonbeing were forged, your family's sustenance,
the formula of laws, written in fox blood,
words of rapture, salt, war, ashes.

And so, born of clay,
volcano clay,
the first human emerged.

VIII

The terror dwells inside, below the terror sleeps—
it is a striated egg living in the fire,
a pale feather—machine or medusa—
rising and falling, running through the veins of the volcano,
until frenetically leaping from its enclosure,
and from an inscrutable larva it changed into a crown,
terrible thunder, a perfect pipe for the storm,
a rose of sulfur, and blood above the crowned god.
And that distant peace, that snow on the lies
of quiet water, on the patience of Llanquihue,
all of it—summer with its quiescent dove,
ended in a shriek of deep fire:
the heavens cracked, the earth galloped,
and when only the sea could respond,
the waters united in a single wave of cowardice,
palpitating, rising through the loftiness,
falling with shivers into hell.

IX

My love, my love, close my eyes, protect them
not only from the volcanic brilliance, not only from
the darkness of terror: I don't want to have eyes.
I don't want that knowledge yet—to experience, to exist.
Close my eyes, protect them from all the tears,
protect them from my weeping and yours, from the perpetual
river of laments, caressing and piercing,
between night and lava—like sulfur's kiss—
the last vestment from a poor homeland, resting on stone,
facing the sea's insistent invitation,
beneath the cordillera's unmerciful bearing.

X

Fear envelops bones like new skin,
envelops blood with night's skin,
the earth moves beneath the soles of the feet—
it is not your hair but the terror in your head,
like long hair made of vertical nails,
and what you see are not shattered streets,
but rather, within you, your own crushed walls,
your frustrated infinity, again the city comes
crashing down: in your silence, only water's threat
is heard, and in the water
drowned horses gallop through your death.

XI

I will return to see how much was respected
by fire, land, and sea—there is no doubt. One day
I will arrive like the emigrants before their defeat:
this remained, this house, this rock, this man.
Kindness has the hands of a slow cyclone

when it comes to reclaiming their miserable treasures.
Forgetfulness and rain wash the finger-stains
of the devoured. Surely everything
will be there—the sailboats
return from the archipelago laden
with sea urchins, tomatoes of iodine,
with the hardwoods of Chacao.
And I will witness the same day's antiquity, named in snow,
with a volcano silenced in fullest brilliance,
the planet's supreme chill already
traveling, en route to its destiny, like a polar wind.
And more than a flower, more than a loaf of bread, more than a man will
   grow
from the same forgotten roots of fear.

XII

Araucaria, who are you? Who am I? A subject!
Suffer! Subject! Run! Here I am! But it is raining.
There is no one else. The tower collapsed. Swallow,
swallow the spoon, the shovel, the hoe,
now I'm dying—where is the Rose? There is no one—
no window, no light—they left, they died.
I went down to the patio—and then there was no land,
everything was rolling, fire around the corner.
You know that Alarcón put his children
on a ship, heading out to sea—but the sea
wasn't there—the sea went away—away, away,
escaped, absconded, the sea fled
and returned in a single wave, in a black wave,
the sea in a black wave,
the sea returned, returned, returned.
In a single wave the Alarcón family perished.

XIII

Sleep, children, beneath my wet wings,
bitter family of the trembling night,
Chileans lost in the terror, nameless
shoeless, without fathers, without mothers, without wisdom:
now beneath the rain we will have
the poncho, and plain as death, beneath my wings,
in the depths of night, we will sleep to awaken:
the enemy earth is our eternal obligation,
our duty is to open our hands and eyes
and to go out to count the dead and what is reborn.
There is no misfortune which the needle
cannot reconstruct, sewing, time sewing like a seamstress.
The red rose will stitch over the scars
and now we have new islands, volcanoes,
new rivers, a newborn ocean,
Let us live again—now—we will exist,
let us put on our faces the only smiles floating in the sea,
let us pick up the burnt hat and the dead surname,
let us again clothe the naked man and woman,
let us build the wall, the door, the city,
let us begin again the industries of love and steel:
let us rescue again our quaking homeland.

MARÍA JACKETTI

I

Cuando llegó a París tuvo mucho que hacer.
Estas eran las verdaderas calles del hombre.
Aquí las había taladrado como a los túneles el gusano
adentro de un queso oscuro, bajo el atroz invierno.
Las casas eran tan grandes que la sabiduría
se empequeñeció y corrió como rata al granero
y sólo fueron habitadas las casas por la sombra,
por la rutina venenosa de los que padecían.
Compró flores, pequeñas flores en el mercado de Halles
y de Clignancourt absorbió el asco militante,
no hubo piedra olvidada para el pequeño Isidoro,
su rostro se fue haciendo delgado como un diente,
delgado y amarillo como la luna menguante en la pampa,
cada vez más parecido a la luna delgada.
La noche le robaba hora por hora el rostro.
La noche de París ya había devorado
todos los regimientos, las dinastías, los héroes,
los niños y los viejos, las prostitutas, los ricos y los pobres,
Ducasse estaba solo y cuanto tuvo de luz lo entregó cuerpo a cuerpo,
contra la devoradora se dispuso a luchar,
fabricó lobos para defender la luz,
acumuló agonía para salvar la vida,
fue más allá del mal para llegar al bien.

II

Lo conocí en el Uruguay cuando era tan pequeño
que se extraviaba en las guitarras del mes de julio,
aquellos días fueron de guerra y de humo,
se desbocaron los ríos, crecieron sin medida las aguas.

No había tiempo para que naciera.
Debió volver muchas veces, remontar el deseo,
viajar hasta su origen, hasta por fin llegar
cuando sangre y tambores golpeaban a la puerta,
y Montevideo ardía como los ojos del puma.
Turbulenta fue aquella época, y de color morado
como un deshilachado pabellón de asesinos.
Desde la selva el viento militar
llegaba en un confuso olor a hierba ardiendo.
Los fusiles quebrados a la vera del río
entraban en el agua y a plena medianoche
se habían convertido en guitarras, el viento
repartía sollozos y besos de las barcarolas.

III

Americano! Pequeño potro pálido
de las praderas! Hijo
de la luna uruguaya!
Escribiste a caballo, galopando
entre la dura hierba y el olor a camino,
a soledad, a noche y herraduras!
Cada uno
de tus cantos fue un lazo,
y Maldoror sentado sobre las calaveras
de las vacas
escribe con su lazo,
es tarde, es una pieza de hotel, la muerte ronda.
Maldoror con su lazo,
escribe que te escribe su larga carta roja.
La vidalita de Maldoror, hacia el Oeste,
las guitarras sin rumbo, cerca del Paraná,
terrenos bajos, el misterioso crepúsculo cayó
como una paletada de sangre sobre la tierra,
las grandes aves carnívoras se despliegan,
sube del Uruguay la noche con sus uvas.
Era tarde, un temblor unánime de ranas,

los insectos metálicos atormentan el cielo,
mientras la inmensa luna se desnuda en la pampa
extendiendo en el frío su sábana amarilla.

IV

El falso cruel de noche prueba sus uñas falsas,
de sus cándidos ojos hace dos agujeros,
con terciopelo negro su razón enmascara,
con un aullido apaga su inclinación celeste.

El sapo de París, la bestia blanda
de la ciudad inmunda lo sigue paso a paso,
lo espera y abre las puertas de su hocico:
el pequeño Ducasse ha sido devorado.

El ataúd delgado parece que llevara
un violín o un pequeño cadáver de gaviota,
son los mínimos huesos del joven desdichado,
y nadie ve pasar el carro que lo lleva,
porque en este ataúd continúa el destierro,
el desterrado sigue desterrado en la muerte.

Entonces escogió la Commune y en las calles
sangrientas, Lautréamont, delgada torre roja,
amparó con su llama la cólera del pueblo,
recogió las banderas del amor derrotado
y en las masacres Maldoror no cayó,
su pecho transparente recibió la metralla
sin que una sola gota de sangre delatara
que el fantasma se había ido volando
y que aquella masacre le devolvía el mundo:
Maldoror reconocía a sus hermanos.

Pero antes de morir volvió su rostro duro
y tocó el pan, acarició la rosa,
soy, dijo, el defensor esencial de la abeja,
sólo de claridad debe vivir el hombre.

V

Del niño misterioso recojamos
cuánto dejó, sus cantos triturados,
las alas tenebrosas de la nave enlutada,
su negra dirección que ahora entendemos.
Ha sido revelada su palabra.
Detrás de cada sombra suya el trigo.
En cada ojo sin luz una pupila.
La rosa en el espacio del hombre.
La esperanza que sube del suplicio.
El amor desbordando de su copa.
El deber hijo puro de la madera.
El rocío que corre saludando a las hojas.
La bondad con más ojos que una estrella.
El honor sin medalla ni castillo.

VI

Entonces la muerte, la muerte de París cayó como una tela,
como horrendo vampiro, como alas de paraguas,
y el héroe desangrado la rechazó creyendo
que era su propia imagen, su anterior criatura,
la imagen espantosa de sus primeros sueños.
"No estoy aquí, me fui. Maldoror ya no existe".
"Soy la alegría de la futura primavera",
dijo, y no era la sombra que sus manos crearon,
no era el silbido del folletín en la niebla,
ni la araña nutrida por su oscura grandeza,
era sólo la muerte de París que llegaba
a preguntar por el indómito uruguayo,
por el niño feroz que quería volver,
que quería sonreír hacia Montevideo,
era sólo la muerte que venía a buscarlo.

I

There was much to do when he arrived in Paris.
These were the authentic streets of man.
Here, they were created like worm tunnels
within a dark cheese, below winter's hardness.
The houses puzzled like mazes—
wisdom withered and ran like a rat in search of a granary.
The houses were only inhabited by shadows—
by the poison routine of the anguished.
He shopped for flowers, little blossoms in the market of Halles,
and from Clignancourt he absorbed militant loathing,
Little Isidoro overlooked no stone.
His face grew as thin as a tooth,
skinny and sallow, a shriveled remembrance of the pampa's moon.
Hour by hour, the wheel of night eclipsed his face.
The Parisian night had already devoured
all the regiments, the dynasties, the heroes,
the children and the aged, the whores, the rich and the destitute.
Ducasse was alone—and he relinquished
the remains of his light, body to body,
prepared to fight the devourer,
inventing wolves to defend the light,
accumulating agony to save his life—
traveling beyond evil—to arrive at goodness.

II

I met him in Uruguay when he was very young,
a nomadic child of July's guitars,
those were days of war and smoke,
the lips of rivers overflowed, waters swelled into chaos.
There was no time for his nativity.

He should have returned many times, to find shelter in the desire,
to journey to his origins, until finally arriving
when blood and drums pounded at the door,
and Montevideo flashed flames like the eyes of a puma.
It was a turbulent age, stained purple
like a twisted arcade of assassins.
From the deep forest, a military gale
arrived spreading the confused fragrance of burnt grass.
Shattered guns at the river's edge
penetrated the water and in midnight's fullness
changed into guitars. The wind
repeated the sobs and kisses of barcaroles.

III

American! Wisp of a pallid colt
from the grasslands. Child
of the Uruguayan moon.
You wrote on horseback, galloping
between the rough turf and the aromatic dust,
alone with the night and horseshoes!
Each of your songs was
a lasso,
and Maldoror, seated on the skulls
of cows
writes with his lasso—
it's late, in a hotel room, death prowls.
Maldoror with his lasso,
writes, writes for you his long red letter.
Maldoror's frail life, going west,
guitars without a destination, near Paraná,
lowlands, the mystic twilight descending,
spreading a bloody trowel across the Earth,
great carnivorous birds extending their wings,
the Uruguayan night rising with its grapes.
So late—a unanimous vibrato of frogs,
metallic insects tormenting the skies,

meanwhile the immense moon disrobes in the pampa
spreading its yellow sheet across the chill.

IV

The cruel nocturnal falsifier tests his spurious talons,
from honest eyes he fashions two holes,
with black velvet, his reason makes a mask,
with a howl, his celestial inclination is smothered.

The toad of Paris, the boneless beast
from the obscene city follows each of his steps,
waits for him, and opens the doors of its thick jaws:
little Ducasse has been devoured.

The slim coffin seems to carry
a violin or a tiny seagull cadaver,
not the minimal bones of an unlucky young man.
No one sees what the passing cart is carrying
because within this coffin exile continues,
the exiled man continues his exile in death.

Then by the Commune's election, and in the
bloody streets, Lautréamont, a slim red tower,
befriended the people's anger with his flames,
gathered the flags of shattered love.
During the massacres, Maldoror did not fall,
his transparent chest received the shrapnel
without relinquishing a drop of blood—
it was as if his ghost had flown away
and that massacre returned him to the world.
Maldoror recognized his brothers.

But before dying, his solid face returned—
he touched bread, caressed the rose,
I am, he said, the bee's essential defender,
only clarity should live in man.

V

From the mystic young man, let us gather
the remains of what was left behind, his shattered songs,
the secret wings of bereavement's ship.
We now perceive his blackened residence—
his word, revealed.
Behind each of his shadows, the wheat.
In each eye, devoid of light, a pupil.
The rose expanding into man's space.
Hope rising from torture.
Love overflowing its cup.
Duty, pure offspring of wood.
Dew running in drops, greeting leaves.
Loving-kindness with more eyes than a star.
Honor—but without medals, without a castle.

VI

Then death, death rained down like rags in Paris,
like an ugly vampire, like the wings of an umbrella,
but the wounded hero rejected it believing
it was his own image, a bygone creation,
the dire image of his first dreams.
"I am not here. I don't exist. Maldoror doesn't exist anymore."
"I am the delight of future springtime,"
he said, and it was not the shadow, creation of his hands,
it was not the whistling of novels penetrating the fog,
it was not the spider, nourished by his dark grandeur.
It was only death Parisian style, arriving,
asking for the indomitable Uruguayan,
for the wild boy who wanted to return.
He longed to smile en route to Montevideo.
It was only death coming to find him.

MARÍA JACKETTI

OCEAN LADY

❋

I

Ocean Lady, bride, hips of the islands,
here, beside me, sing to me, the vanished
songs, signs, numbers from the river of desire.
I want to listen to the invisible, things fallen out of time
onto the equinox's canopy of palm trees.
Give me the secret wine guarded within each syllable,
the comings and goings of waves, races of honey
fallen into the sea's bucket, washed up on the reefs.

II

I don't exist—I lost days because back then,
Ocean Lady, I didn't embrace your flowery guitar.
The dawn's mouth glittered like mother-of-pearl.
Like thunder, surf penetrated the islands,
and everything churned to brilliance, except my life,
except my heart, yearning for orange blossoms.

III

Ocean Lady, give your twilight rest in the castle
which faithfully awaited the passage of your lush hair,
in every wave that the sea raised up from its chasm,
and then you weren't yourself—but instead the fugitive sea,
the sea, the sea, and what could I do?
It was late, another day was opening with my key,
another door, and the sea extended emptiness.

IV

Back then I wandered, wasting my smile.
One by one, my teeth dropped into an iron box.
Furiously, I contemplated saints in mourning,
amber coffins carried by the dawn,
minerals imprisoned in their abyss,
the miserable algae rocking themselves in the fog,
and without touching your eyelids, golden Ocean Lady,
black Ocean Lady, Ocean Lady with transparent hands,
I stretched my senses, until without knowing it,
a sudden rose unfurled, blossoming over the sea.

V

Sing to me, snail; speak to me, bell;
sing to me, patience of underwater wheat,
the quivering king, crowned by vertebrae,
the retrograde moon that cried in the cold.
And if there exists a lost teardrop in the language,
let it slip into my cup.
By drinking it, I will know what I didn't know then.
Sing to me the essence that traveled
from mouth to mouth to mouth, becoming
song without touching earth,
pure in the pure air of honeyed days,
high in the air like the everlasting palm.

VI

Siren, or lush palm tree, foamy dove,
serenity or guitars in slow, high flight,
repeat to me the song circulating in my blood.
It had no voice until you arrived,
arrived quivering in the sea's bubbles,

from hard and golden coasts of nonexistence,
from stories, plunged, page by page, into the water,
to Earth, populated by blackened governments.

VII

I yearn only to become the incarnation of marine stone,
statue, lava, a hard, towering monument
where bygone waves explode,
seas that perished with canticles and travelers.
So, Ocean Lady, when from nonexistence,
your wide eyes appeared, and your bracelets,
jingling in the rain, announced your arrival
to me, a languid crown of the sea's flowers,
my heart exited and got lost in the streets.
Reaching back to that moment: sing to me with guitar-eyes.

From that instant: sigh for me with amethyst grapes,
and apples, and strictly tender dates,
fruits, fruits just stolen from the dawn,
and further wounded by bullets of dew.
And may the wet basket brim with the purest pears,
mangoes ripened to a distant sweetness,
abundant guanabanas, radiant with perfume,
shining crimes hidden by the pomegranate,
the honey in the belly of pale melons.

VIII

Ocean Lady, extend to me the shells of the reef,
to cloak walls with your lightning,
the Spondylus, heroes crowned with thorns,
the empurpled splendor of the murex on its rock.
You know the way: over the ultramarine salt
the Argonaut navigates his snow-ship.

Such feathers! Bring with you the bird
joining the secret depths and heaven,
come wrapped in your newborn nakedness of hummingbirds,
until feather by feather, emeralds fly.

X

Remember: you carry the bird's heart
in its cage: the debate of wings and song,
so many violins, soaring and flashing.
Gather, gather for me, the sounds and jewels,
until wrapped in air and fire, we voyage
accompanied by the congress of pure harmonies
to morning's waterfall of shimmering ingots.
And may our love palpitate like a fish in the cold.

At last, to end, do not return to your sea-stone.
Ocean Lady, my soul, southern amber and grace.

On our ship, our earth, we receive
the pollen and fish of distant isles,
listening, listening to the faraway whisper and barcarole,
the sunrise ritual of lost oars.

Ocean Lady, I am just someone who hoped for you
in the tower of an ethereal lighthouse,
and this is the story where only one tide surges . . .
your aquamarine breasts beneath night's radiance.

There are only two truths in this sonata:
your two dark eyes, open in the water.

MARÍA JACKETTI

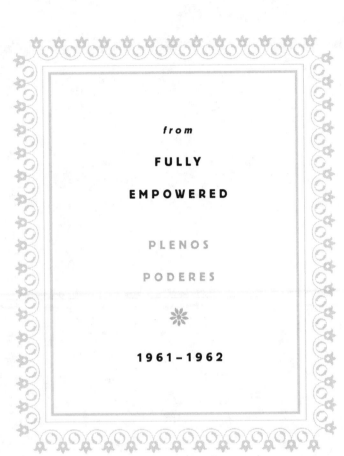

from

FULLY

EMPOWERED

PLENOS

PODERES

1961–1962

DEBER DEL POETA

A quien no escucha el mar en este viernes
por la mañana, quien adentro de algo,
casa, oficina, fábrica o mujer,
o calle o mina o seco calabozo:
a éste yo acudo y sin hablar ni ver
llego y abro la puerta del encierro
y un sin fin se oye vago en la insistencia,
un largo trueno roto se encadena
al peso del planeta y de la espuma,
surgen los ríos roncos del océano,
vibra veloz en su rosal la estrella
y el mar palpita, muere y continúa.

Así por el destino conducido
debo sin tregua oír y conservar
el lamento marino en mi conciencia,
debo sentir el golpe de agua dura
y recogerlo en una taza eterna
para que donde esté el encarcelado,
donde sufra el castigo del otoño
yo esté presente con una ola errante,
yo circule a través de las ventanas
y al oírme levante la mirada
diciendo: cómo me acercaré al océano?
Y yo transmitiré sin decir nada
los ecos estrellados de la ola,
un quebranto de espuma y arenales,
un susurro de sal que se retira,
el grito gris del ave de la costa.

Y así, por mí, la libertad y el mar
responderán al corazón oscuro.

THE POET'S OBLIGATION

To whoever is not listening to the sea
this Friday morning, to whoever is cooped up
in house or office, factory or woman
or street or mine or dry prison cell,
to him I come, and without speaking or looking
I arrive and open the door of his prison,
and a vibration starts up, vague and insistent,
a long rumble of thunder adds itself
to the weight of the planet and the foam,
the groaning rivers of the ocean rise,
the star vibrates quickly in its corona
and the sea beats, dies, and goes on beating.

So, drawn on by my destiny,
I ceaselessly must listen to and keep
the sea's lamenting in my consciousness,
I must feel the crash of the hard water
and gather it up in a perpetual cup
so that, wherever those in prison may be,
wherever they suffer the sentence of the autumn,
I may be present with an errant wave,
I may move in and out of windows,
and hearing me, eyes may lift themselves,
asking "How can I reach the sea?"
And I will pass to them, saying nothing,
the starry echoes of the wave,
a breaking up of foam and quicksand,
a rustling of salt withdrawing itself,
the gray cry of sea birds on the coast.

So, through me, freedom and the sea
will call in answer to the shrouded heart.

ALASTAIR REID

THE WORD

The word
was born in the blood,
grew in the dark body, beating,
and took flight through the lips and the mouth.

Farther away and nearer
still, still it came
from dead fathers and from wandering races,
from lands which had turned to stone,
lands weary of their poor tribes,
for when grief took to the roads
the people set out and arrived
and married new land and water
to grow their words again.
And so this is the inheritance;
this is the wavelength which connects us
with dead men and the dawning
of new beings not yet come to light.

Still the atmosphere quivers
with the first word uttered
dressed up
in terror and sighing.
It emerged
from the darkness
and until now there is no thunder
that ever rumbles with the iron voice
of that word,
the first
word uttered—
perhaps it was only a ripple, a single drop,
and yet its great cataract falls and falls.

Later on, the word fills with meaning.
Always with child, it filled up with lives.
Everything was births and sounds—
affirmation, clarity, strength,

negation, destruction, death—
the verb took over all the power
and blended existence with essence
in the electricity of its grace.

Human word, syllable, flank
of extending light and solid silverwork,
hereditary goblet which receives
the communications of the blood—
here is where silence came together with
the wholeness of the human word,
and, for human beings, not to speak is to die—
language extends even to the hair,
the mouth speaks without the lips moving,
all of a sudden, the eyes are words.

I take the word and pass it through my senses
as though it were no more than a human shape;
its arrangements awe me and I find my way
through each resonance of the spoken word—
I utter and I am and, speechless, I approach
across the edge of words silence itself.

I drink to the word, raising
a word or a shining cup;
in it I drink
the pure wine of language
or inexhaustible water,
maternal source of words,
and cup and water and wine
give rise to my song
because the verb is the source
and vivid life—it is blood,
blood which expresses its substance
and so ordains its own unwinding.
Words give glass quality to glass, blood to blood,
and life to life itself.

ALASTAIR REID

OCEAN

Body more perfect than a wave,
salt washing the sea line,
and the shining bird
flying without ground roots.

ALASTAIR REID

THE SEA

One single being, but there's no blood.
One single caress, death or rose.
The sea comes and reunites our lives
and alone attacks and divides and sings
in night and day and man and creature.
The essence: fire and cold: movement.

MARK EISNER

IT IS BORN

Here I came to the very edge
where nothing at all needs saying,
everything is absorbed through weather and the sea,
and the moon swam back,
its rays all silvered,
and time and again the darkness would be broken
by the crash of a wave,
and every day on the balcony of the sea,
wings open, fire is born,
and everything is blue again like morning.

ALASTAIR REID

PLANET

Are there stones of water on the moon?
Are there waters of gold?
What color is autumn?
Do the days run into one another
until like a shock of hair
they all unravel? How much falls
—paper, wine, hands, dead bodies—
from the earth on that far place?

Is it there that the drowned live?

ALASTAIR REID

SERENATA

Con la mano recojo este vacío,
imponderable noche, familias estrelladas,
un coro más callado que el silencio,
un sonido de luna, algo secreto, un triángulo,
un trapecio de tiza.
Es la noche oceánica, la soledad tercera,
una vacilación abriendo puertas, alas,
la población profunda que no tiene presencia
palpita desbordando los nombres del estuario.

Noche, nombre del mar, patria, racimo, rosa!

SERENADE

With my hand I gather in this emptiness,
the bewildering night, the starry families,
a chorus still more silent than the silence,
a moon sound, something secret, a triangle,
a chalked geometry.

It is the night of the ocean, the third solitude,
a quivering which opens doors and wings.
The mysterious and intangible population
trembles and washes over the names of the estuary.

Night, the sea's name, homeland, roots, rose!

ALASTAIR REID

TO WASH A CHILD

Love, the most immemorial on earth,
washes and combs the effigy of the children,
straightens the feet and knees;
the water rises, the soap slithers,
and the pristine body emerges to breathe
the air of flowers and the mother.

Oh, the sharp watchfulness,
the sweet deceptions,
the loving struggle!

Now the hair is a tangled
pelt crisscrossed by charcoal,
by sawdust and oil,
soot, wires, and crabs,
until love patiently,
patiently,
sets up buckets and sponges,
combs and towels,
and from scrubbing and combing and amber,
from ancient scruples and from jasmine,
emerges the child, cleaner than ever,
running from the mother's arms
to clamber again on its whirlwind,
to look for mud, oil, piss, and ink,
to hurt itself, tumble about on the stones.
In that way, newly washed, the child leaps into life;

for later it will have time for nothing more
than keeping clean, but lifelessly by then.

ALASTAIR REID

ODE TO IRONING

Poetry is white:
it leaves the water wrapped in drops,
it wrinkles and piles up,
the skin of this planet has to be spread out,
the pure whiteness of the sea must be ironed,
and the hands go on and on,
the sacred surfaces are smoothed,
and that's how things are made:
each day hands make the world,
fire joins steel,
the linen, fabric, and cotton cloth arrive
from the combat of the laundries,
and a dove is born out of the light:
chastity returns from the foam.

MARK EISNER

TO THE DEAD POOR MAN

Today we are burying our own poor man;
our poor poor man.

He was always so badly off
that this is the first time
his person is personified.

For he had neither house nor land,
nor alphabet nor sheets,
nor roast meat,
and so from one place to another, on the roads,

he went, dying from lack of life,
dying little by little—
that was the way of it from his birth.

Luckily (and strangely) they were all of the same mind,
from the bishop to the judge,
in assuring him of his share of heaven;
and dead now, properly dead, our own poor man,
oh, our poor poor man,
he will not know what to do with so much sky.
Can he plow it or sow it or harvest it?

He did that always; cruelly
he struggled with raw land,
and now the sky lies easy to his plow,
and later, among the fruits of heaven,
he will have his share, and at his table,
at such a height, everything is set
for him to eat his fill of heaven,
our poor man, who brings, as his fortune
from below, some sixty years of hunger
to be satisfied, finally, as is just and proper,
with no more batterings from life,
without being victimized for eating;
safe as houses in his box under the ground,
now he no longer moves to protect himself,
now he will not struggle over wages.
He never hoped for such justice, did this man.
Suddenly they have filled his cup and it cheers him;
now he has fallen dumb with happiness.

How heavy he is now, the poor poor man!
He was a bag of bones, with black eyes,
and now we know, by the weight of him alone,
the oh so many things he always lacked,
for if this strength had gone on and on,
digging up raw land, combing out stones,
harvesting wheat, soaking clay,
grinding down sulfur, lugging firewood,

if this so weighty man did not have shoes,
oh, misery, if this whole separate man
of tendon and muscle didn't ever have
justice in life, and all men beat him,
all men did him down, and even so
he went on laboring away, now, lifting him up,
in his coffin, on our shoulders,
now at least we know how much he didn't have,
that we did not help him in his life on earth.

Now it dawns on us we are taking on
all that we never gave him, and now it is late;
he weighs on us, and we cannot take his weight.

How many people does our dead one weigh?

He weighs as much as this world does, and we go on
taking this dead one on our shoulders. It's clear
that heaven must abound in bread baking.

ALASTAIR REID

GOODBYES

Goodbye, goodbye, to one place or another,
to every mouth, to every sorrow,
to the insolent moon, to weeks
which wound in the days and disappeared,
goodbye to this voice and that one stained
with amaranth, and goodbye
to the usual bed and plate,
to the twilit setting of all goodbyes,
to the chair that is part of the same twilight,
to the way made by my shoes.

I spread myself, no question;
I turned over whole lives,
changed skin, lamps, and hates,

it was something I had to do,
not by law or whim,
more of a chain reaction;
each new journey enchained me;
I took pleasure in place, in all places.

And, newly arrived, I promptly said goodbye
with still newborn tenderness
as if the bread were to open and suddenly
flee from the world of the table.
So I left behind all languages,
repeated goodbyes like an old door,
changed cinemas, reasons, and tombs,
left everywhere for somewhere else;
I went on being, and being always
half undone with joy,
a bridegroom among sadnesses,
never knowing how or when,
ready to return, never returning.

It's well known that he who returns never left,
so I traced and retraced my life,
changing clothes and planets,
growing used to the company,
to the great whirl of exile,
to the great solitude of bells tolling.

ALASTAIR REID

SPRING

The bird has come
to bring light to birth.
From every trill of his,
water is born.

And between water and light which unwind the air,
now the spring is inaugurated,

now the seed is aware of its own growing;
the root takes shape in the corolla,
at last the eyelids of the pollen open.

All this accomplished by a simple bird
from his perch on a green branch.

ALASTAIR REID

TO DON ASTERIO ALARCÓN,
CLOCKSMITH OF VALPARAÍSO

Smell of a crazy seaport,
Valparaíso has,
smell of shade, of stars,
a suspicion of the moon
and the tails of fish.
The heart takes to shivering
on the tattered stairways
up the shaggy hills.
There, squalor and black eyes
dance in the sea mist
and hang out the flags
of the kingdom in the windows—
the sheets stitched together,
the ancient undershirts,
the long-legged drawers—
and the sea sun salutes the emblems
while the white laundry waves
a threadbare goodbye to the sailors.

Streets of sea and wind,
of the hard day swaddled in air and waves,
alleyways singing upward
in a winding spiral, like shells—
the market afternoon is shining,
the sun touches the merchandise,
shop fronts smile like salesmen

opening windows and dentures,
shoes and thermometers, bottles
enclosing a green darkness,
impossible suits, clothes of gold,
gloomy socks, bland cheeses,
and now I get to the point
of this poem.

There is one window
with a glass eye
and inside,
among chronometers,
Don Asterio Alarcón, the clocksmith.
The street heaves and winds,
burns and bumps,
but behind the glass
the clocksmith,
the old curator of timepieces,
stands motionless
with a single protruding eye,
one amazing eye
which peers into the mystery,
the secret hearts of clocks,
and looks deeply in
until the elusive butterfly
of time in its measure
is trapped in his forehead
and the wings of the watch beat.

Don Asterio Alarcón is the ancient
hero of the minutes,
and boats go through the waves
governed by his fingers,
which gave to the minute hands
clockwork responsibilities,
and a meticulous tick.
Don Asterio in his aquarium
kept watch on the clocks of the sea,
oiled with patient fingers

the blue heart of the seaways.
For fifty steady years,
or eighteen thousand days,
a steady stream kept passing,
children and men and women,
up to the ragged hills or down to the sea,
while the clocksmith
among his clocks,
trapped in the flow of time,
kept smoothly on, as a ship does,
cleanly in the perpetual current,
pacified his wood,
and bit by bit the wise man
emerged from the artisan;
working
with glass and oil,
he cleaned away hate, got rid of fear,
fulfilled his office and his destiny
to this present point where time,
that terrifying flow,
made its pact with him, with Don Asterio,
and he waits for his hour on the dial.

So, whenever I pass
along that vibrating street,
black river of Valparaíso,
I listen for one sound above the others,
one clock among so many clocks,
the tired, insistent, whispering,
and ancient movement
of a great and perfect heart,
the distinguished and humble
tick tock of Don Asterio.

ALASTAIR REID

THE NIGHT IN ISLA NEGRA

Ancient night and the unruly salt
beat at the walls of my house.
The shadow is all one, the sky
throbs now along with the ocean,
and sky and shadow erupt
in the crash of their vast conflict.
All night long they struggle;
nobody knows the name
of the harsh light that keeps slowly opening
like a languid fruit.
So on the coast comes to light,
out of seething shadow, the harsh dawn,
gnawed at by the moving salt,
swept clean by the mass of night,
bloodstained in its sea-washed crater.

ALASTAIR REID

PAST

We have to discard the past
and, as one builds
floor by floor, window by window,
and the building rises,
so do we keep shedding—
first, broken tiles,
then proud doors,
until, from the past,
dust falls
as if it would crash
against the floor,
smoke rises
as if it were on fire,
and each new day
gleams
like an empty

plate.
There is nothing, there was always nothing.
It all has to be filled
with a new, expanding
fruitfulness;
then, down
falls yesterday
as in a well
falls yesterday's water,
into the cistern
of all that is now without voice, without fire.
It is difficult
to get bones used
to disappearing,
to teach eyes
to close,
but
we do it
unwittingly.
Everything was alive,
alive, alive, alive
like a scarlet fish,
but time
passed with cloth and darkness
and kept wiping away
the flash of the fish.
Water water water,
the past goes on falling
although it keeps a grip
on thorns
and on roots.
It went, it went, and now
memories mean nothing.
Now the heavy eyelid
shut out the light of the eye
and what was once alive
is now no longer living;
what we were, we are not.
And with words, although the letters

still have transparency and sound,
they change, and the mouth changes;
the same mouth is now another mouth;
they change, lips, skin, circulation;
another soul took on our skeleton;
what once was in us now is not.
It left, but if they call, we reply
"I am here," and we realize we are not,
that what was once, was and is lost,
lost in the past, and now does not come back.

ALASTAIR REID

EL PUEBLO

De aquel hombre me acuerdo y no han pasado
sino dos siglos desde que lo vi,
no anduvo ni a caballo ni en carroza:
a puro pie
deshizo
las distancias
y no llevaba espada ni armadura,
sino redes al hombro,
hacha o martillo o pala,
nunca apaleó a ninguno de su especie:
su hazaña fue contra el agua o la tierra,
contra el trigo para que hubiera pan,
contra el árbol gigante para que diera leña,
contra los muros para abrir las puertas,
contra la arena construyendo muros
y contra el mar para hacerlo parir.

Lo conocí y aún no se me borra.

Cayeron en pedazos las carrozas,
la guerra destruyó puertas y muros,
la ciudad fue un puñado de cenizas,
se hicieron polvo todos los vestidos,

y él para mí subsiste,
sobrevive en la arena,
cuando antes parecía
todo imborrable menos él.

En el ir y venir de las familias
a veces fue mi padre o mi pariente
o apenas si era él o si no era
tal vez aquel que no volvió a su casa
porque el agua o la tierra lo tragaron
o lo mató una máquina o un árbol
o fue aquel enlutado carpintero
que iba detrás del ataúd, sin lágrimas,
alguien en fin que no tenía nombre,
que se llamaba metal o madera,
y a quien miraron otros desde arriba
sin ver la hormiga
sino el hormiguero
y que cuando sus pies no se movían,
porque el pobre cansado había muerto,
no vieron nunca que no lo veían:
había ya otros pies en donde estuvo.

Los otros pies eran él mismo,
también las otras manos,
el hombre sucedía;
cuando ya parecía transcurrido
era el mismo de nuevo,
allí estaba otra vez cavando tierra,
cortando tela, pero sin camisa,
allí estaba y no estaba, como entonces,
se había ido y estaba de nuevo,
y como nunca tuvo cementerio,
ni tumba, ni su nombre fue grabado
sobre la piedra que cortó sudando,
nunca sabía nadie que llegaba
y nadie supo cuando se moría,
así es que sólo cuando el pobre pudo
resucitó otra vez sin ser notado.

Era el hombre sin duda, sin herencia,
sin vaca, sin bandera,
y no se distinguía entre los otros,
los otros que eran él,
desde arriba era gris como el subsuelo,
como el cuero era pardo,
era amarillo cosechando trigo,
era negro debajo de la mina,
era color de piedra en el castillo,
en el barco pesquero era color de atún
y color de caballo en la pradera:
cómo podía nadie distinguirlo
si era el inseparable, el elemento,
tierra, carbón o mar vestido de hombre?

Donde vivió crecía
cuanto el hombre tocaba:
la piedra hostil,
quebrada
por sus manos,
se convertía en orden
y una a una formaron
la recta claridad del edificio,
hizo el pan con sus manos,
movilizó los trenes,
se poblaron de pueblos las distancias,
otros hombres crecieron,
llegaron las abejas,
y porque el hombre crea y multiplica
la primavera caminó al mercado
entre panaderías y palomas.

El padre de los panes fue olvidado,
él que cortó y anduvo, machacando
y abriendo surcos, acarreando arena,
cuando todo existió ya no existía,
él daba su existencia, eso era todo.
Salió otra parte a trabajar, y luego
se fue a morir rodando

como piedra del río:
aguas abajo lo llevó la muerte.

Yo, que lo conocí, lo vi bajando
hasta no ser sino lo que dejaba:
calles que apenas pudo conocer,
casas que nunca y nunca habitaría.

Y vuelvo a verlo, y cada día espero.

Lo veo en su ataúd y resurrecto.

Lo distingo entre todos
los que son sus iguales
y me parece que no puede ser,
que así no vamos a ninguna parte,
que suceder así no tiene gloria.

Yo creo que en el trono debe estar
este hombre, bien calzado y coronado.

Creo que los que hicieron tantas cosas
deben ser dueños de todas las cosas.
Y los que hacen el pan deben comer!

Y deben tener luz los de la mina!

Basta ya de encadenados grises!

Basta de pálidos desaparecidos!

Ni un hombre más que pase sin que reine.

Ni una sola mujer sin su diadema.

Para todas las manos guantes de oro.

Frutas de sol a todos los oscuros!

Yo conocí aquel hombre y cuando pude,
cuando ya tuve ojos en la cara,
cuando ya tuve la voz en la boca
lo busqué entre las tumbas, y le dije
apretándole un brazo que aún no era polvo:

"Todos se irán, tú quedarás viviente.

Tú encendiste la vida.

Tú hiciste lo que es tuyo."

Por eso nadie se moleste cuando
parece que estoy solo y no estoy solo,
no estoy con nadie y hablo para todos:

Alguien me está escuchando y no lo saben,
pero aquellos que canto y que lo saben
siguen naciendo y llenarán el mundo.

THE PEOPLE

That man I remember well, and at least two centuries
have passed since I last saw him;
he traveled neither on horseback nor in a carriage,
always on foot
he undid
the distances,
carrying neither sword nor weapon
but nets on his shoulder,
ax or hammer or spade;
he never fought with another of his kind—
his struggle was with water or with earth,
with the wheat, for it to become bread,
with the towering tree, for it to yield wood,
with walls, to open doors in them,

with sand, to form it into walls,
and with the sea, to make it bear fruit.

I knew him and he goes on haunting me.

The carriages splintered into pieces,
war destroyed doorways and walls,
the city was a fistful of ashes,
all the dresses shivered into dust,
and for me he persists,
he survives in the sand,
when everything previously
seemed durable except him.

In the comings and goings of families,
sometimes he was my father or my relative
or almost was, or, if not, perhaps
the other one who never came back home
because water or earth swallowed him,
a machine or a tree killed him,
or he was that funeral carpenter
who walked behind the coffin, dry-eyed,
someone who never had a name
except as wood or metal have names,
and on whom others looked from above,
not noticing the ant,
only the anthill;
so that when his feet no longer moved
because, poor and tired, he had died,
they never saw what they were not used to seeing—
already other feet walked in his footsteps.

The other feet were still him,
the other hands as well.
The man persisted.
When it seemed he must be spent,
he was the same man over again;
there he was once more, digging the ground,

cutting cloth, but without a shirt,
he was there and he wasn't, just as before
he had gone away and replaced himself;
and since he never had cemetery
or tomb, or his name engraved
on the stone that he sweated to cut,
nobody ever knew of his arrival
and nobody knew when he died,
so only when the poor man was able
did he come back to life, unnoticed.

He was the man all right, with no inheritance,
no cattle, no coat of arms,
and he did not stand out from others,
others who were himself;
from above he was gray, like clay,
he was drab, like leather,
he was yellow harvesting wheat,
he was black down in the mine,
stone colored in the castle,
in the fishing boat the color of tuna,
horse-colored on the prairies—
how could anyone distinguish him
if he were inseparable from his element,
earth, coal, or sea in a man's form?

Where he lived, everything
the man touched would grow—
the hostile stones
broken
by his hands
took shape and line
and one by one assumed
the sharp forms of buildings;
he made bread with his hands,
set the trains running;
the distances filled with towns,
other men grew,

the bees arrived,
and through the man's creating and multiplying,
spring wandered into the marketplace
between bakeries and doves.

The father of the loaves was forgotten,
the one who cut and trudged, beating
and opening paths, shifting sand;
when everything came into being, he no longer existed.
He gave away his existence, that was all.
He went somewhere else to work and ultimately
he went toward death, rolling
like a river stone;
death carried him off downstream.

I who knew him saw him go down
until he existed only in what he was leaving—
streets he could scarcely be aware of,
houses he never never would inhabit.

And I come back to see him, and every day I wait.

I see him in his coffin and resurrected.

I pick him out from all
the others who are his equals
and it seems to me that this cannot be,
that this way leads us nowhere,
that to continue so has no glory.

I believe that heaven must encompass
this man, properly shod and crowned.

I think that those who made so many things
ought to be owners of everything.
That those who make bread ought to eat.

That those in the mine should have light.

Enough now of gray men in chains!

Enough of the pale lost ones!

Not another man should pass except as a ruler.

Not one woman without her diadem.

Gloves of gold for every hand.

Fruits of the sun for all the shadowy ones!

I knew that man, and when I could,
when I still had eyes in my head,
when I still had a voice in my throat,
I sought him among the tombs and I said to him,
pressing his arm that still was not dust:

"Everything will pass, you will still be living.

You set fire to life.

You made what is yours."

So let no one be perturbed when
I seem to be alone and am not alone;
I am not without company and I speak for all.

Someone is hearing me without knowing it,
but those I sing of, those who know,
go on being born and will overflow the world.

ALASTAIR REID

PLENOS PODERES

A puro sol escribo, a plena calle,
a pleno mar, en donde puedo canto,

sólo la noche errante me detiene
pero en su interrupción recojo espacio,
recojo sombra para mucho tiempo.

El trigo negro de la noche crece
mientras mis ojos miden la pradera
y así de sol a sol hago las llaves:
busco en la oscuridad las cerraduras
y voy abriendo al mar las puertas rotas
hasta llenar armarios con espuma.

Y no me canso de ir y de volver,
no me para la muerte con su piedra,
no me canso de ser y de no ser.

A veces me pregunto si de dónde
si de padre o de madre o cordillera
heredé los deberes minerales,

los hilos de un océano encendido
y sé que sigo y sigo porque sigo
y canto porque canto y porque canto.

No tiene explicación lo que acontece
cuando cierro los ojos y circulo
como entre dos canales submarinos,
uno a morir me lleva en su ramaje
y el otro canta para que yo cante.

Así pues de no ser estoy compuesto
y como el mar asalta el arrecife
con cápsulas saladas de blancura
y retrata la piedra con la ola,
así lo que en la muerte me rodea
abre en mí la ventana de la vida
y en pleno paroxismo estoy durmiendo.
A plena luz camino por la sombra.

FULLY EMPOWERED

I write in the clear sun, in the teeming street,
at full sea tide, in a place where I can sing;
only the wayward night inhibits me,
but, interrupted by it, I recover space,
I gather shadows to last a long time.

The black crop of the night is growing
while my eyes in the meantime measure the plain.
So, from sun to sun, I forge the keys.
In the half-light, I look for locks
and keep on opening broken doors to the sea
until I fill the cupboards up with foam.

And I never weary of going and returning.
Death in its stone aspect does not stop me.
I am weary neither of being nor of nonbeing.

Sometimes I wonder where—
from father or mother or the mountains—
I inherited all my mineral obligations,

the threads spreading from a sea on fire;
and I know I go on and go on because I go on
and I sing because I sing and because I sing.

There is no way of explaining what happens
when I close my eyes and waver
as between two underwater channels—
one lifts me in its branches toward dying
and the other sings in order that I may sing.

And so I am formed out of nonbeing,
and as the sea goes battering at a reef
in wave on wave of salty white-tops
and drags back stones in its ebb,
so what there is of death surrounding me

opens in me a window out to living,
and, in a spasm of being, I am asleep.
In the full light of day, I walk in the shade.

ALASTAIR REID

from

ISLA NEGRA

MEMORIAL DE
ISLA NEGRA

❋

1962–1964

THE FIRST JOURNEY

I don't know when we came to Temuco.
It was vague, being born, and a slow business,
being truly born,
and slowly feeling, knowing, hating, loving.
All that has both flowers and thorns.
From the dusty bosom of my country
they took me, still an infant,
into the rain of Araucania.
The boards of the house
smelled of the woods,
of the deep forest.
From that time on, my love
had wood in it
and everything I touched turned into wood.
They became one in me,
lives and leaves,
certain women and the hazelnut
spring, men and trees.
I love the world of wind and foliage.
I can't tell lips from roots.

From axes and rain, it grew up,
that town of wood
recently carved, like
a new star stained with resin,
and the saw and the sierras
made love day and night,
singing away,
working away,
and that sharp chirp of the cricket
raising its plaint
in the unyielding solitude turns into

my song, my own song.
My heart goes on cutting wood,
singing with the sawmills in the rain,
milling together cold, sawdust, wood smell.

ALASTAIR REID

THE FATHER

My blunt father comes back
from the trains.
We recognize
in the night
the whistle
of the locomotive
perforating the rain
with a wandering moan,
lament of the night,
and later
the door shivering open.
A rush of wind
came in with my father,
and between footsteps and drafts
the house
shook,
the surprised doors
banged with the dry
bark of pistols,
the staircase groaned,
and a loud voice,
complaining, grumbled
while the wild dark,
the waterfall rain
rumbled on the roofs
and, little by little,
drowned the world
and all that could be heard was the wind
battling with the rain.

He was, however, a daily happening.
Captain of his train, of the cold dawn,
and scarcely had the sun
begun to show itself
than there he was with his beard,
his red and green
flags, his lamps prepared,
the engine coal in its little inferno,
the station with trains in the mist,
and his duty to geography.

The railwayman is a sailor on earth
and in the small ports without a sea line—
the forest towns—the train runs, runs,
unbridling the natural world,
completing its navigation of the earth.
When the long train comes to rest,
friends come together,
come in, and the doors of my childhood open,
the table shakes
at the slam of a railwayman's hand,
the thick glasses of companions jump
and the glitter
flashes out
from the eyes of the wine.

My poor, hard father,
there he was at the axis of existence,
virile in friendship, his glass full.
His life was a running campaign,
and between his early risings and his traveling,
between arriving and rushing off,
one day, rainier than other days,
the railwayman, José del Carmen Reyes,
climbed aboard the train of death, and so far has not come back.

ALASTAIR REID

THE FIRST SEA

I discovered the sea. From Carahue
the river Cautín flowed to its estuary
and, in the paddleboats,
dreams and another life began to possess me,
leaving questions in my eyelashes.
A frail child, a bird,
a solitary student or a shadowy fish,
I stood alone in the prow,
aloof
from joy, while
the world
of the little ship,
unaware of me,
unwound the thread
of the accordions.
The passing visitors
of summer and the water
were eating and singing.
I, in the prow, small,
hardly human,
lost,
still without mind or voice,
or any joy,
transfixed by the movement of the water
flowing between the receding mountains—
mine alone were those solitary places,
mine alone that elemental pathway,
mine alone the universe.

Rapture of the rivers,
banks of thicket and fragrance,
sudden boulders, burnt-out trees,
and land, ample and lonely.
Child of those rivers,
I kept on
traveling the earth
along the same river edges

toward the same sea foam
and when the sea of that time
crashed down like a broken tower,
rose curling in its rage,
I broke free of my roots.
My country grew in size.
My world of wood split open.
The prison of the forests
opened a green door,
letting in the wave in all its thunder,
and, with the shock of the sea,
my life widened out into space.

ALASTAIR REID

THE SOUTH

The vast frontier. From
the Bío-Bío
as far as Reloncaví,
by way of
Renaico, Selva Oscura,
Pillanlelbún, Lautaro,
and even further, partridge eggs,
the dense mosses of the jungle,
leaves in leaf mold,
transparent
spiders,
no more than a filigree of nerves,
with clouded webs.
A snake
like a shiver
crosses the dark swamp,
glistens
and disappears.
Discoveries
of the forest,
the sense of being lost

under
the arch, the nave,
the forest twilight
(aimless,
so small) bristling with rodents,
fruits, plumage—
I wander, lost
in the darkest
entrails of greenness.
Screech of glacial birds.
A tree lets fall
something which flies and drops
on my head.

I am alone
in the natal jungle,
in the deep
and black Araucania.
There are wings
which scissor at the silence,
a raindrop which falls
heavy and cold
like a horseshoe.
The forest sounds and is silent—
it is silent when I listen.
It sounds when I am asleep.
I bury
my tired feet
in the rot
of ancient flowers, in the decay
of birds, leaves, and fruit,
blind, despairing,
till a point of light appears—
a house.

I am alive again.
But only from that point,
from my lost steps,
from my bewildered solitude, from fear,

from the entangling vines,
from the torrential green, with no escape,
did I come back with the secret.
Only then and there could I realize it,
on the precipitous edge of fever.
There, in the somber light,
it was decided and made,
my contract with the earth.

ALASTAIR REID

SEX

The door at twilight,
in summer.
The last passing carts
of the Indians,
a wavering light
and the smoke
of forest fires
which comes as far as the streets
with the smell of red,
ash
of the distant burning.

I, in mourning,
grave,
withdrawn,
shorts,
thin legs,
knees,
and eyes on the look for
sudden treasures;
Rosita and Josefina
on the other side
of the street,
all teeth and eyes,
full of light, voices

like small, concealed guitars,
calling me.
And I crossed
the street, confused,
terrified;
and hardly
had I arrived
than they whispered to me,
they took my hands,
they covered my eyes
and they ran with me
and my innocence
to the bakehouse.

Silence of great tables, the serious
place of bread, empty of people;
and there, the two of them
and I, prisoner
in the hands of
the first Rosita
and the final Josefina.
They wanted to
undress me.
I fled, trembling,
but I couldn't
run, my legs
couldn't
carry me. Then
the
enchantresses
brought out
before my eyes
a miracle:
the tiny nest
of a small wild bird
with five little eggs,
with five white grapes,
a small
cluster

of forest life,
and I reached out
my hand
while
they fumbled with my clothes,
touched me,
studied with their great eyes
their first small man.

Heavy footsteps, coughing,
my father arriving
with strangers,
and we ran
deep into the dark,
the two pirates
and I, their prisoner,
huddled
among spiderwebs,
squeezed
under a great table, trembling,
while the miracle,
the nest
with its small light-blue eggs,
fell and eventually the intruders' feet
crushed its shape and its fragrance.
But, with the two girls
in the dark,
and fear,
with the smell of flour,
the phantom steps,
the afternoon gradually darkening,
I felt that something was
changing
in my blood
and that to my mouth,
to my hands,
was rising
an electric
flower,

the
hungry,
shining
flower
of desire.

ALASTAIR REID

LA POESÍA

Y fue a esa edad . . . Llegó la poesía
a buscarme. No sé, no sé de dónde
salió, de invierno o río.
No sé cómo ni cuándo,
no, no eran voces, no eran
palabras, ni silencio,
pero desde una calle me llamaba,
desde las ramas de la noche,
de pronto entre los otros,
entre fuegos violentos
o regresando solo,
allí estaba sin rostro
y me tocaba.

Yo no sabía qué decir, mi boca
no sabía
nombrar,
mis ojos eran ciegos,
y algo golpeaba en mi alma,
fiebre o alas perdidas,
y me fui haciendo solo,
descifrando
aquella quemadura,
y escribí la primera línea vaga,
vaga, sin cuerpo, pura
tontería,
pura sabiduría
del que no sabe nada,

y vi de pronto
el cielo
desgranado
y abierto,
planetas,
plantaciones palpitantes,
la sombra perforada,
acribillada
por flechas, fuego y flores,
la noche arrolladora, el universo.

Y yo, mínimo ser,
ebrio del gran vacío
constelado,
a semejanza, a imagen
del misterio,
me sentí parte pura
del abismo,
rodé con las estrellas,
mi corazón se desató en el viento.

POETRY

And it was at that age . . . poetry arrived
in search of me. I don't know, I don't know where
it came from, from winter or a river.
I don't know how or when,
no, they were not voices, they were not
words, not silence,
but from a street it called me,
from the branches of night,
abruptly from the others,
among raging fires
or returning alone,
there it was, without a face,
and it touched me.

I didn't know what to say, my mouth
had no way
with names,
my eyes were blind.
Something knocked in my soul,
fever or forgotten wings,
and I made my own way,
deciphering
that fire,
and I wrote the first, faint line,
faint, without substance, pure
nonsense,
pure wisdom
of someone who knows nothing;
and suddenly I saw
the heavens
unfastened
and open,
planets,
palpitating plantations,
the darkness perforated,
riddled
with arrows, fire, and flowers,
the overpowering night, the universe.

And I, tiny being,
drunk with the great starry
void,
likeness, image of
mystery,
felt myself a pure part
of the abyss.
I wheeled with the stars.
My heart broke loose with the wind.

ALASTAIR REID

SHYNESS

I scarcely knew, by myself, that I existed,
that I'd be able to be, and go on being.
I was afraid of that, of life itself.
I didn't want to be seen,
I didn't want my existence to be known.
I became pallid, thin, and absentminded.
I didn't want to speak so that nobody
would recognize my voice, I didn't want
to see so that nobody would see me.
Walking, I pressed myself against the wall
like a shadow slipping away.

I would have dressed myself
in red roof tiles, in smoke,
to continue there, but invisible,
to attend everything, but at a distance,
to keep my own obscure identity
fastened to the rhythm of the spring.

A girl's face, the pure surprise
of a laugh dividing the day in two
like the two hemispheres of an orange,
and I shifted to another street,
unnerved by life and tentative,
close to water without tasting its coolness,
close to fire without kissing its flame,
and a mask of pride encased me,
and I was thin and arrogant as a spear,
unlistening, unlistened to
(I made that impossible),
my lament
buried deep
like the whine of a hurt dog
at the bottom of a well.

ALASTAIR REID

SWAN LAKE

Lake Budi, in shadow, dark and heavy stone,
water among the vast unburied forests,
there you opened yourself like an underground door
beside that lonely sea at the world's end.
We galloped along the infinite sand
close to the prodigal and teeming foam,
neither house nor man nor horse,
only time passing and that green and white
shore, that ocean.
Later, into the hills and, suddenly,
the lake, its waters hard and hidden,
compacted light, jewel set in a ring of earth.
A black-and-white flying: the swans took flight,
long necks of night, feet of red leather,
and a placid snow flying over the world.

Oh, the flight from the mirroring water,
a thousand bodies aimed at a beautiful stillness
like the transparent permanence of the lake.
Suddenly, all was racing over the water,
movement, sound, towers of the full moon,
and then, wild wings, which out of the whirlwind
turned into order, flight, realized vastness,
and then absence, a white shivering in the void.

ALASTAIR REID

THE HUMAN CONDITION

Behind me, to the south, the sea
had shattered the land with its glacial hammer.
From the scratched solitude, the silence
suddenly became an archipelago
and green islands girdled
the waist of my country
like pollen or petals from a marine rose

and, even more, the forests lit by fireflies
were endless, the mud was phosphorescent.
The trees trailed long, dry cords
as in a circus, and light went from drop to drop
like a green dancer through the undergrowth.

I grew up fired by silent races,
by axes cutting with a woodsman's pride,
by secret earth smells, udders, and wine.
My spirit was a wineshop lost among the trains
filled with abandoned sleepers and wine casks,
wire, oat, wheat, cochayuyo, wooden slabs,
and winter with its gloomy merchandise.

So my body went on growing, by night,
my arms were snow,
my feet hurricanes,
I grew like a river in a downpour,
I was fertile in everything
that happened to me, germination,
songs from leaf to leaf, scarabs
which procreated, new
roots which rose to
the surface,
storms which still shake
the laurel towers, the scarlet bough
of the hazel tree, the holy
patience of the larch;
and so my adolescence
was landscape, I had
islands, silence, mountains, growing,
volcanic light, mud of the roads,
the wild smoke of burning logs.

ALASTAIR REID

SUPERSTITIONS

Uncle Genaro would come back
from the mountains. The man
hadn't a whole bone in his body.
Everything had been broken by the earth,
horses, bullets, bulls,
stones, snow, his luck.
He slept at times in my room.
He struggled on his stiff legs
to get into bed
as though he were mounting a horse.
He grunted, he cursed, he dragged off
his wet boots, spitting as he did so,
and, in the end, smoking,
he'd start to talk about happenings in the jungle.
That's how I know that the Devil,
breathing sulfur fumes,
appeared to Juan Navarro,
begging him for a light. Luckily,
before he committed himself,
Juan Navarro noticed the tail,
the electric, hairy tail of the Devil,
on the floor, under his poncho,
and, seizing his whip, he scourged
the emptiness, because the Devil
dissolved, became a branch,
air, or the cold night wind.
He's tricky, the old Devil!

Genaro Candia smokes, smokes
while the great rain of July
falls and falls on Temuco,
and so the people of the rain
brought their religions into being.

That waterfalling voice, slow
voice of intervals, of breakings,
voice of boldo tree, of cold air,

of gusts of wind, of thorn,
that voice which reconstructed
footprints of the wounded puma,
the black ways of the condor,
the entanglement of the spring,
when flowers do not come without volcanoes,
hearts without saddles,
vicious animals falling
in the abyss, the spark springing
from a fan of horseshoes,
and later, death alone,
the interminable jungle.
Don Genaro, spare of words,
syllable by syllable, invoked
sweat, blood, ghosts, and wounds,
Uncle Genaro, smoking, smoking.
The bedroom filled up
with dogs, leaves, journeys,
and I listened to how in the lagoons
you watched an innocent, floating skin
which, as you reach to touch it,
turns into a horrendous beast,
daring you to disaster,
to disappearances,
there in the land of the dead
in the depths of who-knows-where,
the headless ones of the woods,
the ones drained by bats
with enormous silky wings.
Everything was slippery.
Any path, any animal
out on its own, a fire
prowling in the fields,
a wanderer under the full moon,
a sleek fox which limped,
a dark leaf which fell.
Hardly have you reached to touch
the cross, the relic,
to cross yourself, than the phosphorus comes,

the burnt horn, the smell of sulfur.
But not only in the open air
does the Evil One approach, the dark deceiver.
In the depths of houses,
a groan, a shadowy lament,
a rattling of chains,
and the dead woman who never misses
her nocturnal appointments,
and Don Francisco Montero
who comes back to claim his horse
there, below, beside the mill,
where he perished with his wife.

Night lasts a long time, rain is long.
I make out the endless glow
of the cigarette, he smokes and smokes,
Genaro Candia, he talks and talks.
I'm afraid. It's raining,
and between the water and the Devil, I fall
into a sulfur ravine,
into hell with its horses,
and runaway mountains.

Many times, listening to the rain,
I fell asleep in the South
while my Uncle Genaro
opened that dark sack
which he brought from the mountains.

ALASTAIR REID

THE ROOMING HOUSE ON THE CALLE MARURI

A street, Maruri.
The houses neither look at nor like each other.
Nevertheless, they are attached,
wall to wall, but
their windows

don't see the street, don't speak.
They are silence.

A paper flies like a grimy leaf
from the tree of winter.

The afternoon kindles a sunset. Disturbed,
the sky spreads fugitive fire.

Black fog invades the balconies.

I open my book. I write
as if I were
in the shaft
of a mine, a damp
abandoned gallery.
I know that now there is nobody,
in the house, in the street, in the bitter city.
I am a prisoner with the door open,
with the world open.
I am a wistful student lost in the twilight,
and I climb to the noodle soup
and descend to my bed and the following day.

ALASTAIR REID

LOVES: TERUSA (I)

And what has become of it, where
is that
onetime love?
Now it is
the grave of a bird, a drop
of black quartz,
a chunk
of wood eroded by the rain.

And that body which shone
like the moon in that remote
Southern spring?
What remains of it?
These hands
which held
all clearness, the murmur
of the gentle river,
wide eyes in the wood,
petrified
like minerals in the night,
those feet
of the young girl of my dreams,
feet of flowers, feet of wheat, feet of cherries,
ready, quick, flying,
between my timid childhood and the world?
Where is my dead love?
Love, love,
where does it go to die?
To secret granaries,
under rosebushes which withered
beneath some seven feet of ash

from those miserable houses
burned out by a village fire?

Oh, love
of that first dawn light,
of fierce noon
with its spears,
love taking in the whole sky
drop by drop
when the great ship of night
passes over the world.
Oh, that love
in the loneliness
of adolescence,
oh, the violet
overflowing
with perfume and dew,
fresh as stars
over the face,
those kisses
crawling over
the skin,
entwining, biting,
from bodies clear and open to
the blue stone of the sailing night.

Terusa, with your wide eyes.
Under the moon
or the winter sun, when
the provinces
take their share of pain, the betrayal
of a vast forgetting,
and you shine, Terusa,
like the burnt crystal
of the topaz,
like the burn
of the carnation,
like the metal which flashes under lightning
and is swallowed by the lips of night.

Terusa,
all open among the poppies,
black
flash
of original pain,
star among the fish
in the light
of a pure genital electricity,
purple bird of the first abyss,
roomless, in the kingdom
of the revealed heart
whose honey nourished the almond trees,
the fiery pollen
of the wild broom,
the lemon bush in its tentative greens,
kingdom of the mysterious mosses.

The bells of Cautín were sounding,
all the petals cried out for something,
the earth was giving nothing up,
the water was winking
endlessly.
It wanted to open up the summer,
to deal it a final wound.
The river that tumbled
in fury from the Andes
turned into a hard star
which pierced the jungle,
the riverbank,
the rocks.
No one lived there—
only water and earth
and the mournful trains,
the winter trains
in their courses
dissecting the lonely
map.
My kingdom,
kingdom of roots

with the glory of mint,
tresses of fern hair,
a damp pubis,
kingdom of my lost childhood,
when I watched the earth being born
and I was a part of
its earthy
damp
wholeness.
Light between water and organism,
in the sprouting of the wheat,
homeland of wood
which died
in the screeching
of the sawmills.
Smoke, sweet-smelling presence
of the wild
twilight,
fettered
like a dangerous prisoner
to the jungle regions,
to Loncoche,
to Quitratúe,
to the dockyards of Maullín,
and I being born
with your love,
Terusa,
with your unleaved love
across my thirsty skin
as if cascades
of orange blossom, amber, and flour
had transgressed my being;
and from that very moment I have carried you,
Terusa,
inexhaustibly
even into oblivion,
across
eroded times,
a marked

aroma,
deep as song or honeysuckle,
or sleep,
or the moon caught up in the jasmine
or the clover dawn close to the water
or the fullness of earth with its rivers
or the delirium of flowers, or sorrow,
or the pull of the magnet or the will
of the shining sea in its never-ending dance.

ALASTAIR REID

LOVES: TERUSA (II)

The year arrives, four numbers
like four lucky birds
perching on a wire
against a backdrop of bare time.
But now
they are not singing.
They consumed the harvest, they defeated
that spring,
and flower upon flower, all that is left
is this vast space.

Now that you come to visit me,
my onetime darling, my love, my invisible girl,
I implore you to lie with me
once more
in the grass.

Now it seems to me
that your head has altered.
Why,
in this coming,
did you cover over with ash
the wondrous coal of your hair

that I ran my hands through
in the starry cold of Temuco?
Where are your eyes?
Why do you narrow them at me
to see if I am the same?
Where did you leave your golden body?
What became of your opening hands
and your jasmine glimmer?

Come into my house, look at the sea with me.
The waves, one by one,
have exhausted
our lives;
it is not just the foam that has disintegrated
but the cherries,
the feet,
the lips
of a time of glass.

Goodbye. I beg you now,
go back
to your amber throne
under the moon,
go back to the honeysuckled balcony,
resume
your burning image,
match your eyes
to those
other eyes,
turn yourself gradually
into that
glowing portrait,
go into it
deeply, deeply
with your smile,
and look at me
from its stillness, until
I see you again

at that point,
at that time,
as the one I once was in your flowering heart.

ALASTAIR REID

BREAD-POETRY

Poetry, my starstruck patrimony.
It was necessary
to go on discovering, hungry, with no one to guide me,
your earthy endowment,
light of the moon and the secret wheat.

Between solitude and crowds, the key
kept getting lost in streets and in the woods,
under stones, in trains.

The first sign is a state of darkness,
deep rapture in a glass of water,
body stuffed without having eaten,
heart a beggar in its pride.

Many things more that books don't mention,
stuffed as they are with joyless splendor:
to go on chipping at a weary stone,
to go on dissolving the iron in the soul
until you become the person who is reading,
until water finds a voice through your mouth.

And that is easier than tomorrow being Thursday
and yet more difficult than to go on being born—
a strange vocation that seeks you out,
and which goes into hiding when we seek it out,
a shadow with a broken roof
and stars shining through its holes.

ALASTAIR REID

MY CRAZY FRIENDS

Quite suddenly, night life dawned on me.
I discovered it, a secret rose
between one yellowing day and the next.
But, for someone newly arrived from the South,
from the regions where nature reigns,
full of fire and blizzards,
the city night seemed like a boat,
a kind of ship's hold.
Doors would open and out of the dark
light spat on us.
Men and women danced
in shoes like shiny black coffins
and glued themselves to one another,
like limpets, amidst tobacco,
rough wine, conversation,
the crude belly laughs of drunks.
At times, some woman, wallowing
in her pale emptiness, would turn on me
her wasted eyes and mouth.
That's where I spent my stormy adolescence—
amidst bottles of wine, spilling
their exploding rubies,
flourishing their wild swords,
their meaningless bravado.
And these friends I had—
Rojas Giménez, lost in his own
fastidiousness,
a theoretical sailor, certifiably
crazy, offering in the smoke
his wayward tenderness
in one drink after another,
until he fell in stages
as if the wine itself
had taken him further and further away from us!
My vulnerable brother, I learned
so much in your company,
I lost so much in the waywardness of your heart,

a broken box,
with no notion of where your tongue was going,
with no notion that you too were going to die,
you who could have taught things to the spring!
And later, like an apparition,
keeping to his dark corner
during parties,
Joaquín Cifuentes arrived,
freed from his chains, a ghostly friend
with his emphatic face in the rain,
his sharp, defining hairline
crossing a forehead open to pain.
He didn't know how to laugh, my new friend;
and in the course of cruel, ashy evenings,
I watched him destroy himself, Horseman of Death.

ALASTAIR REID

FIRST TRAVELINGS

When I first went to sea, I was inexhaustible.
I was younger than the whole world.
And on the seacoast there rose to receive me
the endless tang of the universe.

I had no sense that the world existed.

My faith lay in a buried tower.

I had found so many things in so little,
in my own twilit discoveries,
in the sighs of love, in roots,
that I was the displaced one, the wanderer,
the poor proprietor of my own skeleton.

And I understood then that I was naked,
that I had to dress myself.
I had never thought seriously about shoes.

I didn't speak any languages.
The only book I could read was the book of myself.
The only life I knew was my secret life.
And I understood that I couldn't
summon myself because I wouldn't respond.
I had used up that chance.
Nevermore, nevermore, croaked the raven.

I had to fall back on things like clouds,
on all the hats of the world,
rivers, waiting rooms, doors,
and names, so many names, that simply learning them
would have taken my whole sacred life.

The world was full of women,
jammed like a shop window,
and given all the hair I learned,
the breasts, the wonderful thighs,
I learned that Venus was no mere legend.
She was sure and firm, with two enduring arms,
and her hard mother-of-pearl
weathered my lusty genital ambition.

Everything was new to me. This whole planet
was dying of sheer old age,
but everything was opening for me to experience,
to glimpse that lightning flash.

And with my little pony eyes
I saw that bitter curtain going up,
going up with its fixed and worldly smile,
the curtain opening on a wizened Europe.

ALASTAIR REID

From Singapore on, there was a smell of opium.
The honest Englishman was well aware of it.
In Geneva he denounced
the undercover dealers,
but in the colonies each port
gave off a cloud of legal smoke,
numbered, juicily licensed, legalized.
The gentleman from London,
impeccably dressed like a nightingale
(striped pants, starched armor),
raged against sellers of dreams,
but here in the East
he took off his mask
and peddled lethargy on every corner.

I wanted to know. I went in. Every bench
had its recumbent occupant.
Nobody spoke. Nobody laughed. I thought
they smoked in a total silence,
but pipes crackled beside me
when the needle met the flame,
and with that inhaled coolness,
an ecstatic joy came with the milky smoke,
some far door
opened on a luscious emptiness.
Opium was the flower of torpor,
paralyzed joy,
pure activity without movement.
Everything was pure or seemed pure.
Everything moved like an oiled hinge
to become a sheer existence.
Nothing burned, nobody wept.
There was no room for anguish.
There was no fuel for anger.

I looked around. Poor victims,
slaves, coolies from the rickshaws and plantations,

run–down workhorses,
street dogs,
poor abused people.
Here, after their wounds,
after being not human beings but feet,
after being not men but beasts of burden,
after walking and walking and sweating and sweating,
sweating blood, having no soul,
there they were,
lonely,
stretched out,
lying down at last, the hard-footed people.
Each one had exchanged hunger
for an obscure right to pleasure,
and under the crown of lethargy,
dream or deception, luck or death, they were
at last at rest, what they looked for all their lives,
respected, at last, on a star of their own.

ALASTAIR REID

MONSOONS

Eventually, I went to live across the sea.

My house was set up in magic places,
chapter of waves,
of wind and salt, eye and eyelid
of a stubborn underwater star.
Wondrous the extravagance of the sun,
the ample green of palm trees,
on the edge of a forest of masts and fruit,
with a sea harder than a blue stone,
under a sky new-painted every day,
never the delicate boat of one cloud,
but an absurd gathering—
rumbling thunder and water falling
in cataracts, a hiss of anger—

gravid monsoon exploding overhead,
emptying out the great bag of its power.

ALASTAIR REID

OCTOBER FULLNESS

Little by little, and also in great leaps,
life happened to me,
and how insignificant this business is.
These veins carried
my blood, which I scarcely ever saw,
I breathed the air of so many places
without keeping a sample of any.
In the end, everyone is aware of this:
nobody keeps any of what he has,
and life is only a borrowing of bones.
The best thing was learning not to have too much
either of sorrow or of joy,
to hope for the chance of a last drop,
to ask more from honey and from twilight.

Perhaps it was my punishment.
Perhaps I was condemned to be happy.
Let it be known that nobody
crossed my path without sharing my being.
I plunged up to the neck
into adversities that were not mine,
into all the sufferings of others.
It wasn't a question of applause or profit.
Much less. It was not being able
to live or breathe in this shadow,
the shadow of others like towers,
like bitter trees that bury you,
like cobblestones on the knees.

Our own wounds heal with weeping,
our own wounds heal with singing,

but in our own doorway lie bleeding
widows, Indians, poor men, fishermen.
The miner's child doesn't know his father
amidst all that suffering.

So be it, but my business
was
the fullness of the spirit:
a cry of pleasure choking you,
a sigh from an uprooted plant,
the sum of all action.

It pleased me to grow with the morning,
to bathe in the sun, in the great joy
of sun, salt, sea light, and wave,
and in that unwinding of the foam
my heart began to move,
growing in that essential spasm,
and dying away as it seeped into the sand.

ALASTAIR REID

LOST LETTERS

All the stuff they write about me I read
casually, hardly seeing it,
as if they were not really meant for me,
the appropriate words and the vicious ones.
And not just because I refuse to accept
the truth, good or bad,
the polished apple as a present,
or, on the other hand, the poisoned turd.
It's something else.
It has to do with me, with my skin, my hair,
my teeth,
the way I made my own mistakes.
It concerns my own body, my own shadow.

Why, why, I asked myself, and others asked me,
does someone else, loveless and ready with words,
prise me open and, hammering away
with a nail,
pierce my wood, my sweat,
my stone, my shadow,
the elements that are me?

Why me? I live far away,
I don't exist for them, I don't go out,
I don't come home.
Why do the birds of the alphabet
attack my nails and my eyes?
Have I to please them or can I just be?
Who do I belong to?
How come I mortgaged my being
till I don't belong to myself?
How come I sold my blood?
And who now owns
my indecisions, my hands,
my private pain, my pride?

Sometimes I'm afraid
of walking along the banks of strange rivers,
of looking at volcanoes
I've always known, which have always known me.
Sometimes, from below, from above,
I feel the scrutiny of water and fire.
They think I'm no longer telling the truth.
They think I'm a stranger.

So, saddened,
I read things that may not have been sad,
but friendly or angry,
or full of invisible messages.
For me, however,
so many words
would have kept me from my solitude.
I skimmed them indifferently,

neither offended nor slighted,
as if they were letters,
letters to other people,
others like me, but remote from me,
lost letters.

ALASTAIR REID

AY! MI CIUDAD PERDIDA

Me gustaba Madrid y ya no puedo
verlo, no más, ya nunca más, amarga
es la desesperada certidumbre
como de haberse muerto uno también al tiempo
que morían los míos, como si se me hubiera
ido a la tumba la mitad del alma,
y allí yaciere entre llanuras secas,
prisiones y presidios,
aquel tiempo anterior cuando aún no tenía
sangre la flor, coágulos la luna.
Me gustaba Madrid por arrabales,
por calles que caían a Castilla
como pequeños ríos de ojos negros:
era el final de un día:
calles de cordeleros y toneles,
trenzas de esparto como cabelleras,
duelas arqueadas desde
donde
algún día
iba a volar el vino a un ronco reino,
calles de los carbones,
de las madererías,
calles de las tabernas anegadas
por el caudal
del duro Valdepeñas
y calles solas, secas, de silencio
compacto como adobe,
e ir y saltar los pies sin alfabeto,
sin guía, ni buscar, ni hallar, viviendo
aquello que vivía
callando con aquellos
terrones, ardiendo

con las piedras
y al fin callado el grito de una ventana, el canto
de un pozo, el sello
de una gran carcajada
que rompía
con vidrios
el crepúsculo, y aún
más acá,
en la garganta
de la ciudad tardía,
caballos polvorientos,
carros de ruedas rojas,
y el aroma
de las panaderías al cerrarse
la corola nocturna
mientras enderezaba mi vaga dirección
hacia Cuatro Caminos, al número
3
de la calle Wellingronia
en donde me esperaba
bajo dos ojos con chispas azules
la sonrisa que nunca he vuelto a ver
en el rostro
—plenilunio rosado—
de Vicente Aleixandre
que dejé allí a vivir con sus ausentes.

OH, MY LOST CITY

I liked Madrid and now
I can't see it again, not anymore, a bitter
but desperate certainty, coming
from having died at the time
when my friends died, as if
half of my spirit had gone to the grave
and lay there among dry plains,
prisons and prisoners,

and an earlier time when the towers
were not stained with blood, the moon with blood clots.
I liked Madrid, its outskirts,
its streets that fell away to Castile
like little rivers of black eyes.
It was the ending of a day—
streets of ropeworks and barrels,
tresses of esparto like hair,
bent staves from which
one day
wine
would take flight to its raucous kingdom,
streets of coal,
lumberyards,
streets of taverns overflowing
with an abundance
of the hard wine of Valdepeñas,
and solitary streets, dry,
with a silence as tight as adobe,
and the going and coming of my unlettered feet,
unguided, neither looking nor finding, living
what was lived,
being silent with
those plots, burning
with the stones,
and finally silent, the screech of a window, the song
of a well, the sound
of a great guffaw
which broke
the glass
of twilight, and even
closer,
in the throat
of the evening city,
dusty horses,
carts with red wheels,
and the aroma
of closing bakeries,
the crown of night,

as I turned vaguely toward
Cuatro Caminos,
Calle Wellingtonia,
number 3,
where, with eyes like blue sparks,
face like a pink full moon,
a smile I have never gone back to see,
Vicente Aleixandre
was waiting for me.
I left him there to live with his dead friends.

ALASTAIR REID

TAL VEZ CAMBIÉ DESDE ENTONCES

A mi patria llegué con otros ojos
que la guerra me puso
debajo de los míos.
Otros ojos quemados
en la hoguera,
salpicados
por llanto mío y sangre de los otros,
y comencé a mirar y a ver más bajo,
más al fondo inclemente
de las asociaciones. La verdad
que antes no despegaba de su cielo
como una estrella fue,
se convirtió en campana,
oí que me llamaba
y que se congregaban otros hombres
al llamado. De pronto
las banderas de América,
amarillas, azules, plateadas,
con sol, estrella y amaranto y oro
dejaron a mi vista
territorios desnudos,
pobres gentes de campos y caminos,
labriegos asustados, indios muertos,

a caballo, mirando ya sin ojos,
y luego el boquerón infernal de las minas
con el carbón, el cobre y el hombre devastados,
pero eso no era todo
en las repúblicas,
sino algo sin piedad, sin amasijo:
arriba un galopante, un frío soberbio
con todas sus medallas,
manchado en los martirios
o bien los caballeros en el Club
con vaivén discursivo entre las alas
de la vida dichosa
mientras el pobre ángel oscuro,
el pobre remendado,
de piedra en piedra andaba y anda aún
descalzo y con tan poco qué comer
que nadie sabe cómo sobrevive.

PERHAPS I'VE CHANGED SINCE THEN

I arrived in my country with different eyes
which the war had grafted
underneath my own,
other eyes burned
in the bonfire,
splashed
by my own tears and the blood of the others,
and I began to look and to see deeper,
into the troubled depths
of human connections. The truth
which before did not come loose from the sky
as a star does
changed into a bell.
I realized that it was calling me
and that other men were rallying
to its call. Suddenly
the banners of America,

yellow, blue, silver,
with sun and star and amaranth and gold,
left in my vision
naked territories,
poor people from fields and roads,
frightened farmers, dead Indians,
on horseback, gazing without any eyes,
and then the terrible maw of the mines
with coal, copper, and devastated men,
but that was not all
in the republics:
there was something else, pitiless, unformed.
A man on horseback, a cold arrogance,
all his medals
stained by martyred blood,
or else the gentlemen in the club
in their talkative rocking chairs, on the wings
of a good life,
while the poor anonymous angel,
the poor patched-up one,
walked from stone to stone and is still walking
barefoot and with so little to eat
that nobody knows how he survives.

ALASTAIR REID

REVOLUTIONS

Dignitaries fell,
wrapped in their togas
of worm-eaten mud,
nameless people shouldered spears,
tumbled the walls,
nailed the tyrant to his golden door,
or in shirtsleeves, went
simply
to a small meeting
in factories, offices, mines.

These were
the
in-between
years.
Trujillo of the gold teeth fell
and in Nicaragua
one Somoza, riddled
with bullets,
bled to death in his swamp
for another Somoza-rat
to emerge like a chill
in the place of that dead rat;
but he will not last long.
Honor and dishonor, contrary winds
of those terrible days!
From some still-hidden place, they brought
a vague laurel crown to the poet
and recognized him.
He passed the villages
with his leather drum
and stone trumpet.
Country people with half-shut eyes
who had learned in the dark
and knew hunger like a sacred text
looked at the poet who had crossed
volcanoes, waters, peoples, and plains
and knew who he was.
They sheltered him
under
their foliage.
The poet
was there with his lyre
and his stick, cut in the mountains
from a fragrant tree,
and the more he suffered,
the more he knew,
the more he sang.
He had found

the human family,
his lost mothers,
his fathers,
an infinite number
of grandfathers, of children,
and so he grew used to
having a thousand brothers.
So, he didn't suffer from loneliness.
Besides, with his lyre
and his forest stick
on the bank
of the infinite river
he cooled his feet
among the stones.
Nothing happened, or nothing seemed
to happen—
the water, perhaps, which slithered
on itself,
singing
from transparency.
The iron-colored jungle
surrounded him.
That was the still point,
the bluest, the pure center
of the planet,
and he was there with his lyre,
among boulders
and the sounding
water,
and nothing happened
except the wide silence,
the pulse, the power
of the natural world.
He was, however,
fated for a grave love,
an angry honor.
He came out from the woods
and the waters.

With him went, clear as a sword,
the fire of his song.

ALASTAIR REID

THE UNKNOWN ONE

I want to measure the many things I don't know
and that's how I arrive
aimlessly, I knock and they open, I enter and see
yesterday's pictures on the walls,
the dining room of the man and the woman,
armchairs, beds, saltcellars.
Only then do I understand
that there they don't know me.
I go out and I don't know what streets I'm walking,
nor how many men this street has eaten up,
nor how many poor and tantalizing women,
workers of various breeds
and far from satisfactory rewards.

ALASTAIR REID

INSOMNIA

In the middle of the night I ask myself,
what will happen to Chile?
What will become of my poor, poor, dark country?

From loving this long, thin ship so much,
these stones, these little farms,
the durable rose of the coast
that lives among the foam,
I became one with my country.
I met every one of its sons
and in me the seasons succeeded one another,
weeping or flowering.

I feel that now,
with the dead year of doubt scarcely over,
now that the mistakes which bled us all
are over and we begin to plan again
a better and a just life,
the menace once again appears
and on the walls a rising rancor.

ALASTAIR REID

GOODBYE TO THE SNOW

Chiaretta was there
with his white beard and white jacket,
deep in his memories.
His wife had been weeping
over bad news:
her brother dead in Laos,
far away, and why so far away?
What had he lost in the jungle?
But Isla Negra
rose up
like a lime tower,
stone and sweet smells,
with the emphatic blue
of a strong
and stable sky,
a still place,
always new-painted,
with the same gulls,
bold, starving.
The Isla
buzzing
with bees, vines, men
and women,
solitary on its rock,
clear in its little solitude,
on one side the crazy rich people,

on the other the careful poor.
Room for all.
There's too much light to deny it.
Help yourself to a glass of light,
all the honey of one day,
the whole night with its blue fire,
let's stay at peace,
let's not squabble with Lucas
nor with Piero.
A loaf of light for everyone,
says the Isla,
and there it is with its stored-up light,
as inexhaustible as a cherry tree,
and it's ten years now and I go upstairs.
It's the same,
lime-clear, a hive of verbena,
between chalk and crag
the soft, soft branches,
the wavering scent
of its ruffled vegetation.
From above, the silence
of the sea like a ring,
a blue ring,
the blue sea,
the Isla—
neither wars nor the rich destroyed it,
the poor didn't leave.
Neither the smoke nor the aroma
abandoned that place.
The wasps hummed,
the wine, color of water,
lasted in bottles,
transparent fire,
and the shards of nature
hummed on.

I would come back from far away
in order to leave,
to leave again,

and I knew that to be a kind of dying,
going away while everything stays.
It's dying, with the Isla
flowering,
going away, with everything intact—
hyacinths,
the ship surrounding
the pale pleasure
of the sand
like a devoted swan.
Ten years which could have been a hundred years,
a hundred years without touching or smelling or seeing,
absence, shadow, cold,
and everything there in flower,
full of noises—
always
an edifice of water,
always
a kiss,
always
an orange,
always.

ALASTAIR REID

TIDES

I grew up drenched in natural waters
like the mollusk in the phosphorous sea.
In me the crusty salt resounded
and formed my singular skeleton.
How to explain—almost without
the blue and bitter rhythm of breathing,
one by one the waves repeated
what I sensed and trembled with
until salt and spray formed me:
the wave's rejection and desire,
the green rhythm which at its most secret

raised up a transparent tower.
It kept that secret and all at once
I felt that I was beating with it,
that my song was growing with the water.

ALASTAIR REID

EXILIO

Entre castillos de piedra cansada,
calles de Praga bella,
sonrisas y abedules siberianos,
Capri, fuego en el mar, aroma
de romero amargo
y el último, el amor,
el esencial amor se unió a mi vida
en la paz generosa,
mientras tanto,
entre una mano y otra mano amiga
se iba cavando un agujero oscuro
en la piedra de mi alma
y allí mi patria ardía
llamándome, esperándome, incitándome
a ser, a preservar, a padecer.

El destierro es redondo:
un círculo, un anillo:
le dan vuelta tus pies, cruzas la tierra,
no es tu tierra,
te despierta la luz, y no es tu luz,
la noche llega: faltan tus estrellas,
hallas hermanos: pero no es tu sangre.
Eres como un fantasma avergonzado
de no amar más a los que tanto te aman,
y aún es tan extraño que te falten
las hostiles espinas de tu patria,
el ronco desamparo de tu pueblo,

los asuntos amargos que te esperan
y que te ladrarán desde la puerta.

Pero con corazón irremediable
recordé cada signo innecesario
como si sólo deliciosa miel
se anidara en el árbol de mi tierra
y esperé en cada pájaro
el más remoto trino,
el que me despertó desde la infancia
bajo la luz mojada.
Me pareció mejor la tierra pobre
de mi país, el cráter, las arenas,
el rostro mineral de los desiertos
que la copa de luz que me brindaron.
Me sentí solo en el jardín, perdido:
fui un rústico enemigo de la estatua,
de lo que muchos siglos decidieron
entre abejas de plata y simetría.

Destierros! La distancia
se hace espesa,
respiramos el aire por la herida:
vivir es un precepto obligatorio.
Así es de injusta el alma sin raíces:
rechaza la belleza que le ofrecen:
busca su desdichado territorio:
y sólo allí el martirio o el sosiego.

EXILE

Among castles of tired stone,
streets of beautiful Prague,
smiles and Siberian birches,
Capri, fire in the sea, scent
of harsh rosemary,

and lastly, love,
essential love brought all my life together
in a generous peace,
meanwhile
with one hand and its friend, the other,
a dark hole was being dug out
in the stone of my spirit
and in it my country was burning,
calling me, waiting for me, spurring me on
to be, to preserve, to endure.

Exile is round in shape,
a circle, a ring.
Your feet go in circles, you cross land
and it's not your land.
Light wakes you up and it's not your light.
Night comes down, but your stars are missing.
You discover brothers, but they're not of your blood.
You're like an embarrassed ghost,
not loving more those who love you so much,
and it's still so strange to you that you miss
the hostile prickles of your own country,
the loud helplessness of your own people,
the bitter matters waiting for you
that will be snarling at you from the door.

But inevitably in my heart
I remembered every useless sign
as if only the sweetest honey
gathered in the tree of my own country
and I expected from every bird
the most faraway song
such as woke me from childhood on
in the damp light of dawn.
It seemed better to me, the poor earth
of my country—crater, sand,
the mineral face of the deserts—
than the glass filled with light they toasted me with.
I felt lost and alone in the garden.

I was a rustic enemy of the statues,
of what many centuries had arrived at
among silver bees and symmetry.

Exiles! Distance
grows thicker.
We breathe air through a wound.
To live is a necessary obligation.
So, a spirit without roots is an injustice.
It rejects the beauty that is offered it.
It searches for its own unfortunate country
and only there knows martyrdom or quiet.

ALASTAIR REID

❋

BROTHER CORDILLERA

The priest said only "Brother Water,"
"Brother Fire,"
and "Brother Bird."
There were no cordilleras there.
But he should have said that, because the cordillera
is water, fire, and bird.
It would have been good.
"Brother Cordillera."

My thanks, great brother,
for your existence;
for this splinter that pierced
your stone heart like a sword
and cut deep.
All your grasses bite—
they're hungry.
Your winds weep with rage—
they're hungry.
Your great, mute rocks
are guardians of dead fire
which could not be satisfied.
Up there
it's not green sky,
no,
it's the volcano, waiting.
It destroyed everything, and made it again,
it came down, all its red teeth showing,
it thundered through all its black throats,
and then
out poured the burning semen—
gorges
and ground

received
the slow, thick treasure,
the sulfuric wine
of fire, of death and life,
and all movement petrified:
only smoke
rose from the turbulence.

After, we touch each stone,
we say:
    This one is orange.
    This one is flecked with iron.
    This one is rainbow.
    This is magnetic.
    This has wrinkles.
    This is a dove.
    This has green eyes.

For that's how stones are,
the stones that fell from above.
They were thirsty and they're resting here,
waiting for the snows.
This stone was riddled with holes
from birth.
These bearded mountains
were born that way,
these vertical walls
of copper,
these reddish wounds
on the forehead of the Andes,
and the water that burst from its prison
broke through into song and went its ways.
The turf
that has grown in the high places,
stiff as conquering lances,
silvered spines,
has more now
of white and green.
No tree, no shadows, everything

is open to the light like salt,
coming into existence at a stroke.
It is my country stripped naked,
the action of fire,
of stone, of water,
of the wind
which tidied up the creation;
and here at last we feel naked,
we have arrived at last, without dying,
at the place where the air is born.
At last, we know the earth
and we touch it in its beginnings.

For all these so harsh things
and for the snow, gentle substance,
I give you my thanks, Brother Cordillera.

ALASTAIR REID

WHAT IS BORN WITH ME

I sing to the grass that is born with me
in this free moment, to the fermentations
of cheese, of vinegar, to the secret
spurt of the first semen, I sing
to the song of milk which now comes .
in rising whiteness to the nipples,
I sing to the fertility of the stable,
to the fresh dung of great cows
from whose aroma fly multitudes
of blue wings, I speak
without any shift of what is happening now
to the bumblebee with its honey, to the lichen
in its soundless germination.
Like an everlasting drum
sounds the flow of succession, the course
from being to being, and I'm born, I'm born, I'm born
with all that is being born, I'm one

with growing, with the spread silence
of everything that surrounds me, teeming,
propagating itself in the dense damp,
in threads, in tigers, in jelly.

I belong to fruitfulness
and I'll grow while lives grow.
I'm young with the youthfulness of water,
I'm slow with the slowness of time,
I'm pure with the purity of air,
dark with the wine of night,
and I'll only be still when I've become
so mineral that I neither see nor hear,
nor take part in what is born and grows.

When I picked out the jungle
to learn how to be,
leaf by leaf,
I went on with my lessons
and learned to be root, deep clay,
voiceless earth, transparent night,
and beyond that, bit by bit, the whole jungle.

ALASTAIR REID

APPOINTMENT WITH WINTER

I

I have waited for this winter as no winter
has been waited for by any man before me.
Everyone else had an appointment with joy.
I was the only one waiting for you, dark time.
Is this one like other winters, father and mother, coal fire,
and the neighing of a horse in the street?
Is this one like a winter in the future,
an absolute cold, in which we don't exist,
and nature not realizing we are gone?
No. I laid claim to a solitude surrounded

by a great sash of sheer rain
and here in my own ocean winter found me, with the wind
flying like a bird between two regions of water.
Everything was ready for the sky to weep.
The vast sky with a single eyelid
let fall its tears like glacial swords
and the world shuttered up like an empty
hotel room: sky, rain, and spaces.

II

Center of things, vessel without latitude or end!
Blue heart of the spread water!
Between air and water quivers and dances
some body seeking
its transparent nourishment
as I arrive and enter with my hat,
my dusty boots
worn out by the thirsty roads.
Nobody had arrived
for the solitary ceremony.
I can scarcely feel alone
now that I feel the pureness of the place.
I know I have limitless depths, like the well
which filled us with dread as children;
and that, surrounded by transparency
and the throbbing of the needles,
I am in touch with winter,
with its overwhelming power,
power of its shadowy element,
with the spread and splash
of its late-blooming rose,
until, suddenly, light has gone,
and under the roof
of the dark house
I shall go on speaking to the earth,
although nobody replies.

III

Who doesn't wish for a stubborn spirit?
Who hasn't sharpened the edge of his soul?
When, just as our eyes are opened, we see hate,
and just after learning to walk, we are tripped,
and just for wanting to love, we are hated,
and for no more than touching, we are hurt,
which of us hasn't started to arm himself,
to make himself sharp, somehow,
like a knife, to pay back the hurt?
The sensitive one tries to be cynical,
the gentlest reaches for his sword.
The one who only wanted to be loved
at least once, with the ghost of a kiss,
turns cold and aloof, and doesn't look at the girl
who was waiting for him, open and unhappy.
There is nothing to do. In the streets,
they set up stalls selling masks
and the dealer tries on every one
twilight faces, face of a tiger,
faces sober or virtuous, faces of ancestors,
until the moon dies
and in the lampless night we are all equal.

IV

I had a face which I lost in the sand,
a pale and wistful paper face,
and it was hard for my spirit to change its skin
till it found its true nature,
and could claim that sad right:
to wait for winter, alone, unwitnessed,
to wait, under the wings
of the dark sea cormorant,
for a wave to flow, restored
to the fullness of solitude,
to wait for and to find myself
with a touch of light or mourning
or nothing:

what my reason is scarcely aware of,
my unreason, my heart, my doubts.

V

By now the water is so very old
that it's new. The ancient water went,
breaking through glass into another life,
and the sand did not save up time.
The new sea has a clean shirt.
Identity lost its mirror
and we grow by changing our ways.

VI

Winter, don't come looking for me. I've left.
I belong to later, to now, when the thin rain
arrives and unlooses
its endless needles, the marriage
of the spirit with the dripping trees,
the sea's ash, the crash
of a gold capsule in the foliage,
and my belated eyes
preoccupied with earth, with earth alone.

VII

With earth alone, with earth, wind, sand, and water,
which granted me an absolute clarity.

ALASTAIR REID

THE HERO

The mistress of the castle summoned me
to weep in every one of its rooms.
I didn't know her
but I loved her with a harsh affection
as if all my misfortune came from the fact
that once she undid her hair over me,
shrouding me in shadow.

It was already late.

We went in
among the dead portraits
and our footsteps
sounded
as if
we were going down
to knock
at the door
of weary honor, the blind labyrinth,
and the only truth
were oblivion.

So at every stage
the silence was liquid,
and the castle's hard mistress
and I, her dark companion,
both of us hesitant,
drifted in that cold,
her black hair close to the ceiling.
Above, the dirty gold
of the ancient drawing rooms
blurred into her bare feet.

The thick silence
of the threadbare chambers
troubled me, and I resisted
in the name of the natural,
of pure physics,
but from her depths my mistress
pressed me to go on,
wandering over worn carpets,
weeping in passageways.
Time dawned, pristine, empty,
without words or sustenance.
Everything lay in the past, in a vague dream,
or else time itself
no longer recognized us

and we two were trapped like fish in its net,
prisoners in the still castle.

I hold on to those hours,
like stones or ashes in my hands,
without asking any more from memory.
But if my wanderings
take me close to castle walls,
I put on my mask,
I quicken
my pace by the moat,
I skirt the gloomy lake,
I leave without looking behind. Perhaps
her hair will fall again from a balcony,
and she will pierce my heart
with the sharp points of her tears, to keep me there.

That's why I, sly hunter,
wear a mask in the forest.

ALASTAIR REID

THE FOREST

I looked for the tree's dead root
to bury it over again.
I felt that in the air
that hard hairy clump
meant trouble to the traveler.
When I put it in the ground
it quivered like a hand
and once again perhaps, this time perhaps,
it went back to live among roots.

I'm of that lost race
that lives under the bells of the world.
I don't need eyes.

Thirst defines my country,
and the blind water that feeds me.

Then, from the frayed wood,
I took the goodness
turned up by storm or time.
I looked up. I looked deep in
as if everything was watching.
I couldn't feel alone.
The forest needed me
for its underground work.

And as I dug they watched me,
leafy cotyledons,
close-petaled tulips,
drupes bunched together,
wandering dandelions,
storm-topped beeches.
They watched the quiet intent
of my earth-stained hands
digging a new hole
for roots to resurrect.

Lupine and amaryllis
towered over the ground
up to the leaves and eyes
of the rauli watching me,
and the pristine, quivering maitén
with its garlands of green water;
and I in the jungle, guarding
an irresponsible silence
like an out-of-work butler
with no tools or language.

Nobody knows that I work
as a man who plants roots
among strange things that rustle
and others that suddenly whistle.
When the homogamous helianthuses

form their characteristic cups,
the whole vaginal jungle
is a rich-smelling wineshop,
and I go back and forth, scattering
constellations of pollen
in the looming silence.

ALASTAIR REID

NIGHT

I go into the black air.
Night's on the move,
patience in its foliage,
shifting
its great space,
round,
perforated with stars.
What feathers is it wrapped in?
Or is it naked?
It falls on metallic
mountains
covering them with the salt
of hard stars.
One by one,
every single mountain
goes out,
goes out under its wings,
goes under its black handwork.
At the same time
we are
black mud,
discarded
puppets
who sleep
without being, day clothes thrown aside,
gold spears, tasseled hat,
life with its streets and numbers,

there it all stays,
a heap of poor pride,
a hive without sound,
oh, night, open night,
mouth, boat, bottle,
not just time and shadow,
not just tiredness,
something breaks in, fills up
like a cup,
dark milk,
black salt,
and falls
into
its well,
a destiny,
all that exists burns up, the smoke
goes looking for space to stretch out the night,
but
from tomorrow's
ash
we will be born.

ALASTAIR REID

MEXICAN SERENADE

From Cuernavaca to the sea, Mexico is a spread
of pine groves, brown villages, rivers splintered
by ancient stone, raw land, grass
with amaranth eyes, torpid iguanas,
roofs of orange tile, rock-spines,
mouths of abandoned mines, serpents
of fire, men of dust,
and winding highways, raddled
by the geology of hell itself.

Oh, buried heart, stone and fire,
blunted star,

hostile rose,
powder on the wind!

I lived out the treacheries
of ancient cruelty,
I touched
the perennial rose,
the murmur
of ever-present bees.
Whatever that small people touch
with fingers or wings—
thread, silver, wood,
leather, turquoise, clay—
turns into a practical corolla,
takes on a life, and takes sparkling flight.

Oh, Mexico, from all
the mountains
or deserts
or farmlands
of our blood-embittered territories,
I would single you out
for your living being,
for your ageless dream, your lightning,
for your underworld thick with shadows,
for a brilliance and a love that are still untamed.

Air breathed in,
air for the vain
utterances
of man,
of the man singing to you:
so did the pilgrim pass
from straw to stone, to sombreros,
to looms, to agriculture,
and here I carry in my breast the scar
of loving and knowing you.
And when I close my eyes at night
I hear the threadbare music

of your streets
and I fall asleep as if adrift
in the air of Sinaloa.

Hands brought into being
your scruffy landscape,
hands of unknown men,
hands of the soldier,
the musician, the tiller of the soil.
Your stature was tempered,
and clay and stone, assembled
where the land
married the ocean,
was crowded with thorns,
with cactus
whose green wounds opened
the drunken eyes
of dream and rage.

So, in the undergrowth, they came together,
butterflies and the bones of the dead,
poppies and forgotten gods.

But the gods did not forget.

Mother matter, seed,
earth-womb,
turbulent
clay
of fertility, burning rain
over the red earth,
everywhere
it was the time of hands:
from ancient volcanic ash
pure, dark hands began
the work of
building, building.

As in the far past, perhaps,
when the harsh invader
ruled from afar
and a cold eclipse
covered with its shroud
the golden body of earth,
so did the stonecutter
carve his own cell
out of stone and the sun's presence
spread its day-honey.
The potter filled the market
with the round bulk
of water jugs
and out of green and yellow thread
the weaver fashioned shining butterflies,
till the barren plains flowered
with the dignity of their crafts.

I know
your echoing jungle.
My southern feet explored
the far parts of fragrant Chiapas.
I remember.
The great twilight of blue ash
suddenly descended
and high up there was neither
sky nor light.
It was all leaves.
The heart of the world was foliage.

Since I did not feel
weighed down
by dark earth or green night,
in spite of
misfortune, uncertainty,
perhaps for the first time
I did not feel myself to be
the father of grief

or the guest
of eternal anguish.

The earth, dense, buzzing,
taught me once and for all to be of the earth.
I knew both pain and defeat.
For the first time I learned,
from earthly clay,
it is in his singing
that the solitary man arrives at joy.

The jungle chorus
sounded
like the crackling of fire,
birds like endlessly running water,
harsh cries of startled beasts,
or else a sudden silence
would fall on that tangled globe,
then suddenly the earth would quiver
under a cover of locusts.

I was struck dumb,
awed, overcome by the sense
of some celestial mechanism
moving the night and its sounds.

The sky trembled through the lilies,
the shadows hid their dark stones
and there arose
the thin excitement
of a wave,
the metallic shifting
of a river
of bells.

There, the deep night
took on new eyes,

the world slowly filled
with the color of dark.
The stars throbbed
and I was alone, overcome
by the playing of
the sawmills of night, the vast
song of the secret world
of the locusts.

I returned to my own land, and leaning on
the harsh windowsill of winter,
I watch the persistent waves
in the cold seas off Isla Negra.
The glory of midday
founders under the weight of the salt
and the estuaries of foam grow into
the infinity of time and sand.

I watch the birds,
arrowed like hungry ships
flying over the sea
in search of blue fire,
in search of warm stone.
I think that the triumph of their wings
perhaps will lead them to descend one day
on the coast
of unbridled Mexico.
A thirst that stems from this hemisphere
leads them on,
a mysterious pathway
draws them.

Here, I tell them:
land, come to ground
on the blue phosphorescence
of bright indigo bushes
and scatter the fruits of your flight
along the coasts of Mexico.

To the hungry
and arriving birds,
open up your generous bounty,
your fish of light, the hurricanes
of your buoyant blood.

Oh, Mexico, take in
along with the wings that have flown
from the far south, where the continent
ends in white foam, the body
of unknown America.
Take in the pulse
of our separate being, which knows
your blood, your grain, your helplessness,
your boundless star.
We are of the same growth.
It is in our roots
that we are one.

ALASTAIR REID

PARA LA ENVIDIA

De uno a uno saqué los envidiosos
de mi propia camisa, de mi piel,
los vi junto a mí mismo cada día,
los contemplé
en el reino transparente
de una gota de agua:
los amé cuanto pude: en su desdicha
o en la ecuanimidad de sus trabajos:
y hasta ahora no sé
cómo ni cuándo
substituyeron nardo o limonero
por silenciosa arruga
y una grieta anidó donde se abriera
la estrella regular de la sonrisa.

Aquella grita de un hombre en la boca!

Aquella miel que fue substituida!

El grave viento de la edad
volando
trajo polvo, alimentos,
semillas separadas del amor,
pétalos enrollados de serpiente,
ceniza cruel del odio muerto
y todo
fructificó en la herida de la boca,
funcionó la pasión generatriz
y el triste sedimento del olvido
germinó, levantando la corola,
la medusa violeta de la envidia.

Qué haces tú, Pedro, cuando sacas peces?
Los devuelves al mar, rompes la red,
cierras los ojos ante el incentivo
de la profundidad procreadora?

Ay! Yo confieso mi pecado puro!
Cuanto saqué del mar,
coral, escama,
cola del arcoiris,
pez o palabra o planta plateada
o simplemente piedra submarina,
yo la erigí, le di la luz de mi alma.

Yo, pescador, recogí lo perdido
y no hice daño a nadie en mis trabajos.

No hice daño, o tal vez herí de muerte
al que quiso nacer y recibió
el canto de mi desembocadura
que silenció su condición bravía:
al que no quiso

navegar en mi pecho,
y desató
su propia fuerza,
pero vino el viento
y se llevó su voz y no nacieron
aquellos que querían ver la luz.

Tal vez el hombre crece y no respeta,
como el árbol del bosque, el albedrío
de lo que lo rodea,
y es de pronto
no sólo la raíz, sino la noche,
y no sólo da frutos, sino sombra,
sombra y noche que el tiempo y el follaje
abandonaron en el crecimiento
hasta que desde la humedad yacente
en donde esperan las germinaciones
no se divisan dedos de la luz:
el gratuito sol le fue negado
a la semilla hambrienta
y a plena oscuridad desencadena
el alma un desarrollo atormentado.

Tal vez no sé, no supe, no sabía.

No tuve tiempo en mis preocupaciones
de ver, de oír, de acechar y palpar
lo que estaba pasando, y por amor
pensé que mi deber era cantar,
cantar creciendo y olvidando siempre,
agonizando como resistiendo:
era mi amor, mi oficio
en la mañana entre los carpinteros,
bebiendo con los húsares, de noche,
desatar la escritura de mi canto
y yo creí cumplir,
ardiente o separado

del fuego,
cerca del manantial o en la ceniza,
creí que dando cuanto yo tenía,
hiriéndome para no dormir,
a todo sueño, a toda hora, a toda vida,
con mi sangre y con mis meditaciones,
y con lo que aprendí de cada cosa,
del clavel, de su generosidad,
de la madera y su paz olorosa,
del propio amor, del río, de la muerte,
con lo que me otorgó la ciudad y la tierra,
con lo que yo arranqué de una ola verde,
o de una casa que dejó vacía
la guerra, o de una lámpara
que halló encendida en medio del otoño,
así como del hombre y de sus máquinas,
del pequeño empleado y su aflicción,
o del navío navegando en la niebla:
con todo y, más que todo, con lo que yo debía
a cada hombre por su propia vida
hice yo lo posible por pagar, y no tuve
otra moneda que mi propia sangre.

Ahora qué hago con éste y con el otro?

Qué puedo hacer para restituir
lo que yo no robé? Por qué la primavera
me trajo a mí una corona amarilla
y quién anduvo hostil y enmarañado
buscándola en el bosque? Ahora
tal vez es tarde ya para encontrar
y volcar en la copa del rencor
la verdad atrasada y cristalina.

Tal vez el tiempo endureció la voz,
la boca, la piedad del ofendido,
y ya el reloj no podrá volver
a la consagración de la ternura.

El odio despiadado tuvo tiempo
de construir un pabellón furioso
y destinarme una corona cruel
con espinas sangrientas y oxidadas.
Y no fue por orgullo que guardé
el corazón ausente del terror:
ni de mi dolor ensimismado,
ni de las alegrías que sostengo
dispersé
en la venganza
el poderío.

Fue por otra razón, por indefenso.

Fue porque a cada mordedura
el día
que llegaba
me separaba de un nuevo dolor,
me amarraba las manos y crecía
el liquen en la piedra de mi pecho,
la enredadera se me derramaba,
pequeñas manos verdes me cubrían,
y me fui ya sin puños a los bosques
o me dormí en el título del trébol.

Oh, yo resguardo en mí mismo la avaricia
de mis espadas, lento
en la ira,
gozo
en mi dureza,
pero cuando la tórtola en la torre
trina, y agacha el brazo el alfarero
hacia su barro, haciéndolo vasija,
yo tiemblo y me traspasa
el aire lancinante:
mi corazón se va con la paloma.

Llueve y salgo a probar el aguacero.

Yo salgo a ser lo que amo, la desnuda
existencia del sol en el peñasco,
y lo que crece y crece sin saber
que no puede abolir su crecimiento:
dar grano el trigo: ser innumerable
sin razón: porque así le fue ordenado:
sin orden, sin mandato,
y, entre las rosas que no se reparten,
tal vez esta secreta voluntad,
esta trepidación de pan y arena,
llegaron a imponer su condición
y no soy yo sino materia viva
que fermenta y levanta sus insignias
en la fecundación de cada día.

Tal vez la envidia, cuando
sacó a brillar contra mí la navaja
y se hizo profesión de algunos cuantos,
agregó a mi substancia un alimento
que yo necesitaba en mis trabajos,
un ácido agresivo que me dio
el estímulo brusco de una hora,
la corrosiva lengua contra el agua.

Tal vez la envidia, estrella
hecha de vidrios rotos
caídos
en una calle amarga,
fue una medalla que condecoró
el pan que doy cantando cada día
y a mi buen corazón de panadero.

TO ENVY

I plucked the envious ones, one by one,
from my shirt, from my skin.

I saw them all around me every day.
I brooded on them
in the transparent kingdom
of a drop of water.
I loved them as much as I could, in their misfortune,
or in the equanimity of their labors,
and even now I have no idea
how or when
they replaced lilies and lemon trees
with a silent frown
or, where an ordinary smile should have been,
a gash set in.

That gash of a mouth!

All that honey that was replaced!

The heavy wind of age
brought in its flight
dust, food,
seeds split off from love,
petals wound with snakes,
cruel ash of dead hatred,
and everything
flourished in the wounded mouth.
A web of passions started up
and the woeful dregs of being forgotten
gave root to the spreading tentacles,
the violet medusa of envy.

When you catch fish, Pedro, what do you do?
Do you throw them back, rip up your net,
close your eyes to the urges
in the vast web of procreation?

I confess to my own sin!
Whatever I took from the sea,

coral, fish scales,
rainbow tail,
fish or word or silvered leaf,
or even an underwater stone,
I raised it up, I gave it the light of my spirit.

Fisherman myself, I gathered whatever was lost,
and my efforts harmed no one.

I did no harm, or maybe I did to death
someone who wanted the light himself, and got instead
me, emptying myself in song,
which silenced his untamed ways,
someone who didn't want
to swim in my breast,
and cut out
on his own,
but the wind came
and carried off his voice,
and they were never born,
those who longed to see light.

The tree is part of the forest, but perhaps a man
can grow up ignoring
the bent of everything around him,
and quite suddenly
it's not just roots but darkness,
not just fruit but shadow,
shadow and night which time and foliage
left behind as they grew,
till in the close dampness
where the seeds expected to swell
there is no trace of the fingering light.
The gift of the sun is denied
the hungry seed
and deep in darkness the spirit
unwinds in its own contortions.

Perhaps I don't know, perhaps I didn't know,
perhaps I never knew.

Preoccupied as I was, I had no time
to see, or hear, or seek out, or face
all that was happening, and for love's sake
I believed my obligation was to sing,
to sing as I grew and left my life behind,
out of the pain of the struggle.
It was my dedication, my function,
alongside carpenters in the morning,
drinking at night with the horsemen,
to pour out my song in writing,
and I thought I was doing it,
on fire or far away
from the fire,
close to the source or out of the ashes;
I thought that by giving all I had,
jabbing myself to keep myself awake,
giving my whole vision, my whole time, my whole life,
my blood and all my thinking,
and what I learned from every thing,
the generosity of carnations,
wood and its sweet-smelling peace,
love itself, rivers, death,
all I was given by the city, by the earth,
all I gathered in from a green wave,
or a house left empty by war,
or a lamp I found lit
in the middle of autumn,
and men too, and their machinery,
working men and their troubles,
or the ship steering through the fog:
all that, more than all, all that I owed
to every man for the life in him,
I did what I could to repay, and I had
no other currency but my own blood.

So what do I do now with this man and the other?

What can I do to give back
what I never stole? Why did the spring
bring me a yellow crown
and who, aggrieved and puzzled,
searched for it in the forest?
It's perhaps too late to uncover
the missing clarity of truth
and pour it into his bitter cup.

Maybe time has hardened his voice,
his mouth, his righteousness,
and the clock cannot turn back
to bring us together in tenderness.

Raw hatred took its time
making an outpost of its rage
and prepared for me a savage crown
with rusty, bloodstained spikes.
It wasn't pride that made me keep
my heart at a distance from such terror,
nor did I waste
on revenge
or the pursuit of power
the forces that came from my selfish griefs
or my accumulated joys.

It was something else—my helplessness.

It was because with every taunt
the day
that dawned
detached me from new hurt,
bound my hands, and lichen
grew on the stone of my breast.
I was overgrown by creeping plants,
small green hands covered me,

and I took to the woods, unfisted,
or slept in care of the clover.

Oh, I am most careful with
my sword's keen edge, I'm slow
to anger,
I rejoice in
my hard nature,
but when the turtledove in the tower
croons, and the potter stretches his hands
to his clay, raising a bowl,
I tremble, I am pierced through
by the sharp air.
My heart takes off with the dove.

It rains, and I go out to try the shower.

I go out to the being I love, naked presence
of sun on a rock,
everything growing, growing, unaware
that it cannot put an end to its own growing;
the wheat going to grain, multiplying
far beyond reason, so it was ordained,
without order or instruction;
and, among undivided things,
perhaps this secret urge,
this agitation of bread and sand,
imposed its own conditions,
and I'm not me but living matter
fermenting and forming its own shapes
in the fruitfulness of every day.

Perhaps envy, when it flashed
its knife at me
and became the profession of certain people,
gave to my body an extra food
which I needed in my work,

a fierce acid which gave me
sharp stimulation for an odd hour,
corrosive tongue against the water.

Perhaps envy, a star
made from broken glass
fallen
in a bitter street,
was a medal pinned on
the bread I bring, singing, every day,
and my good baker's heart.

ALASTAIR REID

ARS MAGNETICA

From so much loving and journeying, books emerge.
And if they don't contain kisses or landscapes,
if they don't contain a man with his hands full,
if they don't contain a woman in every drop,
hunger, desire, anger, roads,
they are no use as a shield or as a bell:
they have no eyes, and won't be able to open them,
they have the dead sound of precepts.

I loved the entanglings of genitals,
and out of blood and love I carved my poems.
In hard earth I brought a rose to flower,
fought over by fire and dew.

That's how I could keep on singing.

ALASTAIR REID

TO THOSE AT ODDS

These marriages gone sour,
these discordant couples,
why don't they break up once and for all,
why don't their stories come to an end—
the grumbles of Juan and Juana,
the squabbles of Pedro and Pedra,
the blows between Roso and Rosa?

No one likes to be around
matrimonial swordfish

armed with hard arguments
or dissolving in salt tears.

Please, please agree,
at least to disagree.
Don't come out showing
your knives, your forks, your false teeth.

In the estuary of love
there is still room for tears,
and there is not earth enough
to fill in the tomb of love;
but we don't go to bed at sunset
to wound and bite one another—
that's a matter for dark places.

ALASTAIR REID

DAY DAWNS

Day dawns without debts,
without doubts,
and later
the day changes,
the wheel revolves,
the fire is transfigured.

Nothing is left
of what dawned, the earth consumed itself
grape by grape,
the heart was left without blood,
spring was left without leaves.

Why did all that happen this very day?
Why was it mistaken in its bells?
Or does everything always have to be so?

How to twist, unravel the thread,
keep on pushing the sun back to the shadow,
send back the light until the night
grows big again with day?
May this day be our child,
endless discovery, aura
of time recovered,
conquest of debt and doubt,
so that our life
may simply be
a pure morning substance,
a clear current.

ALASTAIR REID

SOLITUDE

The not-happening was so sudden
that I stayed there forever,
without knowing, without their knowing me,
as if I were under a chair,
as if I were lost in night.
Not being was like that,
and I stayed that way forever.

Afterwards, I asked the others,
the women, the men,
what they were doing so confidently
and how they learned how to live.
They did not actually answer.
They went on dancing and living.

What determines the silence
is what doesn't happen,
and I don't want to keep on talking,
for I stayed there waiting.
In that place, on that day,

I have no idea what happened to me,
but now I am not the same.

ALASTAIR REID

IT IS NOT NECESSARY

It is not necessary to whistle
to be alone,
to live in the dark.

Out in the crowd, under the wide sky,
we remember our separate selves,
the intimate self, the naked self,
the only self who knows how the nails grow,
who knows how his own silence is made
and his own poor words.
There is a public Pedro,
seen in the light, an adequate Bernice,
but inside,
underneath age and clothing,
we still don't have a name,
we are quite different.
Eyes don't close only in order to sleep,
but so as not to see the same sky.

We soon grow tired,
and as if they were sounding the bell
to call us to school,
we return to the hidden flower,
to the bone, the half-hidden root,
and there we suddenly are,
we are the pure, forgotten self,
the true being
within the four walls of our singular skin,
between the two points of living and dying.

ALASTAIR REID

MEMORY

I have to remember everything,
keep track of blades of grass, the threads
of all untidy happenings,
the resting places, inch by inch,
the infinite railroad tracks,
the surfaces of pain.

If I were to misplace one rosebud
and confuse night with a hare,
or even if one whole wall
of my memory were to disintegrate
I am obliged to make over the air,
steam, earth, leaves,
hair, even the bricks,
the thorns which pierced me,
the speed of flight.

Be gentle with the poet.

I was always quick to forget,
and those hands of mine
could only grasp intangibles,
untouchable things
which could only be compared
when they no longer existed.

The smoke was an aroma,
the aroma something like smoke,
the skin of a sleeping body
which came to life with my kisses;
but don't ask me the date
or the name of what I dreamed—
nor can I measure the road
which may have no country
or that truth that changed
or perhaps turned off by day

to become a wandering light,
a firefly in the dark.

ALASTAIR REID

THE LONG DAY CALLED THURSDAY

Hardly had I wakened than I recognized
the day. It was yesterday,
it was yesterday with another name,
a friend I thought was lost
who came back to surprise me.

Thursday, I told it, wait for me.
I'm going to dress and we'll go out together
until you disappear into night.
You'll die, I will go on
awake, and accustomed
to the satisfactions of dark.

But things happened differently,
as I shall tell in intimate detail.

I lingered, lathering my face.
What a pleasure to feel
the foam on my cheeks!
I felt the sea was giving me a present
of a running whiteness.
My face was a separate, vague island
rimmed round by soap reefs,
and when, during the struggle
of the small waves and the strokes
of warm brush and sharpened blade,
I was careless and all at once
badly wounded,
I stained the towels
with drops of my own blood.

I called for styptic, cotton, iodine,
for whole pharmacies to run to help me.
The only response was my face in the mirror,
badly washed, badly wounded.

My bath
encouraged me
with prenatal warmth to submerge myself,
and my body curled up lazily.

That womb
kept me curled up,
waiting to be born, still and liquid,
a flabby substance
enmeshed in nonexistence,
and I put off getting out
for hours on end,
stirring my legs deliciously
in the underwater warmth.

So much time toweling and drying myself,
one sock in the wake of the other,
one trouser leg and its brother—
entering one shoe took an age,
so that when, in my gloomy uncertainty,
I picked out a tie, and at last was leaving on
my explorations, looking for my hat,
I realized that it was much too late.
Night had come down,
and I started again to undress myself,
garment by garment, to slip between the sheets,
until I was soon asleep.

When night passed and through the door
the preceding Thursday entered again,
properly transformed into Friday,
I greeted it with a doubtful laugh,
distrusting its identity.

Wait for me, I said to it, keeping
doors and windows wide open,
and I began my routine again,
from the lathered soap to the hat,
but my feeble effort
came face to face with the arriving night
just when I was about to go out.
And I went back to my meticulous undressing.

All this time they were waiting in the office,
the horrible records, the
numbers flying onto the papers
like tiny, migrating birds,
joined in a threatening deployment.
It seemed to me that everything had gathered
to wait for me for the first time—
my new love who, recently come upon,
was urging me under a tree in the park
to keep the spring in me going.

And the business of eating was ignored
day after day, forced as I was to put on
my accessories, one after the other,
to go through my daily washing and dressing.
The situation was impossible:
my shirt a problem every time,
my underclothes more hostile,
my jacket more interminable.

Until, little by little, I died
of inanition, of not being sure, of nothing,
of being between that day that was returning
and the night waiting like a widow.

When I finally died, it all changed.

Well dressed, a pearl in my tie,
and exquisitely shaved this time,
I wanted to go out, but there was no street,

there was no one in the nonexistent street,
and consequently, no one was waiting for me.

And Thursday would go on all year long.

ALASTAIR REID

WHAT WE ACCEPT WITHOUT WANTING TO

Oh, what longing for no,
no, no, no.
How much life
we spend
or lose
yes yes
yes yes
yes yes.
We were down in the mud that time
and when we fell from the star
further, among buffaloes
on fire
with clashing horns,
when we couldn't move
nearer or further, the moment
of indecision which corrodes
with the slow seep of acid,
finally, in every sense,
we lost our will
and there we stayed, alive but dead.
Because it's always to save
Pedro and his grandmother from suffering—
by that standard
we were measured
all life long
from our eyes to our heels
and by these lights
we were judged;
and later, with no respect at all,

they told us what entrails
we should
sacrifice,
what bones,
teeth and veins
they would graciously remove
from our worn-out skeletons.
And so that Thursday passed
when, among the rocks,
we had no feet and later
no tongue.
We had used it up without knowing,
we said yes without knowing how
and among yeses and yeses
we were left lifeless among the living
and they all looked at us and thought us dead.
We didn't know
what could happen because the others
seemed to agree about being alive
and there we were
without ever being able
to say no, no,
or perhaps no, or ever
no, or always
no no
no no
no no.

ALASTAIR REID

EL FUTURO ES ESPACIO

El futuro es espacio,
espacio color de tierra,
color de nube,
color de agua, de aire,
espacio negro para muchos sueños,

espacio blanco para toda la nieve,
para toda la música.

Atrás quedó el amor desesperado
que no tenía sitio para un beso,
hay lugar para todos en el bosque,
en la calle, en la casa,
hay sitio subterráneo y submarino,
qué placer es hallar por fin,
                              subiendo
un planeta vacío,
grandes estrellas claras como el vodka
tan transparentes y deshabitadas,
y allí llegar con el primer teléfono
para que hablen más tarde tantos hombres
de sus enfermedades.

Lo importante es apenas divisarse,
gritar desde una dura cordillera
y ver en la otra punta
los pies de una mujer recién llegada.

Adelante, salgamos
del río sofocante
en que con otros peces navegamos
desde el alba a la noche migratoria
y ahora en este espacio descubierto
volemos a la pura soledad.

THE FUTURE IS SPACE

The future is space,
earth-colored space,
cloud-colored,
color of water, air,
black space with room for many dreams,

white space with room for all snow,
for all music.

Behind lies despairing love
with no room for a kiss.
There's a place for everyone in forests,
in streets, in houses;
there's an underground space, a submarine space,
but what joy to find in the end,
                              rising,
an empty planet,
great stars clear as vodka,
so uninhabited and so transparent,
and arrive there with the first telephone
so that so many men can later discuss
all their infirmities.

The important thing is to be scarcely aware of oneself,
to scream from a rough mountain range
and see on another peak
the feet of a woman newly arrived.

Come on, let's leave
this suffocating river
in which we swim with other fish
from dawn to shifting night
and now in this discovered space
let's fly to a pure solitude.

ALASTAIR REID

from

ART OF BIRDS

ARTE DE PÁJAROS

✳

1962–1965

MIGRACIÓN

Todo el día una línea y otra línea,
un escuadrón de plumas,
un navío
palpitaba en el aire,
atravesaba
el pequeño infinito
de la ventana desde donde busco,
interrogo, trabajo, acecho, aguardo.

La torre de la arena
y el espacio marino
se unen allí, resuelven
el canto, el movimiento.

Encima se abre el cielo.

Entonces así fue: rectas, agudas,
palpitantes, pasaron
hacia dónde? Hacia el norte, hacia el oeste,
hacia la claridad,
hacia la estrella,
hacia el peñón de soledad y sal
donde el mar desbarata sus relojes.

Era un ángulo de aves
dirigidas
aquella latitud de hierro y nieve
que avanzaba
sin tregua
en su camino rectilíneo:
era la devorante rectitud
de una flecha evidente,
los números del cielo que viajaban
a procrear formados
por imperioso amor y geometría.

Yo me empeñé en mirar hasta perder
los ojos y no he visto
sino el orden del vuelo,
la multitud del ala contra el viento:
vi la serenidad multiplicada
por aquel hemisferio transparente
cruzado por la oscura decisión
de aquellas aves en el firmamento.

No vi sino el camino.

Todo siguió celeste.

Pero en la muchedumbre de las aves
rectas a su destino
una bandada y otra dibujaban
victorias
triangulares
unidas por la voz de un solo vuelo,
por la unidad del fuego,
por la sangre,
por la sed, por el hambre,
por el frío,
por el precario día que lloraba
antes de ser tragado por la noche,
por la erótica urgencia de la vida:
la unidad de los pájaros
volaba
hacia las desdentadas costas negras,
peñascos muertos, islas amarillas,
donde el sol dura más que su jornada

y en el cálido mar se desarrolla
el pabellón plural de las sardinas.

En la piedra asaltada
por los pájaros
se adelantó el secreto:

piedra, humedad, estiércol, soledad,
fermentarán y bajo el sol sangriento
nacerán arenosas criaturas
que alguna vez regresarán volando
hacia la huracanada luz del frío,
hacia los pies antárticos de Chile.

Ahora cruzan, pueblan la distancia
moviendo apenas en la luz las alas
como si en un latido las unieran,

vuelan sin desprenderse

del cuerpo

migratorio

que en tierra se divide
y se dispersa.

Sobre el agua, en el aire,
el ave innumerable va volando,
la embarcación es una,
la nave transparente
construye la unidad con tantas alas,
con tantos ojos hacia el mar abiertos
que es una sola paz la que atraviesa
y sólo un ala inmensa se desplaza.

Ave del mar, espuma migratoria,
ala del sur, del norte, ala de ola,
racimo desplegado por el vuelo,
multiplicado corazón hambriento,
llegarás, ave grande, a desgranar
el collar de los huevos delicados
que empolla el viento y nutren las arenas
hasta que un nuevo vuelo multiplica
otra vez vida, muerte, desarrollo,

gritos mojados, caluroso estiércol,
y otra vez a nacer, a partir, lejos
del páramo y hacia otro páramo.

Lejos
de aquel silencio, huid, aves del frío,
hacia un vasto silencio rocalloso
y desde el nido hasta el errante número,
flechas del mar, dejadme
la húmeda gloria del transcurso,
la permanencia insigne de las plumas
que nacen, mueren, duran y palpitan
creando pez a pez su larga espada,
crueldad contra crueldad la propia luz
y a contraviento y contramar, la vida.

MIGRATION

All day, column after column,
a squadron of feathers,
a fluttering airborne
ship
crossed
the tiny infinity
of the window where I search,
question, work, observe, wait.

The tower of sand
and marine space
join there, comprise
song, movement.

Above, the sky unfolds.

So it was: palpitating,
sharp right angles passed
heading northward, westward,
toward open space,

toward the star,
toward the spire of salt and solitude
where the sea casts its clocks to the winds.

It was an angle of birds
steering for
that latitude of iron and snow,
inexorably advancing along
their rectilinear road:
the skyborne numbers
flew with the hungry rectitude
of a well-aimed arrow, winging
their way to procreate, formed
by urgent love and geometry.

I kept looking as far as
the eye could see and saw
nothing but orderly flight,
the multitude of wings against the wind:
I saw serenity multiplied
in that transparent hemisphere
crossed by the obscure decision
of those birds in the firmament.

I saw only the flyway.

All remained celestial.

But among the throngs of birds
homing for their destination
flock after flock sketched out
triangular
victories
united by the voice of a single flight,
by the unity of fire,
by blood,
by thirst, by hunger,
by the cold,
by the precarious day that wept

before being swallowed by night,
by the erotic urgency of life:
the unity of birds
flew
toward the toothless black coasts,
lifeless pinnacles, yellow isles,
where the sun works overtime

and the plural pavilion of sardines
spreads over the warm sea.

On the stone assaulted
by the birds
the secret was set forth:
stone, moisture, excrement, and solitude
will ferment and beneath the blood-red sun
sandy offspring will be born
and they, too, will one day fly back
to the tempestuous cold light,
to the antarctic feet of Chile.

Now they pass, filling the distance,
a faint flapping of wings against the light,
a throbbing winged unity

that flies without breaking

from the migratory

body

which ashore divides,
disperses.

Above the water, in the sky,
the innumerable bird flies on,
the vessel is one,
the transparent ship
builds unity with so many wings,

with so many eyes opened to the sea,
sails over a singular peacefulness
with the movement of one immense wing.

Seabird, migratory foam,
wing from north and south, wave wing,
cluster deployed by flight,
multiplied hungry heart,
you will arrive, great bird, to strip
from the necklace the fragile eggs to be
hatched by the wind and nourished by the sand
until another flight again
multiplies life, death, growth,
wet cries, hot dung,
being born again, and leaving, far
from the windy waste to another windy waste.

Far
from that silence, flee, polar birds,
to the vast rocky silence
and from the nest to the errant number,
sea arrows, bequeath me
the wet glory of time elapsed,
the renowned permanence of feathers
that are born, that die, endure, and throb,
creating fish by fish their long sword,
cruelty against cruelty, the very light
and against the wind and the sea, life.

JACK SCHMITT

※

WANDERING ALBATROSS
Diomedea exulans

The wind sails the open sea
steered by the albatross
that glides, falls, dances, climbs,
hangs motionless in the fading light,
touches the waves' towers,
settles down in
the disorderly element's
seething mortar
while the salt crowns it with laurels
and the furious foam hisses,
skims the waves
with its great symphonic wings,
leaving above the tempest
a book that flies on forever:
the statute of the wind.

JACK SCHMITT

AMERICAN KESTREL
Falco sparverius cinnamomimus

High noon opened up:
the sun in the center, crowned.
The earth awaited indecisively
some movement in the sky
and everyone remained
indecipherably still.

At that slender second
the hawk hammered its flight,

cut loose from the firmament,
and swooped like a sudden shiver.

The landscape remained serene
and the woodlands were not frightened,
the volcanoes were still aloof,
the river kept proclaiming
its abrupt and wet lineage:
everything kept throbbing
in that green-patterned pause
except a hare, a bird,
something that flew or ran,
something that used to live
on that blood-spattered spot.

JACK SCHMITT

GUANAY CORMORANT
Phalacrocorax bougainvillii

Crucified on the rock,
the motionless black-coated cross
stubbornly posed in twisted profile.
The sun fell on the coastal stones
like a galloping horse:
its shoes unleashed
a million furious sparks,
a million seadrops,
and the crucified steering wheel
did not blink on the cross:
the surf swelled up and gave birth:
the stone trembled in delivery:
the foam whispered softly:
and there, like a hanged Negro,
the cormorant remained dead,
the cormorant remained alive,
remained alive and dead and cross
with its stiff black wings
opened above the water:

remained like a cruel gaffing hook
plunged into the rock's salt
and from so many angry blows,
from so much green and fire and fury,
from the forces gathered
along the howling seacoast
it looked like a menace:
it was the cross and the gallows:
the night nailed to the cross,
the agony of darkness: but
suddenly it fled to the sky,
flew like a black arrow,
and climbed in cyclical form
with its snowy black suit,
with a star's or ship's repose.
And above the unruly ocean—
a gnashing of sea and cold—
it flew flew flew flew
its pure equation in space.

JACK SCHMITT

SLENDER-BILLED PARAKEET
Enicognathus leptorhynchus

The tree had so many leaves
it was toppling with treasure,
from so much green it blinked
and never closed its eyes.

That's no way to sleep.

But the fluttering foliage
went flying off green and alive,
each bud learned to fly,
and the tree was left naked,
weeping in the winter rain.

JACK SCHMITT

GRAY GULL

Larus modestus

The gull adroitly opened,
in sea foam and stupor,
two wandering pointers,
kept stationary with
two wings stretched out in the sky,
two shining secretaries of the light,
until it flew off, however,
to the east and to the west,
to the north and to the snow,
to the Moon and to the Sun.

JACK SCHMITT

MAGELLANIC WOODPECKER

Ipocrantor magellanicus

The woodpecker toco toc:
under the sun the forests distill
water, resin, night, honey,
the hazelnut trees don
galloons of scarlet pomp:
the burned logs bleed on,
the foxes of Boroa are asleep,
the leaves grow silently
while the roots' language
circulates beneath the ground:
suddenly in the green silence
the woodpecker toco toc.

JACK SCHMITT

✳

CHILEAN LAPWING
Belonopterus chilensis

The lapwing flew off flashing
white snow and black snow
and opened its suit
in broad daylight,
in broad morning silver:
its nuptial wings' fan was priceless:
precious the body adorned
by the morning and the plumage.

The velvety bird's
wild extravagance shone
upon the stones of Isla Negra
and I thought: where is it going?

What celestial reception?

What golden water wedding?

What salon of pure purple
among columns of hyacinths,
where only the well-dressed clouds
may accompany it?

Well, I said, perhaps it's going
to crown the tresses
of Pedro Espinosa's friend,
the naiad of the River Genil.

The diviner did no such thing:
it planed down to land
among clumps of stubble

in a fallow wheat field,
and there it launched its language,
its piercing tero tero,
while it pecked, picked,
and dispassionately devoured
a simple earthworm.

JACK SCHMITT

CHILEAN MOCKINGBIRD
Mimus thenca

The long-tailed mockingbird flew
dressed like scissors:
perched on a thread, it listened to
the telegraph's deep voice,
the wire's blue pulse,
heard words, kisses, numbers,
fleet petals from the soul,
then launched its trill,
released a transparent stream,
and scattered its delirium to the winds.

Mockingbird, I did not learn your lesson
of flight and song and thought:
I learned it all from the mist,
the moisture, the silence.
I did not know how to dance and fly
above the peumo trees' beauty,
submerge my soul in the boldu trees,
while away time whistling in the wind.
I did not know about your wisdom,
the speed of your trill,
the republic of your song.

I swear I'll learn whatever you profess:
to know how to fly like an arrow,
to study the secret syllables

of the outdoors and leaves,
to sing with the water and the land,
and to establish in the silence
a crystalline chair of learning.

JACK SCHMITT

DODOBIRD
Autoritarius miliformis

The dodobird, seated,
sensed that it didn't know it,
that it didn't fly and didn't fly
but gave out flight orders
and kept explaining wing by wing
what would happen in the atmosphere:
it made pronouncements about feathers,
revealed the sky and its currents.

The dodobird was born seated.

This sad featherless bird
grew up seated and never had
wings or song or flight.

But the dictator dictated.

It dictated the air, hope,
the sums of coming and going.

And if the matter at hand was lofty,
the dodobird was born above,
it pointed out the skyways,
it would ascend sometime,
but it was now concerned
with numbers, proprieties,
best not fly now:
"Meanwhile, you may fly."
The ferocious dodobird
sits down on its fangs
and spies on others flying:

"Not one bee will fly here
unless I so decree."

And thus the dodobird flies
but does not fly from its chair.

JACK SCHMITT

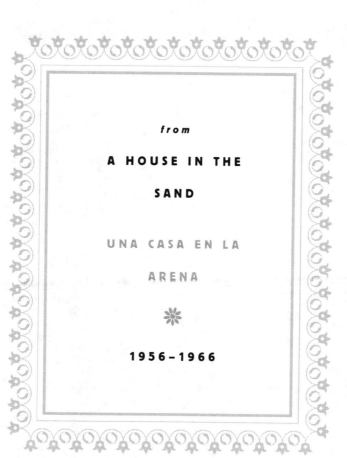

from

**A HOUSE IN THE
SAND**

UNA CASA EN LA
ARENA

❋

1956–1966

AMOR PARA ESTE LIBRO

En estas soledades he sido poderoso
de la misma manera que una herramienta alegre
o como hierba impune que suelta sus espigas
o como un perro que se revuelca en el rocío.
Matilde, el tiempo pasará gastando y encendiendo
otra piel, otras uñas, otros ojos, y entonces
el alga que azotaba nuestras piedras bravías,
la ola que construye, sin cesar, su blancura,
todo tendrá firmeza sin nosotros,
todo estará dispuesto para los nuevos días,
que no conocerán nuestro destino.

Qué dejamos aquí sino el grito perdido
que no conocerán nuestro destino
del queltehue, en la arena del invierno, en la racha
que nos cortó la cara y nos mantuvo
erguidos en la luz de la pureza,
como en el corazón de una estrella preclara?

Qué dejamos viviendo como un nido
de ásperas aves, vivas, entre los matorrales
o estáticas, encima de los fríos peñascos?
Así, pues, si vivir fue sólo anticiparse
a la tierra, a este suelo y su aspereza
líbrame tú, amor mío, de no cumplir, y ayúdame
a volver a mi puesto bajo la tierra hambrienta.

Pedimos al océano su rosa,
su estrella abierta, su contacto amargo,
y al agobiado, al ser hermano, al herido
dimos la libertad recogida en el viento.
Es tarde ya. Tal vez
sólo fue un largo día color de miel y azul,
tal vez sólo una noche, como el párpado
de una grave mirada que abarcó
la medida del mar que nos rodeaba,

y en este territorio fundamos sólo un beso,
sólo inasible amor que aquí se quedará
vagando entre la espuma del mar y las raíces.

LOVE FOR THIS BOOK

In these lonely regions I have been powerful
in the same way as a cheerful tool
or like untrammeled grass which lets loose its seed
or like a dog rolling around in the dew.
Matilde, time will pass wearing out and burning
another skin, other fingernails, other eyes, and then
the algae that lashed our wild rocks,
the waves that unceasingly construct their own whiteness,
all will be firm without us,
all will be ready for the new days,
which will not know our destiny.

What do we leave here but the lost cry
of the seabird, in the sand of winter, in the gusts of wind
that cut our faces and kept us
erect in the light of purity,
as in the heart of an illustrious star?

What do we leave, living like a nest
of surly birds, alive, among the thickets
or static, perched on the frigid cliffs?
So then, if living was nothing more than anticipating
the earth, this soil and its harshness,
deliver me, my love, from not doing my duty, and help me
return to my place beneath the hungry earth.

We asked the ocean for its rose,
its open star, its bitter contact,
and to the overburdened, to the fellow human being, to the wounded
we gave the freedom gathered in the wind.
It's late now. Perhaps

it was only a long day the color of honey and blue,
perhaps only a night, like the eyelid
of a grave look that encompassed
the measure of the sea that surrounded us,
and in this territory we found only a kiss,
only ungraspable love that will remain here
wandering among the sea foam and the roots.

DENNIS MALONEY AND CLARK M. ZLOTCHEW

from

LA BARCAROLA

LA BARCAROLA

❋

1964–1967

THE WATERSONG ENDS

You will know that in that region I once crossed fearfully
the night was stirring with secret sounds, darkness of jungle,
and I crawled along in a truck into that curious universe—
black Asia, forest dark, sacred ash,
and my youth trembling like the wings of a fly
darting from this place to that in uncertain kingdoms.

All at once the wheels came to a stop, the unknown ones climbed down
and there I was, a foreigner, in the solitudes of the jungle,
there, marooned in that truck stranded in night,
twenty years old, waiting for death, shrinking into my language.

Suddenly a drum began, a torch flared, there was a stirring,
and those I had taken for certain as my murderers
were dancing, beneath the towering dark of the jungle
to entertain a traveler strayed into those far regions.
So, when so many omens were pointing the end of my life,
the tall drum, the flowering tresses, the flashing ankles
were dancing and smiling and singing for a foreigner.
I tell you this story, love, because the lesson,
the human lesson, shines through its strange disguises
and there the principles of the dawn were grounded in me—
there my mind awoke to the sense of men as brothers.

That was in Vietnam, the Vietnam of 1928.

Forty years after, on the music of my companions
fell the murdering gas, scorching the feet and the music,
burning the ritual silence of the wilderness,
blasting love and destroying the peace of the children.
"Down with the brutish invader" sound the drums now, gathering
the tiny country into a knot of resistance.

My love, I told you all the happenings in the sea and the day,
and the moon in my watersong was dozing in the water.
The system of my symmetry had so arranged it
with the tingling first kiss of marine spring.

I told you—in carrying through my traveling world the vision of your
    eyes,
the rose in my heart sets up its own flowering place
and I said I give you as well memories of rogues and heroes,
all the thunder of the world rumbles beneath my kisses—
that was the way of the boat unwinding in my watersong.

But these are tainted years, ours; the blood of men far away
tumbles again in the foam, the waves stain us, the moon is spattered.
These faraway agonies are our agonies
and the struggle for the oppressed is a hard vein in my nature.

Perhaps this war will pass like the others which divided us,
leaving us dead, killing us along with the killers
but the shame of this time puts its burning fingers to our faces.
Who will erase the ruthlessness hidden in innocent blood?

My love, all along the broad coastline
from one petal to the next the earth yields up its aroma
and now the insignia of the spring is proclaiming
our eternity, no less painful for being brief.

If the ship never returns to port with its fingers uncallused,
if the watersong followed its course in the thundering sea,
if your golden waist turned beautifully in my hands,
here let us submit to the sea's return, our destiny.
Without more ado, we comply with its tantrums.

Who can tune in to essential secrets of flow and succession
which in sequential stages fill us with sun, then weeping?
A leaf inclines to the great earth at its last branching
and falls in the yellow air as evidence of an advent.
Man turned to his mechanisms and made hideous
his works of art, his lead paintings, his wistful statues of wire,
his books which were aimed at falsifying the lightning;
business deals were made with stains of blood in the mud of the rice
    fields,
and of the hopes of many only a faint skeleton remained—
in the sky, the end of the century was paying what it owed us.

And while they arrived on the moon and dropped tools of gold there,
we never knew, children of the slow half-light,
if what was discovered was a new planet or a new form of death.

For my part and yours, we comply, we share our hopes and winters;
and we have been wounded not only by mortal enemies
but by mortal friends (that seemed all the more bitter),
but bread does not seem to taste sweeter, nor my book, in the
    meantime—
living, we supply the statistics that pain still lacks,
we go on loving love and in our blunt way
we bury the liars and live among the truth-tellers.

My love, night came down, galloping over the spread of the world.

My love, night erases all trace of the sea, the ship heels, is at rest.

My love, night lit up its starry institution.

To the place by the sleeping man, the woman glided in her wakefulness
and in dreams the two descended the rivers which led to the weeping
and grew once again among dark animals and trains loaded with shadows
to the point of being nothing more than pale stones at night.

It is time, love, to break off that somber rose,
shut up the stars and bury the ash in the earth;
and, in the rising of the light, wake with those who awoke
or go on in the dream, reaching the other shore of the sea which has no
    other shore.

ALASTAIR REID

from

**THE HANDS
OF DAY**

LAS MANOS
DEL DÍA

❋

1967–1968

I

GUILTY

I declare myself guilty of not having
made, with these hands they gave me,
a broom.

Why did I make no broom?

Why did they give me hands?

What use have they been
if all I ever did was
watch the stir of the grain,
listen up for the wind
and did not gather straws
still green in the earth
for a broom,
not set the soft stalks to dry
and bind them
in a gold bundle,
and did not lash a wooden stick
to the yellow skirt
till I had a broom for the paths?

So it went.
How did my life
get by
without seeing, and learning,
and gathering and binding
the basic things?

It's too late to deny
I had the time,
the time,
yet the hands were lacking,
so how could I aim
for greatness
if I was never able

to make
a broom,
not one,
not even one?

XL

IN VIETNAM

And who made war?

It's been pounding since the day before yesterday.

I'm afraid.

It pounds like a stone
against the wall,
like thunder with blood,
like a dying mountain.
This is a world
I didn't make.
You didn't make it.
They made it.
Who threatens it with terrible fingers?
Who wants it decapitated?
Wasn't it about to come into being?
And who kills it now it is born?

The cyclist is afraid,
so is the architect.
The mother with a child and her breasts
hides in the mud.
This mother sleeps in the cave and suddenly,
war,
war arrives big,
arrives full of fire
and already dead,

dead
are the mother with her milk and her son.

They died in the mud.

Oh pain! From then
till now,
should one stay covered with mud
up to the temples,
singing and shooting? Holy God!
If only you had been told
before you lived, almost before you lived . . .
If at least
they had whispered it
to your relatives and nonrelatives,
children of love's laughter,
children of human sperm,
of that fragrance
in a new Monday and with a fresh shirt . . .
But they had to die so suddenly,
without ever knowing what it was all about!

They are the same ones
who come to kill us,
yes, the same ones
who come to burn us,
yes, the same ones,
the winners and the braggers,
the smiling ones who enjoyed so much
and took so much,
now
by air
they come, will come, they came,
to kill the world within us.

They have left a pool
made of father, mother, and child.
Let us look
in it,

look for our own blood and bones,
look for them in the mud of Vietnam,
look for them among so many other bones;
they're charred, they no longer belong to anyone
but to everyone,
our bones are burnt,
look for your death in that death,
because they are after you too,
and the fate they bring you is that selfsame mud.

ILAN STAVANS

LVIII
EL PASADO

No volverán aquellos anchos días
que sostuvieron, al pasar, la dicha.

Un rumor de fermentos
como sombrío vino en las bodegas
fue nuestra edad. Adiós,
adiós, resbalan
tantos adioses como las palomas
por el cielo, hacia el Sur, hacia el silencio.

THE PAST

The old abundant days,
transient keepers of happiness, shall come no more.

Our prime
was a rumor of fermentation,
like dark wine in the cellars. Adiós,
adiós, so many goodbyes
slip by, like doves
in the sky, southbound, onward into silence.

ILAN STAVANS

LX
VERB

I'm going to wrinkle this word,
twist it,
yes,
it's too smooth,
as if the tongue
of a big dog or a big river's water
had washed it
for years and years.

I want to see
roughness in the word,
ironlike salt,
earth's
toothless strength,
the blood
of those who spoke out and those who didn't.

I want to see thirst
deep in its syllables.
I want to touch fire
in the sound.
I want to feel
the darkness of a scream.
I want rough words
like virginal stones.

ILAN STAVANS

from

WORLD'S END

FIN DEL MUNDO

❋

1968–1969

✳

THE SEEKER

I left to find what I had lost
in enemy cities:
They closed streets and doors on me.
They attacked me with fire and water.
They threw shit at me.
I just wanted to find
toys broken in dreams:
a crystal horse,
my dug-up watch.

Nobody wanted to understand
my joyless fate,
my absolute disinterest.

In vain I explained to women
I had no desire to steal anything
or kill their grandmothers.
They screamed in fear
as they saw me
emerge from a chest,
or come down the chimney.

Still, for days on end
and nights of violent rain
I kept on moving.
I traversed furtively
hostile mansions
by way of roofs and fences,
and even hid under the rug
as I battled oblivion.

I never found what I looked for.

Nobody had my horse,
my loves, the rose
I lost in my lover's waist
along with countless kisses.

I was jailed, injured,
misunderstood,
treated like a notorious criminal
and I no longer seek my own shadow.
I'm as serious as everyone else,
but I miss what I once loved:
the sweet foliage now opens,
a leaf at a time,
till you are really still—
truly naked.

ILAN STAVANS

THE SADDER CENTURY

The century of émigrés,
the book of homelessness—
gray century, black book.
This is what I ought to leave
written in the open book,
digging it out from the century,
tinting the pages with spilled blood.

I lived the abundance
of those lost in the jungle:
in the jungle of punishment.
I counted the cutoff hands
and the mountains of ash
and the fragmented cries
and the without-eyes glasses
and the headless hair.

Then I searched the world
for those who lost their country,
pointlessly carrying
their defeated little flags,
their Stars of David,
their miserable photographs.

I too knew homelessness.

But as a seasoned wanderer,
I returned empty-handed
to this sea that knows me well.
But others remain
and are still at bay,
leaving behind their loved ones, their errors,

thinking maybe
but knowing never again
and this is how I ended up sobbing
the dusty sob
intoned by the homeless.
This is the way I ended celebrating
with my brothers (those who remain)
the victorious building,
the harvest of new bread.

ILAN STAVANS

from

SEAQUAKE

MAREMOTO

❋

1968

MAREMOTO

Los relojes del mar,
las alcachofas,
las alcancías con sus llamaradas,
los bolsillos del mar
a manos llenas,
las lámparas del agua,
los zapatos, las botas
del océano,
los cefalópodos, las holoturias,
los recalcitrantes cangrejos,
ciertos peces que nadan y suspiran,
los erizos que salen
de los castaños del profundo mar,
los paraguas azules del océano,
los telegramas rotos,
el vals sobre las olas,
todo me lo regala el maremoto.

Las olas regresaron a la Biblia:
hoja por hoja el agua se cerró:
volvió al centro del mar toda la cólera,
pero entre ceja y ceja me quedaron
los variados e inútiles tesoros
que me dejó su amor desmantelado
y su rosa sombría.

Toquen este producto:
aquí mis manos trabajaron
diminutos sarcófagos de sal
destinados a seres y substancias,
feroces en su cárdena belleza,
en sus estigmas calcáreos,
fugaces
porque se alimentarán
nosotros y otros seres
de tanta flor y luz devoradoras.

Lo que dejó en la puerta el maremoto,
la frágil fuerza, el ojo submarino,
los animales ciegos de la ola,
me inducen al conflicto,
al ven y ven y aléjate, oh tormento,
a mi marea oculta por el mar.

Mariscos resbalados en la arena,
brazos resbaladizos,
estómagos del agua,
armaduras abiertas a la entrada
de la repetición y el movimiento,
púas, ventosas, lenguas,
pequeños cuerpos fríos,
maltratados
por la implacable eternidad del agua,
por la ira del viento.

Ser y no ser aquí se amalgamaron
en radiantes y hambrientas estructuras:
arde la vida y sale
a pasear un relámpago la muerte.
Yo sólo soy testigo
de la electricidad y la hermosura
que llenan el sosiego devorante.

SEAQUAKE

The clocks of the sea,
the artichokes,
the blazing money boxes,
the pockets of the sea
full of hands,
the lamps of water,
the shoes and boots
of the ocean,
the mollusks, the sea cucumbers,

the defiant crabs,
certain fish that swim and sigh,
the sea urchins that exit,
the deep sea's chestnuts,
the ocean's azure umbrellas,
the broken telegrams,
the waltz over the waves,
the seaquake gives all of this to me.

The waves returned to the Bible:
page by page the water closed:
all anger returned to the sea's center,
but between my eyes what remains
are the varied and useless treasures
that the sea left me, the ocean's dismantled love
and shadowy rose.

Touch this harvest:
here my hands worked
the diminutive tombs of salt
destined for being and substances,
ferocious in their livid beauty
in their limestone stigmas,
fugitives,
because they will feed us
and other beings
with so much flowering and devouring light.

What the seaquake left at the door,
the fragile force, the submarine eye,
the blind animals of the wave,
push me into the conflict,
Come! And come! Bid farewell! Oh tempest,
to my tide hidden by the sea.

Cockles spilled on the sand,
slippery arms,
stomachs of water,
armor open at the entrance

of the repetition and the movement,
quills, suction cups, tongues,
little cold bodies,
abused
by the implacable eternity of water,
by the wind's anger.

Here, being and not being were combined
in radiant and hungry structures:
life burns and death passes,
like a flash of lightning.
I am the only witness
to the electricity and the splendor
that fills the devouring calmness.

MARÍA JACKETTI AND DENNIS MALONEY

STARFISH

When the stars in the sky
ignore the firmament
and go off to sleep by day,
the stars of the water greet
the sky buried in the sea
inaugurating the duties
of the new undersea heavens.

MARÍA JACKETTI AND DENNIS MALONEY

JAIVA

The violet-colored crab
lurks in the corner of the sea:
its pincers are the two enigmas:
its appetite is an abyss.

Later its armor agonizes
in a hellish bowl
and now it is nothing more than a rose:
the delectable red rose.

MARÍA JACKETTI AND DENNIS MALONEY

FAREWELL TO THE OFFERINGS OF THE SEA

Return, return to the sea
from these pages!

Fishes, mollusks, seaweed,
escapees from the cold,
return to the waist
of the Pacific,
to the giddy kiss
of the wave, to the secret
logic of rock.

Oh hidden ones,
naked ones, submerged ones,
slippery ones,
it is the time
of division and separation:
paper reclaims me,
the ink, the inkwells,
the printing presses, the letters,
the illustrations,
the characters and numbers
jumbled in riverbeds from
where
they ambush me: the women,
and the men
want my love, ask for my company,
the children from Petorca,
from Atacama, from Arauco,

from Loncoche,
also want to play with the poet!

A train waits for me, a ship
loaded with apples,
an airplane, a plow
some thorns.
Goodbye, harvested
fruits of the water, farewell,
imperially dressed
shrimps,
I will return, we will return
to the unity
now interrupted.
I belong to the sand:
I will return to the round sea
and to its flora
and to its fury:
but for now—I'll wander
whistling
through the streets.

MARÍA JACKETTI AND DENNIS MALONEY

from

STILL ANOTHER

DAY

AÚN

❋

1969

VI

Pardon me, if when I want
to tell the story of my life
it's the land I talk about.
This is the land.
It grows in your blood
and you grow.
If it dies in your blood
you die out.

WILLIAM O'DALY

VII

Yumbel!
Yumbel! Yumbel!
From where does your name
come out into the sunshine?
Why does the light
ring in your name?
Why, in the morning
does your name, like the rim of a wheel,
come sounding from the blacksmiths' shops?

WILLIAM O'DALY

XII

Cold tower of the world,
volcano, finger of snow
that followed me through all I did:
the topmast high above my ship
and yet O stunned spring,
intermittent traveler,
in the spider's nest
of Buenos Aires, far

from where I grew up,
where I became me,
in Katiabar, in Sandokán, in Prague,
in Mollendo, in Toledo, in Guayaquil,
with my volcano on my back,
with my snow,
with southern fire and calcified night,
with volcanic tongues, with slow lava
devouring the star.
Igneous debtor, companion of snow,
where I went with me
I went with you,
tower of the secret icehouses,
factory of the patriarchal flames.

WILLIAM O'DALY

XVII

Fue temblorosa la noche de septiembre.
Yo traía en mi ropa
la tristeza del tren que me traía
cruzando una por una las provincias:
yo era ese ser remoto
turbado por el humo del carbón
de la locomotora.
Yo no era.
Tuve que ver entonces con la vida.
Mi poesía me incomunicaba
y me agregaba a todos.
Aquella noche a mí
me tocó declarar la Primavera.
A mí, pobre sombrío,
me hicieron desatar la vestimenta
de la noche desnuda.
Temblé leyendo ante dos mil orejas desiguales
mi canto.
La noche ardió

con todo el fuego oscuro
que se multiplicaba en la ciudad,
en la urgencia imperiosa del contacto.

Murió la soledad aquella vez?
O nací entonces, de mi soledad?

XVII

The September night was trembling.
I carried in my clothes
the sadness of the train that carried me
across the provinces one by one:
I was that distant being
sickened by the carbon fumes
of the locomotive.
I didn't exist, yet.
I had something to discover.
My poetry isolated me
and joined me to everyone.
That night I would
have declared Spring.
A sad beggar,
I was made to untie the vestment
of the naked night.
I trembled reading my song before two thousand
uneven ears.
The night burned
with all the dark fire
that multiplied in the city,
in the urgent need of contact.

Did the loneliness die that night?
Or was I born then, of my solitude?

WILLIAM O'DALY

XX

I have seen other things, perhaps nothing, purple
countries, estuaries that carried from the womb
of the land, the seminal odor of origin,
iron rust countries with caves of diamonds
(the city of Bolívar, there in the Orinoco)
and I was in another kingdom, of the color of amaranth
where men and women all were kings and queens
the color of amaranth.

WILLIAM O'DALY

XXVIII

So long, visitor.
Good day.
My poem happened
for you, for nobody,
for everyone.

I beg you: leave me restless.
I live with the impossible ocean
and silence bleeds me dry.

I die with each wave each day.
I die with each day in each wave.
But the day does not die—
not ever.
It does not die.
And the wave?
It does not die.

Gracias.

WILLIAM O'DALY

from

THE FLAMING

SWORD

LA ESPADA

ENCENDIDA

❋

1969–1970

XVIII
SOMEONE

It moved. It was a man,
the primal man.
His eyes were made for him to defend himself.
His hands were made for him to defend himself.
His brain was made for him to defend himself.
Soon his guts were added
for him to save himself.

He trembled, alone,
between light and darkness.

Something fell like a barren fruit,
something darted in the sun like a lizard before him.
His legs were made for him to escape,
but new threats appeared.

He was so afraid, he found a woman.
She was like a hedgehog, like a chestnut.
She was an edible being,
but man needed her.
The two were unique,
reborn from the earth
and fated for love or destruction.

ILAN STAVANS

from

STONES FROM
THE SKY

LAS PIEDRAS DEL

CIELO

❋

1970

To harden the earth
the rocks took charge:
instantly
they grew wings:
the rocks
that soared:
the survivors
flew up
the lightning bolt,
screamed in the night,
a watermark,
a violet sword,
a meteor.

The succulent
sky
had not only clouds,
not only space smelling of oxygen,
but an earthly stone
flashing here and there
changed into a dove,
changed into a bell,
into immensity, into a piercing
wind:
      into a phosphorescent arrow,
      into salt of the sky.

JAMES NOLAN

II

Quartz opens its eyes in the snow
and grows spiky,
slipping on the white
into its own whiteness:
multiplying the mirrors

it poses in facets, at angles:
white sea urchin
from the depths,
it is son of the salt
that shoots up to heaven,
glacial orange blossom
of silence,
very principle of foam:

by virtue of the earth's pride
the clarity that awaits me.

JAMES NOLAN

V

(What happened to me in Colombia, a country well known for its exquisite emeralds, is hard to say. It came about that there they looked for one for me, they found and cut it and the fingers of all the poets lifted it up to offer me, and at the very height of the hands of all the gathered poets, my heavenly stone, my emerald ascended, slipping up into the air during a storm that shook us with fear. Now in that country the butterflies, especially the ones from the province of Muzo, shine with indescribable brilliance, and on this occasion, after the emerald's ascension and the end of the storm, the space filled with shimmering blue butterflies, eclipsing the sun and wrapping it in huge branches of leaves, as though suddenly in the midst of us, the astonished poets, there had sprouted an enormous blue tree.

This event took place in Colombia, in the province of Charaquira, in October of 194— ... I never recovered the emerald.)

JAMES NOLAN

XI

Del estallido a la ruptura férrea,
de la grieta al camino,
del sismo al fuego, al rodamiento, al río,
se quedó inmóvil aquel corazón
de agua celeste, de oro,
y cada veta de jaspe o sulfuro
fue un movimiento, un ala,
una gota de fuego o de rocío.

Sin mover o crecer vive la piedra?

Tiene labios el ágata marina?

No contestaré yo porque no puedo:
así fue el turbulento génesis
de las piedras ardientes y crecientes
que viven desde entonces en el frío.

XI

From the explosion to the iron split,
from the crevice to the road,
from the quake to the fire,
to the turning, to the river,
that heart of sky-water, heart of gold
stayed still
and each vein of jasper or sulfur
was a rush, was a wing,
was a drop of fire or of dew.

Does the rock live without moving or growing?

Does the marine agate really have lips?

I will not answer because I cannot:
so it was, the churning genesis
of glowing and growing stones
that live on, ever since, in the cold.

JAMES NOLAN

XIII

The lichen on the stone, mesh
of green elastic, enmeshes
the primal hieroglyph,
stretches the scripture
of the sea
around the round rock.
The sun reads it, barnacles fade it,
and from stone to stone
the fish slither by like shivers.
Silently the alphabet goes on
spelling out its sunken syllables
along the immaculate hip of the coast.

On his loom the moss weaver
goes back and forth, higher and higher,
carpeting the caverns of air and water
so that no one dances but the wave
and nothing follows but the wind.

JAMES NOLAN

XV

You should comb over the shore
of Lake Tragosoldo in Antiñana
early, when the dew's still
trembling on the hard cinnamon leaves,
and gather up the damp stones,

lakeside grapes of jasper,
of blazing cobblestone,
little purple pebbles
or rock honeycombs bored out
by volcanoes or bad weather,
by the wind's snout.

Yes, the oblong chrysolite
or the Ethiopian basalt
or the massive map
of the granite
waits for you there, but no one comes
but the anonymous fisherman sunk
in his quivering trade.

Only I keep, sometimes
in the morning,
this appointment with slippery stones,
soaked, crystalline, ashen,
and with hands full
of burnt-out fires,
of secret structures,
of clear almonds
I go back to my family,
to my obligations,
more ignorant than the day I was born,
more simple each day,
each stone.

JAMES NOLAN

XIX

Silence is intensified
into a stone:
broken circles are closed:
the trembling world,
wars, birds, houses,

cities, trains, woods,
the wave that repeats the sea's questions,
the unending passage of dawn,
all arrive at stone, sky nut:
a substantial witness.

The dusty stone on the road
knows Pedro, and his father before,
knows the water from which he was born:
it is the mute word of earth:
it says nothing because it's the heir
of the silence before, of the motionless ocean,
of the empty land.

The stone was there before the wind,
before the man, before the dawn:
its first movement
was the first music of the river.

JAMES NOLAN

XXIII

I am this naked
mineral:
echo of underneath:
I am happy
to have come so far,
from so much earth:
I am the last one, barely
guts, body, hands
that split off
from the motherlode
without knowing why,
without hope of staying,
resigned to this flighty human
fated to live and drop like a leaf.

Ah this destiny
of the darkening incessancy,
of being your own—unsculptured granite,
sheer bulk, irreducible, cold:
I was rock, dark rock
and the parting was violent,
a gash of an alien birth:
I want to go back
to that sure thing,
to home base, to the middle
of the stone mother
from which, I don't know how or when,
I was torn away to be torn apart.

JAMES NOLAN

XXVIII

El cuadrado al cristal llega cayendo
desde su simetría:
aquel que abre las puertas de la tierra
halla en la oscuridad, claro y completo,
la luz de este sistema transparente.

El cubo de la sal, los triangulares
dedos del cuarzo: el agua lineal
de los diamantes: el laberinto
del azufre y su gótico esplendor:
adentro de la nuez de la amatista
la multiplicación de los rectángulos:
todo esto hallé debajo de la tierra:
geometría enterrada:
escuela de la sal: orden del fuego.

XXVIII

The square arrives at the crystal tipping
over from its symmetry:
whoever swings open the doors of the earth
finds in the darkness, clear and complete,
the light of this lucid system.

The salt cube, the triangular
fingers of quartz: the aligned water
of diamonds: the network
of sulfur and its gothic glory:
the multiplication of rectangles
inside the kernel of amethyst:
all this I found under the earth:
buried geometry:
school of salt:
          formula of fire.

JAMES NOLAN

from

BARREN

TERRAIN

GEOGRAFÍA

INFRUCTUOSA

1969–1972

NUMBERED

Today is the twenty-seventh, a twenty-seventh.

Who numbered the days?

What is this about?

I
ask
in this world, on this earth, in this
century, in this time,
in this numerical life, why,
why were we ordered, reduced
to quantities?
Why was daylight divided,
the winter rain,
the bread baked under the sun every summer,
seeds, trains,
silence,
death with its numbered houses
in the immense white cemeteries,
streets in rows?
Each of us by number,
shriek not only those in charge
of camps and ovens,
but also the fleshy,
unavoidable brunettes
and sugar-coated blondes:
we are rolled into numbers
and soon fall off a list
into oblivion.
My name is three-hundred,
forty-six, or seven.
Humbly I keep my books
until I get to zero, and I'm gone.

ILAN STAVANS

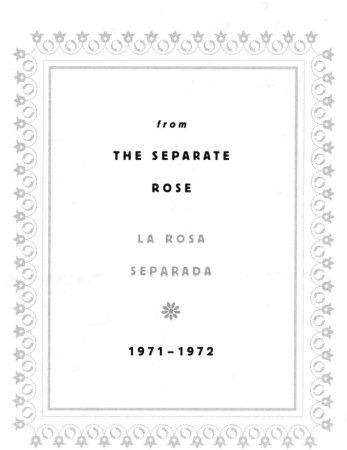

from

THE SEPARATE

ROSE

LA ROSA

SEPARADA

❋

1971–1972

MEN II

The truth is in the prologue. Death to the romantic fool,
to the expert in solitary confinement,
I'm the same as the teacher from Columbia,
the Rotarian from Philadelphia, the merchant
from Paysandú who saved his silver
to come here. We all arrive by different streets,
by unequal languages, at Silence.

WILLIAM O'DALY

MEN IX

They taught us to respect the church,
not to cough, not to spit in the atrium,
not to wash our clothes upon the altar,
but it's not so: life tears apart religions,
and on this island the Wind God inhabits
the only church living and true:
our lives come and go, dying, making love:
here on Easter Island where everything is altar,
where everything is a workroom for the unknown,
a woman nurses her newborn
upon the same steps that her gods tread.

Here, they live! But do we?
We transients, followers of the wrong star,
were shipwrecked on this island as in a lagoon,
like in a lake in which all distances end,
on a motionless journey, so difficult for men.

WILLIAM O'DALY

MEN X

Yes, soon they'll see where they went wrong, before returning
to the flock, to the hive of sad bees,
these tourists convinced they'll soon be back, the ones
who share the black street and live in houses full of antiques
and garbage pails, stepbrothers
in room thirty-three thousand four hundred twenty-seven,
sixth floor, apartment A, B, or J,
facing the warehouse of Astorquiza, Williams and Company,
yes, my poor brother, we're one and the same,
now that we realize we can never stay
here, not even in jail; as of today we know
that this grandeur is too big for us,
that solitude crowds us like the suit of a little boy
who has grown too fast, or the way
darkness embraces the day.

WILLIAM O'DALY

LOS HOMBRES XI

Se ve que hemos nacido para oírnos y vernos,
para medirnos (cuánto saltamos, cuánto ganamos,
                              ganamos, etcétera),
para ignorarnos (sonriendo), para mentirnos,
para el acuerdo, para la indiferencia o para comer juntos.
Pero que no nos muestre nadie la tierra, adquirimos
olvido, olvido hacia los sueños de aire,
y nos quedó sólo un regusto de sangre y polvo
en la lengua: nos tragamos el recuerdo
entre vino y cerveza, lejos, lejos de aquello,
lejos de aquello, de la madre, de la tierra de la vida.

MEN XI

One can see we were born to hear and see each other,
to compete (how high we jump, how often we win, how much
                    we earn, et cetera),
to ignore each other (smiling), to lie
in order to agree or be indifferent or eat together.
But let no one reveal the world to us, for we acquire
oblivion, nothing but dreams of air,
and all that's left is an aftertaste of blood and dust
on the tongue: we swallow the memory
with wine and beer, so far, far from all that,
from the mother, from the land of our lives.

WILLIAM O'DALY

MEN XIV

Such a long, long way we have to go,
even farther from the stone masks
standing erect, in utter silence, and we'll go
wrapped in their pride, in their distance.

What brought us to the island?
It won't be the smile of flowering men,
or the crackling waist of lovely Ataroa,
or the boys on horseback, with their rude eyes,
that we'll take home with us:
just an oceanic emptiness, a poor question
with a thousand answers on contemptuous lips.

WILLIAM O'DALY

from A CALL FOR THE DESTRUCTION OF NIXON AND PRAISE FOR THE CHILEAN REVOLUTION

INCITACIÓN AL
NIXONICIDIO Y ALABANZA
DE LA REVOLUCIÓN
CHILENA

1972–1973

I BEGIN BY INVOKING WALT WHITMAN

Because I love my country
I claim you, essential brother,
old Walt Whitman with your gray hands,

so that, with your special help
line by line, we will tear out by the roots
and destroy this bloodthirsty President Nixon.

There can be no happy man on earth,
no one can work well on this planet
while that nose continues to breathe in Washington.

Asking the old bard to confer with me
I assume the duties of a poet
armed with a terrorist's sonnet

because I must carry out with no regrets
this sentence, never before witnessed,
of shooting a criminal under siege,

who in spite of his trips to the moon
has killed so many here on earth
that the paper flies up and the pen is unsheathed

to set down the name of this villain
who practices genocide from the White House.

TERESA ANDERSON

I SAY GOODBYE TO OTHER SUBJECTS

Love, goodbye until tomorrow, kisses!
My heart, you will have to hold fast to this duty
because I now declare this trial open.

The question at hand is to be or not to be:
If we let the guilty party live
the people will continue to suffer,

and this criminal of a President
will go on robbing Chile of the copper in her customs houses
and disemboweling the innocent in Vietnam.

We can't wait a week
nor even a single day longer
since it is by means of his inhuman atrocities

that we trap this beetle;
and it is a matter of pride for all the people
who have borne the dagger of the news

like a hard and lasting instrument
announcing justice on earth—
for this reason, comrade, the tribunal

of blood that begins now was looking for you;
and although the harsh judge be a poet
the people gave me a rose

so that with my true verse
I can punish the powerful rage
of the immense executioner, commanded

by money his mistress
to burn down garden and gardener
in remote and golden lands.

TERESA ANDERSON

V

THE JUDGMENT

Summoned by me the entire earth
that fits, as you will see, inside my sonnet

will deliver the judgment of spring,

face to face, looking at your skeleton,
so that never again will any mother

bleed into the razed earth—
carrying in the sun, under the sad moon,
a child whom I raise up like a sword,

sister-comrade, over the neck of Nixon.

TERESA ANDERSON

VII

VICTORY

Honor to the longed-for victory
honor to the people who
have come to the time
of establishing their right to live!

But Nixon, like a mouse used to cheese
and saddened by his losses,
said goodbye to Eduardo Frei with a kiss.

He changed ambassadors, changed spies
and decided to close us in with wire:
They would no longer trade with us

so that Chile would die of hunger.

When the Braden Copper Company
wagged its tail
the lean ones helped with the task

crying "Freedom and Saucepans,"

while the bosses turned into altarboys
painted their ugly faces with kindness

and disguising themselves as proletarians
called for a strike of the owners
receiving money from Nixon:

thirty pieces of silver for the traitors.

TERESA ANDERSON

IX

I CALL UPON YOU

We inherit this from the past
and today the face of Chile is magnified
after leaving behind so many sorrows;

I need you, young brother,
young sister, listen to what I am saying:
I do not believe in inhuman hatred,

I do not believe man is the enemy,
I believe that with your hand and with mine
facing the villain and opposing his punishment

we will fill this country with joy
delicious and golden as wheat.

TERESA ANDERSON

XIII
COME WITH ME

For this reason I am here in your company:
for Chile, for her blue sovereignty,

for the ocean of fishermen,
for copper and the struggles in the office,

for the bread of nightingale children,
for the good companion and woman friend,

for the sea, the rose and ear of grain,
for our forgotten countrymen,

students, sailors, and soldiers,
for the people of every land,

for the bells and the roots,
for the roads and the footpaths
that lead to the light of the whole world

and for the liberating will
of red flags in the dawn.

All my happiness flows from this union.

Fight beside me and I will deliver to you
all the weapons of my poetry.

TERESA ANDERSON

XVIII
PORTRAIT OF THE MAN

It is necessary to judge those hands stained
by the dead he killed with his terror;

the dead from under the beaten earth
are rising up like seeds of sorrow.

Because this is a time never before dreamed of.

And Nixon, the trapped mouse,
his eyes wide with fear,

is watching the rebirth of flags shot down.

He was defeated every day in Vietnam.
In Cuba his rage was dissipated
and now in the buried twilight
this rodent wants to gnaw at Chile
not knowing that Chileans of little importance
are going to give him a lesson in honor.

TERESA ANDERSON

XXV
AGAINST DEATH

As punishment the bitter criminal
is driving us to civil war.
He who was overthrown has his mouth full

yet he wants to steal food from others,
and another, poisoned by his wound,
wants to spread its venom around.

Fratricidal claws want to lead us
into a civil war full of contradictions
without knowing that Chilean adversaries

will always love the laws of life.
And even the strongest and most noble
cannot win by bleeding dry the chosen land

and exchanging life for death.

The earth which gave us happiness
which taught us suffering
will one day bloom with every good thing:

Let us not deny the light to the discontented.
Let each of us bring to our disputes
the best of our knowledge and our time.

TERESA ANDERSON

XXX
MAR Y AMOR DE QUEVEDO

Aquí en mi casa de Isla Negra leo
en el mar y en el verso favorito,
en la palpitación y el centelleo,

del mar amargo y del amor maldito,
la misma espuma de la poesía:
el mar que se ilumina en la ruptura

y yo leyendo con melancolía,
a Quevedo, su amor y desventura.

Tal vez es mi destino diferente:
mi pecho militar de combatiente
me inclinó a las guerrillas del Estado:

a conseguir con la paciencia ardiente

de la verdad y del proletariado

el Estatuto de la pobre gente.

THE SEA AND THE LOVE OF QUEVEDO

Here in my house on Isla Negra
in the sea and in my favorite poetry,
in the throbbing and the scintillations

of the bitter sea and ill-starred love,
the same foam of poetry:
the sea which is illuminated by its rupture

and me reading with sadness
of Quevedo's love and misfortune.

Perhaps my destiny is different:
My militant fighter's chest
moved me toward guerrillas in the government

to gain with the ardent patience
of truth and the working class

the Law of the poor.

TERESA ANDERSON

XXXII
SEPTEMBER 4, 1970

A memory: Finally there is unity!
Long live Chile: Joy and Alleluia!
Long live copper, wine, and nitrate.

Long live unity and tenacity.
Yes, sir! Chile has a candidate.
It was hard work, it was a dream,

until today when the struggle was understood.

To march, to march like the light of day.

The President *is Salvador Allende.*

All victory is chilling,
because when the people win, a gust of wind
enters the envious through the backs of their heads.

(One rises, and the other goes down into his cave
fleeing from time and history.)

As long as Allende is rising to victory
the Fascists will run away like cockroaches.

TERESA ANDERSON

from

THE SEA
AND THE BELLS

EL MAR

Y LAS CAMPANAS

1971–1973

BUSCAR

Del ditirambo a la raíz del mar
se extiende un nuevo tipo de vacío:
no quiero más, dice la ola,
que no sigan hablando,
que no siga creciendo
la barba del cemento
en la ciudad:
estamos solos,
queremos gritar por fin,
orinar frente al mar,
ver siete pájaros del mismo color,
tres mil gaviotas verdes,
buscar el amor en la arena,
ensuciar los zapatos,
los libros, el sombrero, el pensamiento
hasta encontrarte, nada,
hasta besarte, nada,
hasta cantarte, nada,
nada sin nada, sin hacer
nada, sin terminar
lo verdadero.

TO SEARCH

From the dithyramb to the root of the sea
stretches a new kind of emptiness:
I don't want much, the wave says,
only for them to stop their chatter,
for the city's cement beard
to stop growing:
we are alone,
we want at last to scream,
to pee facing the ocean,
to see seven birds of the same color,
three thousand green gulls,

to seek out love on the sand,
to break in our shoes, to dirty
our books, our hat, our mind
until we find you, nothing,
until we kiss you, nothing,
until we sing you, nothing,
nothing without nothing, without being
nothing, without putting an end
to truth.

WILLIAM O'DALY

I AM GRATEFUL

I am grateful, violins, for this day
of four chords. Pure
is the sound of the sky,
the blue voice of air.

WILLIAM O'DALY

MY NAME WAS REYES

My name was Reyes, Catrileo,
Arellano, Rodríguez, I have forgotten
my true names.
I was born with a surname
of old oaks, of saplings,
of hissing wood.
I was deposited
among rotting leaves:
this newborn sank down
in the defeat and in the birth
of forests that were falling
and poor houses that had recently been weeping.
I was not born but rather they founded me:
all at once they gave me every name,

every family's name:
I was called thicket, then plum tree,
larch and then wheat,
that is why I am so much and so little,
so wealthy and so destitute,
because I come from below,
from the earth.

WILLIAM O'DALY

I WILL TELL YOU

I will tell you that I lived in a city
on a certain street called Capitán,
that street was jammed with people,
shoe shops, liquor stores,
department stores filled with rubies.
You were not able to come or go,
everywhere there were people
eating or spitting or breathing,
buying and selling clothes.
It all seemed to glitter,
everything was glowing
and everything resounded,
enough to blind or deafen.
A long time has passed since this street,
it's been a long time since I've heard anything,
I changed my life, I live among stones
and the movement of water.
Maybe that street died
a natural death.

WILLIAM O'DALY

A SMALL ANIMAL

A small animal,
pig, bird, or dog,
defenseless,
gristled with feathers or fur,
I heard it all night,
fevered, howling.

It was a vast night
and in Isla Negra, the sea,
all of its thunder, its floating hardware,
its tons of salt, its glass broken
against the immobile rock,
the sea shuddered.

The silence was clear and fierce
after every bolt or shower.

My sleep was stitched
by the spinning of the interrupted night
and then the small, shaggy being,
small bear or sick child,
suffered asphyxia or fever,
little bonfire of sadness, a cry
against the immense night of the ocean,
against the black tower of silence,
wounded animal,
so small,
barely whispering
beneath the emptiness of night,
alone.

WILLIAM O'DALY

IT RAINS

It rains
over the sand, over the roof
the theme
of the rain:
the long Ls of rain fall slowly
over the pages
of my everlasting love,
this salt of every day:
rain, return to your old nest,
return with your needles to the past:
today I long for the whitest space,
winter's whiteness for a branch
of green rosebush and golden roses:
something of infinite spring
that today was waiting, under a cloudless sky
and whiteness was waiting,
when the rain returned
to sadly drum
against the window,
then to dance with unmeasured fury
over my heart and over the roof,
reclaiming
its place,
asking me for a cup
to fill once more with needles,
with transparent time,
with tears.

WILLIAM O'DALY

THIS BROKEN BELL

This broken bell
still wants to sing:
the metal now is green,
the color of woods, this bell,

color of water in stone pools in the forest,
color of day in the leaves.

The bronze cracked and green,
the bell with its mouth open to the ground
and sleeping
was entangled in bindweed,
and the hard golden color of the bronze
turned the color of a frog:
it was the hands of water,
the dampness of the coast,
dealt green to the metal
and tenderness to the bell.

This broken bell
miserable in the rude thicket
of my wild garden,
green bell, wounded,
its scars immersed in the grass:
it calls to no one anymore, no one gathers
around its green goblet
except one butterfly that flutters
over the fallen metal and flies off, escaping
on yellow wings.

WILLIAM O'DALY

from

2000

2000

❋

1971

I

THE MASKS

Pity on these centuries and their happy
or battered survivors, what we did not do
was the fault of no one, steel was missing:
we exhausted it on so much useless destruction,
but none of this matters in the balance:
the years suffered from oozing sores and wars,
years grown weak when hope trembled
at the bottom of the enemy's bottles.
Very well, we will talk sometime, more than once,
with a swallow so that no one can listen:
I am ashamed, we possess the humble decency of widows:
truth died and rotted in so many graves:
it is best to remember what is going to happen:
in this nuptial year there are no defeated ones:
let each one of us put on victorious masks.

RICHARD SCHAAF

IV

LA TIERRA

Amarillo, amarillo sigue siendo
el perro que detrás del otoño circula
haciendo entre las hojas circunferencias de oro,
ladrando hacia los días desconocidos.

Así veréis lo imprevisto de ciertas situaciones:
junto al explorador de las terribles fronteras
que abren el infinito, he aquí el predilecto,
el animal perdido del otoño.
Qué puede cambiar de tierra a tiempo, de sabor a estribor,
de luz velocidad a circunstancia terrestre?
Quién adivinará la semilla en la sombra
si como cabelleras las mismas arboledas

dejan caer rocío sobre las mismas herraduras,
sobre las cabezas que reúne el amor,
sobre las cenizas de corazones muertos?

Este mismo planeta, la alfombra de mil años,
puede florecer pero no acepta la muerte ni el reposo:
las cíclicas cerraduras de la fertilidad
se abren en cada primavera para las llaves del sol
y resuenan los frutos haciéndose cascada,
sube y baja el fulgor de la tierra a la boca
y el humano agradece la bondad de su reino.

Alabada sea la vieja tierra color de excremento,
sus cavidades, sus ovarios sacrosantos,
las bodegas de la sabiduría que encerraron
cobre, petróleo, imanes, ferreterías, pureza,
el relámpago que parecía bajar desde el infierno
fue atesorado por la antigua madre de las raíces
y cada día salió el pan a saludarnos
sin importarle la sangre y la muerte que vestimos los hombres,
la maldita progenie que hace la luz del mundo.

THE EARTH

The dog that backtracks in autumn,
tracing golden circumferences among the leaves,
barking toward unknown days, continues being yellow, yellow.

So shall you see the unforeseen in certain situations:
beside the explorer of terrible frontiers
that open to the infinite, here is my dog:
autumn's stray animal.
How can one move from earth to time, from a savor to starboard,
from the speed of light to earthly circumstance?
Who in the darkness will divine the seed
if, like strands of hair, the leafy groves
let fall dew on horseshoes,

on heads that love unites,
on the ashes of worn-out hearts?

This planet, carpet thousands of years old,
shall flourish but it does not accept death nor repose:
each spring the sun's keys open
fertility's cyclical locks,
and cascading bunches of fruit resound,
the earth's splendor rises and falls to the mouth
and humankind is thankful for the goodness of its kingdom.

Praised be the old land the color of excrement,
her cavities, her sacrosanct ovaries,
the storehouses of wisdom that contained
copper, oil, magnets, ironworks, purity.
The lightning bolt that seemed to fall from hell
was hoarded by the ancient mother of roots
and each day bread came out to greet us,
unperturbed by the blood and death we humans wear,
the accursed progeny who deliver light unto the world.

RICHARD SCHAAF

IX
CELEBRATION

Let us put on our shoes, the pin-striped shirt,
the blue suit though it shines from long wear,
let us light the flares and set off fireworks,
let the wine and beer flow from our necks to our toes,
because duly we must celebrate
this immense number that cost so much time,
so many years and days in bundles,
so many hours, so many millions of minutes:
let us celebrate this inauguration.

Let us uncork all our bottled up happiness
and seek out some lost sweetheart

who accepts a festive nibble.
It is today. Today has arrived. Let us walk on the rug
of the inquiring millennium. The heart, the almond
of the mounting epoch, the definitive grape
will go on depositing themselves in us,
and truth—so long awaited—will arrive.

Meanwhile, one leaf of foliage
advances the beginning of the Age:
branch by branch the trees will intertwine,
leaf by leaf the days will mount up,
and fruit by fruit peace will arrive:
the tree of happiness is prepared
from the struggling bloodroot that survives
searching for water, truth, life.

Today is today. Tomorrow has arrived
prepared through much darkness:
still we don't know if this newly
inaugurated world is bright:
let us brighten it, let us darken it
till it is golden and burnt
like hardened grains of corn:
that each one, the newborns,
the survivors, the blind,
the mute, the maimed and crippled,
may see and may speak,
that they may survive and wander freely,
that they may seize hold of the future fruit
born of the present kingdom that we leave open
as much to the explorer as to the queen,
as much to the inquisitive cosmonaut
as to the traditional farmer,
to the bees that now arrive
to participate in the work of the hive
and, above all, to the peoples newly arrived,
to the peoples increasing from now on
with new flags that were born
in each drop of blood or sweat.

Today is today and yesterday passed, this is certain.

Today is also tomorrow, and I left
with some cold year that passed,
that year left with me and took me with it.

About this there can be no doubt. My skeleton
consisted, at times, in words hard
as bones exposed to the air and rain,
and I was able to celebrate what is happening
leaving behind instead of a song or testimony
a stubborn, enduring skeleton of words.

RICHARD SCHAAF

from

ELEGY

ELEGÍA

❋

1971–1972

XIV

Yevtushenko is a lunatic,
a clown—
so people say with tight mouth.
Come, Yevtushenko!
Let's not talk any more,
since before birth we already said
everything there is to say.
In your poetry
there are fresh rays of moonlight,
electronic petals,
locomotives,
tears,
and, every so often, a welcome!
Arriba! Abajo!
Your pirouettes, your high-minded acrobatics—
why shouldn't you be a clown?

We need another Napoleon
in the world—a battleground clown,
lost later on in the snow;
a Picasso—a cosmic clown,
dancing on the altars
where miracles are performed;
and a Columbus—the rueful clown,
humiliated, clueless,
who found us centuries since.

Only the poet won't be left alone.
They want to take his pirouettes away,
his mortal jump.

Adelante, Yevtushenko!
I'll protect you
against the new Philistines.
Let the circus admire
our own dexterity, our sadness,
the pleasure to be found in playing with light,

so that truth may thunder
between shadows.
Hurrah!
Turn on the lights,
Let's be onstage,
the audience will witness
two joyful birds
ready to mourn humanity.

ILAN STAVANS

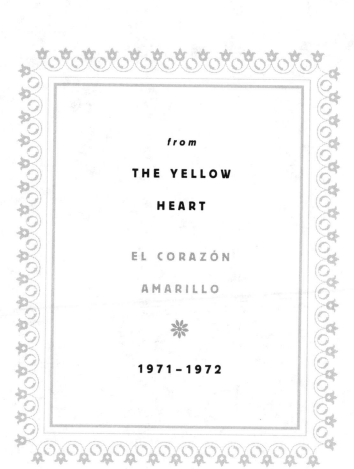

from

THE YELLOW

HEART

EL CORAZÓN

AMARILLO

❋

1971–1972

I STILL GET AROUND

Now and then, I am happy!
I stated before a wise man
who without passion examined me
and pointed out my shortcomings.

Maybe I never found salvation
for my crooked teeth,
each hair on my head
lost its way and fell:
it was better not to argue
the trouble with my cavernous trachea:
as for the rivers in my heart,
they were full of warnings
just as my gloomy liver
that didn't serve as a shield
or this conspiring kidney.
With my saddened prostate
and sudden urges of my urethra,
everything slowly led me
to a final diagnosis.

Staring that sage in the eye
I decided not to succumb
and showed him I was able to see,
to touch, to hear and endure
at the next opportunity.
And so he'd leave me the pleasure
of being loved and of loving:
I sought one love or another
for a month or for a week
or for the next-to-last day.

The wise and contemptuous man
watched me with the indifference
that camels have for the moon
and decided in his pride
to forget my entire organism.

Since then I've never been sure
whether I should obey
his decree of death
or feel as well as my body
tells me that I do.

And confused, I couldn't decide
whether to seriously meditate
or feed myself on carnations.

WILLIAM O'DALY

LOVE SONG

I love you, I love you, is my song
and here my silliness begins.

I love you, I love you my lung,
I love you, I love you my wild grapevine,
and if love is like wine:
you are my predilection
from your hands to your feet:
you are the wineglass of hereafter
and my bottle of destiny.

I love you forwards and backwards,
and I don't have the tone or timbre
to sing you my song,
my endless song.

On my violin that sings out of tune
my violin declares,
I love you, I love you my double bass,
my sweet woman, dark and clear,
my heart, my teeth,
my light and my spoon,
my salt of the dim week,
my clear windowpane moon.

WILLIAM O'DALY

REJECT THE LIGHTNING

Lightning, you committed me
to the slow pace of my work:
with the warning at equinox
of your phosphoric threat
I gathered up my choices,
renounced what wasn't mine
and found at my feet and with my eyes
the abundances of autumn.

The flash taught me to be calm,
not to lose light in the sky,
to search inside of myself
for the galleries of Earth,
to dig in the hard ground
until finding in that hardness
the same site, in its agony,
the meteor was seeking.

I learned the velocity
needed to leave it in space,
and to study my slowness
I formed a frivolous school
like a coterie of fishes
whose daily glide and turn
develops between threats.
This is the style of down below,
of the manifesto under the sea.

And I do not believe that I'll ignore it
because of some damned law:
each with its flashing signal,
with what it had in the world,
and I turn toward my truth
because I am lacking a lie.

WILLIAM O'DALY

When I arrived in Curacautín
it was raining ash
because the volcanoes willed it.

I had to detour to Talca
where they had grown so wide,
those tranquil rivers of Maule,
that I fell asleep on a boat
and went to Valparaíso.

In Valparaíso the houses
were falling around me
and I ate breakfast in the wreckage
of my lost library
between a surviving Baudelaire
and a dismantled Cervantes.

In Santiago the elections
expelled me from the city:
everybody spit in each other's faces
and according to the reporters,
the righteous were in the sky,
and in the streets, assassins.

I made my bed next to a river
that carried more stones than water,
next to some serene oaks,
far from every city,
next to stones that were singing,
and finally I was able to sleep in peace
in certain terror of a star
that was watching me and winking
with a certain malignant insistence.

But the gentle morning
painted the black night blue
and the enemy stars

were swallowed by light
while I sang peacefully
with no catastrophe and no guitar.

WILLIAM O'DALY

MORNING WITH AIR

Prisoner of the outdoors,
a man rolls by at midmorning
like a crystalline globe.
What can he understand or know
if he's caught like a fish
between space and silence,
if innocent bushes
hide flies of evil from him?

It is my duty as a priest,
as a penitent geographer,
as a swindled naturalist,
to open the traveler's eyes:

I halt in the middle of the street
and stop his bicycle:

Have you forgotten, I ask him, villain,
know-nothing full of oxygen,
the hovel of misfortune
and the humiliated corners?

You ignore that, there with a dagger,
here with a club and a thrown stone,
farther away with a black revolver
and in Chicago with a fork
vermin are assassinated,
doves are torn apart
and watermelons have their throats cut?

Be ashamed of oxygen,
I told the surprised traveler,
nobody has the right to surrender his life
to one single clarity.

We need to enter the dark house,
the alley of death,
to touch the blood and the terror,
to share the horrific evil.

The wanderer nailed me
with his two confused eyes
and he moved away in the sunlight
without responding or understanding.

And he left me—poor me—
talking to myself in the street.

WILLIAM O'DALY

EL TIEMPO QUE NO SE PERDIÓ

No se cuentan las ilusiones
ni las comprensiones amargas,
no hay medida para contar
lo que no podría pasarnos,
lo que rondó como abejorro
sin que no nos diéramos cuenta
de lo que estábamos perdiendo.

Perder hasta perder la vida
es vivir la vida y la muerte
y no son cosas pasajeras
sino constantes evidentes
la continuidad del vacío,
el silencio en que cae todo
y por fin nosotros caemos.

Ay! lo que estuvo tan cerca
sin que pudiéramos saber.
Ay! lo que no podía ser
cuando tal vez podía ser.

Tantas alas circunvolaron
las montañas de la tristeza
y tantas ruedas sacudieron
la carretera del destino
que ya no hay nada que perder.

Se terminaron los lamentos.

TIME THAT WASN'T LOST

One doesn't count illusions
nor bitter realizations,
no measure exists to count
what couldn't happen for us,
what circled like a bumblebee,
without our not noticing
what we were losing.

To lose until we lose our life
is to live our life and our death,
and nothing that passes on exists
that doesn't give constant proof
of the continuous emptiness of all,
the silence into which everything falls
and, finally, we fall.

O! what came so close
that we were never able to know.
O! what was never able to be
that maybe could have been.

So many wings flew around
the mountains of sorrow
and so many wheels beat
the highway of our destiny,
we had nothing left to lose.

And our weeping ended.

WILLIAM O'DALY

SUBURBS

I celebrate the virtues and vices
of suburban middle-class people
who overwhelm the refrigerator
and position colorful umbrellas
near the garden that longs for a pool:
for my middle-class brother
this principle of supreme luxury:
what are you and what am I, and we go on deciding
the real truth in this world.

The truth of that dream we buy on credit
of not going to the office on Saturday, at last,
and the merciless bosses whom the worker
manufacturers in indivisible granaries
where executioners were always born
and grow up and always multiply.

We, heroes and poor devils,
the feeble, the braggarts, the unfinished,
and capable of everything impossible
as long as it's not seen or heard,
Don Juans, women and men, who come and go
with the fleeting passage of a runner
or of a shy hotel for travelers.
And we with our small vanities,
our controlled hunger for climbing

and getting as far as everybody else has gotten
because it seems that is the way of the world:
an endless track of champions
and in a corner we, forgotten
maybe because of everybody else,
since they seemed so much like us
until they were robbed of their laurels,
their medals, their titles, their names.

WILLIAM O'DALY

from

WINTER GARDEN

JARDÍN DE INVIERNO

1971–1973

Nobody is missing from the garden. Nobody is here:
only the green and black winter, the day
waking from sleep like a ghost,
a white phantom in cold garments
climbing the steps of a castle. It's an hour
when no one should arrive. Just a few drops
of chilly dew keep falling
from the bare branches of winter
and you and I in this circle of solitude,
invincible and alone, waiting
for no one to arrive, no, nobody will come
with a smile or a medal or a budget
to make us an offer or ask for anything.

This is the hour
of fallen leaves, their dust
scattered over the earth, when
they return to the depths of being and not being
and abandon the gold and the greenery,
until they are roots again,
and again, torn down and being born,
they rise up to know the spring.

O heart lost
inside me, in this man's essence,
what bountiful change inhabits you!
I am not the culprit
who has fled or turned himself in:
misery could not exhaust me!
Your own happiness can grow bitter
if you kiss it every day,
and there is no way of freeing oneself
from the sunlight except to die.

What can I do if the star chose me
to flash with lightning, and if the thorn
guided me to the pain of so many others.

What can I do if every movement
of my hand brought me closer to the rose?
Should I beg forgiveness for this winter,
the most distant, the most unattainable
for that man who used to seek out the chill
without anyone suffering because of his happiness?

And if somewhere on those roads:
—distant France, numerals of fog—
I return to the extent of my life:
a lonely garden, a poor district,
and suddenly this day equal to all others
descends the stairs that do not exist
dressed in irresistible purity,
and there is the odor of sharp solitude,
of humidity, of water, of being born again:
what can I do if I breathe my own air,
why will I feel wounded to death?

WILLIAM O'DALY

GAUTAMA CRISTO

Los nombres de Dios y en particular de su representante
llamado Jesús o Cristo, según textos y bocas,
han sido usados, gastados y dejados
a la orilla del río de las vidas
como las conchas vacías de un molusco.

Sin embargo, al tocar estos nombres sagrados
y desangrados, pétalos heridos,
saldos de los océanos del amor y del miedo,
algo aún permanece: un labio de ágata,
una huella irisada que aún tiembla en la luz.

Mientras se usaban los nombres de Dios
por los mejores y por los peores, por los limpios y por los sucios
por los blancos y los negros, por ensangrentados asesinos

y por las víctimas doradas que ardieron en napalm,
mientras Nixon con las manos
de Caín bendecía a sus condenados a muerte,
mientras menos y menores huellas divinas se hallaron en la playa,
los hombres comenzaron a estudiar los colores,
el porvenir de la miel, el signo del uranio,
buscaron con desconfianza y esperanza las posibilidades
de matarse y de no matarse, de organizarse en hileras,
de ir más allá, de ilimitarse sin reposo.

Los que cruzamos estas edades con gusto a sangre,
a humo de escombros, a ceniza muerta,
y no fuimos capaces de perder la mirada,
a menudo nos detuvimos en los nombres de Dios,
los levantamos con ternura porque nos recordaban
a los antecesores, a los primeros, a los que interrogaron,
a los que encontraron el himno que los unió en la desdicha
y ahora viendo los fragmentos vacíos donde habitó aquel hombre
sentimos estas suaves sustancias
gastadas, malgastadas por la bondad y por la maldad.

GAUTAMA CHRIST

The names of God and especially of his representative
called Jesus or Christ, according to texts and mouths,
have been used up, worn down, and deposited
on the riverbank of our lives
like empty mollusk shells.

Nevertheless, touching these sacred names
drained of their blood, wounded petals,
balances of the oceans of love and of fear,
we know something endures there: an agate lip,
an iridescent footprint still shimmering in the light.

While the names of God were spoken
by the best and the worst, by the clean and the dirty,

by whites and blacks, by bloodstained assassins
and golden brown victims who blazed with napalm,
while Nixon with the hands
of Cain blessed those he had condemned to death,
when fewer and smaller divine footprints were found on the beach,
men began to examine the colors,
the promise of honey, the symbol for uranium,
with suspicion and hope they studied the possibilities
of killing and not killing each other, of organizing themselves in rows,
of going even further, of making themselves limitless, without rest.

We who live through these ages with their bloody flavor,
the smell of smoking rubble, of dead ash,
we who were not able to forget the sight
have often stopped to think in the names of God,
have raised them up tenderly, because they reminded us
of our ancestors, of the first humans, of those who asked questions,
of those who found the hymn that united them in misery
and now seeing the empty fragments where that man lived
we finger those smooth substances
spent, squandered by good and evil.

WILLIAM O'DALY

MODESTLY

We are supposed to know certain common
virtues, vestments for each day of the week
that we see so often they become invisible
and do not surrender us to the mysterious,
to the fire swallower or the spider woman.

Without doubt I praise the wild excellence,
the old-fashioned reverence, the natural see,
the economy of sublime truths that cling
to rock upon rock in succeeding generations,
like certain mollusks who conquered the sea.

We are all the people, the gray links
of lives that repeat themselves until death,
and we never wear unfitting uniforms, no precise tears:
it's proper that we communicate, have clean love, pure bread,
soccer, side streets with garbage in the doorways,
the dogs with complacent tails, the juice of a lemon
with the arrival of the peaceful fish.

I ask permission to be like everybody else,
like the rest of the world and what's more, like anybody else:
I beg you, with all my heart,
if we are talking about me, since we are talking about me,
please resist blasting the trumpet during my visit
and resign yourselves to my quiet absence.

WILLIAM O'DALY

WITH QUEVEDO, IN SPRINGTIME

Everything has flowered in
these fields, apple trees,
hesitant blues, yellow weeds,
and in green grass the poppies thrive.
The inextinguishable sky, the new air
of each day, the invisible shine within,
that gift of a wide and vast springtime.
But spring hasn't come to my room.
Diseases, dubious kisses,
that stuck like the church's ivy
to the black windows of my life
and love alone is never enough, not even the wild
and expansive fragrance of spring.

And, to you, what can these mean now:
the orgiastic light, the evidence unfolding
like a flower, the green song
in the green leaves, the presence
of the sky with its goblet of freshness?

External spring, do not torment me,
unleashing wine and snow in my arms,
corolla and battered bouquet of sorrow,
just for today give me the sleep of nocturnal
leaves, the night of the dead, the metals, the roots,
and so many extinguished springtimes
that awaken to life every spring.

WILLIAM O'DALY

WINTER GARDEN

Winter arrives. Shining dictation
the wet leaves give me,
dressed in silence and yellow.

I am a book of snow,
a spacious hand, an open meadow,
a circle that waits,
I belong to the earth and its winter.

Earth's rumor grew in the leaves,
soon the wheat flared up
punctuated by red flowers like burns,
then autumn arrived to set down
the wine's scripture:
everything passed, the goblet of summer
was a fleeting sky,
the navigating cloud burned out.

I stood on the balcony dark with mourning,
like yesterday with the ivies of my childhood,
hoping the earth would spread its wings
in my uninhabited love.

I knew the rose would fall
and the pit of the passing peach
would sleep and germinate once more,

and I got drunk on the air
until the whole sea became the night
and the red sky turned to ash.

Now the earth lives
numbing its oldest questions,
the skin of its silence stretched out.
Once more I am the silent one
who came out of the distance
wrapped in cold rain and bells:
I owe to earth's pure death
the will to sprout.

WILLIAM O'DALY

IN MEMORY OF MANUEL AND BENJAMÍN

At the same time, two lives of my career,
two from my quarry, two of my labors,
died within hours of each other:
one shrouded in Santiago, the other in Tacna:
two singular beings who have something in common
now, at long last, because they have died.

The first one was somber and kingly,
harsh, with his rugged character,
and seldom spoke a word:
a hard laborer he kept hands
that were always ready to shape
the stone, to hammer the hot metal.
The other one, restless to know things,
a bird hopping branch to branch in life,
the fire at his center like a beautiful beacon
breaking into intermittent rays of light.
                              Two partisans
following two separate visions:
two lonesome nobles who today came together
for me, at the news of their death.

I loved my two contrary friends
who, with their silence, left me speechless
without knowing what to think or say.

So much searching under the skin
and so much walking among souls and roots,
hour by hour so much pecking at paper.

They are quiet now, settling into
a new sphere of darkness,
one with the rectitude of an oak tree,
the other with his mirror and his illusion:
those two who passed through our lives
chiseling time, untangling, opening
furrows, trailing the just word,
the bread of the word every day.

(Even if they didn't have the time to grow tired,
now quiet and finally solemn,
they enter, pressed together, the vast silence
that will slowly grind down their frames.)

Tears were never invented
for those men.
                    And our words
sound as hollow as a new tomb
in which our footsteps sound out of key,
while they remain there alone,
naturally, as they existed.

WILLIAM O'DALY

ANIMAL OF LIGHT

I am in this endless lack of solitude
an animal of light corralled
by his mistakes and by his foliage:
the forest is wide: here my brother creatures

swarm, back away, or roam around,
while I retreat accompanied
by the escort that time chooses:
waves of the sea, stars of the night.

It is small, it is wide, scarce and is everything.
My eyes from looking into so many eyes
and my mouth from so many kisses,
from having swallowed the smoke
of those trains that vanished:
the old merciless stations
and the dust of countless bookshops,
the man I am, the mortal, weary
of eyes, of kisses, of smoke, of roads,
tired of books thicker than the earth.

And today, deep in the lost forest
he hears the rustling of the enemy and flees
not from the others but from himself,
from the interminable conversation,
from the choir that used to sing with us,
and from the meaning of life.

Because one moment, because one voice, because one
syllable or the passing of one silence
or the undying sound of the wave
leave me face to face with the truth,
and there is nothing left to decipher,
nothing more to say: that was all:
the doors of the forest are closed,
the sun circles opening the leaves,
the moon rises like a white fruit,
and man suits himself to his destiny.

WILLIAM O'DALY

Mi perro ha muerto.

Lo enterré en el jardín
junto a una vieja máquina oxidada.

Allí, no más abajo,
ni más arriba,
se juntará conmigo alguna vez.
Ahora él ya se fue con su pelaje,
su mala educación, su nariz fría.
Y yo, materialista que no cree
en el celeste cielo prometido
para ningún humano,
para este perro o para todo perro
creo en el cielo, sí, creo en un cielo
donde yo no entraré, pero él me espera
ondulando su cola de abanico
para que yo al llegar tenga armistades.

Ay no diré la tristeza en la tierra
de no tenerlo más por compañero
que para mí jamás fue un servidor.
Tuvo hacia mí la amistad de un erizo
que conservaba su soberanía,
la amistad de una estrella independiente
sin más intimidad que la precisa,
sin exageraciones:
no se trepaba sobre mi vestuario
llenándome de pelos o de sarna,
no se frotaba contra mi rodilla
como otros perros obsesos sexuales.
No, mi perro me miraba
dándome la atención que necesito,
la atención necesaria
para hacer comprender a un vanidoso
que siendo perro él,
con esos ojos, más puros que los míos,

perdía el tiempo, pero me miraba
con la mirada que me reservó
toda su dulce, su peluda vida,
su silenciosa vida,
cerca de mí, sin molestarme nunca,
y sin pedirme nada.

Ay cuántas veces quise tener cola
andando junto a él por las orillas
del mar, en el Invierno de Isla Negra,
en la gran soledad: arriba el aire
traspasado de pájaros glaciales
y mi perro brincando, hirsuto, lleno
de voltaje marino en movimiento:
mi perro vagabundo y olfatorio
enarbolando su cola dorada
frente a frente al Océano y su espuma.

Alegre, alegre, alegre
como los perros saben ser felices,
sin nada más, con el absolutismo
de la naturaleza descarada.
No hay adiós a mi perro que se ha muerto.
Y no hay ni hubo mentira entre nosotros.

Ya se fue y lo enterré, y eso era todo.

A DOG HAS DIED

My dog has died.

I buried him in the garden
beside a rusty old engine.

There, not too deep,
not too shallow,
he will greet me sometime.

He already left with his coat,
his bad manners, his cold nose.
And I, a materialist who does not believe
in the starry heaven promised
to a human being,
for this dog and for every dog
I believe in heaven, yes, I believe in a heaven
that I will never enter, but he waits for me
wagging his big fan of a tail
so I, soon to arrive, will feel welcomed.

No, I will not speak about my sadness on earth
at not having him as a companion anymore,
he never stooped to becoming my servant.
He offered me the friendship of a sea urchin
who always kept his sovereignty,
the friendship of an independent star
with no more intimacy than necessary,
with no exaggerations:
he never used to climb over my clothes
covering me with hair or with mange,
he never used to rub against my knee
like other dogs, obsessed with sex.
No, my dog used to watch me
giving me the attention I need,
yet only the attention necessary
to let a vain person know
that he being a dog,
with those eyes, more pure than mine,
was wasting time, but he watched
with a look that reserved for me
every bit of sweetness, his shaggy life,
his silent life,
sitting nearby, never bothering me,
never asking anything of me.

O, how many times I wanted to have a tail
walking next to him on the seashore,
in the Isla Negra winter,

in the vast solitude: above us
glacial birds pierced the air
and my dog frolicking, bristly hair, full
of the sea's voltage in motion:
my dog wandering and sniffing around,
brandishing his golden tail
in the face of the ocean and its spume.

O merry, merry, merry,
like only dogs know how to be happy
and nothing more, with an absolute
shameless nature.
There are no goodbyes for my dog who has died.
And there never were and are no lies between us.

He has gone and I buried him, and that was all.

WILLIAM O'DALY

LA ESTRELLA

Bueno, ya no volví, ya no padezco
de no volver, se decidió la arena
y como parte de ola y de pasaje,
sílaba de la sal, piojo del agua,
yo, soberano, esclavo de la costa
me sometí, me encadené a mi roca.

No hay albedrío para los que somos
fragmento del asombro,
no hay salida para este volver
a uno mismo, a la piedra de uno mismo,
ya no hay más estrella que el mar.

THE STAR

Well, I never went back, I no longer suffer
from not going back, the sand willed it
and as part wave and part channel,
syllable of salt, leech of water,
I, sovereign, slave of the coast
surrendered, chained to my rock.

There is no freedom anymore for us
who are fragments of the mystery,
there is no way out for returning
to oneself, to the stone of oneself,
no other stars remain except the sea.

WILLIAM O'DALY

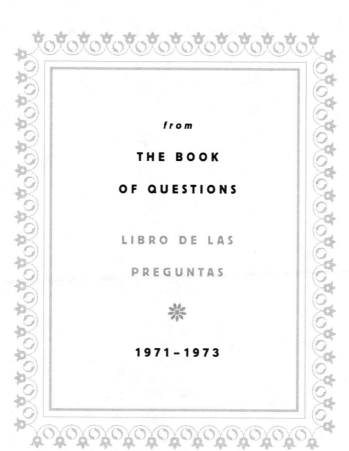

from

THE BOOK
OF QUESTIONS

LIBRO DE LAS

PREGUNTAS

❋

1971–1973

I

Why don't the immense airplanes
fly around with their children?

Which yellow bird
fills its nest with lemons?

Why don't they train helicopters
to suck honey from the sunlight?

Where did the full moon leave
its sack of flour tonight?

WILLIAM O'DALY

VII

Is peace the peace of the dove?
Does the leopard wage war?

Why does the professor teach
the geography of death?

What happens to swallows
who are late for school?

Is it true they scatter
transparent letters across the sky?

WILLIAM O'DALY

IX

Es este mismo el sol de ayer
o es otro el fuego de su fuego?

Cómo agradecer a las nubes
esa abundancia fugitiva?

De dónde viene el nubarrón
con sus sacos negros de llanto?

Dónde están los nombres aquellos
dulces como tortas de antaño?

Dónde se fueron las Donaldas,
las Clorindas, las Eduvigis?

IX

Is the sun the same as yesterday's
or is this fire different from that fire?

How do we thank the clouds
for their fleeting abundance?

From where does the thundercloud come
with its black sacks of tears?

Where are all those names
sweet as cakes of yesteryear?

Where did they go, the Donaldas,
the Clorindas, the Eduvigises?

WILLIAM O'DALY

X

What will they think of my hat,
the Polish, in a hundred years?

What will they say about my poetry
who never touched my blood?

How do we measure the foam
that slips from the beer?

What does a fly do, imprisoned
in one of Petrarch's sonnets?

WILLIAM O'DALY

XI

How long do others speak
if we have already spoken?

What would José Martí say
about the pedagogue Marinello?

How old is November anyway?

What does autumn go on paying for
with so much yellow money?

What is the name of the cocktail
that mixes vodka and lightning bolts?

WILLIAM O'DALY

XXI

And when light was forged
did it happen in Venezuela?

Where is the center of the sea?
Why do waves never go there?

Is it true that the meteor
was a dove of amethyst?

Am I allowed to ask my book
whether it's true I wrote it?

WILLIAM O'DALY

XXXIX

No sientes también el peligro
en la carcajada del mar?

No ves en la seda sangrienta
de la amapola una amenaza?

No ves que florece el manzano
para morir en la manzana?

No lloras rodeado de risa
con las botellas del olvido?

XXXIX

Do you not also sense danger
in the sea's laughter?

Do you not see a threat
in the bloody silk of the poppy?

Do you not see that the apple tree flowers
only to die in the apple?

Do you not weep surrounded by laughter
with bottles of oblivion?

WILLIAM O'DALY

XLI

How long does a rhinoceros last
after he's moved to compassion?

What's new for the leaves
of recent spring?

In winter, do the leaves live
in hiding with the roots?

What did the tree learn from the earth
to be able to talk with the sky?

WILLIAM O'DALY

XLV

Is the yellow of the forest
the same as last year's?

And does the black flight
of the relentless seabird repeat itself?

And is where space ends
called death or infinity?

What weighs more heavily on the belt,
sadnesses or memories?

WILLIAM O'DALY

LXV

Does the drop of metal shine
like a syllable in my song?

Does a word sometimes
slither like a serpent?

Didn't a name like an orange
creep into your heart?

From which river do fish come?
From the word *silversmithing*?

When they stow too many vowels
don't sailing ships wreck?

WILLIAM O'DALY

LXXII

If sweet water flows in all the rivers,
from where does the ocean take its salt?

How do the seasons know
that they should change their costumes?

Why, so listless in winter,
are they so passionate after?

And how do the roots know
they should rise up toward the sun?

And later, wave at the air
with such flowers and colors?

Is it always the same Spring
who reprises her role, forever?

RAFAEL CAMPO

from

SELECTED FAILINGS

DEFECTOS ESCOGIDOS

❊

1971–1973

Toda la noche me pasé la vida
sacando cuentas,
pero no de vacas,
pero no de libras,
pero no de francos,
pero no de dólares,
no, nada de eso.

Toda la vida me pasé la noche
sacando cuentas,
pero no de coches,
pero no de gatos,
pero no de amores,
no.

Toda la vida me pasé la luz
sacando cuentas,
pero no de libros,
pero no de perros,
pero no de cifras,
no.

Toda la luna me pasé la noche
sacando cuentas,
pero no de besos,
pero no de novias,
pero no de camas,
no.

Toda la noche me pasé las olas
sacando cuentas,
pero no de botellas,
pero no de dientes,
pero no de copas,
no.

Toda la guerra me pasé la paz
sacando cuentas,

pero no de muertos,
pero no de flores,
no.

Toda la lluvia me pasé la tierra
haciendo cuentas,
pero no de caminos,
pero no de canciones,
no.

Toda la tierra me pasé la sombra
sacando cuentas,
pero no de cabellos,
no de arrugas,
no de cosas perdidas,
no.

Toda la muerte me pasé la vida
sacando cuentas:
pero de qué se trata
no me acuerdo,
no.

Toda la vida me pasé la muerte
sacando cuentas
y si salí perdiendo
o si salí ganando
yo no lo sé, la tierra
no lo sabe.

Etcétera.

SAD SONG TO BORE EVERYONE

I wasted my life all night
doing some counting

not cows,
not pounds,
not francs, not dollars,
no, nothing like that.

I wasted my life all night
doing some counting,
not cars,
not cats,
not loves,
no.

I wasted my life in the light,
doing some counting,
not books,
not dogs,
not numbers,
no.

I wasted the moon all night
doing some counting,
not kisses,
not brides,
not beds,
no.

I wasted the night in the waves,
doing some counting,
not bottles,
not teeth,
not cups,
no.

I wasted the war in peace
doing some counting,
not the dead,
not flowers,
no.

I wasted the rain on the land
doing some counting,
not roads,
not songs,
no.

I wasted the land in shadow
doing some counting,
not hair,
not wrinkles,
not lost things,
no.

I wasted death in life
doing some counting,
and does it add up?
I don't remember,
no.

I wasted life in death
doing some counting,
and if I show a loss
or a surplus,
I don't know,
and neither does the land.

Et cetera.

ILAN STAVANS

EL GRAN ORINADOR

El gran orinador era amarillo
y el chorro que cayó
era una lluvia color de bronce
sobre las cúpulas de las iglesias,
sobre los techos de los automóviles,
sobre las fábricas y los cementerios,
sobre la multitud y sus jardines.

Quién era, dónde estaba?

Era una densidad, líquido espeso
lo que caía
como desde un caballo
y asustados transeúntes
sin paraguas
buscaban hacia el cielo,
mientras las avenidas se anegaban
y por debajo de las puertas
entraban los orines incansables
que iban llenando acequias, corrompiendo
pisos de mármol, alfombras,
escaleras.

Nada se divisaba. Dónde
estaba el peligro?

Qué iba a pasar en el mundo?

El gran orinador desde su altura
callaba y orinaba.

Qué quiere decir esto?

Soy un simple poeta,
no tengo empeño en descifrar enigmas,
ni en proponer paraguas especiales.

Hasta luego! Saludo y me retiro
a un país donde no me hagan preguntas.

THE GREAT URINATOR

The great urinator was yellow
and the stream that came down
was bronze-colored rain

on the domes of churches,
on the roofs of cars,
on factories and cemeteries,
on the populace and their gardens.

Who was it, where was it?

It was a density, thick liquid
falling as from
a horse,
and frightened passersby
with no umbrellas
looked up skyward,
meanwhile avenues were flooding
and urine inexhaustibly flowing
underneath doors,
backing up drains, disintegrating
marble floors, carpets,
staircases.

Nothing could be detected. Where
was this peril?

What was going to happen to the world?

From on high the great urinator
was silent and urinated.

What does this signify?

I am a pale and artless poet
not here to work out riddles
or recommend special umbrellas.

Hasta la vista! I greet you and go off
to a country where they won't ask me questions.

JOHN FELSTINER

HOMAGE

FOURTEEN OTHER WAYS
OF LOOKING AT
PABLO NERUDA

❋

SONG OF PROTEST

I

PUERTO RICO, PUERTO POBRE

It is late, at this stage, for a beginning,
nevertheless this is my feeling:
here as in other times I come forth
to sing or to die: here I begin.
And there is no power that can silence me
except the sad magnitude of time
and of its ally: death with its plow
for the farming of bones.
I have chosen a theme hot
with blood, with palm trees and silence,
it is about an island surrounded
by many waters and infinite death:
there the pain of those who wait grows
and a river of lamentation bleeds,
it is a poor and incarcerated island,
ash-colored days come and go,
the light flies off and returns to the palms,
the night travels in its black ship
and there she is, there is the prisoner,
the island surrounded by suffering.
And our blood bleeds into hers
because a golden claw separates her
from her lovers and her birthright.

XV

I COME FROM THE SOUTH

I was born to sing these sorrows,
to expose destructive beasts,
to contain shamelessness with a scourge,

to touch inhuman scars.
I am of American parentage,
born from Araucanian ashes,
for when the invader searched for gold
my country attacked him with fire and pain.
In other lands he dressed in gold:
here the conqueror did not conquer:
greedy Pedro de Valdivia
found what he looked for in my country:
he died underneath a cinnamon tree
with molten gold in his throat.
I represent tribes that fell
defending their beloved banners
with nothing left but silence and rain
after the splendor of their battles,
but I continue their action
and throughout all of America
I stir up the grief of my people,
I incite the root of their swords,
I caress the memory of their heroes,
I water their subterranean hopes,
for to what purpose my songs,
the natural gift of beauty and words,
if it does not serve my people
to struggle and walk with me?
So I go throughout oppressed America
lighting fuses and lamps,
tyrants deny me a passport
because my poetry frightens them:
if they bolt the doors against me,
I come, like light, through windows,
if they ignite the territories against me
I enter by rivers flowing with water,
my poetry reaches into prisons
to converse with him who looks for me,
with the fugitive I count stars
all night, in the morning I part:
the ocean's reefs do not detain me:
machine guns do not stop me:

my poems are the eyes of dawn,
they're fists of stone and winged hearts.
When people recognize me on the street,
in copper or barley fields,
from trains that cross the countryside,
on bittersweet plantations,
if greeted in remote ports
or in infernal subterranean mines
it is my poetry that has passed there
with its wheel of love and vengeance
to establish worldwide clarity
to give light to those who hope for it
to advance victory to those who struggle
to give the earth to those who work it.

APRIL BERNARD

THE SEA AND THE BELLS

FROM MY JOURNEY

From my journey I circle back—
why?
Why didn't I return to my homeland,
the streets, countries, continents, islands
I once owned and called home?
Why, instead, did this borderland choose me;
and what does this haven offer
but a wind that whips at my face
and flowers blackened and beaten down
by the long winter?
Oh, they accuse me, saying: He is
so lazy, Master of Rust,
who cannot bear to leave
his hard haven—
he just slowed, then stopped
until his eyes turned to stone
and the ivy veiled his gaze.

ROBERT BLY

I WISH THE WOODCUTTER WOULD WAKE UP

West of the Colorado River
there's a place I love.
I take refuge there with everything alive
in me, with everything
that I have been, that I am, that I believe in.
Some high red rocks are there, the wild
air with its thousand hands
has turned them into human buildings.
The blind scarlet rose from the depths
and changed in these rocks to copper, fire, and energy.
America spread out like a buffalo skin,
light and transparent night of galloping,
near your high places covered with stars
I drink down your cup of green dew.

Yes, through acrid Arizona and Wisconsin full of knots,
as far as Milwaukee, raised to keep back the wind and the snow
or in the burning swamps of West Palm,
near the pine trees of Tacoma, in the thick odor
of your forests which is like steel,
I walked weighing down the mother earth,
blue leaves, waterfalls of stones,
hurricanes vibrating as all music does,
rivers that muttered prayers like monasteries,
geese and apples, territories and waters,
infinite silence in which the wheat could be born.

I was able there, in my deep stony core, to stretch my eyes, ears, hands,
far out into the air until I heard
books, locomotives, snow, battles,
factories, cemeteries, footsteps, plants,
and the moon on a ship from Manhattan,
the song of the machine that is weaving,

the iron spoon that eats the earth,
the drill that strikes like a condor,
and everything that cuts, presses, sews:
creatures and wheels repeating themselves and being born.

I love the farmer's small house. New mothers are asleep
with a good smell like the sap of the tamarind, clothes
just ironed. Fires are burning in a thousand homes,
with drying onions hanging around the fireplace.
(When they are singing near the river the men's voices
are deep as the stones at the river bottom;
and tobacco rose from its wide leaves
and entered these houses like a spirit of the fire.)
Come deeper into Missouri, look at the cheese and the flour,
the boards aromatic and red as violins,
the man moving like a ship among the barley,
the blue-black colt just home from a ride smells
the odor of bread and alfalfa:
bells, poppies, blacksmith shops,
and in the run-down movies in the small towns
love opens its mouth full of teeth
in a dream born of the earth.
What we love is your peace, not your mask.
Your warrior's face is not handsome.
North America, you are handsome and spacious.
You come, like a washerwoman, from
a simple cradle, near your rivers, pale.
Built up from the unknown,
what is sweet in you is your hivelike peace.
We love the man with his hands red
from the Oregon clay, your Negro boy
who brought you the music born
in his country of tusks: we love
your city, your substance,
your light, your machines, the energy
of the West, the harmless
honey from hives and little towns,
the huge farm boy, on his tractor,
the oats which you inherited

from Jefferson, the noisy wheel
that measures your oceanic earth,
the factory smoke and the kiss,
the thousandth, of a new colony:
what we love is your workingman's blood:
your unpretentious hand covered with oil.

For years now under the prairie night
in a heavy silence on the buffalo skin
syllables have been asleep, poems
about what I was before I was born, what we were.
Melville is a sea fir, the curve of the keel
springs from his branches, an arm
of timber and ship. Whitman impossible to count
as grain, Poe in his mathematical
darkness, Dreiser, Wolfe,
fresh wounds of our own absence,
Lockridge more recently, all bound to the depths,
how many others, bound to the darkness:
over them the same dawn of the hemisphere burns,
and out of them what we are has come.
Powerful foot soldiers, blind captains,
frightened at times among actions and leaves,
checked in their work by joy and by mourning,
under the plains crossed by traffic,
how many dead men in the fields never visited before:
innocent ones tortured, prophets only now published,
on the buffalo skin of the prairies.

From France, and Okinawa, and the atolls
of Leyte (Norman Mailer has written it out)
and the infuriated air and the waves,
almost all the men have come back now,
almost all . . . The history of mud and sweat
was green and sour; they did not hear
the singing of the reefs long enough
and perhaps never touched the islands, those wreaths of brilliance and
    perfume,
except to die:

dung and blood
hounded them, the filth and the rats,
and a fatigued and ruined heart that went on fighting.
But they have come back,
                              you have received them
into the immensity of the open lands
and they have closed (those who came back) like a flower
with thousands of nameless petals
to be reborn and forget.

THE STRIKE

The idle factory came to seem strange.
A silence in the plant, a distance
between machine and man, as if a thread had been cut
between two planets, an absence
of human hands that use up time
making things, and the naked
rooms without work and without noise.
When man deserted the lairs
of the turbine, when he tore off
the arms of the fire, so that the inner organs
of the furnace died, and pulled out the eyes
of the wheel, so that the dizzy light
paused in its invisible circle,
the eyes of the great energies,
of the pure circles of force,
of the stupendous power,
what remained was a heap of pointless pieces of steel,
and in the shops without men a widowed air
and the lonesome odor of oil.

Nothing existed without that fragment
hammering, without Ramírez,
without the man in torn overalls.
Nothing was left but the hides of the engines,
heaps of power gone dead,

like black whales in the polluted
depths of a sluggish sea,
or mountain ranges suddenly drowned
under the loneliness of outer space.

VOYAGES AND HOMECOMINGS

ODE TO THE WATERMELON

The tree of intense
summer,
hard,
is all blue sky,
yellow sun,
fatigue in drops,
a sword
above the highways,
a scorched shoe
in the cities:
the brightness and the world
weigh us down,
hit us
in the eyes
with clouds of dust,
with sudden golden blows,
they torture
our feet
with tiny thorns,
with hot stones,
and the mouth
suffers
more than all the toes:
the throat
becomes thirsty,
the teeth,
the lips, the tongue:
we want to drink
waterfalls,

the dark blue night,
the South Pole,
and then
the coolest of all
the planets crosses
the sky,
the round, magnificent,
star-filled watermelon.

It's a fruit from the thirst-tree.
It's the green whale of the summer.

The dry universe
all at once
given dark stars
by this firmament of coolness
lets the swelling
fruit
come down:
its hemispheres open
showing a flag
green, white, red,
that dissolves into
wild rivers, sugar,
delight!

Jewel box of water, phlegmatic
queen
of the fruit shops,
warehouse
of profundity, moon
on earth!
You are pure,
rubies fall apart
in your abundance,
and we
want
to bite into you,
to bury our

face
in you, and
our hair, and
the soul!
When we're thirsty
we glimpse you
like
a mine or a mountain
of fantastic food,
but
among our longings and our teeth
you change
simply
into cool light
that slips in turn into
springwater
that touched us once
singing.
And that is why
you don't weigh us down
in the siesta hour
that's like an oven,
you don't weigh us down,
you just
go by
and your heart, some cold ember,
turned itself into a single
drop of water.

ONE HUNDRED LOVE SONNETS

XLIV

You will know that I do and do not love you
just as life is of two minds,
a word is one wing of silence,
and fire is half made of ice.

I love you just so I can begin to love you,
to begin anew at the infinite
and to be able never to stop loving you:
For these reasons, I do not love you yet.

I do and do not love you as if I held
in my hands the keys to every happiness
and an uncertain, unhappy fate.

My love has two lifetimes to love you.
That's how I can love you when I don't,
and still love you when I do.

LXVI

I don't love you only because I love you
and from loving you I start not loving you,
and yet from waiting for you when I don't expect you
my cold heart begins to burn for you.

I love you only because it is you I love,
I hate you endlessly, and in hating you I beg you,
and it's the measure of my vagrant love
not to see you and yet to love you blindly too.

Maybe January's light will consume
my entire heart in its cruel rays,
robbing me of my key to the quiet sublime.

In this story, only I die today,
and I will die of love because I love you,
because I love you, my love, mercilessly, crazed.

XCIV

Should I die, survive me with a force so pure
that you awaken fury from the pale, chill world,
in all directions raise your indelible eyes,
day in, day out, sound your mouth's guitar.

I don't want your footsteps to vacillate
nor your smile wane, I don't want my bequeathed joy
to die. Don't come knocking at my chest, I'm away.
Dwell in my absence as you would in my estate.

Absence is such a vast house
that you will walk through its walls
and hang paintings in the air.

Absence is such a transparent house
that without my own life I will watch you live
and if I see you suffer, my love, I will die again.

CANTO GENERAL

THE CELESTIAL POETS

What did you do, you Gideans,
intellectualizers, Rilkeans,
mystifiers, false existential
sorcerers, surrealist
butterflies incandescent
in the tomb, Europhile
cadavers in fashion,
pale worms in the capitalist
cheese, what did you do
confronted with the reign of anguish,
in the face of this dark human being,
this kicked-around dignity,
this head immersed
in manure, this essence
of coarse and trampled lives?

You did nothing but take flight:
sold a stack of debris,
searched for celestial hair,
cowardly plants, fingernail clippings,
"Pure Beauty," "spells,"
works of the timid
good for averting the eyes,
for the confusion of delicate
pupils, surviving
on a plate of dirty leftovers
tossed at you by the masters,
not seeing the stone in agony,
no defense, no conquest,
more blind than wreaths
at the cemetery, when rain
falls on the flowers still
and rotten among the tombs.

IN SALVADOR, DEATH

In Salvador, death still patrols.
The blood of dead campesinos
has not dried, it does not dry with time,
the rain does not wipe it off the roads.
Fifteen thousand machine-gunned:
Martínez was the murderer's name.
To this day the taste of blood lingers
in the land, bread and wine of Salvador.

OCTOPI

Oh octopus, oh fierce monk,
the trembling of your garb
flows across the salt of the rock,
satanic and slippery.
Oh visceral testimony,
branch of frozen rays,
head of a monarchy
all arms and foreboding:
portrait of shivering,
plural cloud of black rain.

ELEMENTAL ODES

ODE TO THE BOOK I

Book, when I close you
life itself opens.
I hear
broken screams
in the harbor.
The copper slugs
cross the sandy areas,
descending to Tocopilla.
It is night.
Between the islands
our ocean
palpitates with fish.
It touches the feet, the thighs,
the chalky ribs
of my homeland.
Night touches the shoreline
and rises while singing
at daybreak
like a guitar awakening.

I feel the irresistible force
of the ocean's call. I am
called by the wind,
and called by Rodríguez,
José Antonio,
I received a telegram
from the "Mina" worker's union
and the one I love
(I won't tell you her name)
waits for me in Bucalemu.

Book, you haven't been able
to enwrap me,

you haven't covered me
with typography,
with celestial impressions,
you haven't been able
to trap my eyes between covers,
I leave you so I can populate groves
with the hoarse family of my song,
to work burning metals
or to eat grilled meat
at the fireside in the mountains.
I love books
that are explorers,
books with forest and snow,
depth and sky,
but
I despise
the book of spiders
that employs thought
to weave its venomous wires
to trap the young
and unsuspecting fly.
Book, free me.
I don't want to be entombed
like a volume,
I don't come from a tome,
my poems don't eat poems,
they devour
passionate events,
they're nurtured by the open air
and fed by the earth
and by men.
Book, let me wander the road
with dust in my low shoes
and without mythology:
go back to the library
while I go into the streets.

I've learned to take life
from life,

to love after a single kiss,
and I didn't teach anything to anyone
except what I myself lived,
what I shared with other men,
what I fought along with them:
what I expressed from all of us in my song.

ODE TO THE BOOK II

Book,
beautiful
book,
little forest,
leaf
after leaf,
your paper
smells
of the elements,
you are
daily and nocturnal,
grain,
ocean;
in your ancient pages
bear hunters,
bonfires
along the Mississippi,
canoes
in the islands;
later on
roads
and more roads,
revelations,
rebellious
towns,
Rimbaud, like an injured
blood-soaked fish
gasping in the mud,

and the beauty
of brotherhood,
stone by stone
building the human castle,
grief interwoven
with firmness,
solidarity;
occult
book
passed from pocket
to pocket,
a secret
lamp,
a red star.

We
the wandering
poets
explored
the world,
life welcomed us
at every door,
we joined
in the earthly struggle.
What was our victory?
A book,
a book filled
with human connections,
with shirts,
without isolation, with men
and tools,
a book
is our victory.

A book ripens and falls
like all fruits,
it has light
and shadow,
but its pages

are torn away,
it gets lost
in the streets,
buried in the earth.
Book of poetry
dawning,
come back again
to hold snow or moss
in your pages
so that the footsteps
or the eyes
can leave
their traces;
once again
describe the world for us
of freshwater springs
in the thickets,
groves of tall trees,
the polar
planets,
and human beings
on the roads,
on the new roads,
advancing
in the jungle,
on the water,
in the sky,
in the naked solitude of the sea,
human beings
discovering
the ultimate secrets,
human beings
returning
with a book,
the hunter coming home
with a book,
the farmer
working the land
with a book.

ELEMENTAL ODES

ODE TO TIME

Inside your body, your age
is growing,
inside my body, my age
places foot after wandering foot.
Time is unwavering,
it never rings its bell for time out,
it increases, it journeys,
it shows up within us
like water that deepens
within our own watching,
until next to the chestnut burning
that is your eyes
a slender grass blade arrives,
and the trace of a tiny river,
and a small dry star
ascends to your lips.
Then time raises
its threads in your hair,
and still in my heart
your fragrance of honeysuckle
lives like a fire.
It is beautiful,
how, as we live,
we grow old in the living.
Each day
was a transparent stone,
each night for us was a rose of blackness,
and this crease that has come to your face,
to mine,
is its stone or its flower,
the souvenir and memory of a bolt of lightning.
My eyes were consumed
by your loveliness,

but you have become my eyes.
I exhausted your twin breasts
under my kisses it seems,
but all have viewed in my joy
their secret splendor.
Love, it doesn't matter
if time
(that same time that lifted
my body and your softness
as if they were two rising flames
or two stalks of wheat growing side by side)
tomorrow keeps them aloft and living
or mills them away—
the same invisible fingers
erasing the very existence that kept us apart
will give us our victory,
of being a single being under the earth.

GALWAY KINNELL

RESIDENCE ON EARTH

I EXPLAIN A FEW THINGS

You will ask: But where are the lilacs?
And the metaphysics covered with poppies?
And the rain that often struck
his words, filling them
with holes and birds?

Let me tell you what's happening with me.

I lived in a barrio
of Madrid, with bells,
with clocks, with trees.

From there you could see
the parched face of Castile
like an ocean of leather.
                    My house was called
the house of flowers, because from everywhere
geraniums burst: it was
a beautiful house,
with dogs and children.
                    Raul, do you remember?
Do you remember, Rafael?
                    Federico, do you remember
under the ground,
do you remember my house with balconies
where the June light drowned the flowers in your mouth?
                              Brother, brother!

Everything
was loud voices, salt of goods,
crowds of pulsating bread,
marketplaces in my barrio of Arguelles with its statue
like a pale inkwell set down among the hake:

oil flowed into spoons,
a deep throbbing
of feet and hands filled the streets,
meters, liters, the hard
edges of life,
                heaps of fish,
geometry of roofs under a cold sun in which
the weathervane grew tired,
delirious fine ivory of potatoes,
tomatoes, more tomatoes, all the way to the sea.

And one morning it all was burning,
and one morning bonfires
sprang out of the earth
devouring humans,
and from then on fire,
gunpowder from then on,
and from then on blood.

Bandidos with planes and Moors,
bandidos with rings, and duchesses,
bandidos with black friars signing the cross
coming down from the sky to kill children,
and in the streets the blood of the children
ran simply, like blood of children.

Jackals the jackals would despise,
stones the dry thistle would bite on and spit out,
vipers the vipers would abominate.

Facing you I have seen the blood
of Spain rise up
to drown you in a single wave
of pride and knives.

Traitors,
generals:
look at my dead house,
look at Spain broken:

from every house burning metal comes out
instead of flowers,
from every crater of Spain
comes Spain
from every dead child comes a rifle with eyes,
from every crime bullets are born
that one day will find out in you
the site of the heart.

You will ask: why doesn't his poetry
speak to us of dreams, of leaves
of the great volcanoes of his native land?

Come and see the blood in the streets,
come and see
the blood in the streets,
come and see the blood
in the streets!

ELEMENTAL ODES

ODE TO SALT

In the salt mines
I saw the salt
in this shaker.
I know you won't believe me,
but there
it sings,
the salt sings, the skin
of the salt mines
sings
with a mouth choking
on dirt.
Alone
when I heard
the voice
of salt,
I trembled
in the empty
desert.
Near Antofagasta
the whole
salted plain
shouts out
in its
cracked
voice
a pitiful
song.

Then in its caverns
jewels of rock salt, a mountain
of light buried under earth,
transparent cathedral,

crystal of the sea, oblivion
of the waves.
And now on each table
of the world
your agile
essence,
salt,
spreading
a vital luster
on
our food.
Preserver
of the ancient
stores in the holds
of ships, you were
the explorer
of the seas,
matter
foretold
in the secret, half-open
trails of foam.
Dust of water, the tongue
receives through you a kiss
from the marine night:
taste melds
your oceanity
into each rich morsel
and thus the least
wave
of the saltshaker
teaches us
not merely domestic purity
but also the essential flavor of the infinite.

W. S. MERWIN

TWENTY LOVE POEMS

V

SO THAT YOU WILL HEAR ME

So that you will hear me
my words
sometimes grow thin
as the tracks of the gulls on the beaches.

Necklace, drunken bell
for your hands smooth as grapes.

And I watch my words from a long way off.
They are more yours than mine.
They climb on my old suffering like ivy.

It climbs the same way on damp walls.
You are to blame for this cruel sport.
They are fleeing from my dark lair.
You fill everything, you fill everything.

Before you they peopled the solitude that you occupy.
and they are more used to my sadness than you are.

Now I want them to say what I want to say to you
to make you hear as I want you to hear me.

The wind of anguish still hauls on them as usual.
Sometimes hurricanes of dreams still knock them over.
You listen to other voices in my painful voice.

Lament of old mouths, blood of old supplications.
Love me, companion. Don't forsake me. Follow me.
Follow me, companion, on this wave of anguish.

But my words become stained with your love.
You occupy everything, you occupy everything.

I am making them into an endless necklace
for your white hands, smooth as grapes.

XVI
IN MY SKY AT TWILIGHT

This poem is a paraphrase of the thirtieth poem in Rabindranath Tagore's
The Gardener.

In my sky at twilight you are like a cloud
and your form and color are the way I love them.
You are mine, mine, woman with sweet lips,
and in your life my infinite dreams live.

The lamp of my soul dyes your feet,
My sour wine is sweeter on your lips,
oh reaper of my evening song,
how solitary dreams believe you to be mine!

You are mine, mine, I go shouting it to the afternoon's
wind, and the wind hauls on my widowed voice.
Huntress of the depths of my eyes, your plunder
stills your nocturnal regard as though it were water.

You are taken in the net of my music, my love,
and my nets of music are wide as the sky.
My soul is born on the shore of your eyes of mourning.
In your eyes of mourning the land of dreams begins.

ELEMENTAL ODES

ODE TO A HARE-BOY

In the light of autumn
and the open road,
the boy
holds up in his hands
not a blossom
nor a lantern
but a dead hare.

The automobiles scan
the freezing camber,
no faces showing
from behind
windshields,
their eyes
of iron,
their ears
set against everything,
their gear-teeth quick
as flashes of lightning,
skidding
towards the sea and the cities
while an autumn-
boy
with a hare,
standoffish
as a thistle,
hard
as a flint,
raises
there
a hand
to the shudder-sighs
of the cars.

Nobody
slows down.

They're dun-dullish,
the high ridges,
the hills
the color of a puma
on the run,
violet
now
the silence,
and like
two embers,
two
black
diamonds,
the eyes
of the hare-boy,
now
two points
set
on a knife,
two little black blade-tips,
the eyes
of the boy
who's all at a loss,
offering up his hare
to the huge
autumn
of the open road.

GARY SOTO

HOUSE

Maybe this is the house where I lived
when I did not exist, when the earth did not exist,
when everything was moon or stone or shadow,
when the motionless light had yet to rise.
Maybe then this stone was
my house, my windows or my eyes.
It reminds me, this granite rose,
of something that inhabited me or that I inhabited,
cave or cosmic head of dreams,
cup or castle or ship or source of my beginning.
I touch the rock's tenacious effort,
its bulwark beaten in the brine,
and I know that here remain my crevices,
the wrinkled substance that climbed
from the depths to my soul—
I was stone, will be stone. That is why
I touch this stone, and for me it has not died:
it's what I was, what I will be, rest
from a battle as long as time.

NEW ELEMENTAL ODES

ODE TO THE SMELL OF FIREWOOD

It was late.
I opened the door
and the stars
were shining
in the cold.
　　　　And the sea
was galloping
in the night.

The intense
aroma
of firewood
slipped from the house
like a hand.

As if the tree
still lived,
still breathed,
the aroma was visible.

Visible
as a dress.

Visible
as a broken branch.

I walked
around
in the house
enveloped
by the fragrant
dark.

Outside,
the sky's
sharp points
sparkled
like magnetic stones,
and the door of firewood
touched
my heart
like fingers,
like jasmine,
like certain memories.

It was not the piercing
odor of pine,
no,
nor of the torn bark
of eucalyptus,
neither
was it
the green perfume
of the vineyard,
but something more secret,
because that fragrance
existed
just once,
just once,
and there, with all that I have seen in the world,
in my own
house at night
by the winter sea,
there waiting for me
the odor
of the deepest rose,
the wounded heart of the earth,
something
that entered me like a wave
cut loose from time
and was lost within myself

when I opened the door
in the night.

ODE TO A PAIR OF SOCKS

Maru Mota brought me
a pair
of socks
that she knitted with her
shepherdess hands,
two socks soft
as rabbits.
I put my feet
into them
as into
two
cases
knitted
with threads of
twilight
and sheeps wool.

Wild socks,
my feet were
two wool
fish,
two big sharks
of ultramarine
crossed
by a golden braid,
two giant blackbirds,
two cannons:
my feet
were honored
in this way
by these

heavenly
socks.
They were
so beautiful
that for the first time
my feet seemed to me
unacceptable
like two decrepit
firemen, firemen
unworthy
of that
embroidered
fire,
of those shining
socks.

Anyway
I resisted
the sharp temptation
to save them
the way schoolboys
keep
lightning bugs,
the way scholars
collect
rare books,
I resisted
the mad impulse
to put them
in a golden
cage
and each day
to feed them birdseed
and the meat of a rosy melon.
Like explorers
in the forest
who give up the finest
young deer
to the roasting spit

and eat it
with regret,
I stretched out
my feet
and put on
the
lovely
socks
and then
my shoes.

And this is
the moral of my ode:
beauty is twice
beautiful
and goodness is doubly
good
when
it concerns two wool
socks
in winter.

ODE TO ENCHANTED LIGHT

The light under the trees,
the light from high heaven.
The green
arbor
light
that flashes
in the leaf
and falls like fresh
white sand.

A grasshopper lifts
its sawing sound
over the clearness.

The world
is a full glass
of water.

JAMES WRIGHT

CANTO GENERAL

TOUSSAINT L'OUVERTURE

Out of its own tangled sweetness
Haiti raises mournful petals,
and elaborate gardens, magnificent
structures, and rocks the sea
as a dark grandfather rocks
his ancient dignity of skin and space.

Toussaint L'Ouverture knits together
the vegetable kingdom,
the majesty chained,
the monotonous voice of the drums
and attacks, cuts off retreats, rises,
orders, expels, defies
like a natural monarch,
until he falls into the shadowy net
and they carry him over the seas,
dragged along and trampled down
like the return of his race,
thrown into the secret death
of the ship holds and the cellars.
But on the island the boulders burn,
the hidden branches speak,
hopes are passed on,
the walls of the fortress rise.
Liberty is your own forest,
dark brother, don't lose
the memory of your sufferings,
may the ancestral heroes
have your magic sea foam in their keeping.

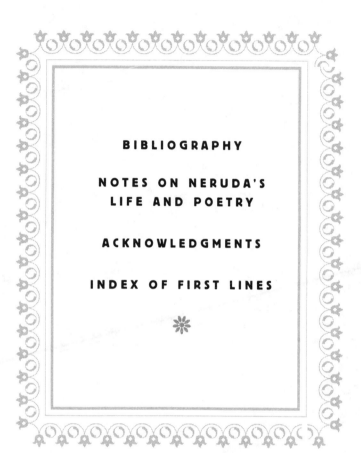

BIBLIOGRAPHY

NOTES ON NERUDA'S
LIFE AND POETRY

ACKNOWLEDGMENTS

INDEX OF FIRST LINES

❊

I don't intend to offer a complete annotation of the material included in this volume. Instead, my objective in this section is to equip the reader with basic historical and biographical information and to offer signposts to deeper knowledge.

SPANISH EDITIONS

The authoritative edition of Neruda's work has been done by Hernán Loyola, with the assistance of Saúl Yurkievich. Their five-volume set *Pablo Neruda: Obras Completas* (Barcelona: Galaxia Gutenberg/Círculo de Lectores, 1999) is an inestimable resource. The first three volumes are devoted to the poetry. For a detailed bibliographical reference on the original Spanish publication of every collection of poetry, from *Book of Twilight* to *The Sea and the Bells*, see the section "Notes on Neruda's Life and Poetry." Another significant volume is *Yo acuso: Discursos parlamentarios* (1945–1948), edited by Leonidas Aguirre Silva (Santiago de Chile: Editorial Oveja Negra, 2002).

It is important to mention that throughout the Chilean's life, he repeatedly embarked on translations of his own from other languages (French, English, Russian, and German) into Spanish. This is a complete list of the titles he brought out. The date in parentheses is that of the translation's publication:

La ciudad durmiente, by Marcel Schwob (1923)
El incendio terrestre, by Marcel Schwob (1923)
Páginas escogidas de Anatole France (1924)
A fragment of Los cuadernos de Malte Laurids Brigge, by Rainer Maria
    Rilke (1926)
El enemigo, by Charles Baudelaire (1933)
Two stanzas of Música de cámara, by James Joyce (1933)
Visiones de las hijas de Albión, by William Blake (1935)
El viajero mental, by William Blake (1935)
La voz de Henri Martin, by Nazim Hikmet (1951)

El recuerdo, by Stephan Hermlin (1949)
For the Reader, by Walter Lowenfels (1955)
El pasaporte, by Vladimir Mayakovsky (1955)
Granada, by Mikhail Svetlov (1968)
El mar, by Yevgeny Yevtushenko (1968)
Romeo y Julieta, by William Shakespeare (1964)

TRANSLATIONS INTO ENGLISH

Neruda's poetry has been available in English versions since after World War II. Here is a complete list of translations of full-fledged individual collections of poetry as well as of anthologies, in chronological order. Unless otherwise noted, all entries were originally published in the United States:

Selected Poems, 1944. Trans. Angel Flores. Privately printed.

Residence on Earth and Other Poems, 1946. Trans. Angel Flores. Norfolk, Conn.: New Directions.

Let the Rail Splitter Awake and Other Poems, 1950. Trans. Samuel Sillen. New York: Masses & Mainstream.

Elementary Odes, 1961. Trans. Carlos Lozano. New York: A Cypress Book.

Selected Poems, 1961. Trans. Ben Belitt. New York: Grove Press.

Bestiary, 1965. Trans. Elsa Neuberger. New York: Harcourt Brace & World.

The Heights of Macchu Picchu, 1966. Trans. Nathaniel Tarn. New York: Farrar, Straus and Giroux.

We Are Many, 1967. Trans. Alastair Reid. London: Cape Goliard.

Twenty Poems, 1967; *Neruda and Vallejo: Selected Poems*, 1971. Trans. Robert Bly, John Knoepfle, and James Wright. Boston, Mass.: Beacon Press.

A New Decade: Poems, 1958–1967, 1969. Trans. Ben Belitt. New York: Grove Press.

Twenty Love Poems and a Song of Despair, 1969. Trans. W. S. Merwin. Harmondsworth, England, and New York: Penguin Books.

Pablo Neruda: The Early Poems, 1969. Trans. David Ossman and Carlos G. Hagen. New York: New River Press.

Selected Poems, 1970. Trans. Anthony Kerrigan, W. S. Merwin, Alastair Reid, and Nathaniel Tarn. New York: Delacorte Press.

New Poems, 1968–1970, 1972. Trans. Ben Belitt and Alastair Reid. New York: Grove Press.

The Captain's Verses, 1972. Trans. Donald D. Walsh. New York: New Directions.

Residence on Earth, 1973. Trans. Donald D. Walsh. New York: New Directions.

Five Decades: A Selection (Poems 1925–1970), 1974. Trans. Ben Belitt. New York: Grove Press.

Extravagaria, 1974. Trans. Alastair Reid. New York: Farrar, Straus and Giroux.

Fully Empowered, 1975. Trans. Alastair Reid. New York: Farrar, Straus and Giroux.

Pablo Neruda: A Basic Anthology, 1975. Ed. Robert Pring-Mill. Oxford, England: Dolphin Book Co.

Song of Protest, 1976. Trans. Miguel Algarín. New York: William Morrow.

Incitement to Nixonicide and Praise for the Chilean Revolution, 1979. Trans. Steve Kowit. Houston, Tex.: Quixote Press.

A Call for the Destruction of Nixon and Praise for the Chilean Revolution, 1980. Trans. Teresa Anderson. Cambridge, Mass.: West End Press.

Translating Neruda: The Way to Macchu Picchu, 1980. Trans. John Felstiner. Stanford, Calif.: Stanford University Press.

Isla Negra: A Notebook, 1981. Trans. Alastair Reid. New York: Farrar, Straus and Giroux.

Skystones, 1981. Trans. Ben Belitt. Easthampton, Mass.: Emanon Press.

Elegy, 1983. Trans. Jack Hirschman. San Francisco, Calif.: David Books.

Still Another Day, 1984. Trans. William O'Daly. Port Townsend, Wash.: Copper Canyon Press.

Eight Odes, 1984. Trans. Ken Norris. Ste. Anne de Bellevue, Québec: The Muses' Company.

Art of Birds, 1985. Trans. Jack Schmitt. Austin: University of Texas Press.

The Separate Rose, 1985. Trans. William O'Daly. Port Townsend, Wash.: Copper Canyon Press.

One Hundred Love Sonnets, 1986. Trans. Stephen Tapscott. Austin: University of Texas Press.

The Stones of Chile, 1986. Trans. Dennis Maloney. Fredonia, N.Y.: White Pine Press.

Winter Garden, 1986. Trans. William O'Daly. Port Townsend, Wash.: Copper Canyon Press.

Stones of the Sky, 1987. Trans. James Nolan. Port Townsend, Wash.: Copper Canyon Press.

The House at Isla Negra, 1988. Trans. Dennis Maloney and Clark M. Zlotchew. Fredonia, N.Y.: White Pine Press.

Late and Posthumous Poems (1968–1974), 1988. Trans. Ben Belitt. New York: Grove Press.

The Sea and the Bells, 1988. Trans. William O'Daly. Port Townsend, Wash.: Copper Canyon Press.

The House in the Sand, 1990. Trans. Dennis Maloney and Clark M. Zlotchew. Minneapolis: Milkweed Editions.

The Yellow Heart, 1990. Trans. William O'Daly. Port Townsend, Wash.: Copper Canyon Press.

Selected Odes of Pablo Neruda, 1991. Trans. Margaret Sayers Peden. Berkeley: University of California Press.

The Book of Questions, 1991. Trans. William O'Daly. Port Townsend, Wash.: Copper Canyon Press.

Canto General, 1991. Trans. Jack Schmitt. Berkeley: University of California Press.

Spain in the Heart: Hymn to the Glories of the People at War, 1993. Trans. Richard Schaaf. Washington, D.C.: Azul Editions.

2000, 1993. Trans. Richard Schaaf. Falls Church, Va.: Azul Editions.

Seaquake, 1993. Trans. María Jacketti and Dennis Maloney. Fredonia, N.Y.: White Pine Press.

Twenty Poems of Love and a Sad Song of Hopelessness, 1994. Trans. Giovanni Previtali. Santa Rosa, Calif.: Plumtree Press.

Odes to Common Things, 1994. Trans. Ken Krabbenhoft. Boston: Little, Brown, and Company.

Neruda's Garden: An Anthology of Odes, 1995. Trans. María Jacketti. Pittsburgh: Latin American Literary Review Press.

Odes to Opposites, 1995. Trans. Ken Krabbenhoft. Boston: Little, Brown.

Ceremonial Songs, 1996. Trans. María Jacketti. Pittsburgh: Latin American Literary Review Press.

Full Woman, Fleshly Apple, Hot Moon: Selected Poems, 1997. Trans. Stephen Mitchell. New York: HarperFlamingo.

Ode to Typography, 1998. Trans. Stephen Kessler. Berkeley: P. Koch.

Neruda at Isla Negra, 1998. Trans. María Jacketti, Dennis Maloney, and Clark M. Zlotchew. Fredonia, N.Y.: White Pine Press.

Machu Picchu, 2001. Trans. Stephen Kessler. Boston: Bulfinch Press Book, Little, Brown, and Company.

Seven Poems, 2001. Trans. Audrey Lumsden Kouvel. Millwood, N.Y.: Haybarn Press.

For readers interested in a meditation on the art of translating Neruda, I recommend John Felstiner's *Translating Neruda: The Way to Macchu Picchu* (Stanford, Calif.: Stanford University Press, 1980). Equally noteworthy is the essay by Alastair Reid, "Basilisk's Eggs," in *Whereabouts: Notes on Being a Foreigner* (San Francisco: North Point Press, 1987). There is also Ben Belitt's *Adam's Dream: A Preface to Translation* (New York: Grove Press, 1979).

The list of nonfiction and a play by Neruda available in English is comparatively shorter than that of his poetry:

Toward the Splendid City: Nobel Lecture, 1972. Trans. Margaret Sayers Peden. New York: Farrar, Straus and Giroux.
Splendor and Death of Joaquín Murieta, 1972. Trans. Ben Belitt. New York: Farrar, Straus and Giroux.
Memoirs, 1977. Trans. Hardie St. Martin. New York: Farrar, Straus and Giroux.
Passions and Impressions, 1983. Trans. Margaret Sayers Peden. New York: Farrar, Straus and Giroux.

BIOGRAPHICAL AND CRITICAL WORKS

Since the sixties, Neruda has become a veritable academic industry. There are a couple of valuable bibliographies: *Pablo Neruda: An Annotated Bibliography of Biographical and Critical Studies*, edited by Hensley C. Woodbridge and David S. Zubatsky (New York and London: Garland, 1988); and *Pablo Neruda: Bibliografía*, by Horacio Jorge Becco (Buenos Aires: Casa Pardo, 1975). Although these volumes catalog a wide range of scholarly sources, little is actually readable. The tendency is to simplify, to conceptualize, and to deconstruct the poet. The critical books that are thought-provoking and of enduring value are these:

Alonso, Amado. *Poesía y estilo de Pablo Neruda: Interpretación de una poesía hermética*. Buenos Aires: Losada, 1940.
Aragon, Louis. *Elégie à Pablo Neruda*. Paris: Gallimard, 1966.
Bellini, Giuseppe. *La poesia di Pablo Neruda: Da "Estravagario" al "Memorial de Isla Negra."* Padova, Italy: Liviana Editrice, 1966.

Bloom, Harold, ed. *Pablo Neruda.* New York: Chelsea House, 1989.

Concha, Jaime. *Tres estudios sobre Pablo Neruda,* vol. 1. Hispanic Studies/University of South Carolina. Palma de Mallorca: Mosén Alcover, 1974.

Cortínez, Carlos. *Comentario crítico de "Residencia en la Tierra" (poemas I–X).* Santiago: Editorial Andrés Bello, 1985.

Costa, René de. *The Poetry of Pablo Neruda.* Cambridge: Harvard University Press, 1979.

Durán, Manuel, with Margery Safir. *Earth Tones: The Poetry of Pablo Neruda.* Bloomington: Indiana University Press, 1981.

Flores, Angel, ed. *Nuevas aproximaciones a Pablo Neruda.* Mexico City: Fondo de Cultura Económica, 1987.

Gilbert, Rita. *Seven Voices.* New York: Alfred A. Knopf, 1973.

Larrea, Juan. *Del surrealismo a Macchu Picchu.* Mexico: Joaquín Mortiz, 1967.

Longo, Teresa, ed. *Pablo Neruda and the U.S. Culture Industry at the Turn of the Century.* New York: Routledge, 2002.

Lowenfels, Walter, ed. *For Neruda, for Chile: An International Anthology.* Boston: Beacon Press, 1975.

Loyola, Hernán. *Ser y morir de Pablo Neruda, 1918–1945.* Santiago: Editorial Santiago, 1967.

Meléndez, Concha. *Pablo Neruda: Vida y obra.* New York: Instituto de las Españas en los Estados Unidos, 1936.

Poirot, Luis. *Pablo Neruda: Absence and Presence.* New York: W. W. Norton, 1990.

Riess, J. Frank. *The World and the Stone: Language and Imagery in Neruda's "Canto General."* London and New York: Oxford University Press, 1972.

Rodríguez Monegal, Emir, with Enrico Mario Santí, eds. *Pablo Neruda.* Madrid: Taurus, 1980.

Santí, Enrico Mario. *Pablo Neruda: The Poetics of Prophecy.* Ithaca, N.Y.: Cornell University Press, 1982.

Sicard, Alain. *El pensamiento poético de Pablo Neruda.* Madrid: Editorial Gredos, 1981.

Suárez Rivero, Eliana. *El gran amor de Pablo Neruda: Estudio crítico de su poesía.* Madrid: Editorial Plaza Mayor, 1971.

Teitelboim, Volodia. *Voy a vivirme: Variaciones y complementos nerudianos.* Santiago: Dolmen Ediciones, 1998.

Yurkievich, Saúl. *Fundadores de la nueva poesía latinoamericana: Vallejo, Huidobro, Borges, Neruda, Paz.* Barcelona: Barral Editores, 1971.

Neruda remains a character in search of the right biographer. There are some twenty small biographies; actually, the majority are so uncritical they fall under the category of hagiography. A solid biography, albeit too impressionistic and subjective for my taste—at times it verges on personal memoir—is by Volodia Teitelboim: *Neruda: An Intimate Biography*, translated into English by Beverly J. DeLong-Tonelli (Austin: University of Texas Press, 1991). There is also the encyclopedic *El viajero inmóvil: Introducción a Pablo Neruda* (Buenos Aires: Losada, 1966), by Emir Rodríguez Monegal. For years on the faculty at Yale University, Rodríguez Monegal was also the biographer of Jorge Luis Borges and Horacio Quiroga. His efforts were handicapped by the psychoanalytic emphasis he felt compelled to provide. Also useful are two volumes by Margarita Aguirre: *Genio y figura de Pablo Neruda* (Buenos Aires: Editorial Universitaria, 1964) and *Las vidas de Pablo Neruda* (Mexico City: Grijalbo, 1973); and one by Alvaro Sarmiento: *Neruda: Entierro y testamento* (Las Palmas, Canary Islands: Inventarios Provisionales, 1974).

In the category of personal accounts, the autobiography of Neruda's third wife, Matilde Urrutia (1912–1985), *Mi vida junto a Pablo Neruda: Memorias* (Barcelona: Seix Barral, 1986), is particularly important. She was not only the raison d'être of *One Hundred Love Sonnets* but also the source of peace and domesticity in his mature life, and the keeper of the flame after his death. Also valuable is *Retrato de familia: Neruda (1904–1920)* (San Juan, Puerto Rico: Editorial de la Universidad de Puerto Rico, 1996), by Bernardo Reyes. Also about Neruda's love life are the biography of Fernando Sáez, *Delia del Carril: La mujer argentina del poeta Neruda* (Buenos Aires: Editorial Sudamericana, 1998) and *Cartas de amor de Pablo Neruda* (Madrid: Ediciones Rodas, 1975), edited by Sergio Fernández Larraín. *Pablo Neruda: Cartas a Laura* (Madrid: Instituto de Cooperación Iberoamericana, 1980) collects the poet's letters to his sister. *Neruda total* (Santiago: Ediciones Systhema, 1991) by Eulogio Suárez has some useful information, and so do *Nerudiario* (Santiago: Planeta Chilena, 1999) by José Miguel Varas and *Neruda en Valparaíso* (Valparaíso: Ediciones Universitarias, 1983) by Sara Vidal. Finally, I recommend the memoir by Jorge Edwards, *Adiós, poeta . . .* (Barcelona: Tusquets, 1990).

Neruda has been a fixture of fiction for decades. First and foremost is the novel *Ardiente paciencia* (Buenos Aires: Editorial Sudamericana, 1985) by Antonio Skármeta, translated into English as *Burning Patience* (also *The Postman of Neruda*) by Katherine Silver (New York: Pantheon Books, 1987). He is also a character in *La casa de los espíritus* (Barcelona: Plaza y Janés, 1982) by Isabel Allende, translated as *The House of the Spirits* by Magda Bogin (New York: Alfred A. Knopf, 1985). And he appears in André Maurois's *Les roses de septembre* (Paris: Flammarion, 1956).

Neruda was eulogized by scores of his contemporaries, from Federico García Lorca to Octavio Paz. The number of special Neruda issues of periodicals is voluminous. For instance, the Spaniard Vicente Aleixandre and the Brazilian Jorge Amado celebrated Neruda in a significant special issue of *Revista Iberoamericana*, vol. 39, nos. 82–83 (January–June 1973); and he was praised by the Guatemalan Miguel Angel Asturias and the Frenchman Louis Aragon in another useful special issue of *Anales de Literatura Hispanoamericana*, vol. 2, nos. 2–3 (1973–1974). See also *Anales de la Universidad de Chile*, vol. 129, nos. 157–160 (January–December 1971); *Ínsula*, vol. 29, no. 330 (May 1974); *Modern Poetry Review*, vol. 5, no. 1 (Spring 1974); and *Review* (Spring 1974). Also of value is Angel Flores's *Aproximaciones a Pablo Neruda* (Barcelona: Libres de Sinera, 1974).

In film, Neruda has been the subject of a documentary in 16 millimeters directed by Harold Mantell: *Yo Soy Pablo Neruda* (Princeton, N.J.: Films for the Humanities). Of course, there is the popular Italian movie *Il postino* (Miramax, 1995), directed by Michael Radford and based on *Ardiente paciencia*. The cast includes Philippe Noiret, Massimo Troisi, and Maria Grazia Cucinotta.

Musical compositions and adaptations based on Neruda's poetry have been plentiful too. These include the sound recording by Mikis Theodorakis of *Canto General* (Cologne, Germany: Intuition Records, 1993). Luciano Berio adapted texts by the Chilean into English, French, German, Hebrew, Italian, and Spanish in *Coro per voci e strumenti* (Milan: Universal Edition, 1976; Berlin: Deutsche Grammophon, 1980). And in 2000, Berio produced *Ekphrasis: Continuo II* for forty voices and orchestra (Salzburg, Austria: Col Legno), which includes partial lyrics by Neruda. The instrumentalist Dean Anderson adapted a cycle of the Chilean's poems for soprano, three violoncellos, percussion, and taped voices in *Divinations* (Acton, Mass.: Neuma Records, 1996). This adaptation includes music by Alvin Etler, Peter Child, Matt Marvuglio, William Kraft, and Shirish Korde. The Swedish composer Allan Pettersson used parts of *Canto General* in his *Symphonies, no. 12: De döda på torget* (Sweden: Caprice, 1978).

Samuel Barber used portions of *Twenty Love Poems and a Song of Despair* in *The Lovers*, opus 43 (New York: G. Schirmer, 1972), written for baritone, mixed chorus, and orchestra. Todd Brief incorporated poems by Neruda in *Cantares* (New York: CRI, 1986), which is a musical arrangement for soprano and large orchestra. The mezzo-soprano Jan DeGaetani, in her *Volume 3* (New York: Bridge, 1995), also included adaptations of Neruda. Morton Subotnick did choral pieces based on works by Emily Dickinson and Pablo Neruda in *Parallel Lives* (New York: Composers Recordings, 1983). Peter Child used the Chilean, as well as the poetry of Ernesto Cardenal and Pablo Antonio Cuadra, in his *String Quartet, no. 2: Estrella* (New York: New World Records, 2002). And in *Epitaffio, Nos. 1–3* (Mainz, Germany: Ars Viva Verlag, 1974), Luigi Nono invoked the Spanish Civil War through the poetry of Neruda and Federico García Lorca.

Finally, there are recordings of Neruda reciting his own poetry. Valuable among them is the vinyl recording *Pablo Neruda Reading His Poetry* (Caedmon, 1967).

I have glossed here each collection of poetry, including those not represented in this volume. The Spanish title appears first, followed by the translated title in brackets. When more than two versions of a title are available in translation, my choice represents the most recognized version. Books marked by an asterisk are not fully available in English.

To enlighten the poet's odyssey, quotations are occasionally drawn from his prose volumes *Confieso que he vivido* (*Memoirs*, 1974), and *Para nacer he nacido* (*Passions and Impressions*, 1978), as well as from biographical and critical works. In these annotations I have sought to offer information that might provide "a living context," as Neruda himself once put it. To achieve this end, I have made use of biographical material. Just as in the table of contents, the books are organized in chronological order according to the date of composition, not the date of publication. This is done to attest to the poet's artistic development: earlier on in his career, because not every volume finished was published immediately; conversely, in his mature years, because various books were outgrowths of previous ones. More than any other work, for these comments I've consulted, and made substantial use of, the *Complete Works*. I'm indebted to Hernán Loyola for his panoramic knowledge. Poems are ordered in the table of contents according to Neruda's strict design. The roman numerals that often precede them, as well as the names of sections within certain collections, designate the exact places they belong to.

CREPUSCULARIO*
[BOOK OF TWILIGHT]

The book was written between 1920 and 1923, when Neruda was not yet twenty years of age. His first publication, under the name of Neftalí Reyes, was an article entitled "*Entusiasmo y perseverancia*," printed in 1917 in the daily *La Mañana* of Temuco, Chile. In successive years a series of poems appeared in magazines such as *Corre-Vuela* under the same name.

His father and mother were José del Carmen Reyes Morales and Rosa Basoalto de Reyes. In his *Memoirs*, Neruda stated: "My father had come [to Temuco, "the farthest outpost of Chilean life in the southern territories," where the poet attended a boys' school until he completed his sixth-year studies in the humanities in 1920] from Parral, where I was born. There, in central Chile, vineyards thrive and wine is plentiful. My mother . . . died before I could have a memory of her, before I knew it was she my eyes gazed upon. I was born on July 12, 1904, and a month later, in August, wasted away by tuberculosis, my mother was gone . . . My grandfather, Don José Angel Reyes, had little land and many children . . . [My own father] left his father's farm while he was still very young and worked as a laborer at the dry docks of the port of Talcahuano, eventually becoming a rail-road man in Temuco [where he moved in 1906 and remarried]. He was a conductor on a ballast train" (translation by Hardie St. Martin).

The pseudonym Pablo Neruda became a definitive fixture in 1920, around the time he conceived a couple of unpublished books: *Las ínsulas extrañas* (The Strange Isles) and *Los cansancios inútiles* (The Useless Tiredness). Portions of these volumes would become *Crepusculario* (the title is a made-up word), 180 pages long, which was published in Santiago by Editorial Claridad in 1923. Several of the poems in the collection were influenced by the Symbolist aesthetic that prevailed in Latin America at the time, and by the *Modernista* revolution (1885–1915), led by Rubén Darío and José Martí, the first to model an authentic transcontinental literary movement from the Mexican provinces to the Argentine pampas and the Caribbean basin. This movement ought not to be confused with European Modernism. Influenced by French Parnassianism and Symbolism, the *Modernistas* sought to inject a fresh drive into Spanish-language letters on this side of the Atlantic Ocean. They reacted against the naturalism of the nineteenth century by making Quevedo's language more urbane.

In *Book of Twilight* Neruda experimented with agricultural images and began to define his own *soledad*—solitude—which would eventually become his poetic staple. At the time of composition, he was reading Pushkin, Dostoyevsky, and Andreyev. The volume had unusual success for a debut collection by someone so young. The first poem I selected, "Love," is from the second section: *"Farewell y los sollozos"* (Farewell and Sobs). "If God Is in My Verse" and "My Soul" are from the third section, *"Los crepúsculos de Maruri"* (Maruri's Twilights). By the time *Book of Twilight* appeared, Neruda had moved to Chile's capital to become a French teacher at the Instituto Pedagógico, and from there on to the globe entire. At the age of twenty-three, he was named consul in Burma.

While written between 1923 and the early parts of 1924, this volume of 34 pages was not published until a decade later; Empresa Letras brought it out in Santiago in 1933, as number 2 in the series *Cuadernos de Poesía*. Shortly after he began *Book of Twilight*, Neruda sought ways to support himself. He contributed to newspapers, and translated and edited an anthology of the work of Anatole France. He also began *Venture of the Infinite Man*, a book influenced by Surrealism.

VEINTE POEMAS DE AMOR Y UNA CANCIÓN DESESPERADA

[TWENTY LOVE POEMS AND A SONG OF DESPAIR]

This collection, from which I've selected approximately half of the content, was Neruda's first substantial success, commercial and critical. It established him as an erotic poet and has remained a perennial favorite around the globe. The book of 96 pages was written between 1923 and 1924, and published in 1924 in Santiago by Nascimento. I've selected thirteen poems (a couple are part of the section "Homage"), as well as the song that comes as a coda and serves as a counterpoint—on the polarities love and non-love—to the rest of the book. In the essay *"Exégesis y soledad"* (Exegesis and Solitude), published in the newspaper *La Nación* on August 20, 1924, the poet explained how the book came to be: "I've only put a song to my life and to the love of several dear women I've known."

The leitmotiv of *Twenty Love Poems and a Song of Despair* is of an adolescent lover trained in the art of longing. As in "Love" in *Book of Twilight*, the poet is at once adult and child. He sings in order to survive, to overcome the misery of obsession. "I no longer love her, that's certain, but maybe I love her," poem XX states. "Though this be the last pain that she makes me suffer / and these the last verses that I write for her." The critic Manuel Durán once rightly described this as the onset of "the nature period" in Neruda's arc, not, obviously, in the sense of melancholy sunsets and ferocious storms but as an age in which he "describes what is to be seen or found at the other end of the senses."

Neruda once told how he wrote "The Song of Despair" in a long, slender-bodied lifeboat left over after a shipwreck. He composed the song after reading the novel *Jean-Christophe*, by Romain Rolland. He also talked about the women in *Twenty Love Poems and a Song of Despair*. "I'm always asked who the women are . . . The two women who weave in and out of these melancholy and passionate poems correspond, let's say, to Marisol and Marisombra: Sea and Sun, Sea and Shadow. Marisol is love in the enchanted countryside, with stars in bold relief at night, and dark eyes like the wet sky of Temuco. She appears with all her joyfulness and her lively beauty on almost every page, surrounded by the waters of the port and by a half-moon over the mountains. Marisombra is the student in the city. Gray beret, very gentle eyes, the ever-present honeysuckle fragrance of my foot-loose and fancy-free student days, the physical peace of the passionate meetings in the city's hideaways" (translation by Hardie St. Martin).

TENTATIVA DEL HOMBRE INFINITO*
[VENTURE OF THE INFINITE MAN]

Written in 1924 and the early parts of 1925, this volume, 44 pages long, was published in Santiago by Nascimento in 1926, around the time Neruda edited the magazine *Caballo de Bastos* and contributed to various periodicals. He was also beginning to conceive *Residence on Earth*. In 1926 he translated a fragment of the *Notebooks of Malte Laurids Brigge* by Rainer Maria Rilke. Portions of *The Ardent Slingsman* and *Venture of the Infinite Man* were translated by David Ossman and Carlos G. Hagen in *Pablo Neruda: The Early Poems* (1969). The collection also includes four early uncollected poems, as well as parts of *Book of Twilight* and *Twenty Love Poems and a Song of Despair.*

In 1926 Neruda published his only novel, *El habitante y la esperanza** (*The Habitant and His Hope*).

RESIDENCIA EN LA TIERRA
[RESIDENCE ON EARTH I AND II, THIRD RESIDENCE]

In 1927, at age twenty-three, Neruda was named consul ad honorem in Rangoon, Burma. His travels would take him first to Buenos Aires, then to Lisbon, Madrid, Paris, and Marseilles. A year later he was transferred to Colombo, Ceylon, in 1929 to Batavia, Java, and in 1931 to Singapore. He returned to Chile the following year. In his *Memoirs* Neruda described the way *Residence on Earth I* was written over this period, between 1925 and 1931, while he was abroad, suffering from a feeling of solitude and remoteness. This was thus, in his own words, "a dark and gloomy but essential book within my work." The volume of 176 pages was published in Santiago by Nascimento in 1933. (It was also in 1933 that Neruda met Federico García Lorca.) Various portions of the book appeared separately. *Residence on Earth* marks a clear shift, from the personal poetry of the first two installments to the socially and politically conscious poetry of *Tercera Residencia* (111 pages), which was released in Buenos Aires by Neruda's longtime publisher Editorial Losada, S.A., in 1947.

Residence on Earth includes some of Neruda's most famous poems, such as "Ars Poetica," "Ode to Federico García Lorca," and the entire sequence *España en el corazón* (Spain in Our Heart), the product of his experience in the Iberian peninsula at the time of the Spanish Civil War. Other authors and intellectuals, among them Ernest Hemingway, George Orwell, and Arthur Koestler, also felt compelled to be part of the popular upheaval, but they witnessed the events through the eyes of the foreign brigades. Thanks to his language and his sympathies with the Spanish poets of the era, Neruda instead was at "the heart," as his title rightly claims.

In 1934 Neruda had traveled to Barcelona to become Chile's consul in the Catalan metropolis. Around this time he delivered a lecture in Madrid at which he was introduced by García Lorca. In 1935, shortly after he met and fell in love with Delia del Carril, an Argentine also known as *la hormiguita* (the little ant), his diplomatic duties were moved to Madrid. A year later, as the Spanish Civil War broke out, he began *España en el corazón: Himno a las glorias del pueblo en la guerra*. Forty-seven pages long, it appeared in Santiago under the imprint of Ercilla in 1937. The book, which became part of *Tercera Residencia*, was also issued in 1938 by Spanish Republican soldiers on the battlefront. "I should explain that my book *España en el corazón* has never seemed to me an easy book to understand," said Neruda in his *Memoirs*. "It tries to be clear, but it is steeped in the torment of overwhelming and painful events."

"Alliance (Sonata)" is a reference to the alliance with the night established by the poet. Hernán Loyola suggests that the poet used the word *sonata* in his titles for songs of nostalgia and sadness. The Joachim in "Joachim's Absence" is Joaquín Cifuentes Sepúlveda (1900–1929), a Chilean poet who died of syphilis in Buenos Aires. The title "Walking Around" was originally in English. It has been suggested that it may refer to James Joyce, in particular to *Chamber Music*, which Neruda translated in this period. "Ode to Federico García Lorca" might have been written as a sign of gratitude by Neruda to the Andalusian for his friendship and welcome in 1934. (For a comment by García Lorca on Neruda, see the epigraph to this volume.) Tina Modotti was a famous Italian photographer in Mexico, a member of the Communist Party who befriended the artists José Clemente Orozco, Diego Rivera, and Frida Kahlo.

Canto General is arguably Neruda's most ambitious volume. It follows the pattern of transgeographic, suprahistorical poems such as Joel Barlow's *Columbiad* in English and *La Araucana* by Alonso Ercilla y Zúñiga in Spanish. Neruda worked on it for twelve years. It is also his longest and most sustained effort at a poetic vision of history. He attempted a chronicle of the Americas from before the arrival of Columbus in the first poem, "*Amor America* (1400)," to the present time of the last poem, "I End Here (1949)." It is an epic that concerns itself with the social and political factors that shaped the so-called New World. References to mythical and actual figures are abundant. The book was published in Mexico by Talleres Gráficos de la Nación in 1950 in 567 pages, with illustrations by the muralists Diego Rivera and David Alfaro Siqueiros. Neruda imagines a past that mixes the Spanish and indigenous people and ultimately serves his Marxist politics. He sings to the Communist Party and praises humble, common people.

Canto General was a resounding success. Various sections, such as *The Heights of Macchu Picchu*, appeared separately. Critics have compared the overall collection with Dante's *Divine Comedy* in the odyssey it maps out, the conversion it entails, and the ascent that is achieved in the Macchu Picchu section. (Neruda visited the pre-Inca ruins in 1943.) The literary critic Roberto González Echeverría argues that it is here "that Neruda's vision is refocused by the presence of these ruins, testament to a utopia in the past, an allegiance of a collectivity with nature to create beauty and justice. It is an allegiance also marred by violence, abuse and betrayal." He adds, "It is also here that the poet meets death" (introduction to *Canto General*, trans. Jack Schmitt, 1991). Rapa Nui is the name by which the inhabitants refer to Easter Island in the South Pacific, 2,300 miles west of Chile's shores. Neruda would visit the island in 1971 and sing to it in *The Separate Rose*.

In 1937, while in Paris, Neruda met the Peruvian poet César Vallejo (1892–1938), author of *España, aparta de mí este cáliz* (*Spain, Take This Cup from Me*). They became friends. He wrote, "The great *cholo*" was "a poet whose poetry had a rough surface, as rugged to the touch as a wild animal's skin, but it was magnificent poetry with extraordinary power. Incidentally, we had a little run-in right after we met. It was in La Rotonde. We were introduced, and in his precise Peruvian accent, he greeted me with: 'You are the greatest of all our poets. Only Rubén Darío can compare with you.' 'Vallejo,' I said, 'if you want us to be friends, don't ever say anything like that to me again. I don't know where we'd end up if we started treating each other like writers.'" Neruda added, "Vallejo was shorter than I, thinner, more heavy-boned. He was also more Indian than I, with very dark eyes and a very tall, domed forehead. He had a handsome Inca face, saddened by an air of unmistakable majesty. Vain like all poets, he loved it when people talked to him this way about his Indian features. He would hold his head high to let me admire it and say, 'I've got something, haven't I?' And then laugh at himself quietly."

In contrast, Neruda's appreciation of the other Latin American master, Vicente Huidobro (1893–1948), author of *Altazor*, is far more measured in tone. Huidobro, the Chilean argued, "was Vallejo's opposite in so many ways. Huidobro would let a lock of hair hang over his forehead, insert his fingers in his vest, push out his chest, and ask: 'Have you noticed how much I look like Napoleon Bonaparte?'" Elsewhere in the *Memoirs* Neruda said, Huidobro "crowned himself the 'God of Poetry' and did not think it was right that I, so much younger than he, should be part of his Olympus. I never understood what that Olympus was all about. Huidobro's group creationized, surrealized, and devoured the latest fashions from Paris. I was infinitely inferior, a hopeless country boy from the backwoods, a hayseed. Huidobro was not content to be the extraordinarily gifted poet he really was. He also wanted to be Superman" (translation by Hardie St. Martin).

This was a period of intense political efforts on behalf of Spain's leftist forces. Neruda founded the Alianza de Intelectuales de Chile para la Defensa de la Cultura. The following year he intensified his efforts in favor of peace and equality in Spain, offering lectures and readings throughout the country. In 1939 his duties as consul were transferred to Paris, and in 1940 he returned to Chile. Shortly after, he traveled to Guatemala and Mexico. In Cuernavaca, some sixty miles from Mexico's capital, Nazi sympathizers attacked him. Then, in the early forties, he traveled to Cuba and a year later published *Nuevo canto de amor a Stalingrado* (New Song of Love to Stalingrad). Neruda had slowly become a supporter of the USSR and would visit it for the first time in 1949. His shift toward Stalinism would lead to breaks with several friends and colleagues, among them Octavio

Paz. He also visited the United States, Panama, Colombia, and Peru. And in 1945 his political career beyond the diplomatic service began as Neruda was elected senator for the provinces of Tarapacá and Antofagasta. On July 8, he became a member of Chile's Communist Party.

He wrote *Alturas de Macchu Picchu* (*The Heights of Macchu Picchu*) this same year, although the volume was not published until 1948 in Santiago, by Iberoamérica/Archivo de la Palabra. Volodia Teitelboim argues, "His poem is not travel literature nor a hymn in praise of ancient gods. For [Neruda], it is principally a passage across a long ancient frontier that separated him from pre-Columbian history, where he is convinced that at least a part of his own history comes from." In his *Memoirs*, Neruda wrote, "When my poem *Alturas de Macchu Picchu* was first published, no one in Chile dared mention it . . . Its publisher went to the offices of Chile's bulkiest newspaper, *El Mercurio*, which has been in existence almost a hundred and fifty years; he had with him a paid announcement of the book's publication. They accepted it on condition that my name be removed. 'But Neruda is the author,' [the publisher] protested. 'It doesn't matter,' they said . . . What good had the newspaper's hundred and fifty years of life been to it? In all that time, it had not learned to respect the truth, or the facts, or poetry" (translation by Hardie St. Martin).

In November 1947, shortly after he was awarded Mexico's prestigious Aztec Eagle Prize, Neruda published *"Carta íntima para millones de hombres"* (Short Letter for a Million Men) in *El Nacional*, the newspaper in Caracas. At the time censorship of the press was in effect. As a result of this letter, Chile's president began judicial proceedings against the poet. In January 1948, Neruda gave a speech in the senate, which was later published as *Yo acuso* (*I Accuse*). The following month Chile's Supreme Court upheld Neruda's removal, then ordered his arrest. As a result, he was forced to go into hiding, and in 1949 he left his native country, crossing the Andes on horseback toward Argentina.

This was a journey that would have a deep effect on him. In his Nobel Prize address, the poet wrote: "In those inaccessible regions one travels through great forests as if through tunnels, and along that dark and forbidden route there were no tracks, no trails, I and my four companions, in a snaking cavalcade—overcoming the obstacles of imposing trees, impassable rivers, enormous outcroppings of rock, desolate snow—had to seek—more accurately, to reckon—the route to my freedom. The men accompanying me knew the direction we must travel, the potential routes through the heavy outgrowth. But to be more certain on their return—

after they had abandoned me to my fate—from their horses they slashed at the bark with their machetes, blazing a trail on tower trees" (translation by Margaret Sayers Peden). This odyssey established Neruda as a poet of exile, a state of life and mind that marked the poetry of the twentieth century. His roaming life—his ups and downs across the Americas, his ins and outs through the chambers of homelessness—established him as the essential voice of displacement.

LOS VERSOS DEL CAPITÁN
[THE CAPTAIN'S VERSES]

In 1951 Neruda toured Italy. His travels across Europe and the Far East intensified. The following year *The Captain's Verses* (184 pages) was published privately and anonymously in Naples, by Imprenta L'Arte Tipografica. Many of the love poems in the book were written about Matilde Urrutia, but Neruda didn't want to hurt her predecessor, Delia del Carril. Later, when he reunited with Urrutia, his name was put on the book, first when it was issued publicly by Losada in Argentina in 1962. (Urrutia describes their love affair in *Mi vida junto a Pablo Neruda: Memorias*.) This was one of Neruda's most controversial books. He argued in his *Memoirs*, "It remained a secret for a long time, for a long time it did not carry my name on its cover, as if I were disowning it or as if the book itself did not know who its father was. There are natural children, offspring of natural love, and, in that sense, *Los versos del Capitán* was a natural book."

Why the anonymity? Neruda confessed: "The real truth is that I did not want those poems to wound Delia, whom I was leaving. Delia del Carril, sweetest of consorts, thread of steel and honey tied to me during the years when my poetry sang most, was my perfect mate for eighteen years. This book, filled with sudden and burning love, would have reached her like a rock hurled against her gentleness. That, only that, was the profound, personal, respectable reason for my anonymity" (translation by Hardie St. Martin).

And in an "Explanation" prefacing the 1962 edition, Neruda wrote, "In some ways I think that all books should be anonymous. But between removing my name from all my books and restoring it to the most mysterious one, I yielded, finally, though with no great pleasure. Why did I preserve the mystery so long? For no reason and for all reasons, for this and for that, for improper joys, for alien sufferings. When Paolo Ricci, luminous companion, printed it for the first time in Naples in 1952, we thought that the few copies that he prepared with superb care would disappear and leave no trace in the southern sands. It didn't turn out that way. And the life that demanded its secret explosion now imposes it on me as the presence of lasting love. And so I present this book with no further explanation, as if it were mine and not mine: it is enough that it should be able to go through the world on its own and grow by itself. Now that I recognize it I hope that its furious blood will recognize me, too" (translation by Donald W. Walsh). In the early fifties the poet again returned to the Soviet Union.

LAS UVAS Y EL VIENTO*
[THE GRAPES AND THE WIND]

This travel book, with its cult of Joseph Stalin, was published in 1954. Almost forgotten today, it resulted from various trips Neruda took abroad between 1950 and 1954. The poet attempted a sequel of sorts to *Canto General*, following an itinerant journey through the countries of the so-called Eastern Bloc that lay behind the Iron Curtain. In their reviews critics attacked Neruda as a "servant of the Communist Party" and a puppet of the Soviet regime. The journal *Ercilla*, in its March 23, 1954, issue, published a questionnaire in which authors were asked: Should a poet be also a militant or ought he to stay in an ivory tower? In the Soviet Union, though, *The Grapes and the Wind* was awarded the first Stalin Prize for Peace (its name was changed from the Lenin Peace Prize to honor the Soviet dictator, who would die in 1953). Neruda was fifty-two when he received the award. A few months earlier he had organized the Continental Congress of Culture, which was held in Santiago. The endeavor was meant to orchestrate the voices of intellectuals from all across the Americas committed to social justice. Among the participants were Cuba's Nicolás Guillén, Mexico's Diego Rivera, and Brazil's Jorge Amado.

ODAS ELEMENTALES, NUEVAS ODAS ELEMENTALES,
TERCER LIBRO DE LAS ODAS
[ELEMENTAL ODES, NEW ELEMENTAL ODES,
THIRD BOOK OF ODES]

About their title, Margaret Sayers Peden, responsible for some of the best translations of the odes, wrote: "The Spanish qualifier *elemental* is equivalent in English to both 'elemental' and 'elementary' . . . The belittling connotations of 'elementary' are not appropriate, however. If Neruda had been an artist, one would say that his odes are too painterly to merit such a reading." *Elemental*, then, should be read as synonymous with *fundmental*. (In 1961 Carlos Lozano translated the book as *Elementary Odes*. See the bibliography, "Translations into English.")

It has been said that what the ghazel is to Federico García Lorca, the ode is to Neruda. The comparison is only partially valid: the Spaniard was flexible, but, assassinated by the fascists in Spain's Civil War, he didn't have a long career in which to experiment. The Chilean, by contrast, used the ode at different times in his life. *Residence on Earth* includes "Ode with a Lament," "Ode to Federico García Lorca," "Solar Ode to the Army of the People," and "Seventh of November: Ode to a Day of Victories." And then there are these three books. *Odas elementales* (*Elemental Odes*), 254 pages long, was published by Losada in Buenos Aires in 1954. Neruda then worked on *Nuevas odas elementales* (*New Elemental Odes*) throughout 1955, and the volume appeared in 1956 (Buenos Aires, Losada, 184 pages). *Tercer libro de las odas* (*Third Book of Odes*, 207 pages) was composed between 1956 and 1957 and released by Losada toward the end of 1957. There is also the 1961 volume *Ceremonial Songs*, but Neruda referred to those poems not as odes, but as chants.

Neruda originally intended to publish the odes in newspapers. As a poetic form, the ode dates back to Homer, Pindar, and Horace. From the seventeenth century on, Ben Jonson, John Milton, John Dryden, and William Wordsworth adapted the form to English poetry, and in German it was employed by G. R. Weckherlin and Schiller. Less significantly, in the Hispanic tradition the ode was also used in public events as an organized, highly sophisticated hymn, sometimes of considerable length. The Chilean paid tribute to the classics but appropriated the form for his own purposes. He used his odes to praise common things: a village movie house, an onion, a dictionary.

He stated in his *Memoirs*: "In *Odas elementales*, I decided to deal with things from their beginnings, starting with the primary state, from birth onward. I wanted to describe many things that had been sung and said over and over again. My intention was to start like the boy chewing on his pencil, setting to work on his composition assignment about the sun, the blackboard, the clock, or the family. Nothing was to be omitted from my field of action; walking or flying, I had to touch on everything, expressing myself as clearly and freshly as possible." The poet added, "An Uruguayan critic was shocked because I compared some stones to small ducks. He had established that small ducks, and some other kinds of small animals, are not material for poetry. Literary refinement has come to this kind of flippancy. They are trying to force creative artists to deal only with the sublime themes. But they are wrong. We'll even make poetry from those things most scorned by the arbiters of good taste" (translation by Hardie St. Martin).

ESTRAVAGARIO
[EXTRAVAGARIA]

"Of all my books," Neruda stated in his *Memoirs*, "*Estravagario* (*Extravagaria*) is not the one that sings most but the one that has the best leaps. Its leaping poems skip over distinction, respect, mutual protection, establishments, and obligations, to sponsor reverent irreverence. Because of its disrespect, it's my most personal book. Because of its range, it is one of the most important. For my taste, it's a terrific book, with the tang of salt that the truth always has" (translation by Hardie St. Martin). The volume marks a kind of return to the self. Neruda has just had a period of remarkable social and political poetry, and this volume brings him back, in some ways, to where he began as a poet: the subject of love. Again, Matilde Urrutia is its inspiration. But the volume is also hermetic, to the point that some critics consider it linked to *Residence on Earth*. The critic René de Costa describes it in *The Poetry of Pablo Neruda* (1979) as a "conversation work." De Costa adds, "In it the author not only refuses to take himself seriously, but he also presents his work in such a way as to challenge the reading public's sense of decorum."

Estravagario—the title is an invented word that invokes a gathering of inordinate, in other words, *extravagant*, items—was published in Buenos Aires by Losada in 1958 in 343 pages. Its predominant poetic form is the *endecasílablo*, the eleven-syllable line that has a solid tradition in Hispanic culture. The section *Navegaciones y regresos* (*Voyages and Homecomings*), in fact a separate book but linked in theme and style, was written between 1957 and 1959. It was an outgrowth of 146 pages of *Estravagario* that was released in Buenos Aires by Losada in 1959.

The Uruguayan critic Emir Rodríguez Monegal, in *El viajero inmóvil* (1966), describes Neruda's work from the late fifties to the early seventies as "autumnal." He sees him as a poet who "contemplates himself in the mirror of his life." This was surely a period in which the Chilean looked back at his life and career with a sense of accomplishment but also a feeling of skepticism. Manuel Durán and Margery Safir divide the earlier poetry by Neruda into three categories: love poetry, nature poetry, and public poetry. But they describe his last decades in a fourth category: personal poetry. Durán and Safir, in their book *Earth Tones* (1981), offer a note of caution: "There is no work of Neruda's that cannot be called 'personal' to the degree that the poet's individual vision is presented, even where he adopts the role of public bard and addresses subjects of immediate social concern." Still, they add, "Neruda plunged into personal, often autobiographical, poetry at a time when his public role had never been more in evidence . . . He was both a highly esteemed member of the establishment and a rebel poet, a paradox that could not have failed to delight him."

CIEN SONETOS DE AMOR
[ONE HUNDRED LOVE SONNETS]

In 1954 the poet donated his library to the Universidad de Chile and established the Fundación Neruda para el Desarrollo de la Poesía. A year later he and Delia del Carril separated, ending a long and passionate relationship. Del Carril was one of Neruda's three major female companions: María Antonieta Hagenaar Vogelzanz and Matilde Urrutia were the other two. Urrutia had been the inspiration of *The Captain's Verses*. She was also the presence behind *One Hundred Love Sonnets*, as well as *La barcarola*.

Hagenaar, Neruda's first wife, was an Indonesian of Dutch ancestry who lived in Java. Neruda called her Maruca. They married in Batavia in 1930 and had one child, Malva Marina (1934–1942), about whom little is known. In his *Memoirs*, Neruda described Hagenaar thus: "I became very fond of her. She was a tall, gentle girl and knew nothing of the world of arts and letters." According to Margarita Aguirre's *Genio y figura de Pablo Neruda* (1964), this ignorance also applied to language: "She doesn't know any Spanish," Aguirre wrote, "but she's learning it."

Houses were the other companions in Neruda's life. "I am frightened by houses I have lived in," he wrote once. "The arms of their compasses are opened wide, waiting: they want to swallow you and bury you in their rooms, and I remember each of them with fondness. I couldn't enumerate them, and I couldn't go back to live in them, because I don't like resurrections. Space, time, life, and oblivion not only invade a house to spin cobwebs in all the corners; they also store a record of everything that happened in certain rooms: the love, illness, misery, and happiness that will not be relegated to the past but want to live on" (translation by Margaret Sayers Peden). At the time of the separation from del Carril, Neruda started to build his new house, "La Chascona," and founded a new journal, *La Gaceta de Chile*. He had fallen in love with Matilde Urrutia, and in 1957 he began to write a series of poems for her. He interrupted the quest to return to the third *Residence on Earth*, and then to *Extravagaria*, but returned to it soon after. The 126-page book appeared in 1959 in Santiago, published by Prensa de la Editorial Universitaria.

CANCIÓN DE GESTA
[SONG OF PROTEST]

In 1957 the *Obras Completas* was published by Losada in Argentina. The following year Neruda took part in the presidential campaign in Chile, touring the country and speaking at mass rallies. He then traveled to Venezuela. It was at the end of that year that Fidel Castro, from the Sierra Maestra, orchestrated his revolution in Cuba. Neruda had by that time begun *Song of Protest*, which, at least initially, dealt with the political and social condition of Puerto Rico and Cuba. It was first inspired by his acquaintance with the Puerto Rican independence activist Antonio Santaella Blanco. But mesmerized by Castro, the poet expanded the volume, which he imagined to be somewhat modeled after his book on the Spanish Civil War. *Song of Protest* (74 pages) was published in Havana by Imprenta Nacional de Cuba in 1960. The first edition was of 25,000 copies. Miguel Algarín, the English translator whose renditions appear here, is the mainland Puerto Rican author of *Mongo Affair* and *Love Is Hard Work: Memorias de Loisaida*. He founded and promoted the Nuyorrican Poets' Café in Manhattan.

Also in 1960, Picasso illustrated Neruda's poem "Toro" in a French edition translated by Jean Marcenac.

LAS PIEDRAS DE CHILE
[THE STONES OF CHILE]

Stones, precious and mundane, attracted Neruda dearly. In the preface to *The Stones of Chile*, published in Buenos Aires by Losada in 1961, with 133 pages and photographs by Antonio Quintana, the poet claims that it was conceived some twenty years earlier, when he was working on *Canto General*.

The 115-page book was published in Buenos Aires in 1961. "The Unburied Woman of Paita" is a tribute to the *libertador* Simón Bolívar's lover, Manuela Sáenz (ca. 1797–1856). Isadore Ducasse, aka the Count of Lautréamont, a precursor of the Surrealists, was the author of the cult volume *Les chants de Maldoror*. He was born in Uruguay to French parents in 1846 and died mysteriously in 1870, at the age of twenty-four. The pseudonym *Lautréamont*, in Flaubert's tongue, is a play on words with "the other world." Neruda's poem is one of his attempts to reclaim Ducasse as part of the canon of Latin American letters. Other intellectuals from the region, most prominently Emir Rodríguez Monegal, have joined the effort. In 1938 the Surrealist André Breton wrote a provocative introduction to Ducasse's *Oeuvres complètes*.

PLENOS PODERES
[FULLY EMPOWERED]

Fully Empowered was written between 1961 and 1962. (It was also in 1961 that the millionth copy of *Twenty Love Poems and a Song of Despair* was issued, breaking all sales expectations for a tiny volume of youthful poetry.) *Fully Empowered* (88 pages) was published by Losada in Buenos Aires in 1962.

MEMORIAL DE ISLA NEGRA
[ISLA NEGRA]

Conceived between 1962 and 1964, the section *"Donde nace la lluvia"* (Where the Rain Is Born) first appeared in Alpignano (Torino, Italy), under the aegis of Alberto Tallone, in 1963, in a fifty-copy edition of 122 pages. It was reprinted by Losada in 1964. Losada published part II, *"La luna en el laberinto"* (The Moon in the Labyrinth), in 1964. Parts III through V—*"El fuego cruel"* (Cruel Fire), *"El cazador de raíces"* (The Hunter After Roots), and *"Sonata crítica"* (Critical Sonata)—appeared in 1964. (The last part was replaced by *La barcarola*.)

In his prose collection *Passions and Impressions*, Neruda included these paragraphs dated September 1969: "Everything flowers in Isla Negra. The tiniest yellow flowers survive the long winters to become blue, then later, with spring, magenta. The sea flowers the year round. Its rose is white. Its petals are stars of salt . . . And just this last winter the needleworkers of Isla Negra have begun to flower. Each of the houses I have known for thirty years displayed on its exterior an embroidery like a flower. Before, these houses were dark and silent; and suddenly they were alight with colored threads of blue innocence, violet profundity, red clarity. The embroiderers are simple women, and they embroider with the color of their hearts. Their names are Mercedes, like the wife of José Luis, or Eufemia, or Pura, or Adela, or Adelaida. Their names are simple names, as names should be. They have the names that flowers would have if they could choose their names. And they embroider with their names, with the pure colors of earth, sun, water, and springtime . . . There is nothing more beautiful than these embroideries, illustrious in their purity, radiant in a joy that has transcended suffering" (translation by Margaret Sayers Peden).

The architect of the house at Isla Negra was the Spanish Republican Germán Rodríguez, and the building foreman was Alejandro García. In the beechwood beams, Neruda would have his carpenter, Rafita, carve the names of deceased friends. Volodia Teitelboim writes that in the house, "the poet feels like something more than a ship's captain. When he's at Isla Negra the house is like a government palace when the king or president is in residence. The flag waves on its pole, as Neruda's presence . . . is announced by a blue banner with a horizontal fish enclosed in two contiguous circles."

In 1964 the National Library in Chile commemorated Neruda's sixtieth birthday with a series of events. That same year his Spanish translation of *Romeo and Juliet* had its debut at the Instituto del Teatro de la Universidad de Chile. In an essay written to commemorate the four hundredth anniversary of the Bard's birth, the Chilean meditated on his education and admiration: "Goneril, Regan, Hamlet, Angus, Duncan, Glansdale, Mortimer, Ariel, Leontes . . . These names from Shakespeare were part of our childhood; they crystallized and became the substance of our dreams. Even when we could scarcely read, we knew that behind the names lay a continent with rivers and kings, clans and castles and archipelagos, that someday we would explore. The names of these somber, or radiant, protagonists revealed to us the texture of poetry, the first peal of a great bell. Later, much later, come the days and years when we discover the lines and lives of these names. We discover suffering and remorse, martyrdom and cruelty, beings of blood, creatures of air, voices illuminated for a magic feast, banquets attended by bloodstained ghosts. All that action, all those souls, all those passions—all that life. In every epoch, one bard assumes responsibility for the dreams and the wisdom of the age: he expresses the growth, the expansion, of that world. His name is Alighieri, Victor Hugo, Lope de Vega, Walt Whitman. Above all, his name is Shakespeare" (translated by Margaret Sayers Peden).

In 1965 Neruda was awarded a doctorate honoris causa from Oxford University, hosted by the underappreciated scholar R.D.F. Pring-Mill, whose reviews in the *Times Literary Supplement* in the seventies offered a context for Neruda in the English-speaking world. In 1975 Pring-Mill edited *Pablo Neruda: A Basic Anthology.* He also translated "The Liberators" (*Canto General*) in 1965 and a year later wrote the preface to Nathaniel Tarn's translation of *The Heights of Macchu Picchu.*

In his late teens, Neruda lived on Maruri Street, No. 513. This is where he wrote his first book. The site is invoked in the poem "The Rooming House on the Calle Maruri."

ARTE DE PÁJAROS
[ART OF BIRDS]

Flocks and particular birds abound in Neruda's oeuvre, from *Canto General* onward. In *Passions and Impressions*, there is a 1963 preface by the poet to the volume *Arte de pájaros*. It contains the following sentences: "From snows to sands, over volcanoes, beaches, pastures, rivers, rocks, thatched roofs, roads, waves, everywhere, the birds. Birds, little birds, gigantic birds, birdy birds, wordy birds! Not all flying, some spying; some singing, some winging; flashing like a golden beam, blending into ash and night. And their flight! Flight in the wide freedom of the air, fleet as arrows or slow as ships. Different styles of flight, some cleaving the sky, some piercing it with knives; and sometimes, with the overflowing multitudes of migration, flooding the universe with liquid birddom" (translation by Margaret Sayers Peden). *Art of Birds* was published in a private edition of 105 pages in Santiago by the Society of Friends of Contemporary Art in 1966. It has been suggested that the poet conceived of it while in Moscow, as he participated in the celebration of the orbits of the Soviet space capsules *Vostok III* and *Vostok IV.* Hernán Loyola, in *Obras Completas*, suggests throwing the net farther back, perhaps to *Twenty Love Poems and a Song of Despair.*

Neruda sings in this book to his house in Isla Negra, which had been a fixture in his life for years. After the poet has mapped the interior and exterior of the place, the concluding love poem, "Love for This Book," a recognition of Matilde's presence and domain, takes the house and the sea to the frontier. The 56-page volume, with photographs by Sergio Larraín, was published by Lumen in Barcelona in 1966. That same year the poet traveled to New York City as a guest of P.E.N., where he was introduced by Archibald MacLeish. His marriage to Matilde Urrutia, which had taken place abroad, became legal in Chile at this time.

LA BARCAROLA*

Buenos Aires: Losada, 1967, 163 pages. Neruda initially conceived this cyclical poem as part of *Memorial de Isla Negra*. The clear influence of Rubén Darío can be felt in these domestic pages. Neruda once wrote: "I wrote a big book of poetry, I called it *La barcarola*, and it was a kind of ballad; I dabbled a little in all the materials I like to use, sometimes water or wheat, sometimes simple sand, an occasional hard and precise crag or quarry, and always the sea with its silence and its thunder, eternities at my disposal right outside my window and within reach of my paper, and in this book there are some episodes that not only sing but tell a story, because long ago that's how it was, poetry sang and told a story, and that's the way I am, too, old-fashioned" (translation by Margaret Sayers Peden).

That same year the debut of his play *Fulgor y muerte de Joaquín Murieta (Splendor and Death of Joaquín Murieta)*, about a border bandit famous among Chicanos in the United States, took place at the Instituto de Teatro de la Universidad de Chile. The play announces Neruda's empathy with the growing Hispanic community in the United States, which in the following decades would grow exponentially, reaching over 35.3 million documented citizens in the year 2000. Since strictly speaking Neruda didn't conceive this play as poetry, I didn't include a fragment from Ben Belitt's English translation of 1972. Still, the play is fascinating, if not altogether successful. (I discuss it along with other texts on Murieta—the last name is often spelled with a double *r*—in *The Hispanic Condition* (1995; rev. ed. 2001). About Murieta, Neruda said, "It so happens that when the news of the discovery of gold in California spread through the world, a large number of Chileans went north to seek their fortune. They set out from Valparaíso, then the most important port along the southern coast. These men were miners, farmers, fishermen, and adventurers, drawn by the lure of glittering adventure. In Chile they'd learned how to get along in a poor and rugged land . . . Among them was the famous Joaquín Murieta, the most notorious of Chilean outlaws. But was he simply an outlaw, a renegade? This is the theme of my poem. Murieta was lucky. He found gold, he married a Chilean girl, but as he continued his dogged search for fresh lodes, he was overtaken by a tragedy that changed his life . . . Mexicans, Chileans, Central Americans, all lived in the poor barrios of the towns that sprung up like mushrooms around San Francisco. There, every night, you could hear the throbbing of guitars and the songs of the brown-skinned continent. Soon the profusion of foreigners, gold, song, and happiness incited violence. The North Americans formed bands of white vigilantes that raided these settlements by night—burning, razing, and killing. There seems little doubt that the idea for the Ku Klux Klan was born there. The same frenzied racism that typifies the Klan even today motivated those crusading Yankees who wanted to clean out all the Latin Americans from California, and, it follows, to get their hands on the Latins' strikes. In one of these raids, the wife of Joaquín Murieta was murdered . . . Murieta's birthplace is disputed by Mexico and Chile. The debate persists in the midst of fable and legend, but, for me, Murieta was Chilean. His story intrigued me because of the racial conflict and the extent of the greed and blood surrounding the man—real and legendary" (translation by Margaret Sayers Peden).

LAS MANOS DEL DÍA
[THE HANDS OF DAY]

The nostalgic tone in *The Hands of Day* recalls the Neruda of *Residence on Earth*. It was published in Buenos Aires by Losada in 1968, as a volume of 117 pages.

FIN DEL MUNDO*
[WORLD'S END]

This collection represents a full-fledged return to the poet's poetical obsessions. In it Neruda reacts to the major events of recent years: the Soviet invasion of Prague in 1968 as well as the American marine invasion of

Santo Domingo, Dominican Republic, in 1966. The theme of utopianism and the apocalyptic notion of the end of history are on display. Neruda pondered other titles, such as *Juicio final* (Final Judgment), before settling on the one known to posterity. *World's End* (246 pages) was released by the Society of Contemporary Art in Santiago in 1969.

MAREMOTO
[SEAQUAKE]

In 1970 Neruda campaigned actively in favor of Salvador Allende's presidential bid in Chile. In a speech he stated, "President-to-be of Chile: I hope that you will often call on writers and artists, and that once in power you will talk with us, and listen. You will always find in us the greatest loyalty to the destiny of our nation, and the greatest selflessness." When Allende became president, the poet was named ambassador to France. That year in Santiago the Society of Contemporary Art published *Seaquake* (82 pages). It is possible that, given the themes of these poems, they were originally intended for or resulted as an outgrowth from *World's End*.

AÚN
[STILL ANOTHER DAY]

In content, although not in pages, this is the shortest of Neruda's books. The twenty-eight poems of *Still Another Day* appear to have been written between July 5 and 6, 1969. William O'Daly describes this volume as "a farewell to the Chilean people." It was first published in Santiago by Nascimiento in 1969 in 68 pages. There is a return here to the theme of solitude that permeates *Residence on Earth*.

LA ESPADA ENCENDIDA*
[THE FLAMING SWORD]

Hernán Loyola links the theme of this collection, written between 1969 and 1970, and published in Buenos Aires by Losada in 1970 (152 pages), to a translation done by Neruda decades before of Marcel Schwob's *El incendio terrestre*. In other words, though the plot appears to be biblical, in truth it is mythical. Neruda makes reference to a book by Julio Vicuña Cifuentes (*Mitos y supersticiones de Chile*, Santiago, 1915) that served as inspiration. *The Flaming Sword* opens with a notice explaining that it is a fable about a fugitive who survives the apocalyptic times of humankind. He establishes a kingdom in the *"espaciosas soledades magallánicas"* (the spacious Magellanic solitudes), until he comes across a young woman from an aural city. A flaming sword leads them to a new, savage Garden of Eden. Then, after the death of God, under an enlightened volcano, these "Adamic creatures" become conscious of their own divinity. The poem I have selected, "XVIII Someone," depicts the first encounter between man and woman.

LAS PIEDRAS DEL CIELO
[STONES FROM THE SKY]

On October 21, 1971, Neruda received the Nobel Prize for Literature. He was the second Chilean to be granted such an honor, after Gabriela Mistral (1889–1957). She and Neruda nurtured a close relationship. Other awardees from Latin America are Miguel Angel Asturias (Guatemala), Gabriel García Márquez (Colombia), and Octavio Paz (Mexico). "Ladies and gentlemen," Neruda said in his speech, "I never found in books any formula for writing poetry; and I, in turn, do not intend to leave in print a word of advice, a method, or a style that will allow young poets to receive from me some drop of supposed wisdom." He added, "There is no unassailable solitude. All roads lead to the same point: to the communication of who we are. And we must travel across lonely and rugged terrain, through isolation and silence, to reach the magic zone where we can dance an awkward dance or sing a melancholy song; but in the dance and the song are consummated the most ancient rituals of awareness—the awareness of being men, and of believing in a common destiny." He concluded with a phrase by Rimbaud—*"A l'aurore, armés d'une ardente patience, nous entrerons aux splendides Villes"*—and stated, "I believe in that prophecy by the seer Rimbaud. I come from a dark province, from a country separated from others by a severe geography. I was the most abandoned of poets, and my poetry was regional, sorrowful, steeped in rain. But I always had confidence in man. I never lost hope. That may be why I am here with my poetry, and with my flag" (translation by Margaret Sayers Peden; the entire speech is included in *The Oxford Book of Latin American Essays* [1997], edited by Ilan Stavans).

Released the same year he received the Nobel Prize, *Stones from the Sky* (91 pages) was published by Losada in Buenos Aires. It is a celebration of the mineral varieties found in the poet's native country.

This 152-page volume is another Neruda collection shaped by sheer serendipity. It was published in Buenos Aires by Losada in 1972. The poem I selected, "Numbered," is part of a total of thirty-three. The numerical theme was a fixture of the poet's later period. (See also "Sad Song to Bore Everyone," part of *Selected Failings.*) At times Neruda seemed disheartened by his work. Had he made proper use of his talents and time on earth? By this time, of course, the poet was a magisterial figure in his milieu. His success was far-reaching. But success and fame in the Hispanic world are a curse: the more one thrives, the more venomous the attacks become. Selden Rodman, author of *Tongues of Fallen Angels,* who interviewed a number of authors from the region and visited the poet in Isla Negra, wrote that since the death of Gabriela Mistral in New York in 1957, "Neruda has so completely dominated Chilean poetry that there have been only two ways for other Chilean poets to survive: to hate him or to join him." The epithets targeted at him by friends and foes in his lifetime were sumptuous: "bourgeois imperialist," "a great bad poet," "an enemy of the workers," and "an imbecile valued for his nearsightedness."

LA ROSA SEPARADA
[THE SEPARATE ROSE]

In *The Separate Rose* Neruda muses on death with a kind of peace. He sings to the island of Pascua (Rapa Nui, invoked in *Canto General* as well), turning it—its landscape, to which he devotes ten poems, and its inhabitants, to which he devotes fourteen (plus a poem that serves as introduction)—into a metaphor. Neruda visited the island with a team of Chile's Canal 13 TV. *La rosa separada* (48 pages) was first published in Paris by Editions du Dragon in 1972. It contained engravings by Enrique Zañartu. The first Spanish-language edition by Losada (Buenos Aires, 116 pages) appeared posthumously.

In 1972 Neruda began the final process of editing his *Memoirs. Passions and Impressions,* his other volume of reminiscences, is a collection of assorted prose first published in 1978 and edited by Matilde Urrutia and Miguel Otero Silva.

This 211-page volume, written hastily and published months before the poet's death, was released by Quimantú in 1973. Like *The Grapes and the Wind*, it is an example of Neruda the political poet as a pamphleteer. He intended it as a contribution to the campaign for parliamentary elections in March. Soon he would also call for the intellectuals in Europe and Latin America to prevent a civil war in Chile and to help contain the interventionist foreign policies of the United States. The situation of Chile the previous year had been critical: there was an internal conspiracy to overthrow Salvador Allende, and foreign pressure had resulted in severe economic difficulties. As ambassador to France, Neruda had tried to help from afar. He resigned from the post in November, then returned to Santiago to see the situation with his own eyes. Also in 1972 he had traveled to New York City to deliver a fateful speech at the American P.E.N. The reverberations of that speech, in which he talked of "renegotiating" his relationship to Walt Whitman and the English language, eventually made the Cubans turn against Neruda.

The Spanish Golden Age conceptual poet Francisco de Quevedo y Villegas (1580–1645), author of memorable poems, novels such as *El buscón* (The Swindler), and satirical essays, was one of the acknowledged influences on Neruda. The Chilean celebrated Quevedo's condemnation of corruption and dishonesty.

POSTHUMOUS WORK

Neruda died of cancer on September 23, 1973, in Santiago. Soon after his death his house in Valparaíso and the one in Santiago, where the wake was held, were ransacked and vandalized.

Seven books were published posthumously: *El mar y las campanas** (*The Sea and the Bells*), Buenos Aires, Losada, 1973 (108 pages); *2000*, Buenos Aires, Losada, 1974 (50 pages); *Elegía* (*Elegy*), Buenos Aires, Losada, 1974 (130 pages); *El corazón amarillo* (*The Yellow Heart*), Buenos Aires, Losada, 1974 (110 pages); *Jardín de invierno* (*Winter Garden*), Buenos Aires, Losada, 1974 (104 pages); *Libro de las preguntas* (*The Book of Questions*), Buenos Aires, Losada, 1974 (99 pages); and *Defectos escogidos** (*Selected Failings*),

Buenos Aires, Losada, 1974 (105 pages). According to a back-cover note in *The Sea and the Bells*, Neruda had been planning to commemorate his seventieth birthday, due in July 1974, with the publication of eight collections of poetry: the seven just listed plus *The Separate Rose*, which had appeared in France but had not yet been released in the Hispanic world. (It is important to note that the poet wanted *Selected Failings* to appear last, perhaps as a sign of self-criticism.) The sequential publication was prevented not only by Neruda's death, but by General Augusto Pinochet's military coup d'état, which put a halt to Chile's democracy. One can only speculate whether these volumes were shaped as the poet wanted them. At any rate, in them he continues to explore common themes that had become leitmotivs throughout his life: man versus nature, social systems, and love.

Yevgeny Aleksandrovich Yevtushenko (b. 1933) is the Russian author of the poem "Babi Yar." His books include *A Dove in Santiago: A Novella in Verse* (1978).

ACKNOWLEDGMENTS

Many people have been instrumental in the preparation of *The Poetry of Pablo Neruda*. First and foremost, I wish to express my wholehearted gratitude to my friend Jonathan Galassi. His superb comments on the manuscript were at once adventurous and pragmatic. And he walked through the maze of agents and copyright owners with conviction and fortitude I found enviable. His assistant James Wilson was an invaluable resource, always prompt in his replies, friendly in his disposition, invaluable as a playmate.

I'm fortunate to have Martín Espada as a neighbor. Our regular breakfasts at the restaurant La Veracruzana were turned into translation workshops. He offered improvements to various translations and read the introduction and portions of the manuscript with a rigorous eye. Jay Parini posed the idea to me in the form of a set of questions in 2000, as we conversed about John Steinbeck at the Mercantile Library of New York: "Why does Neruda's oeuvre in English need to be so obnoxiously dispersed? Might there be a way to appreciate him in full? Why don't you build *a Nerudian aleph*?" The concept struck me as bizarre. As I pondered it, a serendipitous event took place: my former student Jesse H. Lytle and his fiancée, Anne, honored me with the invitation to read at their wedding in Northampton, Massachusetts, in Spanish and English, "Your Laughter," which is part of *The Captain's Verses*. The experience was exhilarating. Suddenly, I was overwhelmed by the need to reread the Chilean poet's oeuvre from start to finish. It took me months to complete the task. The further I got into it, the louder Parini's words resonated in my mind. I described the resonance to Galassi over lunch on an autumn day in New York. His response was enthusiastic. He suggested I embark on a comprehensive compendium of Neruda's career in English.

Margaret Sayers Peden has been my hero and my model. She has granted me her advice and expertise without hesitation. Michael Millman at Penguin Classics offered guidance and support, as did John Felstiner at Stanford University. Felstiner also sent me valuable material and assisted me in establishing contact with various Neruda specialists. Mark Eisner came for an autumn visit to Amherst, Massachusetts, and in Frost Library, amid views of the outside foliage, we circumnavigated Neruda's earthly and posthumous life. I also enjoyed the insightful discussion—syncopated by a tittering Zabar's marmalade jar—with my friends Betty Ferber and Homero Aridjis. Dennis Maloney and María Jacketti served as correspondents. Stephen F. White, of the Rubén Darío club, clarified for me questions about Federico García Lorca and showed me an inspired rendition of "Ode to Federico García Lorca" he produced along with Greg Simon. Robert Bly sent a letter that brought me solace. I also discussed Neruda with my soul mate Ariel Dorfman. Susan Brown did a superb job in copyediting the mountainous manuscript. Frieda Duggan was a diligent production editor. Erika Seidman in the permissions department at Farrar, Straus and Giroux was indefatigable in the campaign to enlist all involved parties in the endeavor. Her descent into the grotto of copyright ownership was an adventure worth recounting someday. My student Aaron Britt set out on a quest to reproduce with a single Xerox machine an urtext broken into infinite parts dispersed over a large galaxy of libraries. He was patient, persistent, and passionate. His help and recommendations were precious. Carina Pons and Carmen Pinilla at the Carmen Balcells Literary Agency in Barcelona endorsed the project and served as mediators with the Fundación Pablo Neruda. I'm indebted to the translators who agreed to look again at their versions. Finally, it was a pleasure to work—by mail, phone, fax, and e-mail or, better still, tête-à-tête and line by line—on the fresh versions done by the English-language poets April Bernard, Rafael Campo, Martín Espada, Edward Hirsch, Jane Hirshfield, Galway Kinnell, Philip Levine, Paul Muldoon, Gary Soto, and Mark Strand.

Thanks to the following individuals and publishers for their permission to use material:

Azul Editions for the following poems from *Spain in the Heart*, translated by Richard Schaaf: "Invocation," "Bombardment/Curse," "Spain Poor Through the Fault of the Rich," "Tradition," "Madrid (1936)," "Song for the Mothers of Slain Militiamen," "Battle of the Jarama River," "Almería," "General Franco in Hell," "Triumph," "Landscape After a Battle," "Madrid (1937)," "Solar Ode to the Army of the People." Used by permission of Richard Schaaf.

Azul Editions for the following poems from *2000*, translated by Richard Schaaf: "I The Masks," "IV The Earth," "IX Celebration." Used by permission of Richard Schaaf.

Beacon Press for "I Wish the Woodcutter Would Wake Up," "The Strike," "Ode to the Watermelon," translated by Robert Bly; and "Toussaint L'Ouverture," translated by James Wright, from *Neruda and Vallejo: Selected Poems*, edited by Robert Bly. © 1971 by Robert Bly. Used by permission of Robert Bly.

Bernard, April: "From My Journey" from *The Sea and the Bells*. © 2003 by April Bernard. Used by permission of the translator.

Farrar, Straus and Giroux for the following poems from *The Heights of Macchu Picchu*, translated by Nathaniel Tarn: "ɪ From Air to Air," "ɪɪɪ Being Like Maize," "ᴠ It Was Not You," "ᴠɪɪɪ Come Up with Me, American Love," "ɪx Interstellar Eagle," "x Stone Within Stone," "xɪɪ Arise to Birth." Used by permission of the publisher.

Farrar, Straus and Giroux for the following poems from *Extravagaria*, translated by Alastair Reid: "To rise to the sky . . . ," "I Ask for Silence," "And the City Now Has Gone," "Repertoire," "With Her," "Point," "Fear," "How Much Happens in a Day," "Soliloquy at Twilight," "V," "Horses," "We Are Many," "To the Foot from Its Child," "This Is Where We Live," "Getaway," "The Unhappy One," "Pastoral," "Autumn Testament." Used by permission of the publisher.

Farrar, Straus and Giroux for the following poems from *Fully Empowered*, translated by Alastair Reid: "The Poet's Obligation," "The Word," "Ocean," "It Is Born," "Planet," "Serenade," "To Wash a Child," "To the Dead Poor Man," "Goodbyes," "Spring," "To Don Asterio Alarcón, Clocksmith of Valparaíso," "The Night in Isla Negra," "Past," "The People," "Fully Empowered." Used by permission of the publisher.

Farrar, Straus and Giroux for the following poems from *Isla Negra*, translated by Alastair Reid: "The First Journey," "The Father," "The First Sea," "The South," "Sex," "Poetry," "Shyness," "Swan Lake," "The Human Condition," "Superstitions," "The Rooming House on the Calle Maruri," "Loves: Terusa (I)," "Loves: Terusa (II)," "Bread-Poetry," "My Crazy Friends," "First Travelings," "Opium in the East," "Monsoons," "October Fullness," "Lost Letters," "Oh, My Lost City," "Perhaps I've Changed Since Then," "Revolutions," "The Unknown One," "Insomnia," "Goodbye to the Snow," "Tides," "Exile," "Brother Cordillera," "What Is Born with Me," "Appointment with Winter," "The Hero," "The Forest," "Night," "Mexican Serenade," "To Envy," "Ars Magnetica," "To Those at Odds," "Day Dawns," "Solitude," "It Is Not Necessary," "Memory," "The Long Day Called Thursday," "What We Accept Without Wanting To," "The Future Is Space." Used by permission of the publisher.

Felstiner, John: "Dead Gallop" and "What Spain Was Like" from *Residence on Earth*; "ɪᴠ Cortés" and "xᴠ Rider in the Rain" from *Canto General*; "Guilty" from *The Hands of Day*; "The Great Urinator" from *Selected Failings*. Used by permission of the translator.

Ferber, Betty: "I'm Asking for Silence" from *Extravagaria*. © 2003 by Betty Ferber. Used by permission of the translator.

Harcourt, Brace for material from *Bestiary*, translated by Elsa Neuberger. Used by permission of the publisher.

HarperCollins for the poem "Ode to the Artichoke" from *Elemental Odes*, translated by Stephen Mitchell. © by Stephen Mitchell. Used by permission of the publisher.

Hirsch, Edward: "Ode to the Book I" and "Ode to the Book II" from *Elemental Odes*. © 2003 by Edward Hirsch. Used by permission of the translator.

Hirshfield, Jane: "Ode to Time" from *Elemental Odes*. © 2003 by Jane Hirshfield. Used by permission of the translator.

Kinnell, Galway: "I Explain a Few Things" from *Residence on Earth*. Used by permission of the translator.

Earth," "Ode to My Suit," "Ode to Sadness," "Ode to Criticism (II)," "Ode to the Dictionary," "Ode to the Seagull," "Ode to Firefoot," "Ode to Bees," "Ode to Bicycles," "Ode to a Village Movie Theater," "Ode to Age," "Ode to a Stamp Album," "Ode to Maize," "Ode to an Aged Poet" from *Elemental Odes*, by Pablo Neruda. Selected, translated, and introduced by Margaret Sayers Peden. London: Libris, 1991. Published in the United States as *Selected Odes of Pablo Neruda*, by University of California Press, Berkeley and Los Angeles. © Libris, 1991. Used by permission of the translator.

Simon, Greg, for permission to use "Ode to Walt Whitman." © 2003 by Greg Simon. Used by permission of the translator.

Soto, Gary: "House" from *Ceremonial Songs*. © 2003 by Gary Soto. Used by permission of the translator.

Stavans, Ilan: "Love," "If God Is in My Verse," "My Soul" from *Book of Twilight*; "**XL** In Vietnam," "**LVIII** The Past," "**LX** Verb" from *The Hands of Day*; "**VII** The Seeker," "**IX** The Sadder Century" from *World's End*; "**XVIII** Someone" from *The Flaming Sword*; "Numbered" from *Barren Terrain*; "**XIV**" from *Elegy*; "Sad Song to Bore Everyone" from *Selected Failings*. © 2003 by Ilan Stavans. Used by permission of the translator.

Strand, Mark: "Ode to the Smell of Firewood," "Ode to a Pair of Socks," "Ode to Enchanted Light," first published in *Nimrod*, vol. 18, no. 1 (Fall–Winter 1973). © 1973 by Mark Strand. Used by permission of the translator.

University of California Press for the following poems from *Canto General*, translated by Jack Schmitt: "**I** *Amor America* (1400)," "Vegetation," "**III** The Birds Arrive," "**IV** The Rivers Come Forth," "Orinoco," "Amazon," "**V** Minerals," "**VI** Man," "**I** They Come Through the Islands (1493)," "**V** Cholula," "**VI** Alvarado," "**VII** Guatemala," "**IX** The Head on the Spear," "**X** Homage to Balboa," "**XV** The Red Line," "**XVI** Elegy," "**XX** Land and Man Unite," "**XXII** Ercilla," "**I** Cuauhtemoc (1520)," "**II** Brother Bartolomé de Las Casas," "**III** Advancing in the Lands of Chile," "**VIII** Lautaro (1550)," "**XI** Lautaro Against the Centaur (1554)," "**XVII** Commoners from Socorro (1781)," "**XVIII** Tupac Amaru (1781)," "**XIX** Insurgent America (1800)," "**XXI** San Martín (1810)," "**XXVII** Guayaquil (1822)," "**XXXVII** Sandino (1926)," "**XLII** The Tyrants Again," "**XLIII** The Day Will Come," "Perhaps, perhaps oblivion," "**I**: The Hangmen," "Doctor Francia," "Rosas (1829–1849)," "Estrada," "Machado," "Martínez (1932)," "**II**: The Oligarchies," "Election in Chimborongo (1947)," "Diplomats (1948)," "The Bordellos," "Standard Oil Co.," "United Fruit Co.," "The Beggars," "The Indians," "The Judges," "**IV**: Chronicle of 1948 (America)," "Paraguay," "Cuba," "The Traitor," "I Accuse," "The Victorious People," "**I** From Above (1942)," "**II** An Assassin Sleeps," "**III** On the Coast," "**IV** Winter in the South, on Horseback," "**V** Crimes," "**VI** Youth," "**VII** Climates," "**VIII** Varadero in Cuba," "**XI** Hunger in the South," "**XIII** A Rose," "**XIV** Life and Death of a Butterfly," "**XV** The Man Buried in the Pampa," "**XVIII** America," "**XIX** America, I Do Not Invoke Your Name in Vain," "Eternity," "**II** I Want to Return to the South (1941)," "**V** Saddlery," "Pottery Shop," "**VII** Atacama," "**X** Untilled Zones," "**XII** Botany," "**XVI** Chile's Seas," "**I** Cristóbal Miranda (Shoveler, Tocopilla)," "**VII** Antonio Bernales (Fisherman, Colombia)," "**XII** Maestro Huerta (From the 'La Despreciada' Mine, Antofagasta)," "**XVI** Catastrophe in Sewell," "**XVII** The Earth's Name Is Juan," "**III** Beyond Your Lands, America," "**I** Through the dead of night," "**IV** A young couple opened a door," "**X** And so, from night to night," "**XII** To all, to you," "**XIII** American sand, solemn," "**II** Brother Pablo," "**VII** Gold," "**X** The Poet," "**XI** Death in the World," "**XII** Mankind," "**I** Letter to Miguel Otero Silva, in Caracas (1949)," "**V** To Miguel Hernández, Murdered in the Prisons of Spain," "**VIII** Chile's Voices,"

Throughout the Caribbean." English translation copyright © 1976 by Miguel Algarín. Used by permission of HarperCollins Inc.

Thanks to Farrar, Straus and Giroux for permission to quote from *Memoirs* and *Passions and Impressions*. Also, my sincere gratitude to the Fundación Pablo Neruda in Chile and to the Carmen Balcells Literary Agency in Spain for permission to use the originals throughout this volume.